GRAND DESIGNS AND VISIONS OF UNITY

The New Cold War History

JOHN LEWIS GADDIS, EDITOR

GRAND

DESIGNS

AND

VISIONS

OF UNITY

The Atlantic Powers
and the Reorganization
of Western Europe,
1955–1963

JEFFREY GLEN GIAUQUE

 The University of North Carolina Press

Chapel Hill and London

© 2002 The University of North Carolina Press
All rights reserved
Manufactured in the United States of America
Designed by April Leidig-Higgins
Set in Minion by Copperline Book Services, Inc.

The paper in this book meets the guidelines for
permanence and durability of the Committee on
Production Guidelines for Book Longevity of the
Council on Library Resources.

Library of Congress Cataloging-in-Publication Data
Giauque, Jeffrey Glen.
Grand designs and visions of unity: the Atlantic
powers and the reorganization of Western Europe,
1955–1963 / Jeffrey Glen Giauque.
p. cm.—(The New Cold War history)
Includes bibliographical references and index.
ISBN 0-8078-2679-0 (cloth: alk. paper)
ISBN 0-8078-5344-5 (pbk.: alk. paper)
1. National security—Europe—History—20th
century. 2. Europe—Relations—United States.
3. United States—Relations—Europe. 4. European
Economic Community. 5. North Atlantic Treaty Organization. I. Title. II. Series.
D843 .G4478 2002   327'.094'09045—dc21
2001047647

06 05 04 03 02   5 4 3 2 1

To my family

CONTENTS

ACKNOWLEDGMENTS

I thank my parents, Brent and Susan Giauque, and my sisters, Natalie and Amy, for their support throughout my academic career, without which none of my accomplishments would have been possible.

I thank the archivists in four countries at nearly a dozen archives who endured my endless requests for more files and made it possible for me to complete my research in the time available.

This research was supported by grants from the Ohio State University History Department and Graduate School, the Phyllis Krumm Memorial International Scholarship fund, the U.S. Department of Education, and the German Academic Exchange Service (Deutscher Akademischer Austauschdienst). Crucial additional financial support was provided by my parents.

I am grateful to both *International History Review* and *Contemporary European History* for publishing portions of my research and granting permission to reprint the material here.

Finally, I wish to thank all those who read drafts of the manuscript and did much to improve the substance and style of the text. Chief among these was my Ph.D. adviser, Carole Fink, who has now read the text, in all its forms, nearly as many times as I have. I would also like to thank Michael Hogan, John Gaddis, and the readers and editors of the University of North Carolina Press for their helpful suggestions. Needless to say, I alone am responsible for any shortcomings that may remain. The views expressed in this book are my own views and not necessarily those of the Department of State or the U.S. government.

ABBREVIATIONS

The following abbreviations are used throughout the book.

BDI	Bundesverband der Deutschen Industrie
Benelux	Belgium, Netherlands, Luxembourg
CAP	Common Agricultural Policy
CDU	Christlich-Demokratische Union
CET	Common External Tariff
CFEP	Council on Foreign Economic Policy
CNPF	Conseil National du Patronat Français
CSU	Christlich-Soziale Union
ECSC	European Coal and Steel Community
EDC	European Defense Community
EEC	European Economic Community
EFTA	European Free Trade Association
Euratom	European Atomic Energy Community
FDP	Freie Demokratische Partei
FTA	Free Trade Area
GATT	General Agreement on Tariffs and Trade
GDR	German Democratic Republic
MLF	Multi-Lateral (Nuclear) Force
MNF	Multi-National (Nuclear) Force
MRP	Mouvement Républicain Populaire
NATO	North Atlantic Treaty Organization
OECD	Organization for Economic Cooperation and Development
OEEC	Organization for European Economic Cooperation
SACEUR	Supreme Allied Commander Europe
SFIO	Section Française de l'Internationale Ouvrière
SPD	Sozialdemokratische Partei Deutschlands
USSR	Union of Soviet Socialist Republics
WEU	Western European Union

GRAND DESIGNS AND
VISIONS OF UNITY

INTRODUCTION

France, Germany and Italy were devastated, but these three countries are regaining the elements of their power and there is no reason to abandon the direction of Europe to the Anglo-Saxons, especially the Americans. It is a bad idea, because our peoples will lose interest in the actions of their governments. A state cannot survive unless its people are convinced that their government is responsible for their fate and not some organization with an acronym name or some foreign country, however friendly it may be.
—Charles de Gaulle, 24 June 1959

Between 1955 and 1963, Western European and transatlantic relations witnessed a period of political and economic ferment as a wide variety of proposals for unity and cooperation appeared on both sides of the Atlantic. Among the accomplishments of the period were the creation of the European Common Market, the antecedent of today's European Union, and the Organization for Economic Cooperation and Development (OECD), the main transatlantic organization for economic cooperation to this day, as well as the cementing of the postwar rapprochement between France and Germany in treaty form in 1963. Other proposed institutions and arrangements did not come into being. These included a political union to provide Western Europe greater cohesion in foreign policy and a voice in global affairs, a structured Atlantic political and economic community to strengthen the connections between the United States and its European partners, and the admission of Britain to the Common Market to increase the political and economic weight of the European community.

In retrospect, it is not surprising that the late 1950s and early 1960s was a time to explore new forms of cooperation in Western Europe. Throughout much of the world, both inside and outside the Cold War blocs, this was an era of adaptation to a bilateral international system that placed overwhelming power in the hands of the United States and Soviet Union. Nineteen fifty-five marked the formal construction of the Warsaw Pact, which represented the Soviet response to the Atlantic alliance, the creation of NATO, and the rearming of West Germany.[1] The same year also witnessed the beginning of the nonaligned movement at the Bandung conference, reflecting the increasing assertiveness of Europe's former colonies at a time when decolonization was at its peak. The United States was actively intervening around the world to support friendly governments and remove hostile ones. In a world dominated by two superpowers and moving toward regional and political blocs, Western Europe had to move quickly or be left behind and reduced to insignificance.

European countries struggled to find new, post-imperial roles in the world, both to reassert their status and importance and to reaffirm their own national identities. At a time when Europe's decline seemed manifest in myriad ways and when painful adjustments to a reduced status were still being made, cooperation and unity offered both immediate symbols of recovery and potential concrete gains, particularly over the long term. The European task would be to alter the structures of the western Cold War international system. At the moment these were based primarily on NATO and other American-dominated alliances, American economic support of the continent and of international trade structures such as GATT and Bretton Woods, and the presence of U.S. troops in Europe and elsewhere. All these contributed to European recovery and security, but they also enshrined American dominance. Because the East-West conflict largely paralyzed the United Nations, these structures predominated not only in Europe, but also in most of the noncommunist world. If Europe were to regain an independent voice, it would have to build up its own structures for unity in order to speak as one and deal with the United States on more equal terms.

Efforts at Western European and Atlantic integration predated 1955, but during that year an important shift occurred. Between 1947 and 1954, the Western European countries and their American allies had focused on building a bulwark against the USSR, based largely on reconciling themselves to the political, economic, and military recovery of West Germany. The threat of a military attack from the East seemed very real, particularly after the outbreak of the Korean War, and German support was needed to counter it. During this period, all cooperative efforts, including the Marshall Plan and the creation of the Organization for European Economic Cooperation (OEEC), the predecessor of the OECD, were intended primarily to increase Western Europe's capacity to resist the USSR militarily and its ability to halt the spread of communist influence within its borders, as well as to reduce America's burden on the continent. In this first phase of European and Atlantic cooperation and integration, the successes were either clearly military, from the creation of NATO to the 1954 arrangements that enabled Germany to join the alliance, or were fairly limited in scope, from the use of the OEEC to coordinate the distribution of Marshall Plan aid to the creation of the European Coal and Steel Community (ECSC) to consolidate elements of Western European heavy industry and facilitate acceptance of German economic recovery. More ambitious and less well-defined efforts, such as those to build a supranational European military organization (the European Defense Community [EDC]) or a political or customs union in Western Europe, failed as a result of the absence of consensus on anything more than sectoral measures.[2]

By 1955 most of the issues that had led to this first phase of European integration had been resolved in one way or another. Marshall Plan aid had been successfully distributed and employed, and Western Europe was well on its way to economic recovery and growth. The Soviet military threat to Western Europe had been countered via NATO and the likelihood of a direct military attack from the East gradually decreased after Stalin's death in early 1953. Détente remained a long way off, but the Cold War was entering a phase of greater stability in Europe that would require adjustments from Western countries. Germany had been tentatively accepted as an integral part of Western Europe, and the United States had taken up a political and military partnership with the continent.

Throughout most of the Cold War, the Soviet Union opposed the unification efforts of Western Europe since the Kremlin realized that unity would make Europe much more resistant to both Soviet lures and threats. Soviet leaders used both the carrot and the stick to attempt to derail the unity process, from the Marshall Plan to the Common Market to the Franco-German treaty of 1963. These efforts were uniformly unsuccessful, and the USSR was generally powerless to stop the unity effort. If anything, Soviet bluster helped the Europeans to overcome their differences and move toward unity. Soviet pressures helped bring about the Franco-German rapprochement and convinced the United States to accept European trade discrimination for the sake of greater political and economic unity on the continent. Whenever the Europeans had a falling out, the Soviets were always there to remind them why unity was necessary, whether blockading Berlin in 1948–49 and menacing it in 1958–62, invading Hungary in 1956, or threatening Britain and France with nuclear attack during the Suez crisis. However, the Soviet threat was most important in motivating European unity in the earliest days of the Cold War. Thereafter its significance receded and other causes came to the forefront, but throughout the Cold War, and even after its end, uncertainty regarding the USSR or Russia was often in the back of European minds and helped them to overcome differences that might otherwise have been more difficult to resolve.[3]

With the most immediate concerns settled by the mid-1950s, Western European leaders reexamined their basic ideas on cooperation and unity. The second phase of the debate over European and Atlantic relations was in some ways more dynamic than the first, since economic recovery and the relative receding of the Soviet threat allowed Europeans and Americans to contemplate the relations and institutions they wanted to build rather than those that had to be constructed out of necessity. At the same time the second phase was more realistic than the first, since the Europeans and Americans had learned the limits of supranational integration during the earlier period, particularly as a result of the rejection of the EDC by the French National Assembly in August 1954. No longer under pressure for immediate, sweeping measures, they could explore less radical options. This shift led to a wide variety of new proposals for cooperation, but also produced considerable disunity, as each major member of the Western camp developed its own vision of the future shape of Europe that would best promote its own national interests. The combination of competition and cooperation produced progress but also a great deal of rancor among the Atlantic powers, which now allowed their disputes to overshadow their underlying areas of agreement. Facing a less direct Soviet threat, they resumed the traditional European contest for power and influence, but with new rules, new language, and a new forcefulness. Indeed, by the late 1950s and early 1960s the Atlantic powers spent at least as much energy competing with one another as they did cooperating to face the Soviets.

This book is the story of how the four largest Atlantic powers, Britain, France, Germany, and the United States, sought to reshape their partnership to adapt it to a changing world in which European empires were fading rapidly, the Soviet-communist challenge was moving from Europe to the developing world, and the United States could no longer carry the entire political and economic burden of the West on its own, yet hesitated to share leadership with Europe. The book takes a thematic approach to European and Atlantic relations in the 1950s and 1960s. It examines the "grand designs" that each country developed to advance its own European and Atlantic interests, which often defined these national priorities as synonymous with "common" Western interests, the specific proposals for cooperation and unity, and the reactions of the others. It considers both the plans that were achieved, such as those leading to the Common Market, and those that failed, such as the early efforts to create a European political union. The case studies in this book demonstrate the swings between cooperation and competition among the four Atlantic powers as well as the constant shift in alignments between them. Up to now, many historians have overlooked the volatility of this period and reduced it to a contest for influence between France and the United States. While there were major disagreements between Paris and Washington, there were numerous examples of Franco-American cooperation as well. Moreover, there were many instances when the United States and its nominal "special" partner, Britain, disagreed and worked against one another. The case study approach enables us to investigate not only the connections between various issues, but also larger themes such as the reasons for the long-term failure of European political union.

Although this book includes economic and military subjects, its focus is political and diplomatic. The principal actors are government leaders, their advisers, and their representatives in foreign relations, since it was they who conceived, implemented, and contested each other's plans to reshape European and Atlantic relations. Other elements, both inside and outside government, that affected the formation of policy are included in each chapter. In instances where external forces played a decisive role, such as the challenges mounted by the ministry of economics in Bonn for control over Germany's European policy or the threats to British Common Market entry posed by domestic opposition in the early 1960s, their impact is analyzed in greater detail. With this approach in mind, we can now sketch the basic plans of the four countries for European and Atlantic relations.

The United States, despite the shift from a Republican to a Democratic administration in 1961, followed a consistent policy between 1955 and 1963. Washington had favored the creation of an integrated, supranational Western Europe since the late 1940s. President Dwight D. Eisenhower believed that unity beyond the national level would create a stronger, more self-sufficient Cold War ally, able to bear more of the economic and military burden of matching the USSR in Europe, thus allowing the United States to focus on containing Soviet and communist expansion elsewhere in the world. Permanent linkage of Germany to the United States and Western Europe was also a top priority for Washington. Eisenhower hoped that European integration would include as many countries as possible, especially Great Britain. After their failed efforts to promote the EDC against the will of many Europeans, Eisenhower and his secretary of state, John Foster Dulles, now wanted the latter to initiate all future integration efforts. After the EDC, the United States played an increasingly peripheral role in European unity, a development Eisenhower hoped would encourage the Europeans to take more responsibility for their affairs. From 1955 onward, Washington took a pragmatic, short-term approach, supporting almost any proposal to advance European unity. Nevertheless, America's long-term goal remained some form of supranational union. Absent an impairment to Europe's political and economic relations with the United States or to the Atlantic alliance or NATO, Eisenhower and Dulles would have supported almost any plan of European integration.[4]

West Germany's European and Atlantic blueprint, as consistent in principle as that of the Americans, underwent greater variation in practice. This was the result of internal debates and struggles for power between both individuals and government ministries as the country came of age in the international community. Chancellor Konrad Adenauer was a staunch supporter of European integration and Atlantic cooperation as the best means to restore German sovereignty, allow Germany to take its place as an equal partner in Europe and NATO, and promote all its interests. After 1955, he and his subordinates disagreed over the precise mix of cooperation and integration to follow and on the relative priority of relations with each of their major partners. Nevertheless, the German leadership all agreed that close political and economic relations with Western Europe and the United States were the keys to security, stability, economic development, political influence, and, over the long term, dealing with the USSR from a position of strength to achieve reunification.[5]

The British Conservative governments of Anthony Eden (1955–57) and Harold Macmillan (1957–63) had an uneasy relationship with Western Europe. Although, as we will see, the outer trappings of their European policy changed considerably, the overwhelming impression is nevertheless one of continuity. British governments since the end of World War II had focused on maintaining their country's global status by exerting influence in each of three "circles," the United States, the Commonwealth, and Europe, in that order. Whereas continental leaders pursued unity to enhance Europe's global influence, for Britain integration into a unified European system meant renouncing its traditional role in world affairs. Unlike the continental countries, all of which had been defeated and occupied by one side or the other during the war, Britain and its system of government had survived seemingly intact and its leaders and people thus saw no reason to abandon their sovereignty. Thus, London restricted itself to promoting purely cooperative European arrangements and viewed more ambitious plans, whether the United Kingdom participated or not, as a threat. However, by remaining aloof, Britain risked losing its political importance in Europe and suffering the consequences of economic isolation from the continent as well. It was for this reason that Eden and Macmillan repeatedly tried to divert European unity from a supranational to a cooperative basis and to submerge it in a wider Atlantic forum that maintained America's ties to the continent and linked Britain's three circles.[6]

The French vision of Europe, outwardly the most complicated and inconsistent between 1955 and 1963, nevertheless exhibited elements of continuity. The last leaders of the Fourth Republic generally supported limited European integration and Atlantic cooperation in order to increase their country's political and economic strength and influence and control a resurgent West Germany. Despite their doubts about the integrated NATO alliance, particularly after the Suez debacle in 1956, they accepted a major American role in Europe and sought to increase their own influence through cooperation with Washington. Because of its lingering doubts about Germany, France also welcomed an active British role on the continent. With the return to power of Charles de Gaulle and the formation of the Fifth Republic in 1958, many French policies changed, but the underlying goals for Europe remained. Rejecting supranational integration in any form, whether in the organization of European affairs or in NATO, as a threat to the French state and the autonomy of its people, de Gaulle attempted to shift European and Atlantic relations to a purely intergovernmental basis. Like his predecessors, he sought to use European cooperation to control Germany and increase French influence, but unlike them, de Gaulle was convinced that France could achieve these goals without the direct participation of Britain and the United States in Europe. He thus promoted an Atlantic arrangement whereby France would achieve hegemony in Western Europe and join a global partnership with Britain and the United States, which would both withdraw to their respective spheres of influence and leave Europe under the domination of Paris. As long as Britain was more interested in the Commonwealth and America than Europe, it could not be a real part of the latter. De Gaulle welcomed the alliance with the United States, but his sense of history and his problematic wartime relations with the Americans led him to question reliance on Washington and to reject its leadership. He believed that America tended to fluctuate between isolation and hegemony in its relations with Europe, neither of which was acceptable for France and Europe. The former would lead to abandonment while the latter could lead to annihilation without representation. This handful of basic goals and assumptions constituted de Gaulle's rough blueprint for the future of Europe, but he was flexible, at least initially, on how they were to be achieved.[7]

During the past ten years, the scholarship on Western European integration has greatly expanded as more and more documents have been released. Because this book examines the foreign policies of four countries, the institutions of European integration, the role of the Cold War in European and Atlantic relations, and the development of the Atlantic alliance, it is not possible to evaluate all the specialized literature in this introduction. Instead, each chapter includes a section on the historiography relevant to its particular thematic subject. For now, only general characteristics of the existing literature will be noted. First of all, most historical studies have been written without access, or with incomplete access, to the primary source materials that have only become available during the last few years. Many of the existing works by biographers, political scientists, and diplomats provide invaluable insights but lack the perspective and interests of the historian.[8] Second, much of the historical and archival-based work that has appeared more recently on the subjects of this book has been narrowly focused, from analyses of the foreign policy of one country, to bilateral studies, to biographies of individual policy makers, to histories of European integration focusing on the development of community institutions, to technical studies of various negotiations in the community.[9] Finally, most of the historiography on the European community per se centers on a few basic debates: the significance of supranationalism versus cooperation in the history of the community, the relative importance of government leaders, federalist bureaucrats, and "functional" pressures for unity, whether the unity effort strengthens or weakens the nation-state, and the relative significance of the United States in European integration.[10]

While these are important debates and readers will learn the author's views on all of them, they are matters of nuance that can never be decisively settled and thus should not exclusively define the study of European integration. This book differs from all the existing literature in several important ways. It offers a truly multinational and multiarchival perspective to demonstrate how cooperation and competition between national "grand designs" shaped the development of European and Atlantic relations over an extended period. The consideration of a variety of political and economic topics over nearly a decade allows wider themes, linkages, and continuities to appear that no book limited to one country, government, or subject can offer. Finally, the book is based on access to virtually all of the important archival collections of the political and foreign policy leaders of all four countries.

The structure of the book reflects its thematic approach. Each of the seven chapters analyzes one of the major issues in European and Atlantic integration in the late 1950s and early 1960s, beginning with an introduction to the subject and a discussion of the historiography. Each chapter details the positions of the four major Atlantic powers, analyzes their interactions, links the topic with other contemporary affairs, and narrates the course of developments. Each chapter offers conclusions on the outcome of events and draws connections between the topic at hand and wider European and Atlantic relations.

Chapter 1 describes the origins and early development of the European Common Market, the heart of European integration down to the present day. It details the views of American, German, and French leaders toward the idea of a customs union and explains why they ultimately supported it as a means of promoting national interests. The chapter examines the British decision to remain aloof and British efforts to derail or replace the new continental institution. It argues that the creation and success of the Common Market led to a diplomatic realignment in Western Europe, by transforming the foundations and assumptions on which the Atlantic powers had previously based their European policies.

Chapter 2 relates the British effort to replace or complement the Common Market with a wider and looser free trade area. Such an organization, aimed at protecting British political and economic interests in Europe, offered a challenge to the incipient, supranational Common Market. The chapter considers whether the British offered a viable alternative to Europe or simply played the role of spoiler. It analyzes the reasons for French opposition to the British plans and the ultimate American and German decisions to support Paris against London and torpedo the British proposals.

Although the significance of de Gaulle's return to power and his views on Western Europe are dealt with in Chapters 1 and 2, his wider plans for the continent are addressed at greater length in Chapter 3. The key to all of the French leader's ambitions for Europe was a long-term entente with Adenauer's Germany. De Gaulle hoped to use Germany as a junior partner in his effort to seize hegemony in Western Europe, reduce British and American influence on the continent, and consolidate Europe's political and economic weight to deal with the Soviet bloc from a position of strength. Chapter 3 examines the first phase of de Gaulle's effort to win Germany to his side, between 1958 and 1960. Before he could launch his sweeping plans, de Gaulle had to reassure the Germans of his commitment to European integration, German political and security interests, and the Atlantic alliance.

Chapter 4 details the American response to the rapid development of the Common Market and the political and economic cohesion of its six members after 1955. The Americans had long favored European integration, but had no wish to see Western Europe become an autarkic or neutralist "Third Force" in the Cold War. To prevent this, both the Eisenhower and Kennedy administrations worked to find means to match steps toward European unity with greater Atlantic political and economic ties. The result was an often contradictory and haphazard proposal for an Atlantic political and economic community. This plan provoked ambivalent reactions from all the major Western European states, which supported it erratically according to their own national and European priorities.

Chapter 5 considers the European efforts to build a political union in the late 1950s and early 1960s to complement the Common Market. Although the concept was most closely associated with de Gaulle and formed an integral part of his grand design for Europe, all the continental leaders supported the idea in principle. The chapter analyzes the way in which the political union, which even the Americans and British initially supported, became a divisive issue because of its Gaullist links and ultimately failed.

Chapter 6 picks up the British side. After their failure to replace or contain the Common Market in the late 1950s, the British concluded that they could only influence the process of European integration from the inside. Between 1961 and 1963 they applied for admission to the Common Market in the hope of transforming it to suit their own needs. In the face of implacable French political and economic opposition, Britain tried and failed to win the Americans and Germans over to its approach to Europe. London ultimately failed to convince either Washington or Bonn to support its application wholeheartedly, enabling de Gaulle to veto British membership in the end.

Chapter 7 details the development of the Franco-German relationship from mid-1960 through 1963. Having established a solid entente with Adenauer in 1960–61, but failing to advance his political union plans with the six Common Market members, in 1962–63 de Gaulle pursued a bilateral Franco-German relationship to dominate Western Europe. He exploited Adenauer's doubts on Britain and America's commitments to the continent and the chancellor's desire to cement the bilateral rapprochement to create the Franco-German treaty of January 1963. However, in an ironic turn of fate, wider Franco-German misunderstandings and disagreements reduced the impact of the treaty and brought a government to power in Germany that distrusted de Gaulle and was determined to resist his European agenda in cooperation with the British and Americans.

The Conclusion draws all the threads together and considers the short- and long-term significance of the successes and failures of this second phase of European and Atlantic cooperative efforts (1955–63). It analyzes the significance of the period for European integration, the Cold War, American relations with Europe, and the foreign policies of each of the four Atlantic powers, weighing the balance between transitory and enduring factors in each country's designs.

CHAPTER ONE

THE ORIGINS AND DEVELOPMENT OF

THE COMMON MARKET, 1955-1960

European nations must learn the biblical precept that to save their lives they must lose them.—Dwight D. Eisenhower, comments to German finance minister Franz Etzel, 6 February 1957

Europe in the Plans of Germany, the United States, Britain, and France

After the defeat of the European Defense Community (EDC) in August 1954 at the hands of the French National Assembly and its subsequent replacement with the Western European Union (WEU) in late 1954, the process of Western European organization reached a turning point. The initial period of cooperation between 1947 and 1950 had been shaped by fears of the USSR, the need to coordinate recovery from the war, and British efforts to thwart supranational integration. A second phase between 1950 and 1954 was dominated by French promotion of greater supranationalism to control Germany. The institutions created during the period of British predominance, largely cooperative in nature and typified by the Organization for European Economic Cooperation (OEEC), and those created at French initiative, such as the supranational European Coal and Steel Community (ECSC), would remain in force. Nevertheless, the failure of the EDC signaled the end of the era of French leadership, leaving the field open for new initiatives.

During the next five years, between 1955 and 1960, such initiatives came from a variety of directions, from Western European leaders, nongovernmental pressure groups, and also from the United States. These new ideas ultimately laid the groundwork for the formation of the European Economic Community, more frequently known as the Common Market. Historians and political scientists have often studied this period, but none has focused on the rivalries within the Atlantic alliance as the key factor shaping Western Europe and its institutions.[1] Between the mid-1950s and the early 1960s the major Atlantic countries waged a fairly traditional power struggle, complete with shifting allegiances and limited only by the Cold War necessity of maintaining the Atlantic alliance itself, by novel means. By promoting their own plans and resisting or supporting those of others, each of the four major Atlantic powers contributed to the birth and development of the Common Market.

Although Jean Monnet and the leaders of the Benelux countries are credited with the original ideas for the Common Market and the relaunching of Europe in 1955, German chancellor Konrad Adenauer and his foreign ministry quickly adopted them.[2] Bonn's leaders hoped to use a common market to advance German interests on many fronts, including opening markets and establishing economic links to the West to replace the political and military ties lost in the failure of the EDC. The Germans expected the Common Market to overcome the residue of past conflicts in Europe, foster Franco-German reconciliation, and thwart any temptation of future German leaders for a new "Rapallo" with the USSR. They also sought greater ties with the West to promote Germany's economic development, political stability, and democracy, as well as its external security. If the Soviet Union aimed at dividing the West, a common economic area would thwart Moscow's designs. Finally, German leaders favored further progress in integration to assure the maintenance of existing institutions such as the Coal and Steel Community.[3]

Postwar German leaders blamed European disunity for the devastation and division of their country and the continent's decline. Adenauer viewed the two world wars as European "civil" wars that had decimated the continent's human and material resources, sacrificed its overseas possessions and influence, and allowed it to be dominated by outside powers: "Germany and France are neighbors who waged war against each other again and again over the centuries. This was a European madness that must end once and for all."[4] Integration provided a chance to halt this conflict and restore Europe's position in the world. A strong and unified Europe could deal with both the United States and USSR from a position of strength and promote both German and European interests. It could force the United States to acknowledge European concerns and enable Germany to negotiate reunification with the Soviets someday on a basis acceptable to the West, all while reassuring its neighbors of its stability and commitment to European cooperation.[5]

Many German political leaders also felt that in an interdependent world dominated by two superpowers, the European nation-state had become obsolete. Looking back to their own history, the Germans rediscovered the Zollverein ("Tariff Union") of the early nineteenth century. In the words of Adenauer, it too "had initially been limited to economics but had led to political unity," as the economic ties it created among dozens of small states had ultimately provided the building blocks for political unification. Although they knew that the European case was more complicated, Adenauer and his follow-ers suggested that gradual economic unification via a European common mar-ket could similarly lead to a political entity able to serve the interests of Europe as well as its national components.[6]

Foreign Minister Heinrich von Brentano (1955–61), who shared most of the chancellor's basic views, was convinced that Europe must not halt after the EDC's failure. Although von Brentano saw European integration primarily as a link be-tween France and Germany, he and Adenauer both hoped that Western Euro-pean unity would be as wide as possible. After all, the greater its membership, the greater the group's political and economic weight. Von Brentano also shared the chancellor's conviction that, "over the long term, economic cooperation be-tween various countries cannot be realized without the development of politi-cal coordination as well."[7] As realists who understood the impediments to po-litical and economic integration, Adenauer and von Brentano hoped to limit it to the scale of the possible (that of the six members of the ECSC, known simply as "the Six") at the outset, while leaving the door open for future members. Rec-ognizing that an arrangement with France was the key to European unity, they were prepared to make extensive political and economic concessions to French interests in order to advance their fundamental goal of continental unity.

While there was general agreement within the German government on the broad design delineated above, there was sharp disagreement over how to achieve it. Minister of Economics Ludwig Erhard, the father of the "wirtschafts-wunder," led the resistance to Adenauer and von Brentano's short-term strategy. He feared that a narrow and autarkic common market limited to the Six would damage German political and economic interests by dividing Western Europe into two blocs and threatening to cut off vital German markets in Britain and the other excluded countries. He felt that Adenauer was much too conciliatory toward France and complained, "The French are always making new demands. When you concede them half of what they demand, they act like they are mak-ing a great sacrifice."[8] He favored a looser free trade arrangement embracing all of Western Europe. Until Adenauer's retirement in 1963, Erhard helped shape and modify German foreign policy, but never managed to replace the chancel-lor's conceptions with his own.

In contrast to their German counterparts, American leaders during the lat-ter years of the Eisenhower administration generally agreed on how best to ad-vance their country's interests in Europe. Although Eisenhower and his secre-tary of state, John Foster Dulles, had no particular blueprint, the consolidation of Western Europe was essential to America's diplomatic, political, and eco-nomic interests.[9] Eisenhower tended to frame his views on European integra-tion in the most dramatic terms. He referred to European unity as the "salvation" of the western world, as a guarantee of the security, prosperity, and strength of Europe and the West as a whole, and as the surest way to assure world peace. "This project would be to the benefit of the United States, of the Atlantic community, and of all the world." On the other hand, Eisenhower described the consequences of the failure of integration in the darkest possible terms: "If they [the Europeans] did not join together, deterioration and ultimate disaster were inevitable."[10] Like Adenauer, Eisenhower found an analogy for European integration in his own country's history. He often evoked America's evolution from a loose confederation of states to a strong federation as an example for Europe, notwithstanding the vast differences between the European and American cases, and stated that he hoped to "live long enough to see the creation of a United States of Europe."[11] Eisenhower understood that Western Europe had the economic and human resources to become a global superpower alongside the United States and the Soviet Union. With this third great concentration of power lined up alongside the United States, the global balance would shift decisively in favor of the West. A unified Western Europe could act as a powerful magnet on the Soviet satellites in Eastern Europe and slowly dissolve the communist bloc by peaceful means.[12]

Eisenhower was shrewd enough to realize that as Western Europe recovered its economic strength and political stability, it would become restless under American leadership and desire more independence within the Atlantic alliance and greater influence in the world. The United States could not withdraw from Western Europe and leave a vacuum for the USSR to exploit, but a unified Europe could both fill the void and meet the European desire for greater autonomy. Eisenhower, who was not afraid to use the term "Third Force," believed that a unified Europe would inevitably act with a high degree of independence from the United States and welcomed this prospect. A European "third great power bloc" would remain a close American ally, if for no other reason than the weight of common interests, and it would be able to bear a much larger degree of the political and military burden of the Cold War.[13] Eisenhower, who was always concerned with America's vast global responsibilities, sought means to reduce its burden and make it more sustainable over the long term by making Europe more responsible for its own defense.[14] He thus focused American support on the ambitious integration efforts of the Six rather than on wider and looser cooperative arrangements. He hoped for a strong supranational Europe that would include all the countries of Western Europe; but like the Germans he understood that it must start from a smaller base. He wished for the British to join Europe, but refused to hold up the whole process to wait for them.[15]

John Foster Dulles shared many of Eisenhower's views on Europe, particularly its need for self-reliance to create and focus a Third Force. Unlike Eisenhower, Dulles was led more by fear of Europe's future, of the prospects of neutralism and of an eventual deal with the USSR that might harm U.S. interests. From his own historical perspective and experience with the 1919 Paris peace conference and the failed Treaty of Versailles, Dulles recognized the dangers of American neglect and of European weakness and national rivalries and therefore dedicated himself to supporting European unity. Much more frightening than the possibility that a unified Europe might not always agree with the United States were the risks that a divided Western Europe might return to its old habits of internal conflict or prove unable to match the economic strength of the more centralized Eastern bloc. Dulles also made a virtue of necessity in another area. He welcomed the "realization by the Western European nations that they could not invariably count on the United States standing with them in the face of every difficulty they encountered in every part of the world. This realization is leading these nations to the belief that they must have real and intrinsic strength of their own and that such strength can only derive from genuine European unity. European integration might prove to be a welcome by-product of the current friction with our allies."[16]

Eisenhower and Dulles had learned hard lessons from the EDC episode. They now understood that all initiative for integration must come from the Europeans themselves and reflect real European ambitions rather than simply desperate and reluctant European responses to American pressures. For this reason, both men understood that the United States could advance European unity more by supporting European initiatives than by sponsoring any particular proposals themselves. They also realized that American indifference or hostility could slow or arrest the integration process and that the United States could not simply remain on the sidelines. Eisenhower and Dulles thus frequently assured European leaders that they supported integration in principle and would favor any particular proposal that advanced it.[17]

The British perspective toward Europe differed markedly from the German and American views and was based primarily on maintaining the three circles. Without the Commonwealth, Britain would become just another European country, unable to act as a global partner of the United States. But a Europe unified without the United Kingdom would become America's main ally regardless of Britain's links with its former colonies. If Britain could maintain its juggling act and retain its privileged relations with all three areas, it might be able to act as a bridge between Europe, the United States, and the wider world and play a leading role in the Cold War.[18] British leaders based their policy in Europe on promoting sufficient unity and cooperation to foster security and economic development (and British influence on the continent), without leading to supra-national unity that would confront Britain with the choice of joining and aban-doning its global interests or of standing aside, losing its influence on the conti-nent, and becoming little more than an American satellite. Both Labour and Conservative leaders believed that Britain remained a level above the continen-tal states; perhaps not equal to the two superpowers, but still able to play an in-dependent role in the Cold War and global affairs.[19]

Given their general worldview, the governments of Anthony Eden and Harold Macmillan opposed the idea of a European common market. To join threatened their special ties with the United States and the Commonwealth; to stand aside meant suffering economic discrimination and exclusion from a political and economic bloc that might eventually eclipse the United Kingdom as the main partner of the United States and a major player in the world. British opposition to the Common Market, both in theory and manifestation, was primarily polit-ical. Although voices in the government's economic departments occasionally argued that Britain's long-term economic interests were in Europe, they could not yet overcome the weight of the entrenched political opposition.[20] From a political perspective, European integration was a threat to be overcome (or di-verted) by whatever means necessary.[21] British leaders criticized efforts of the Six to achieve supranational integration as inherently unstable and dangerous. A limited group would divide Western Europe into competing economic blocs, and political divisions would inevitably follow. As they had done ever since the United States began promoting supranational cooperation with the Marshall Plan in 1947, the British countered these threats with proposals for wider coop-erative arrangements to achieve a truly unified Europe that could attract the Eu-ropean neutrals and the Soviet satellites.[22] At a time when European efforts at supranational unity seemed to have reached a dead end, such British positions were not unreasonable. The British simply did not believe the Common Market could work in practice and there was little evidence to suggest that they were wrong.

In a departure from the views of Churchill, the Eden and Macmillan govern-ments always viewed France as their main European rival. They accused the French of focusing on their narrow economic interests and aiming to dominate the continent and urged Paris to demonstrate a more flexible, altruistic spirit.[23] The Eden and Macmillan governments viewed Germany as a temporary tool of the French, if possible to be wooed to the British side, but in the long term as a potential threat that might dominate the continent and lead it in directions in-imical to British, European, and Atlantic interests. Macmillan summed up the strengths of his problematic partners as follows: "The Germans were becoming conscious of their [economic] strength and their ultimate superiority, but always feared being 'outsmarted' by the extraordinary skill of French diplomacy, equally agile and resourceful in victory and in defeat."[24]

Viewing Europe through their political lens, British leaders assumed that theirs was the objective view of continental affairs, that divergent views reflected wrongheadedness, and that successful diplomacy was a matter of political will and courage. If the French and Germans opted for forms of integration that excluded Britain from Europe, this reflected a conscious political choice rather than a decision based on economic realities. Throughout the period 1955 to 1963, British leaders insisted that if continental leaders really wished to solve their differences with the United Kingdom, they could easily make the necessary political and economic sacrifices.[25]

The French view of Europe underwent the greatest change between 1955 and 1960. This resulted not only from the transition from the Fourth to the Fifth Republic, but also from France's success in transforming the idea of a common market into a positive national as well as European goal. The leaders of both republics supported some form of further integration to clamp Germany to the West, create a counterweight to the USSR, and provide Europe with more influence with its American partner. The essential change in French policy came about as a result of the disasters in Indochina, Algeria, and Egypt (Suez), as French leaders thought less of a global power base and more of a European foundation with substantial overseas interests. Unlike the British, rather than insist on the equality of all their interests and risk losing all of them, the French made Europe the key to everything else. America's evident indifference and hostility toward French interests outside of Europe reinforced this renunciation and shift of foundation.

Like their American counterparts, French leaders had learned important lessons from the EDC episode. They accepted the idea that economic unity must be the foundation of integration and that political unity would have to wait. Without ruling out further supranationalism, they insisted that it remain within narrow political limits acceptable to the French public and the National Assembly. In searching for concrete and pragmatic means of furthering the solidarity of the Six, the French underwent a fundamental shift in their thinking. In 1955–56 they still largely focused on organizing as much of Western Europe as possible, including the full participation of Britain. The foreign ministry saw it as "politically dangerous to cut [Western] Europe in two, abandoning some European countries to the lures of great powers outside the continent."[26] However, in the course of the negotiations among the Six, the French recognized that the German government was determined, for political reasons, to organize a common market in accordance with French views. France was handed the prospect of a protected economic sphere and a continental bloc it could dominate. First cautiously, then with determination, French leaders abandoned an arrangement with Britain and moved forward to create a new Europe under their leadership. In this revolution the French shifted from doubt, even hostility, toward the idea of a common market in 1955–56 to almost fanatical defense of the institution in the years that followed.[27]

In general, public opinion and the views of national interest groups did not play a decisive role in the formation and early development of the Common Market, particularly in Britain and America. In the United States, public opinion supported European integration in the abstract, but was highly ignorant of the details. Only at the very end of the Eisenhower administration and under President John F. Kennedy would American business leaders and elite opinion become more concerned about the organization of Europe, a result of transatlantic trade disagreements, a worsening American balance of payments, and the widening Franco-American political conflict. Between 1955 and 1960 the Eisenhower government and the State Department had a free hand to pursue the European policy they desired.[28]

Throughout much of the late 1950s, public opinion in Britain was little better informed than that in the United States, and to the extent that the public formed views on European issues, it followed the policy of the government without hesitation. Polls suggested that Britons supported cooperation with Europe in principle but were largely unaware of the nuances between the various forms of cooperation and integration.[29] This lack of interest and knowledge resulted in part from the indifference of the British media toward European integration down to 1960 and the fact that Parliament and most government departments viewed European developments as irrelevant to Britain. Since there were few strong opinions on Europe and since the Conservative governments themselves opposed any sweeping change in Britain's aloof stance, public and elite opinion supported them in promoting alternatives to supranational integration and the Common Market.[30]

Public opinion and special interests played greater roles in France and Germany, but in most cases they supported the goals of the government and did not constitute a hindrance on policy. In Germany, integration was a partisan issue through much of the 1950s, with the Christian Democratic/Christian Socialist (CDU/CSU) government in favor and the Social Democratic (SPD) opposition against, for fear that integration with the West would damage the chances of German reunification. This opposition never succeeded in blocking the government's pro-European course, and, by the late 1950s, a consensus in favor of both European integration and Atlantic cooperation emerged, as the SPD began to adopt many of the government's foreign policy views.[31] Although polls suggested that most Germans had far less interest in integration than in reunification, public opinion was not an impediment to government policy.[32] Trade unions and business leaders tended to support, or at least accept, integration out of awareness of the political benefits and hopes for economic growth. These forces, sometimes skeptical over specific measures of integration and critical of the limited forum of the Six, caused problems for the Adenauer government when it attempted to chart a narrow continental course.[33]

In France public and parliamentary opinion were divided on Europe and did place limits on government action, which should hardly be surprising after the setback administered by the National Assembly in its rejection of the EDC. From this point onward a top priority of French governments was to prevent another such disaster. Initially both public opinion and business and labor groups were dubious over the idea of a common market, and their hesitations forced French leaders to move cautiously. However, when it became clear that Paris could obtain strong assurances from its five partners to protect the French economy, opinion gradually warmed to the common market idea. Indeed, the very doubts of the public and Parliament on the common market concept turned out to be an important asset for Paris, as it enabled French negotiators to obtain concessions their partners might otherwise have rejected.[34]

From the EDC Failure to Messina, 1955

After the collapse of the EDC and its replacement with the WEU in late 1954, the French and the Germans intended to move forward in the economic and political organization of Western Europe, but they also had reasons for caution. The EDC debacle was a disaster for Adenauer's entire foreign policy. In the words of one of the chancellor's closest advisers, this setback "initially threatened to bring down the entire edifice of European unity and dealt Adenauer a hard personal blow."[35] His policies of integration with the West and establishing an entente with France seemed discredited. The chancellor and the foreign ministry, trying to validate their chosen course, moved ahead with the integration process, but acted cautiously to avoid another spectacular defeat. Adenauer focused on new, practical steps for European cooperation and counted on Franco-German collaboration to achieve it. Germany's long-term goals had not changed. Adenauer and his confidants still favored supranationalism over informal cooperation to make Western Europe a potential equal of the United States and USSR, but they were willing to begin with more pragmatic sectoral steps and work gradually toward a real economic and political unity.[36]

This same caution typified the French attitude toward Europe in late 1954 and early 1955. The government of national unity of Prime Minister Edgar Faure (Radical) and Foreign Minister Antoine Pinay (Independent) wished to demonstrate to the Germans, to the French public, and to the rest of Europe that France had not abandoned the cause of European integration by its rejection of the EDC. As the ambassador in Bonn put it, "The Franco-German entente is indispensable to European integration. . . . The Paris [WEU] accords did not repudiate [integration], but rather expressly encouraged it."[37] Although much more pro-European than its predecessor (the Mendès-France government that had presided over the demise of the EDC), the Faure government was initially cautious on further European steps in order to avoid jeopardizing the ratification of the WEU accords. The French were determined to bolster Adenauer's position, but they were as anxious as the Germans to avoid another setback that might halt the integration process once and for all. For this reason, Faure and Pinay aimed at a less ambitious design.[38] Despite its military nature, the WEU offered a model for a new, more practical approach to Europe, emphasizing cooperation over integration. French ideas on how to proceed remained very vague, but Pinay hoped to find some arrangement that could include both Britain and the continental states. After the EDC debacle, the French themselves took no initiative, but waited for others to do so.[39]

Thus, the Monnet and Benelux proposals for a meeting of the foreign ministers of the Six found France and Germany willing to move forward but uncertain on the proper course. The summit was ultimately held in early June in Messina, an old Sicilian city just across the strait from the Italian mainland. As a long-time trading post and connection between Europe and the wider world, Messina seemed an appropriate location for launching ambitious new plans for economic unity. The Monnet-Benelux plans envisioned both general and sectoral integration. The Germans greeted the idea of general economic integration more enthusiastically than the French. On the subject of supranationalism, however, Erhard's doubts and the bruising EDC experience made the German position cautious. Moreover, during the Messina conference German leaders were preoccupied by the imminent Geneva four-power meeting dealing with all the outstanding German issues dividing East and West. Fearing that their Western partners might abandon their interests for the sake of détente with the USSR, German leaders urged the delegates at Messina that European integration must move forward pragmatically or be swept away by larger forces. Fears of Soviet pressure and possible four-power arrangements established without German input made Bonn willing to compromise a great deal to move European unity forward.[40]

The Germans not only set aside supranationalism for the moment, but also focused on developments among the Six, which they believed capable of making more rapid and sweeping commitments than the rest of Western Europe. Bonn advocated the formation of a customs union, as a quick sign of progress that presented opportunities for economic expansion, demonstrated Germany's growing linkage with the West, and left open the possibility of future political integration and supranationalism. State Secretary Walter Hallstein urged the Six to move quickly before nationalism revived and the spirit of cooperation receded. Europe must "face directly the problem of new structures that would combine prudence and progress as well as powers to allow for common decision making."[41] Europe's future depended on unity, its sole protection against the USSR. Hallstein accepted the pragmatic solution of sectoral integration, but insisted the future must remain open for supranationalism and the gradual development of a broader common market. The Germans maintained that a low-tariff common market of the Six would not alienate the rest of Western Europe but would lay the foundation for European strength and unity.[42]

Despite efforts to coordinate their position with the Germans, the French attitude at Messina conflicted with Bonn's on many points. This reflected France's different view of the international situation as well as the divisions among its leaders on how best to proceed. Foreign Minister Pinay considered the Germans' approach to economic integration overly ambitious and a danger to the French economy.[43] The German plan for a very low common tariff, influenced by Erhard and his ministry, threatened to flood France with foreign competition without any real political or economic benefits in return. At Messina, Pinay urged the Six to focus on sectoral integration, which promised rapid progress, and to avoid divisive supranational issues. Although the Quai d'Orsay was divided and some officials sided with Pinay, a consensus gradually emerged that France should support a common market that it could reshape to its liking.[44] According to the foreign ministry, the three key aspects of French European policy were "to control Germany without discriminating against it, obtain better [economic] results by combining workers, techniques, financing, production and markets, and take a conscious political step to bring about the unity of Europe." All this would also increase the power and influence of France and protect and develop the French economy. France should not reject the idea of general economic integration out of hand, but maintain a reserved position until it could negotiate positive terms.[45] Another reason for France's "wait and see" attitude was its hope that Britain would participate in the new European arrangements, providing stability and serving as another control on Germany. Although unwilling to postpone the building of Europe if the British remained hostile to all unity, France still preferred to make every effort to facilitate their participation.[46]

The two key protagonists, France and Germany, left the Messina conference viewing each other as the main obstacle to progress in Europe. The French realized that while Hallstein had officially led the German delegation, Erhard had greatly influenced the German position. Pinay knew that the latter "saw greater prospects for the German economy in global free trade than in a dirigiste organization limited to six countries."[47] The French faulted the German attitude as both overly ambitious in its appeal for general economic integration, and not ambitious enough in its failure to envision any concrete steps of economic harmonization and protection to make such integration possible for France. Despite their own caution, the Germans viewed Pinay's focus on purely sectoral integration as uninspiring and insufficient to provide their country with the links to the West they required. Adenauer noted that while he had "instructed Professor Hallstein to push forward on [European integration] at Messina, the French would not go along. . . . This was an election year in France and there was no uniform opinion in France with respect to European integration."[48] Each side was clearly going to have to move a long way toward the views of the other if the European relaunch was to amount to anything. For now, the Six agreed to establish a study committee in Brussels to consider the options available and invited the British to participate.

In 1955, the United States played the role of benevolent onlooker toward Europe. American leaders viewed the WEU as an acceptable framework for German rearmament and for integrating Germany into the Atlantic alliance, but it was not a sufficient substitute for the EDC in linking Germany and the West; Dulles was certain that "the long-range integration of Europe will be slower."[49] During the early months of the year, American leaders kept a low profile in European affairs, but did not hide their hope to see the European movement regain its momentum. They feared that the failure of the EDC might yet have dangerous effects on German opinion and undermine Adenauer. Concluding from the fate of the EDC that Britain would not participate in any supranational European project, American leaders focused on the Six alone.[50] The United States would continue to support wider European movements alongside the efforts of the Six since wider unity was the ultimate American goal, but it was clear to all where the real U.S. sympathies lay for the short term.

Eisenhower and Dulles welcomed the proposals of the Messina conference as meeting enough U.S. criteria for Europe to merit their support.[51] However, U.S. observers regretted the timidity of the French and the Germans and questioned whether anything substantial would materialize. They shared the German view of France as a major obstacle but decided to take a hands-off policy, avoid pressuring the French, and wait for the European situation to become more clear, because "Europeans would resent any U.S. initiative at this stage that might appear to seek to prejudice or shape European action—e.g., force it along supranational lines."[52] This reserve did not prevent American leaders from doing all they could to encourage a positive German attitude in the hope that France would eventually follow along.[53]

The British, like the Americans, were relegated to the awkward position of outside observers. In early 1955 Britain's leaders supported the idea of a European relaunch. They understood the appeal of the European idea as a counterweight to communism and neutralism and, like the French, they hoped that the WEU accords could serve as a foundation for future steps.[54] Unlike the French, they based their policy solely on the WEU and other existing institutions in order to assure that no further integration took place without their influence. After the EDC debacle the British viewed the French as the main obstacle to any form of European progress. The Foreign Office predicted that blind obstructionism might well reduce France to a "negligible factor in the western world," and warned that keeping France aligned with the West might be more difficult than doing so with Germany.[55] London simply did not believe that France was capable of major steps forward.

Although it backed greater European cooperation in the abstract, the Eden government feared that the specific proposals discussed at Messina could damage British interests. Unlike the French or Germans, who debated a general versus a sectoral approach but supported the Messina goal of renewed efforts at integration, the British government opposed the entire objective of the conference. For one thing, the creation of new economic institutions among the Six would overlap with and threaten the OEEC, which Britain dominated. Second, a continental common market would discriminate against British trade and could even lead to the creation of a hostile political bloc. The British cabinet, aware that it was incapable of reversing the gains achieved at Messina and fearing to damage its continental influence by denouncing the efforts of the Six, sent a representative to the post-Messina talks to try to channel them in the least dangerous directions possible.[56] This set the pattern for Britain's wavering between 1955 and 1960 between participation and aloofness as the best means to stop the European movement. When the British representative failed to derail integration during the latter half of 1955 and Britain recognized it could not collaborate with the Six without endangering its extra-European ties, it shifted its efforts to obstructing, controlling, or replacing the common market idea from the outside.[57]

The Brussels Negotiations and the Treaty of Rome, 1956–1957

Between the Messina conference in June 1955 and the signature of the treaties of Rome in March 1957, the German government acted as the decisive force behind the creation of a European economic community. Adenauer, the foreign ministry, and the German negotiators remained convinced that a common market could serve as the foundation for all their European plans, whether for the Six or a wider European grouping. Within the Six, they could gradually expand the economic base with supranational institutions, including a directly elected European parliament, to give it both a political and a democratic character.[58] After the Geneva conference in July 1955 failed to solve any major German issues or decrease East-West tensions significantly, German leaders viewed progress on European integration as a means to fill the void.[59] They achieved a key national goal by assuring the de facto inclusion of East Germany in the Common Market via a provision stating that the border between the two German states would not be subject to the common external tariff. Thus the Common Market would not further divide Germany.[60]

Undeterred by Britain's objections, the Germans insisted that the Six must develop their own unity and institutions first. Bonn interpreted British passivity and subsequent obstruction as an indication that the United Kingdom still had a long way to go before accepting European unity and might have to be left behind for some time.[61] The Six would move forward with any others ready to make the same commitments in order to deal with the rest of Western Europe and the world from a position of strength. If the Six made progress in the economic sphere, the British might support the use of the WEU for greater political unity and even an ultimate European federation.[62] The more headway the Six made, the greater would be the interest of Britain and others in participating.[63]

Throughout the negotiations, German leaders were frustrated by France's political instability and dilatory attitude. Although Adenauer was committed to the common market idea, in 1956 his doubts about France led him to consider fallback options.[64] Bonn feared that France, having rejected supranational integration in the EDC, had not yet taken a clear, decisive position on European unity. The French expressed mounting fears of German domination, diminishing perceptions of the Soviet threat, a vague inclination for wider ties with Britain, and a penchant for using the continent as a prop to support their global policies. The Paris embassy reported to Bonn, "One could sum up the present European policy of the French government as follows: in the face of its North African problems [Algeria], France seeks understanding partners, but refuses to bind itself too tightly to those partners."[65] Given their doubts based on their previous negotiating experience with the French, the Germans sought to construct an economic union that France could not undermine or obstruct. Adenauer prevailed over Erhard in Germany's call for ever greater doses of supranationalism, supporting the creation of a strong executive body or commission to represent the interests of the community as a whole and, if need be, to override the resistance of a single recalcitrant member.[66] The Germans also hoped to include majority voting and a specific schedule of steps toward future integration to prevent France from stopping the Common Market in mid-course. Adenauer himself noted, "Majority voting opens the possibility of advancing the Common Market even against French opposition."[67]

Because Bonn's political will for the Common Market had become so strong, the German negotiators overcame domestic opposition and made major concessions to the French to bring it about.[68] For example, when the French initially favored a European atomic community over an economic union, Bonn concurred, even though the idea had little appeal in Germany.[69] Bonn understood that the way to overcome French caution and build a solid foundation for Western Europe was through compromise.[70] But before Adenauer could finalize the deal with the French, he and the Auswärtiges Amt (the German foreign ministry) had to fend off efforts by Erhard and his ministry to redirect Bonn's policy. Erhard argued that the Six must take a less complicated and less "perfectionist" approach to European cooperation and build a simpler free trade area that would include all of Western Europe. According to Erhard, such an arrangement would be much easier to negotiate, would not divide Western Europe, and, accompanied by cultural and political cooperation among all the OEEC countries, would enjoy wider support than a narrow, dirigiste common market: "A Europe manipulated by bureaucrats that reflected more mutual distrust than solidarity and came across as entirely materialistic would be more of a danger than a benefit."[71] Adenauer trumped Erhard's objections in 1956 by insisting on the political necessity of success in the Brussels negotiations. The Auswärtiges Amt also rebutted Erhard's theses, insisting that the negotiations for a free trade area would squander the progress of the last year and a half and raise suspicion of Germany's commitment to European integration, without ensuring Britain's participation and support.[72]

Adenauer reaped the fruits of his victory in November 1956, when he met the new Socialist prime minister of France, Guy Mollet, to hammer out the remaining problems in the Common Market negotiations. There were other good omens, including the recent agreement to return the Saar to German sovereignty.[73] These decisive Franco-German negotiations in Paris took place even as the Suez crisis was reaching its humiliating denouement for the French and British. In fact, Eden's phone call announcing the British withdrawal came in the middle of the Mollet-Adenauer discussions. The French and German leaders, who spent most of their time discussing Hungary and Suez, simply directed their subordinates to settle the outstanding Common Market issues and inform them of the results. Adenauer felt that the Suez outcome demonstrated American arrogance and disregard for European interests and the reason why Europe needed to free itself from total dependence on the United States. The Soviet nuclear threats directed at Britain and France during the crisis proved once again that both superpowers were capable of exploiting Europe's weakness. When Soviet tanks crushed the Hungarian uprising, it demonstrated the hollowness of American "rollback" rhetoric and exposed Western Europe's powerlessness in its own backyard. In order to protect their interests on the continent and beyond, the Europeans needed to organize, as Mollet and most French leaders realized, though theirs was precisely the opposite conclusion of the British.[74] The idea of a common market, and the continental political grouping it implied, now had a much greater political appeal in France than it had previously. This new perspective, when combined with Adenauer's willingness to make economic concessions, ensured the meeting's success. It marked a decisive step in France's evolution from the main skeptic to the main proponent of the Common Market.[75]

Adenauer's concessions, which fell into two broad categories, moved the common market idea away from the original Messina conception and toward what the French had hoped for all along. In November, Adenauer agreed to many of the French demands for general economic harmonization to accompany the lowering of tariffs in the Common Market. These included the harmonization of wages and welfare policy, temporary special advantages for French exports, including protection against imports from the Five (West Germany, Italy, and Benelux), and concessions on the atomic community that would enable the French to maintain an independent military nuclear program.[76] In early 1957 the chancellor agreed to the implementation of a common agricultural policy that would promote French agriculture and offer it opportunities for expansion among the Five, largely at the expense of German farmers accustomed to a protected domestic market. Adenauer also accepted French demands that their overseas territories be linked with the Common Market. Although many Germans opposed any association of the Common Market with French colonialism, as did the United States and Britain, Adenauer accepted France's political requirements for its participation.[77]

These German concessions made it possible for the Six to sign the treaties of Rome, creating the Common Market and Euratom[78] in March 1957, with ratification taking place in all six countries by the end of the year. Although their original ideas on an economic union had been transformed, German leaders remained confident that the supranational measures they had managed to include, such as an eventual shift to majority voting in the council of ministers, the creation of the Commission as an independent supranational body, and the semi-detailed plans for progressive stages of development, would create a basis for the eventual political and economic consolidation of Western Europe. The signature of the treaties did not end the struggles with the French or within the German government. Bonn continued to push for the establishment of all the European institutions in one place and with as many links as possible in order to maximize their integrative ability and prevent competition among them. However, the foreign ministry insisted that the European capital must not be Paris, because, when in their own capital, "the French are prisoners of their conventional social cliques."[79] The Germans also pushed for strong political leadership for the Commission and other executive bodies of the communities rather than leave them in the hands of technocrats uninterested in the larger political motives behind them. To set an example, Hallstein gave up his position in the Auswärtiges Amt to become the first president of the Commission. On the internal front, the Auswärtiges Amt continued to insist on its primacy in the formation of Germany's European policy and opposed both the intrusions of the ministry of economics and the idea of creating a European ministry.[80]

The French road to the decisive meeting of November 1956 and the signing of the Treaty of Rome was much more circuitous than that of the Germans. After the Messina conference and through most of 1956, the French remained highly dubious on the whole idea of a common market. Although both the Faure-Pinay government of 1955 and that of Mollet and Christian Pineau from February 1956 to May 1957 were relatively pro-European, they continued to believe that sectoral integration, most notably in the atomic area, offered greater benefits to France and greater chances for progress among the Six. They preferred to proceed very slowly on the Common Market until they could be certain that it was viable and could be transformed sufficiently to protect and promote French economic and political interests. They doubted whether their country, with its shaky financial situation, could weather the economic liberalization that a common market would require and feared a backlash comparable to the EDC failure. Mollet and Pineau felt that "there was no possibility that [the] French assembly would accept at this time a common market treaty. [Such a step] would not be possible for France without a great deal of prior negotiations and also a great deal of education in France."[81] Moreover, Western Europe was initially not either government's highest priority. Mollet initially focused on ambitious disarmament initiatives toward the USSR and only when the Kremlin rejected these did Paris turn its full attention to Western Europe. Since it was the Soviets who rejected any verification measures on disarmament and thus prevented improved relations, Mollet hoped that the French public and assembly would now give greater support to western unity efforts.[82]

French leaders were also preoccupied with the idea of associating Britain with Europe. They not only consulted their British counterparts on developments among the Six, but were highly sensitive to British suspicions. France still hoped to avoid any step that could lead to an irrevocable division of Western Europe, particularly a risky step that might compromise French economic interests. The French remained dubious about being left alone in a Europe potentially dominated by the Germans. They feared that both the OEEC and the WEU might be casualties of a split between Britain and the continent. Also, they sought to protect their ties with their overseas territories, and the foreign ministry insisted that France would not "sacrifice [its] African role to [its] European one."[83] Finally, French leaders feared that the consolidation of the Six might weaken rather than strengthen Europe by inducing the smaller excluded states to fall into the orbit of either the United States or the USSR.[84] In sum, the French hesitated to move forward on an integration limited to the Six until they could be absolutely certain that no wider organization of Western Europe was possible and that the more narrow arrangement could be made to serve their interests. Like the Germans, the French understood the difference between supranational and purely cooperative arrangements and preferred the former for consolidating the continent, but they were long hesitant to abandon one for the other and hoped that the two could somehow move forward in tandem. France was prepared to make sacrifices only if wider progress proved impossible and if the prospects of the Six offered overwhelming benefits.[85]

However, balancing France's caution and delay were reasons for action and haste. Mollet, Pineau, and the foreign ministry understood that their country had lost the initiative in Europe as a result of the EDC debacle and wished to gain it back. A policy of obstructionism would further reduce France's influence. The Americans informed the French that they hoped France would "retain the leadership role it has always held in the European enterprise."[86] To achieve a status in the Atlantic alliance equal to Britain and the United States, France had to become the leading power of continental Europe. The longer it opposed European consolidation, the greater the chance it might be supplanted in this role by Germany. Worse, if France frustrated Adenauer's efforts to achieve supranational integration, Germany might abandon this policy, strike a more independent pose on the international stage, and again menace France. For Germany to turn to the British or become the leader of Western Europe on its own would be bad enough, but a German turn eastward would be disastrous. Given the growing German frustration at French tactics in 1956, none of these possibilities seemed farfetched.[87]

French leaders gradually accepted the Common Market when they became convinced that they had sufficient influence over the Five to shape the idea to their requirements. The "firm German will to succeed," demonstrated by Bonn's readiness to meet all of France's economic concerns, was crucial. These concessions demonstrated the strength of Bonn's commitment to a Franco-German entente. They offered the political basis for the organization of the continent under French influence, a bloc with the potential political and economic weight to deal with both the United States and USSR from a position of strength and serve as a foundation for wider European unity. Pineau argued that if the institutions of the new organizations could be established in Paris, the city would be "the definitive future capital of Europe" and France would become the center of a new European grouping and the magnet for all future European developments. It could both limit supranationalism as it saw fit and protect itself against German power.[88]

This idea of Franco-German collaboration as the basis of the Common Market coalesced only after one last supreme French effort at an arrangement with Britain. During the fall of 1956, Prime Minister Mollet, in the midst of the close Franco-British collaboration during the Suez crisis and in the face of slow progress in the negotiations of the Six, made a breathtaking offer to the British. Mollet called for the formation of a Franco-British union of the sort proposed in 1940 by Winston Churchill to prevent France from signing an armistice with Nazi Germany. During the desperate days preceding the fall of France, leaders as disparate as Jean Monnet and Charles de Gaulle had supported the idea as a means of keeping France in the war. The 1956 Mollet proposal called for common citizenship, economic union, French admission to the British Commonwealth, and close Franco-British cooperation all over the world. According to Pineau, "Mollet was ready to base his entire foreign policy on the entente cordiale."[89] This would have amounted to a French move away from the Six and a shift of their influence to a radically different base. The proposal reflected all the lingering French doubts on Germany and on continental integration as well as the enduring strength of French interest in ties with Britain.[90]

Despite the bold nature of the French offer and the dramatic references to the wartime alliance, the British delivered a disappointing response to Mollet. The Eden cabinet concluded that the French offer presented no advantages, since Britain still wanted an economic association with Western Europe as a whole, not an "organic association with France alone."[91] Moreover, London considered a politically unstable and economically weak France a poor choice for a privileged partnership. It welcomed neither the prospect of France gaining a foothold in the British Commonwealth nor the idea of casting the rest of Europe adrift. Although the British might quibble over details, they valued European cooperation as a means of controlling Germany. Thus the British rebuffed Mollet's proposals and announced that Franco-British cooperation would develop via existing institutions and arrangements.[92]

This blunt rejection, plus the dreary outcome of the Suez crisis, including the French feelings of abandonment by Britain as well as the United States, along with Germany's overt determination to do whatever necessary to make possible a continental common market, finally crystallized French thinking. The foreign ministry argued that Britain's new ardor for a free trade arrangement to associate the United Kingdom with Europe indicated that the negotiations among the Six had drawn it toward Europe: "Progress [in Britain's ties with the continent] has always followed initiatives taken by the Six alone."[93] Mollet and the Quai d'Orsay hoped that this tendency would survive the Suez debacle, and that Britain would recognize Europe as the key to protecting its national and transnational interests and balancing the United States.[94] The installation of Harold Macmillan, "the British statesman most favorable towards European integration,"[95] as prime minister in January 1957 augured well. Thus for a time it seemed that France might have the best of both worlds, a close association among the Six and wider arrangements with the rest of Western Europe. But if not, the events of October and November 1956 had convinced the French to move forward without the British. They now shared the conviction of Adenauer and von Brentano that Britain might be peripheral to Europe and that a Franco-German entente was the crucial element, particularly at a moment when Bonn was determined to make most of the necessary concessions.[96] By continuing to reject Bonn's overtures, France risked German abandonment of the whole idea of a common market in favor of an Erhard-sponsored or British-style free trade arrangement that would offer no protection to the French economy. The new threat France faced was not Britain's rejection, but its luring of the Germans, which would leave France in economic danger, political isolation, and without influence in Europe.[97]

While the Six negotiated the Treaty of Rome, the British felt a growing sense of frustration. Despite their efforts to convince the Americans of the dangers of the Common Market, the United States supported the idea. Eden believed that the Americans exhibited the same naive beliefs that had led them to promote the EDC.[98] With the Europeans, on the other hand, the British generally avoided the jeremiads they used with the Americans. Except for a brief unsuccessful attack on the common market idea in late 1955, they promoted alternatives, most notably the Free Trade Area (FTA). The British also made a show of supporting the atomic community, although the Eden government was actually indifferent toward the idea.[99] Finally, British diplomats and government leaders dealt cautiously with the Six to prevent any of them from using British criticisms to torpedo plans they themselves did not like and to shift the blame to Britain. All this gave an impression of drift in British policy.[100]

Throughout the Brussels negotiations, the British consoled themselves with two ideas. First, as discussed in the next chapter, they believed it possible to create a free trade area to complement the Common Market and protect their political and economic interests. Second, they continued to believe, even beyond the signing of the Treaty of Rome, that the Common Market would fail, primarily because the French economy would be incapable of adapting to it.[101] Indeed, well into 1958 the French themselves had serious doubts on their ability to implement all the treaty requirements on time.[102] Once the Common Market failed, the British could move in and pick up the pieces, just as they had used the WEU to recoup the EDC failure. Whether through a free trade area or some other mechanism, Britain would make its way back into Europe and take control once again.[103] Britain's policy of restraining the Six also included the promotion of the existing Western European cooperative institutions, such as the OEEC, the Council of Europe, and the WEU. All these institutions, created during periods of British predominance, had been designed to organize Europe into a loose cooperative arrangement. The British strongly defended these institutions, as alternatives to the plans of the Six, as fallback options should the integrative efforts of the latter collapse, and as containment devices should they succeed.[104]

There was little opposition to this broad British policy on Europe within the Foreign Office between 1955 and 1957. One critic was the ambassador to France, Sir Gladwyn Jebb, who believed that Britain must fully join Europe to maintain its influence and help stabilize the continent. He felt that London was wrong to believe that it could "induce Western Europe to broaden its political and economic base into something rather more Atlantic than European" and feared that the only real choice for Britain might be between "American dominion" and "European confederation." He feared that every effort to reinforce Britain's ties with the United States and the Commonwealth would only further alienate the Europeans and make Britain more peripheral to continental developments. Despite his keen analysis, Jebb's influence was limited for two reasons. First, it was a disagreement over means, not ends. Jebb simply felt that the government was attempting to advance its European goals in the wrong way and that participation, not aloofness, was the more effective way to influence Europe. Second, Jebb's views found no support from his Foreign Office colleagues.[105]

Even after Suez, British leaders continued to favor the United States over Western Europe at every opportunity. They drew a very different lesson from the debacle than did their continental counterparts.[106] Indeed, most major events and crises outside of Europe led the British to the opposite conclusion of the French and Germans. In virtually every instance, the British judged that the price for maintaining their overseas possessions and influence was to align themselves as closely as possible with the United States. This contrasted sharply with the decision of the Germans and French to overcome their differences as a means of lessening their dependence on Washington. The British rejected Mollet's "Union" offer in September–October 1956 and then signed a "Declaration of Interdependence" with the United States in October 1957. Although London recognized the importance of Franco-British ties, it could not overcome its view of the Common Market as, in the words of Foreign Secretary Selwyn Lloyd, a "French-led movement towards European economic autarky."[107]

The American attitude toward the idea of a common market was broadly similar to that of the French. In 1956, the United States, still with doubts over its practicality, preferred that the Six focus on sectoral integration, particularly in the atomic area, where more rapid progress seemed possible. As negotiations among the Six progressed in late 1956 and early 1957, American leaders grew more hopeful and provided quiet but crucial support. The State Department argued that the unity movement was "not directed toward the creation of a neutral third force or really a third force at all, but rather directed toward increasing Europe's strength and voice within the Atlantic Alliance [and] European influence in the United Nations and in other areas of the world where the Europeans feel they must be heard with some authority."[108] The United States refuted Britain's private, and, in late 1955, public attacks on the Brussels talks. Dulles noted that "it was the president's view that if Britain had given strong support to [the] EDC at an earlier time, [the] EDC would have been a success. British support came too late." The United States would seek to persuade London to take a more positive attitude toward the common market proposal, since it did not want to "see [the] British mistake over [the] EDC repeated."[109] This solid American backing helped overcome the hesitations of the Six on moving forward in the face of British resistance.

Like the British, the Americans viewed France as the key to Europe, but drew very different conclusions. Eisenhower and Dulles saw France as a declining power beset with political instability, financial problems, and colonial conflicts that offered the Soviet Union fertile ground to expand its influence, both in Europe and in the former French empire.[110] The National Security Council argued that "France's basic post-war problem has been—and is—to work out a new relationship with its overseas territories and adjust to the status of a continental nation, without provoking internal convulsions" and hoped that the European idea could replace nationalism and imperialism with the prospect of a leading role in a unified continent.[111] Washington also expected integration to solve France's economic problems and contribute to its political stability. While American leaders viewed Britain as peripheral to Western European developments, they deemed France essential to the construction of European unity.[112] Thus, although Washington was often frustrated at French obstructionism, it was more patient with Paris than with London. For example, the United States agreed to the association of the former French colonies with the Common Market even though it opposed such preferential arrangements in principle.[113] At the same time, U.S. leaders, like the Germans, promoted as much supranationalism as possible in the Treaty of Rome to ensure that France carried out its commitments and accepted the stabilizing influence of its European partners.[114]

The November 1956 report of the U.S. Council on Foreign Economic Policy (CFEP) best sums up the American strategic view of a European common market during the Brussels negotiations. It argued that the United States must support the European idea primarily for political reasons and tolerate a degree of economic discrimination in return. The Common Market would provide Europe with economic growth and stability, improve its global position, foster liberal-multilateral world trade, and build up the political and economic strength of the free world. "By further strengthening the bonds between France and Germany, [it] would reduce the danger of another war arising in Western Europe. [It] would strengthen Europe, politically and economically, against Soviet imperialism." Because the expanding European economies would gradually need to import more products and revise discriminatory tariffs, "there [was] good reason to believe that the net long-run effects would benefit the U.S. economy as a whole, and the world economy as well." Despite a few minor criticisms, the report generally endorsed Europe's emergence as an independent force allied to the United States in the common Cold War struggle. It was this conclusion that led American leaders to accept even the unpalatable aspects of the Common Market, to work behind the scenes to assure the signing and ratification of the Treaty of Rome in 1957, and to help ease the Common Market through the GATT thereafter.[115]

De Gaulle and the Common Market, 1958–1959

The Treaty of Rome officially took effect in January 1958 and the implementation of its economic provisions began a year later. As the Common Market became a reality, the positions of the major Atlantic powers changed in a variety of ways. These shifts grew out of the uneasy compromises between France and Germany that had made the treaty possible. Because the treaty included only an outline of future developments, a prolonged struggle ensued over the shape and meaning of the new Common Market in practice. All those concerned believed that they could still have a decisive impact on its ultimate form. The change was most dramatic after Charles de Gaulle returned to power in mid-1958, when he launched a sustained attack on the supranational mechanisms that France had conceded to Germany.

The last governments of the Fourth Republic, particularly the Mollet-Pineau government of February 1956 to May 1957, had produced the great change in the French attitude toward the idea of a common market. Once the Treaty of Rome was signed, with all its political and economic benefits for France, its preservation became a top priority of French diplomacy. There would be a very sharp French reaction to any effort to subvert the Common Market, whether from within or without. The last governments of the Fourth Republic still hoped for British participation, but they also realized the risks posed by the British conception of Europe. For the time being, they preferred to limit the cooperation among the Six to economics, in the hope that some means could be found to associate Britain with the continent before major steps toward political integration were taken.[116]

When de Gaulle returned to power, first as the last prime minister of the Fourth Republic from June to December 1958 and then as the first president of the Fifth in January 1959, he modified the French strategic vision of Europe and the Common Market in a number of important ways. A long-time opponent of supranationalism and a critic of almost every European treaty France had signed, he was aware that the French negotiators had done all they could to limit the supranational content of the Treaty of Rome, but he believed he could reduce it further. He decided to do so on a de facto basis rather than insist on formal revisions that might endanger the advantages the treaty provided France. De Gaulle shared his predecessors' confidence that France would now modernize and become more outward looking within the protected sphere of the Common Market. He differed from them in his dismissal of any British role on the continent and his greater determination to exploit the political opportunities offered by the existence of the Common Market.[117]

More than his predecessors, de Gaulle developed a detailed vision of the future of France and its role in Europe. He viewed the Common Market as the necessary economic base for the political Europe that he hoped to create. Moreover, while leaders of the Fourth Republic had expressed a mix of idealism and practical power politics, de Gaulle held the former in disdain and upheld the latter relentlessly. In July 1958 he informed his subordinates of his intention to build up Europe as the foundation for France's global power to replace its crumbling empire: "The primary objective of French policy is the construction of a solid Franco-African political and economic bloc. This bloc must be solidly linked to a Western Europe where France plays a major, if not preponderant, role." France needed Western Europe, and Germany in particular, in order to establish a political-strategic equilibrium with the Soviet Union and to carry out an independent foreign policy vis-à-vis the United States. De Gaulle hoped to use this European power base not only to maintain French influence in Africa, but also to force the United States and Britain to reform the Atlantic alliance and establish a tripartite leadership arrangement in which the three "global" powers in the alliance would act as a directorate and coordinate their policies all over the world. De Gaulle believed that German leaders would tolerate such a discriminatory arrangement in return for the added European security and stability provided by a close arrangement with France.[118]

Although previous French leaders had shared many of these ideas, the Gaullist worldview was distinctive in its exclusion of Britain from Europe. Instead of seeing the United Kingdom as a vital partner, de Gaulle considered Britain an external element, one of the three co-leaders of the Atlantic alliance to be sure, but without any role on the continent. Britain would focus on its leadership of the Commonwealth, while France would speak for Europe.[119] This attitude spelled the end to any French interest in British efforts at association with Europe. It signaled a new determination to move Europe forward without Britain and to exclude the British if they tried to force their way in. Ever the strategist, de Gaulle was prepared to play Britain and the United States off each other on the future of the Atlantic alliance. He used Europe to counter American leadership and used America's support for European integration to rebuff British challenges.[120]

During his first years in power de Gaulle concentrated on fending off outside challenges to his plans for Europe, cementing the Franco-German relationship, and limiting the supranational elements of the Common Market. Since the first two points are the subjects of Chapters 2 and 3, only the third is dealt with here. Unlike previous French leaders, who had envisioned France exerting its influence as part of some larger European concert, de Gaulle's France would maintain its identity and represent the rest of Europe. The president and his subordinates, particularly Prime Minister Michel Debré, another longtime critic of supranationalism, kept a constant eye on the activities of the Commission and blocked all its efforts to function as the nucleus of a European government, whether by establishing its own diplomatic posts or holding meetings with the leaders of nonmember countries.[121] France also opposed plans to fuse the executive bodies of the three European communities (the Common Market, ECSC, and Euratom) that risked increasing the power of a single governing commission. Portraying this idea as a pseudo-reform, the French made the radical proposal of fusing the three communities themselves, hoping to reduce their supranational tendencies to the least common denominator.[122] Finally, the de Gaulle government continued to hope that the seat of Europe could be shifted to Paris from Brussels, where it was temporarily located due to the inability of the Six to agree on a permanent location. The foreign ministry hoped that if the French gave Adenauer strong assurances of their commitment to unity, then "the satisfaction that he would gain at the thought that Europe was moving towards political unity would convince him to envisage the installation in Paris of certain institutions of the Six."[123]

Germany's reaction to the implementation of the Common Market and to de Gaulle's return to power demonstrates the predominant elements of continuity in its view of Europe. The Treaty of Rome, once signed and ratified, became the foundation of Bonn's foreign policy despite continued infighting between the foreign ministry and the ministry of economics.[124] The two primary considerations in German policy toward Europe in 1958–59 were the maintenance of the Common Market, with all its supranational aspects, and the search for some form of association with Britain. If the Common Market could be maintained intact, it would increase Bonn's influence on Paris. Unwilling to allow the British to torpedo the Common Market, the Germans also refused to allow de Gaulle to freeze them out entirely. Even before de Gaulle's return, the Germans sought ways to wean the French away from their protectionist tendencies. The foreign ministry noted that because "an isolationist France as one of the core countries of Europe would be a serious danger for [Germany] and its other neighbors," Bonn must convince the French to explore wider economic and political ties in Western Europe.[125]

As we shall see in Chapter 3, the Germans initially feared that de Gaulle would reject or eviscerate the Common Market when he returned to power.[126] However, during the latter half of 1958 the French leader made it clear that he would accept the Common Market and implement the Treaty of Rome in full. Nevertheless, German leaders correctly regarded de Gaulle as a threat to the supranational Europe they hoped to create; they worked to defend their ambitions against this new internal threat just as they did against the external British challenge. They feared that de Gaulle would bring Europe to a standstill, that he would accept the economic benefits of the Common Market for France, but obstruct the steps toward unity that they expected to receive as compensation for the economic concessions they had made. They recognized that de Gaulle intended to use Europe more forcefully than his predecessors as a means to promote French interests and to replace American predominance in Europe with that of France. The foreign ministry feared that de Gaulle saw no contradiction for France between "a close tie with Germany on the one hand and a world leadership role without direct German participation on the other," and that they would have little influence in a French-led Europe.[127] German leaders developed almost a siege mentality toward de Gaulle. After relatively rapid progress in European consolidation between 1955 and 1957, Germany would now have to focus on controlling de Gaulle and preventing him from dismantling or manipulating the existing arrangements.[128]

German leaders hesitated to confront de Gaulle directly, for fear that such a confrontation might lead the French leader to abandon integration entirely. Instead they chose to promote the supranational aspects of the Common Market, in the hope of outflanking France. Bonn held strong cards, because Germany had assumed a considerable burden of aid to France's remaining overseas territories and made concessions to meet France's insistence on a high external tariff. German diplomats expected France to reciprocate by accepting close ties with the United States, giving full support to NATO, and abandoning efforts at hegemony over Western Europe.[129] The Germans hoped to break de Gaulle's resistance to supranational integration by a policy of small, concrete steps.[130] Thus Bonn insisted on a strong and independent Commission as the representative of the community as a whole. It also supported both the fusion of the three executive bodies of the communities and of the communities themselves, not like the French as a means to limit supranationalism, but in order to concentrate all its force in one place.[131]

Despite their alarm over de Gaulle's plans and their desire to create a broader Europe as a complement to the Six, German leaders understood that they had no choice but to align with France over Britain when forced to choose. This awareness was most clear during moments of major East-West conflict and contact. Just as the Geneva conference had increased Germany's support for the Messina conference in 1955 and the Suez and Hungarian crises had led Adenauer to settle with Mollet in November 1956, so the second Berlin crisis that began in November 1958 led the chancellor to focus all his diplomatic efforts on an entente with de Gaulle. The Germans recognized that their desire to develop as much supranationalism as possible within the Common Market implied de facto acceptance of a division between the Six and the rest of Europe. Although Adenauer continued to pay lip service to the advantages of British participation in Europe and offered to act as a bridge to London, Bonn tacitly placed this issue on the back burner after the 1958 outbreak of the new East-West crisis. To express the linkage between the Berlin crisis and the Common Market in another way, we may quote Adenauer's biographer: "Trust and mistrust were closely linked in Adenauer's relations with de Gaulle, now as later. Thus he [Adenauer] sought a firm embrace with the unpredictable partner across the Rhine in order to prevent him from being tempted to turn towards the even more unpredictable enemy to the East."[132]

The British attitude toward Europe in 1958 and 1959 continued to fluctuate between engagement and aloofness. British leaders, uncertain whether the Common Market would last, still hoped to contain or transform it. They became increasingly frustrated at what occasionally seemed to be a conspiracy of all their major "allies" to keep them out of Europe. The Franco-German-American front in favor of the Common Market left them isolated. They employed distinct arguments with each, but none were very successful.

The British had long viewed France as their main obstacle, and the return of de Gaulle in 1958 reinforced this belief. The leaders of the Fourth Republic had disliked British attacks on the Common Market, but they had been reluctant to build Europe without Britain. De Gaulle, however, appeared to be working actively to exclude the United Kingdom by creating a protectionist economic bloc that would discriminate against its trade and eliminate all British influence on the continent. In response, the British vacillated between threats to isolate France and efforts to convince de Gaulle of the need for wider European unity. Macmillan informed de Gaulle that if something were not done, "a very dangerous situation would result. French protectionism would be confronted by British insularity. If we were threatened with high tariffs from the Six, there would be very strong reactions in Great Britain."[133] Given the determination of the Six to thwart any British spoiling campaign, efforts to isolate France had little hope of success and Macmillan's exhortations of de Gaulle had no impact whatsoever. Britain's only hope was that de Gaulle's hostility to supranationalism would keep the European door open for Britain simply by limiting the consolidation of the Six.[134]

Britain's leaders regarded the Germans as de Gaulle's underlings in his effort to exclude them from Europe and used a combination of threats and protestations of commitment to Europe to influence them. Macmillan argued that "Dr. Adenauer, in particular, fears the effects of Soviet political pressure on an isolated Western Germany, and also believes that only a Franco-German political alliance can prevent the Anglo-Saxons from doing a deal with the Russians over Eastern Europe at Germany's expense. He is, therefore, prepared to pay an economic price for French political help."[135] However, this very German dependence on Western unity made it the weak link in de Gaulle's design, since Bonn could not afford to alienate London and divide Western Europe. After all, the Germans needed British support in the Berlin crisis too. If direct pressure on de Gaulle failed, perhaps an indirect approach would be more successful. During times of Franco-German tension the British arguments carried some weight in Bonn, but Adenauer and von Brentano hesitated to break publicly with the French or contemplate a diplomatic realignment. Macmillan's efforts to defuse East-West tensions did not help. His unilateral March 1959 trip to Moscow to negotiate with the Soviets may have been primarily for domestic consumption prior to parliamentary elections, but Bonn interpreted it as a sign of British readiness to abandon Berlin. Macmillan hoped to overcome these German doubts through proclamations of Britain's desire to be part of a wider, cooperative Europe.[136]

The British also failed to win American leaders over to their view of the Common Market and to convince them of the dire consequences of excluding the United Kingdom from Europe. They hoped that once the United States began to suffer economic discrimination from the Six and witness de Gaulle's efforts to exclude the "Anglo-Saxons" from Europe, Washington would rally to Britain's side, bring the continentals to heel, and help London organize a wider, looser arrangement. The cabinet hoped to "seize upon . . . the indication that the United States were prepared to take a more active and official part in co-operating with Europe in the OEEC to find a solution of a large number of problems of the West."[137]

The main reason for Britain's failure was that America's view of Europe and the Common Market had remained largely unchanged in 1958–59. Indeed, American leaders were more intent on promoting further political integration than in assuaging British fears of exclusion or the threat of de Gaulle's leading the continent on an independent course. They were still concerned over the future of Germany, particularly the post-Adenauer era, and sought to institutionalize the country's ties to the West in new ways. The United States endorsed an expansive role for the Commission, worked with it and the other collective European bodies, and treated the Six as a group as often as possible.[138] Like Bonn, Washington concluded that de Gaulle's return to power meant that Europe had entered a period of consolidation with no major new steps possible.[139] The United States also recognized de Gaulle's larger designs to use Europe to enhance France's status as one of the three directing powers of the Atlantic alliance. Rather than confront de Gaulle directly, the Eisenhower administration "studied" his various proposals, while quietly promoting supranationalism among his five partners. Washington's greatest fear of de Gaulle at this point was not that he would lead Europe away from the United States, but rather that his hostility to supranationalism would undermine the entire integration process.[140] Because Britain and France had each, in their own ways, presented rival visions of Europe and the United States was dubious of both, American leaders increasingly supported Adenauer as a fellow defender of a supranational Europe closely tied to the United States.[141]

America's endorsement of supranationalism in Europe did not mean the sacrifice of its national interests. Contrary to British conclusions, American leaders recognized the dangers of European consolidation to U.S. economic interests. America's deteriorating balance of payments with Europe in the late 1950s, a result of the European economic recovery as well as the huge U.S. military presence on the continent, required Washington to seek means to guarantee U.S. access to European markets even as it promoted further integration. Once the Common Market was in place, America's policy toward Western Europe became increasingly pragmatic, propelled by the realization that the United States must play a more direct role in the organization of the continent and in the diminution of its rivalries in order to safeguard both America's political goals and its economic interests. The State Department summed up the situation as follows: "The question is whether this group [the Common Market], which has well developed international economic institutions, will develop into a form of political consultation which would enable the continental states to operate as a bloc within the alliance. Current French policy seems bent on steering it in that direction, emphasizing a tight customs union excluding outsiders and dealing with other nations as a single trading block."[142]

The "Acceleration" Issue and the Solidification of the Common Market, 1960

By the fall of 1959 the Commission and members of the Six proposed to accelerate the implementation of the Common Market. The successful application of the first measures of tariff rapprochement in January 1959 made it seem that the Common Market could be constructed more quickly than originally anticipated. Much of the slowness built into the original plan was the result of French demands during the negotiations. Now that France had become one of the champions of the full implementation and defense of the Common Market and de Gaulle's government had stabilized its currency and finances, acceleration seemed only logical. However, the issue was not as straightforward as it might seem. The acceleration of the Common Market, an economic step on the surface, had important political overtones. It required that Germany and the Benelux countries raise their external tariffs for the first time, thereby demonstrating a commitment comparable to France and Italy, which had already reduced their external tariffs in January 1959.[143] It also represented a decisive break with Britain and other countries outside the Six, forcing them to accept the permanence and power of the Common Market. Acceleration would demonstrate the viability of the community and dispel any illusions that it would not survive.

In the early months of 1960, the debate on acceleration provoked Britain's last effort to halt the Common Market from the outside. Macmillan pulled out all the stops, issuing inflammatory threats and evoking historical analogies that compared the Common Market to Napoleon's continental system and Germany's efforts to dominate the continent during the two World Wars. "He did not think it was to the U.S. advantage to have the U.K. ruined economically" and hoped that both sides "would recoil from recreating the post-Austerlitz, World War I and World War II situation, and not repeat that kind of a division of Europe."[144] Macmillan decried "a boastful, powerful 'Empire of Charlemagne'— now under French control but later bound to come under German control" that might force Britain to "take [its] troops out of Germany" to save money and make up for the economic dislocations. "These were not threats but facts."[145] Aimed primarily at swaying American leaders, the British campaign was also intended to influence France and Germany.[146] If Britain could pressure the latter duo to delay or cancel the acceleration, then it might still be able to stop the Common Market and achieve its hopes for a wider arrangement.

U.S. leaders refused to support the British, precisely because they regarded acceleration as a guarantee of the survival of the Common Market. By proposing to link acceleration with a 20 percent cut in the level of their ultimate external tariff, the Six had made an unequivocal commitment to the global liberalization of trade and ensured a positive American reaction. American leaders expected Britain and the rest of Europe to accept the existence of the Common Market once and for all and pursue friendly relations with the Six.[147] Eisenhower and the State Department thus threw their support behind acceleration, from its origins in late 1959 to its actual implementation in January 1961. They encouraged Adenauer and the Germans to be bold and supported the French argument that acceleration would actually help solve European trading problems by giving the Common Market the strength and cohesion to negotiate with outside countries. The State Department countered British objections in both public and private, reminding Macmillan that "we had supported the Six primarily on political grounds as the best way we knew to tie Germany irrevocably to the West. It was important that the Six feel sure they are really under way toward their ultimate objective. The main issue seems to be to reduce the degree of discrimination rather than the principle of any discrimination."[148]

De Gaulle championed acceleration even more than the United States. Indeed, the French turned the debate into an acid test of the viability of the Common Market itself. Because the British sought to block acceleration, France pursued it singlemindedly to thwart this and any possible future threats to the Common Market. "If the acceleration project failed," noted the Quai d'Orsay, "the enemies of the Treaty of Rome would be reinforced and the European project weakened."[149] Until the Six had consolidated their economic arrangement and Britain had recognized its existence, France refused to acknowledge the economic damage Britain would suffer. Throughout 1960 France dismissed British pleas to slow down as a pretext for sabotage and refused to negotiate any wider arrangement.[150] France, which feared that Germany and Benelux might yet abandon or downgrade the Common Market in favor of some arrangement with the British, hoped to force its partners to make a decisive choice by turning the issue into a test of the whole future of European unity.[151] Paris hoped this would be a model for the Six forming a common front in the face of strong outside opposition. The French also pushed hard for acceleration to take advantage of Eisenhower's support. With a new administration taking office in January 1961, they could not be certain of future U.S. policies toward European integration. To ensure Washington's goodwill and withhold any special concessions to

Britain, France insisted that the external tariff cuts accompanying the acceleration proposal be extended to all the members of the GATT and not simply to the rest of Western Europe.[152]

Since the two major outsiders, the United States and Britain, were divided, and since a Franco-German agreement was, as always, crucial to progress among the Six, the outcome of the acceleration episode came down to the German decision on the matter. Adenauer and the foreign ministry, as might be expected, favored the idea as a means to cement the existence of the Common Market quickly and thwart all its opponents, especially those in Germany.[153] Von Brentano feared that all the opposing forces in Germany, including the ministry of economics, the Bundesverband der Deutschen Industrie (BDI, the League of German Industry), the labor unions, the parliamentary opposition of the SPD, and the doubters in the governing coalition, amounted to an unholy alliance to torpedo the Common Market itself. He informed the French that "the best means of facing the Soviet offensive on the economic level was to strengthen the links among the Six as soon as possible."[154] All of the forces in opposition, which feared a sharp political and economic break with Britain and the rest of Western Europe, wanted the government to move more cautiously. The situation was complicated by the fact that in order to assure the French and the Americans of Germany's commitment to integration and strengthen the Common Market, the German government had already announced, in November 1959, that it approved acceleration in principle.[155]

The internal debate over acceleration was revealing. Adenauer and the foreign ministry reiterated the familiar political motivations for German commitment to the Common Market, and the opposition, led by Erhard, cited economic as well as political considerations. Erhard feared that Germany would be cut off from foreign markets outside the Six and that acceleration, by alienating Britain and the rest of Europe, would lead to a trade war and possible political conflicts as well.[156] Erhard's concerns, reinforced by the widespread opposition outside the government, forced Adenauer to retreat for the first time. In April 1960 the German cabinet requested a delay. Bonn proposed a compromise whereby acceleration was to be postponed, but not canceled, in order to provide more time to study its consequences and continue to search for an arrangement with Britain and the rest of Europe. Erhard's victory in this relatively minor episode emboldened the vice chancellor for future challenges to Adenauer and demonstrated how a broad coalition could be constructed to thwart his will.[157]

Predictably, the French were furious, and criticized the Germans for threatening the future of the Common Market and voiding the acceleration of its political and psychological significance.[158] To placate Paris and maintain the delicate balance within the German cabinet, Bonn agreed to carry out the acceleration by the end of the year regardless of how relations with Britain progressed. The six-month delay proved relatively inconsequential and even Maurice Couve de Murville, de Gaulle's foreign minister, noted that "the European economic community emerged undeniably stronger and in a good position to negotiate with other countries."[159] In the interim, economic discussions took place between the British and Germans, but they led nowhere. With the backing of the United States, France, and Germany, the acceleration of tariff harmonization was carried out in January 1961 over British objections. The result demonstrated the extent of Britain's isolation and the futility of its tactics of dividing the Six and resisting the economic community from the outside. The Common Market had become a reality.

Conclusion

The negotiation and development of the Common Market between 1955 and 1960 made it clear that Germany had become a key player in all European developments. The phases of British (1947–49) and French (1950–54) leadership in European unity were followed by a new period of German centrality. German concessions to French needs and demands had made the Common Market possible. Germany's tacit acceptance of the exclusion of Britain and its compromise on the acceleration of the customs union had ensured its progress. Disagreement within the cabinet over how to achieve these goals did not end in 1960 but continued for the remainder of Adenauer's tenure in office. Nevertheless, by 1960 the chancellor and the foreign ministry had succeeded in making the maintenance and development of the Six the foundation of German foreign policy. Even Erhard's one great "victory," the six-month delay in the acceleration of the Common Market, represented a minor pause. Most German leaders continued to believe that they could overcome de Gaulle's doubts on supranationalism and create an integrated Europe. As to Britain, Adenauer and the foreign ministry had grown less willing to make sacrifices or endanger the Franco-German entente or the Common Market to ensure its place in Europe.

America's support had played an important role in enabling Germany to transform the Common Market from idea to reality. Eisenhower consistently supported European supranationalism and defended it from internal and external attacks. Washington recognized that the phases of British and French initiatives for unity in Western Europe were over. Germany now led the integration effort, France was both an ally and an occasional obstacle, and Britain was a frustrating opponent whose resistance could only be overcome by the progress of the Six.

Despite the Eisenhower administration's consistent support of integration, there were also signs in Washington of a shift in attitudes toward Europe. State Department officials began to express fears, absent only a few years before, of a European Third Force.[160] They saw a revival of European nationalism in de Gaulle's designs, worried over the prospects of economic discrimination against the United States and a less-than-reliable partner in the Cold War, and hoped for new Atlantic arrangements to limit the dangers. These concerns, muted during the Eisenhower administration when State Department officials primarily sought to resolve the tension between U.S. political support for integration and its economic concerns, emerged strongly during the Kennedy presidency. In this sense, the origins of Kennedy's Atlantic Community can be found in the last years of Eisenhower's second term.

Between 1955 and 1960 Britain's Conservative leaders concluded that France had become the main obstacle to their leadership of Europe. The acceleration episode convinced Macmillan and others in London that the Common Market was unmovable from the outside. Britain's resistance had only reduced its influence on the continent and led to isolation. Shortly after the Six agreed to carry out the acceleration at the end of the year, the Foreign Office recommended that Britain switch tactics. A governmental report concluded that the Common Market was likely to endure. The Six would become a major political and economic power, dominated by France and Germany, and eclipse Britain as the main European ally of the United States. By joining the Common Market, the United Kingdom could prevent this, channel its development, and accomplish everything it had failed to do from the outside. Not everyone in the cabinet agreed, but when the report was debated in July 1960, a decisive shift in thinking was discernible. From this time onward, Britain embarked on a course of maintaining its global position from within Europe and accepted a more tightly linked Europe than before. However, this shift, more tactical than strategic, took place without an alteration of Britain's fundamental opposition to supranationalism and its belief in the maintenance of the Commonwealth. Still, the creation of the Common Market was beginning to alter the British worldview, and more changes would follow.[161]

By far the most dramatic shift in policy took place in France. In 1955 Paris still questioned Germany's stability, ambitions, and commitment to the West, but five years later the de Gaulle government viewed Bonn as its key partner. By this time, Paris's confidence in Adenauer was so strong that even in times of Franco-German tensions, when the Germans flirted with the British, France retained its sangfroid and waited for Bonn to return to its real interests.[162] Both before and under de Gaulle, France followed a dual policy toward the United States. It took advantage of American support of European integration to block British attacks on the Six and encourage the Germans, but planned to use European unity to reduce American predominance. De Gaulle elevated the latter from a long-term goal to an immediate priority. French policy toward Britain underwent the greatest change between 1955 and 1960. Initially, French governments had felt that Britain was indispensable to Europe, but their success in shaping the Common Market to reflect their own ambitions, combined with de Gaulle's return to power, transformed the French perspective. With the signing of the Treaty of Rome, France began erecting barriers to British participation in Europe and de Gaulle only reinforced a decision already tacitly made to opt for Germany and the continent over the United Kingdom. This was a reversal of France's diplomatic alignment with Britain and against Germany from the early twentieth century and all the more remarkable less than a decade and a half after the end of the war.

The five-year period from the proposal of the Common Market in 1955, through the signing of the Rome Treaties in 1957, to the reaffirmation of the Six in the acceleration episode in 1960, had a number of important long-term effects as well. First, the EDC setback was overcome and the Six established the institution that has served as the core of all European unity efforts ever since. Much about the Common Market remained to be settled, and its future was by no means assured in 1960, but it had faced and survived a series of severe tests. Second, the Six managed a transition from the idealistic and supranational-focused period of integration of the early 1950s to a more pragmatic approach that retained a degree of supranationalism but that clearly emphasized cooperation and compromise among countries, a trend that would continue thereafter. Third, the countries of Western Europe managed to use the Cold War and Soviet pressures for constructive purposes. Just as instances of American unilateralism motivated the Six to move faster toward unity, so Soviet threats and aggressive actions such as the invasion of Hungary and the Berlin crisis motivated the Western Europeans to settle their economic disagreements. Soviet criticisms of every step toward unity only convinced the Six that they were moving in the correct direction. The Cold War was not the decisive factor behind European integration at this point, but the Soviet danger and the predominance of the two superpowers did help to push it forward and overcome stumbling blocks.

Finally, the 1955–60 period cemented many national views toward integration that have endured ever since. France and Germany became the main actors in European unity and cooperation, and their collaboration was the key to all progress. The French loss of interest in a British role in Europe turned out to be a lasting long-term shift. Britain's separation from the Six predated this period, but the years between 1955 and 1960 represented the last opportunity for the United Kingdom to join the Six on the ground floor or channel them in other directions. Its failure to do so subsequently left it in a position of attempting to catch up to the Six or slow them down. Lastly, the years of the formation of the

Common Market witnessed the first real American doubts about European integration and the mix of political and economic hopes and fears that have characterized the past four decades of Atlantic relations.

The creation of the Common Market, which each of the four major Atlantic powers tried to shape to promote its own interests, in turn forced each of them to reevaluate all their European policies and to adjust them to its creation. In this way it set the stage for all the European and Atlantic struggles of the next decade. Like a rock thrown into a small pond, the Common Market produced ripples that extended outward, reached the shore, and reflected back toward the center of the pond in new ways. The remainder of this book is the story of those ripples.

CHAPTER TWO

THE EUROPEAN AND AMERICAN

REJECTION OF BRITAIN'S ALTERNATIVES

TO THE COMMON MARKET, 1956–1960

No Frenchman will ever say that he accepts something in principle and not intend to keep his word, while the English see nothing wrong with appearing to agree in principle while reserving the option to go back on their agreement in practice.
—Maurice Couve de Murville, comments to John F. Kennedy, 25 May 1963

The Choices Facing Europe

Between July 1956 and the end of 1960 two methods of organizing the political and economic relations among the states of Western Europe struggled for ascendancy. The formation of the Common Market offered one option for the organization of the western half of the continent, a supranational tariff union with aspirations for greater political cooperation and economic integration. However, only six continental states, France, West Germany, Italy, and the Benelux countries, proved willing to accept the economic burdens and loss of sovereignty such an institution required. Even before the signing of the Treaty of Rome, several Western European countries left out of the Common Market, led by Britain, began to plan ways to assure that the division of Europe into the Six and the "Non-Six" did not damage their interests. The alternatives the British developed posed serious challenges to the Common Market during the final period of its negotiation and during its formative years. Although the Common Market ultimately withstood Britain's efforts to transform or replace it, its survival was not inevitable and the alternatives the British proposed merit greater attention than they have received from historians. Britain and the Non-Six did not seek merely to block or reverse the creation of the Common Market, but offered an entirely different basis for the political and economic organization of Western Europe, an alternative not chosen, but an important critique nonetheless.

British leaders, as soon as they realized that the negotiators of the Six might actually succeed, developed an alternative that would protect their interests and replace or contain the Common Market. This alternative became known as the Free Trade Area (FTA), and the British championed its creation between 1956 and 1960. Compared to the complicated, supranational Common Market, the FTA would be simple. All seventeen members of the OEEC would gradually eliminate their tariffs, but only on their trade with one another. For trade with all other countries, each member of the FTA could set its tariffs at whatever levels it preferred. There would be no common external tariff, no harmonization of economic or social policy, and no supranationalism. Because of their desire to maintain their own agricultural support system, exclude continental agriculture from U.K. markets, and continue to rely on Commonwealth imports to make up any shortfall, British leaders insisted on limiting the FTA to industrial goods. British trade and other ties with the continent would be protected, the danger of the division of Western Europe dispelled, and Britain could maintain its special relations with the United States and the Commonwealth.[1]

This British proposal posed serious challenges to the goals of the Six and confronted them with a stark choice. They could continue their efforts, begun at Messina in 1955, to build a "little" European continental political and economic union centered on a common market. Or they could opt for a larger, looser economic association with all of Western Europe that would not advance European unity a great deal but also would not further divide the continent. As a seemingly less burdensome alternative to an integrated economic community, the FTA alternative might well drain away support for the Common Market among the Six and prevent its creation. Even if the Common Market survived, if both organizations came into existence at the same time, the larger FTA could easily submerge the Common Market and render it a minor regional association. Supporters of integration also realized that the political goals of the Six could easily be swept aside if the Common Market were overwhelmed by a larger and looser economic organization. Its external tariff and efforts at economic harmonization would be rendered superfluous and its decisions would always be subordinate to the larger FTA.

The conflict between these two very different means of organizing Western Europe was fought out in a long series of formal and informal negotiations between July 1956 and December 1958. The negotiations ceased in late 1958, but the British continued to champion the FTA for the next two years as an ultimate goal. All these debates centered on seemingly technical and esoteric issues, such as the relative speed of implementation of the Common Market and the FTA, the harmonization of economic and social policy, the inclusion or exclusion of agriculture in the FTA, and the consequences of the absence of a common external tariff. Although political leaders often exhibited frustration at the lack of progress that resulted from the long debates on these issues, the points raised in the technical arguments reflected larger political issues and symbolized the contradictions between two divergent designs for Western Europe.

Britain's free trade alternatives to the Common Market make little appearance in the historiography.[2] The few specialized or archival-based books and articles that address the FTA or EFTA tend to focus on the positions of one or two countries and accord little attention to interactions with others.[3] Usually the British proposals, if examined at all, are treated as nothing more than efforts to obstruct the Common Market and not as a real alternative for the organization of Western Europe. Because the topic is usually dealt with in such cursory fashion, oversimplifications and mistakes on both national positions and the wider significance of the issue are frequent.[4] None of the existing studies offers the multilateral perspective that is necessary to understand the development and ultimate failure of the British proposals.

As in the case of the formation of the Common Market, the governments of the four Atlantic powers had a relatively free hand in their deliberations over a free trade zone for Western Europe. In Britain forces outside of government played almost no role. To the extent that they did become involved, the public, media, industry, and unions all tended to support the free trade proposals, since they were so uniformly favorable to British interests. Parliament and all the major political parties supported the plan. Only in 1960, when it became clear that the plan had failed and a rethinking of British policy was necessary, did forces outside of government become actively interested in relations with Europe and begin to exert pressure on the government.[5] American business supported the FTA as a means to dilute the protectionism of the Common Market and prevent a European trade war. However, the Eisenhower administration and State Department placated these concerns by urging the Six to compromise on reducing tariffs and protecting American economic interests.[6]

In Germany, public opinion was divided on the choice between Common Market and the FTA. Public support for Britain, combined with Erhard's personal popularity, strengthened those who favored the FTA. This included the leaders of German industry (the BDI), the opposition SPD and FDP, and even segments of the CDU/CSU in the Bundestag. When the Bundestag ratified the Treaties of Rome in 1957, it attached a resolution calling for the subsequent creation of an FTA to complement the Common Market. All this reinforced the caution of Adenauer and the foreign ministry throughout the FTA negotiations, but did not determine their course. Since it was Paris that ultimately rejected the FTA and since Adenauer did not require a vote of the Bundestag for his tacit support of the French decision, he retained the last word in German policy.[7]

French public opinion and special interest groups were initially as divided on the FTA as they were on the Common Market, but over time economic concerns turned opinion against the British proposals. At first, there was considerable support for a greater British role on the continent, and the National Assembly voted favorably on an FTA in principle in January 1957. However, over time the economic consequences of the FTA appeared even more challenging than those of the Common Market. French industry, headed by the Conseil National du Patronat Français (CNPF), led the opposition to the FTA, accusing their British competitors of attempting to gain the benefits of the Common Market without taking on any of its burdens. The leaders of the Fourth Republic used this obstreperousness for hard bargaining and stalling for time. When de Gaulle returned to power and ended the free trade negotiations, the public, Parliament, and business interests were prepared to support his arguments that the British proposals were simply unacceptable for France.[8]

How Will Europe Be Organized?, July 1956–September 1957

After their abortive attempts to halt the discussions of the Six in late 1955, Britain's leaders faced the startling prospect that the negotiations in Brussels might succeed, despite the seemingly insuperable differences over agriculture, supranationalism, economic harmonization, and inclusion of overseas territories.[9] Throughout the Brussels negotiations Britain tried to stop or divert supranational integration, but by mid-1956 it seemed it must promote a constructive alternative if it were to influence the Six. Based on ideas developed by the Treasury and Board of Trade, Britain in July 1956 called for the creation of a free trade area to include all seventeen members of the OEEC and preserve the unity of Western Europe. London hoped that this proposal would have one of two effects. Ideally, it might lead the Six to abandon their negotiations on a customs union and fall into the British wake. If so, the threat of a common market would be eliminated and London would call the tune in Western Europe once again. Or, if the Six persisted and the Common Market came into existence, then at least there would be an FTA to surround it, prevent any economic discrimination, and limit its political significance.[10]

During the autumn of 1956 Britain proposed that the Six slow their negotiations to enable the seventeen OEEC countries to negotiate an FTA and activate it at the same time as the Common Market. British leaders also specified that the Common Market and the FTA must have similar or identical procedures and institutions, including comparable methods for lowering tariffs, advancing from one stage of tariff reductions to another, and reconciling disputes. According to the British, without the coordination of FTA and Common Market tariff reductions, there would be discrimination and an economic rift. For this reason, all

OEEC members now needed to "demonstrate a great deal of audacity" to ensure the unity of all of Western Europe.[11] From the outset, British leaders attempted to make nondiscrimination a cardinal principle of the negotiations, a direct challenge to the very nature of the tariff union the Six sought to create. Close linkage of the Common Market and the FTA of the sort the British demanded would limit the maneuvering room of the Six in Brussels and reduce the significance of any institution they created. Because Eden and other British leaders were convinced that "France would accept a common market only on the basis of a high protective tariff," they insisted that the FTA was necessary to protect British trade with the continent.[12]

Britain portrayed its FTA proposal as a major shift from its traditional aloofness from Europe and a signal of its commitment to continental affairs. However, British leaders also emphasized that relations with the United States and the Commonwealth remained paramount to them and chided the Six for pressuring them to choose between Europe and their overseas ties. At the same press conference in October 1956 at which he formally announced the British intention to pursue an FTA, Chancellor of the Exchequer Harold Macmillan restated Britain's loyalty to the Commonwealth.[13] This would give Britain the best of both worlds: economic ties with Europe and the Commonwealth as well as the independence to pursue its other global interests.

Even as they promoted the FTA, the British defended the wider European institutions that already existed, such as the OEEC and WEU, and warned that they would suffer if six of their members began to discriminate against the others. In late 1956 and early 1957, Foreign Secretary Selwyn Lloyd even proposed a "Grand Design" to revitalize and extend the OEEC, NATO, and other European umbrella institutions. He called for the subordination of all smaller organizations, such as the customs union the Six sought to create, to the OEEC and described them as purely "regional" groupings. This was a blatant effort to place the Common Market, even before it came into existence, under the control of the OEEC. The Foreign Office sought to put a more positive spin on the idea for the Americans, stating that the British merely sought to ensure that "the European Community develops as part of the Atlantic community and that energies are not wasted on attempting to develop a European military, foreign, or economic policy independent of the United States of America."[14]

In case the carrot of greater British participation in Europe did not sway the Six, the Eden and Macmillan governments also hinted that they would make use of the stick if necessary. Although they later developed a number of dramatic threats in case the Six refused to accept an FTA to complement the Common Market, the British initially issued vague warnings of the danger of dividing Western Europe in the face of the danger from the East. They warned that if rebuffed by the Six, Britain would withdraw from continental affairs and focus on its relations with the United States and the Commonwealth.[15] On at least one early occasion the British made these hints more explicit. In July 1957 Selwyn Lloyd informed the French that if the FTA did not materialize, the British would have to "use all the means at their disposal to demolish the Common Market."[16]

As we have seen in the previous chapter, France and Germany were alarmed by British hostility to the Common Market but held the line against their efforts to subvert it. Both desired British participation in Europe, but resisted London's pressure to abandon the Common Market or to bring it and the FTA into existence at the same time. Nevertheless, from the outset the German government was divided over the FTA. Erhard welcomed the British proposals as a counter to Adenauer's firm support of the Common Market. The minister of economics announced to the cabinet that "the Common Market and free trade zone must be viewed as a functional whole. The Common Market was not the center of everything, but rather just one part of the free trade zone."[17] Both must come into being at the same time and reduce tariffs at the same pace. In Erhard's view, the FTA would diminish the Common Market's significance and steer the German economy on a path toward global free trade and expansion and away from protectionism and stagnation. It would also assure the maintenance of Western European unity.

Unlike Erhard, both Adenauer and the foreign ministry preferred to move as quickly as possible to bring the common market negotiations to a successful conclusion. They supported closer British ties with the continent, noting that just as conciliatory German relations with France had improved their country's standing in the eyes of the United States, so "an understanding German policy toward Great Britain would secure [their] reputation as a loyal and farsighted ally."[18] They thus accepted the FTA as a means to assure the unity of Western Europe, but still believed that the creation of the Common Market must take priority. Formal FTA negotiations must await the signing and ratification of the Common Market and Euratom treaties so as not to obstruct or delay their completion.[19] Adenauer overruled Erhard and rejected both the abandonment of the Common Market and anything that subordinated it to any other organization. The chancellor and the foreign ministry recognized that Britain's "Grand Design" and its insistence on linking the Common Market and the FTA were aimed at subverting the independence of the Six and must be rejected.[20]

The initial French reaction to the British free trade proposals proved similar, but not identical, to that of the Germans. Like Bonn, Paris supported greater British association with the continent. Indeed, foreign ministry officials repeatedly noted that this political factor constituted the single greatest advantage of the ostensibly economic FTA proposal. French officials initially assumed that the free trade discussions would ultimately succeed and stated that the negotiations would focus primarily on balancing the benefits and risks the FTA would entail.[21] A note written by the Quai d'Orsay in May 1957 listing the political benefits of the FTA could easily have been produced by the British Foreign Office, as it stated the importance of "associating Great Britain as closely as possible with the continent" and preventing "the division of Europe into two groups or several groups of countries." French support of the FTA would assure broad European unity, prevent the formation of trade blocs, and maintain the solidarity of the Six.[22]

Despite this support for an FTA in principle, Paris agreed with Bonn that free trade negotiations could not slow progress toward the Common Market. Foreign Minister Pineau portrayed the Common Market as the economic foundation upon which any FTA would be constructed, but conceded that France would not promote any further integration (beyond the Common Market) among the Six until it had given the British proposals a fair hearing.[23] French diplomats argued bluntly that the signing and ratification of the Common Market and Euratom treaties would facilitate the subsequent creation of a free trade area and that, conversely, "if there is no Common Market, then there will be no free trade zone."[24] They understood that it was only the progress of the Six toward integration that had motivated British overtures toward the continent in the first place and that if the progress of the Six should stop, British interest in the continent would evaporate.[25]

The French were also cautious on the FTA because they perceived significant political and economic dangers in it. In addition to having to face competition from Germany and the other Common Market members, the FTA would immediately confront the French economy with unrestrained competition from Britain and ten additional countries. The French economy, although growing stronger and gradually liberalizing its exchanges, could only take on so many new challenges at once. The Common Market was a higher priority, because it provided for greater protection.[26] The FTA lacked any of the guarantees that the French ultimately received in the Treaty of Rome. These included the equalization of the conditions of competition (such as wage levels) among the Six, alignment of their social (welfare) and financial policies, common agricultural arrangements, and steps to prevent diversions of trade.[27] The FTA also lacked a common external tariff, which meant that the Six could face a flood of goods from outside Europe that would render their own common tariff meaningless. The French feared that products from the Commonwealth would enter Britain duty-free and then be shipped on to the Six via the FTA, thereby evading the Common Market's external tariff. In short, the FTA would expose the French economy not only to the competition of eleven additional European countries, but also to that of other countries all over the world.[28] The French also disliked the British insistence on the exclusion of agriculture from the FTA. They argued that as conceived by the British, the FTA would serve the economic interests of industrial powers such as Britain and Germany and slight countries with large agricultural sectors, such as France. The exclusion of agriculture might also endanger the provisions of the Common Market, which had been developed to protect French agriculture and provide it opportunities for export expansion. Moreover, the Quai d'Orsay noted that French "public opinion would have difficulty accepting a treaty that appeared to give more advantages to the United Kingdom than to [France]."[29]

In addition to these economic concerns, French leaders also sensed political dangers in the FTA. While sharing London's view on consolidating European organizations, Paris feared that the United Kingdom sought to drown the Common Market in a vast FTA before the former could even come into existence. The British "Grand Design" only reinforced such fears.[30] Even those less distrustful of British motives feared that the negotiation and creation of the FTA could divide the Six and void the Common Market of any significance. After all, in the words of the foreign ministry, "How could the independence and the initiative of the Common Market be reconciled with the need to harmonize its policy with that of the free trade zone?"[31] The fact that Erhard and many Benelux officials exhibited much greater interest in the FTA than in the Common Market only confirmed French apprehensions and led them to insist that the FTA not call any aspect of the Common Market into question or divide its members in any way.[32]

As a result of these political and economic concerns regarding the FTA, the French insisted on a number of points to protect their interests. First, negotiations on the FTA must await the signing and ratification of the treaties of the Six. Second, any free trade negotiations must proceed slowly and examine all the technical issues carefully.[33] Any FTA to be created must be very similar to the Common Market, so that the latter's provisions for economic harmonization, trade stability, and agriculture would not be voided. All this would make the negotiation of the FTA very difficult and undermine the entire British conception.[34]

The initial American reaction to the British FTA proposals mirrored that of the Germans and the French, supportive in the abstract, but concerned over certain implications and unwilling to let London derail the negotiations for the Common Market. The Eisenhower administration and the State Department welcomed the end of Britain's attacks on the Common Market of late 1955 and supported its apparent effort at rapprochement with the continent. Without studying the FTA and its implications carefully, American officials began to call for the successful negotiation of both the Common Market and the FTA. American analysts tended to group the two proposals together as means to further the political and economic cohesion of Western Europe and promote multilateral trade and Atlantic cooperation. For example, the major November 1956 study by the Council on Foreign Economic Policy stated, "The United States' position with respect to current Western European proposals for a common market and free trade area grows out of our consistent support of measures for political and economic cohesion of Western Europe," and "The United States welcomes the initiative recently taken by European countries for the establishment of a common market and a European free trade area."[35] As always, the Cold War background and the need to build European strength and unity were crucial to determining Washington's policy. With its FTA, Britain could maintain a leadership role in Europe, contributing to continental stability, blocking neutralism, keeping its troops in Germany, and reducing the dangers of communist takeovers in France and Italy.[36]

Notwithstanding this generally positive reaction, American support of the FTA was soon marked by important caveats. U.S. officials initially believed that most, if not all, of the seventeen OEEC members also favored the FTA as a means to adjust Europe to the creation of the Common Market and assure European cohesion and cooperation. However, because the FTA lacked the supranational political dimension of the Common Market, it had a lower priority. Eisenhower and Dulles argued that the FTA proposal must not slow the completion of the Brussels negotiations or damage the Common Market in any way. In July 1957, Dulles informed the embassy in London that if the British were "thinking in terms [of] trying to delay formal entry into force [of the] Common Market and Euratom treaties in order to allow time for completion and/or ratification [of an] FTA treaty you should discreetly endeavor [to] throw cold water on [the] idea."[37] Washington rejected the "Grand Design" as a device to delay or block the integration of the Six and concluded that it blurred the important distinction between purely cooperative and supranational institutions, a tactic the British had used in the past. Although it valued cooperative organizations such as the OEEC, supranational institutions such as the Common Market took European collaboration to an entirely new level.[38] This view reinforced the Franco-German opposition to the "Grand Design" and the rapid creation of an FTA. Indeed, American enthusiasm for the FTA waned the more closely the idea was examined. It would discriminate against American trade, and the worsening balance of payments made the United States less willing to tolerate this. The Americans could accept such discrimination from the Common Market for the sake of European political integration and linking Germany permanently to the West, but the FTA would mean discrimination by seventeen countries instead of just six and would not offer political integration in return. Dulles warned the

British that "serious problems would arise if tariffs were raised against U.S. goods."[39]

With their free trade proposals in 1956 the British offered a nonsupranational, economic-based form of all-European cooperation as an alternative to, or a control over, the Common Market. But France and Germany, supported by the United States, insisted on completing the Brussels negotiations and ratifying the Rome treaties before considering the British proposals. This prevented the British from simply replacing the Common Market before it came into existence.[40] British leaders concluded that the French, and possibly the others, had only paid lip service to the FTA in order to reduce domestic and international opposition to the creation of the Common Market. They feared that once the Common Market was born, the continental states would refuse to complement it with an FTA. The French embassy in London noted that Paris would have to convince the British that it "would not lose interest in the free trade zone once it had the ratification of the treaties of Rome in hand."[41]

Although the debates over the FTA were not yet a Franco-British conflict, it was apparent that these two countries held very different views on the organization of Western Europe and that their plans would not be easily reconciled. While both countries supported the idea of a free trade zone, the conditions each had already attached would render agreement almost impossible after the ratification of the Rome treaties.[42] Others would join the dispute, with Eisenhower, Adenauer, and the Italians siding with the French on the primacy of the European communities, and Erhard, Benelux, and the other Western European countries following the British lead.

France versus Britain: Common Market versus Free Trade Area, October 1957–May 1958

After the Six ratified the Rome treaties during the summer and autumn of 1957, Britain convened formal negotiations on the FTA under the auspices of the OEEC in a special committee led by the British paymaster general, Reginald Maudling. This group, meeting irregularly in Paris between October 1957 and November 1958, worked to resolve the technical disagreements and produce a treaty. As the talks progressed, it became clear that most of the seventeen OEEC members would accept the British conditions with minor modification. Only the French voiced opposition to almost every condition of the free trade zone, with the result that during this period it was they, and not the British, who became isolated. In this situation the French hesitated to break off the negotiations and resorted to issuing counterproposals unacceptable to the British and stalling for time.

Britain now considered the period between the ratification of the Rome treaties and the date set for the implementation of the Common External Tariff (CET), January 1959, to be its prime opportunity to negotiate a free trade area. If the FTA were formed quickly, it could still reduce the Common Market to insignificance. British delegates tried to expedite the negotiations, warning their partners against becoming bogged down in technical discussions and criticizing France's dilatory tactics, which threatened to overwhelm the discussions with technical quarrels. Maudling also stoked the fears of protectionism among those outside the Common Market as well as their concerns on the "serious political implications of a Little Europe under German domination."[43]

In order to overcome French opposition and gain support among the other OEEC members, the British focused on the political aspects of the FTA. They argued that many of the same technical debates on agriculture and tariffs had threatened to deadlock the Common Market negotiations, but that the political will of the governments of the Six had compelled the negotiators to make compromises. The leaders of the OEEC countries must now demonstrate a similar political will to maintain European unity by signing an accord in principle for the FTA and worrying later about the technical details and hypothetical problems that the accord might create. Macmillan informed Adenauer that "the fate of European unity lay in [Adenauer's] hands. [His] influence on the French would be decisive. The technical problems would be easy to solve if the will to do so existed."[44]

In order to reassure the French and others, British leaders emphasized that they accepted the Common Market and sought only to complement it with an inclusive free trade area.[45] The British accompanied such assurances with strong-arm tactics. They reiterated the now-familiar line that a common market without an FTA would lead to both the economic and political division of Europe. They also issued a number of other, more specific, political threats designed for particular audiences. In order to alarm the Germans and induce them to intercede with the French, Macmillan claimed that British public opinion would not pay to defend a country that discriminated against it economically and hinted at the withdrawal of British troops from the continent. "A[n economic] division would inevitably have repercussions on the strategic conceptions of European defense. If Great Britain were closed out of Europe, then it would have to seek other connections both in and outside of Europe."[46] British leaders not only threatened the French that they would attack the Common Market in the GATT and rally the Commonwealth and developing world against the Six, but also warned that an FTA failure would force them to distance themselves from Europe and reconsider all their ties with the continent.[47]

German leaders did not see the Common Market and the FTA as mutually exclusive. Erhard adhered to the British line that the Common Market merely constituted the core of an all-European FTA and believed that Germany could mediate between the British and French. He reminded both the British and his own chancellor that "the federal government was committed by a resolution of the Bundestag to work for the creation of a free trade zone to complement the Common Market."[48] Even Adenauer acknowledged Germany's commitment to achieve an FTA in order to prevent the further division of the continent. With France more unstable than ever in the spring of 1958 as a result of the ongoing Algerian war and its inability to form a durable government, Germany still viewed British involvement as crucial to European unity and strength.[49] After an April 1958 British-German summit, Adenauer joined Macmillan in issuing a statement emphasizing their mutual commitment to the FTA.[50]

In their new role as mediators between the British and French, the Germans made a series of compromise proposals. They suggested that the British accept some agricultural arrangements, a degree of economic harmonization, and flexibility on the move from one stage of tariff reductions to another. However, their main attempts at conciliation were directed at France. German diplomats urged the French to concede on the FTA's timetable and basic nature. To avoid discrimination, Bonn proposed that the Common Market and the FTA be implemented at the same time. Moreover, it maintained that to insist on identical conditions for the two organizations would injure the smaller organization. The Germans upheld the necessity of a multinational arrangement and deemed ad hoc reactions to trade problems as inadequate.[51] Germany's Cold War concerns, together with its economic worries, accounted for this emphasis.

The German government also hoped to use the FTA negotiations for its own political purposes. According to the Treaty of Rome, the Commission, the executive organ of the Common Market, was empowered to negotiate treaties of association for the Six. The French, however, finding themselves isolated in the Maudling committee, refused to let the Commission negotiate in their name. Because the Germans wished to expand the supranational aspects of the Common Market, as well as to attenuate French obstruction, they urged their partners to allow the Commission to play a greater role in the FTA negotiations, which would demonstrate the viability of the Common Market both to its members and to outsiders who might still hope that it would fail.[52]

Many German officials not only shared Britain's support of the FTA, but issued similar warnings against its failure. Britain would form closer ties with the Commonwealth and the Non-Six and the OEEC would likely collapse, whereupon British retaliation against the Six would be inevitable. London would form its own trade bloc and pull its troops out of Europe.[53] Like the British, German negotiators became increasingly frustrated with France's tactics, which seemed to undermine all the negotiations.[54] By the spring of 1958 Erhard complained to the French that "it appeared that of the six members of the Common Market, five were disposed to conclude an accord acceptable to the other eleven countries of the OEEC, while only one, France, rendered such an accord impossible by its refusal to go along." Erhard informed the French that their "fears seemed to have little foundation and their attitude threatened to lead to a serious crisis with Great Britain and a lasting division of Europe for which France would bear the responsibility and from which the Soviet Union would be the beneficiary."[55] Under strong domestic pressure in favor of the FTA, Adenauer made similar comments to reassure the British.

U.S. support for the FTA was more qualified than that of the Germans. While welcoming both the Common Market and the FTA, American leaders emphasized that both must follow liberal trade relations with third countries.[56] Washington saw the FTA's advantages in primarily "negative" (or preventative) terms. Rather than the "positive" results produced by the Common Market (Franco-German rapprochement, supranational integration, and so on), the FTA would prevent unfavorable developments. "A breakdown in negotiations might adversely affect our political and strategic objectives and our interest in a multilateral trading system."[57] Specifically, the United States feared the division of Europe into trade blocs, the isolation of Britain from the continent, and preferential European deals made at the expense of American interests. As the debate intensified, American officials were careful not to take sides. They were confident that France would ultimately choose to maintain British involvement in continental affairs as a counterweight to Germany but they were reluctant to pressure Paris, because maintaining French support for supranational integration remained a more important American goal than the FTA.[58] For the same reason the United States warned London against using the GATT to coerce the French during the negotiations and told them to cease their "undercover resistance" to the Common Market.[59] U.S. officials, unconvinced that the Common Market and FTA had to develop at the same pace, recommended that the seventeen OEEC members avoid a deadlock and conduct slow and patient deliberations. Like Paris, Washington wished to protect the Common Market while exploring the goals of broader, more liberal trade and continuing to build a front against the Soviet bloc.[60]

In the Maudling committee the French opposed Britain on practically every point. When the British called for the exclusion of agriculture from the FTA, the French insisted on its inclusion, just as they had successfully done with the Common Market. The British sought to limit the scope of the FTA to the elimination of trade barriers, but the French demanded that it also coordinate external tariffs and conditions of competition among its members and include restrictive "rules of origin" (the definition of products made within the zone and thus able to circulate freely) to prevent outside goods from flooding French markets. When the British stated that the FTA should move automatically from one stage of tariff reductions to another, the French required that a unanimous vote of all seventeen members take place between each phase. The British favored rapid negotiation of an accord in principle and delaying discussion of details until later, but the French refused to sign any such blank check, insisting on the completion of detailed studies of the effects of the FTA on every economic sector before the signing of any accord. When the British proposed that the Common Market and the FTA move at the same speed, the French demanded that the FTA reduce tariffs at a slower pace in order to assure that the Common Market not be dissolved in the larger organization.[61] On each of these points the British sought to strengthen the FTA at the expense of the Common Market while the French worked to transform the former into an extension of the latter.

Because of the complete deadlock reached by early 1958, many French officials considered breaking off the negotiations entirely, but were aware of the political risks this would entail. With the Fourth Republic collapsing around them, French leaders and officials could not afford to jeopardize their relations with Britain and Germany, risk British disengagement from Europe, damage the cohesion of the Six, or tempt any of the Non-Six toward neutralism. Indeed, some foreign ministry officials still supported an FTA accord that would maintain European unity, placate France's Common Market partners, and provide opportunities for the expansion of French influence into Eastern Europe. They emphasized that the FTA constituted a better magnet than the Common Market for countries like Yugoslavia and Finland that wished to distance themselves from the USSR and sought closer ties with the West, but did not dare associate themselves with the Common Market because of its political-supranational dimension. These foreign ministry officials saw a sort of slippery slope toward neutralism in Europe if the FTA failed: "If the Europe of the Six disassociated itself too much from the other countries of Europe, such as the Scandinavian countries, western cohesion would suffer. The tendency towards neutralism in these countries might increase. If neutralism gained ground in Europe, it might have an impact on German opinion and thus undermine everything that we have undertaken."[62]

However, despite these strong political priorities, French economic worries and fears for the Common Market increasingly outweighed the positive political aspects of the free trade zone. In order to square the circle, the Quai d'Orsay spent early 1958 developing a proposal to begin the FTA talks on a new basis. The French aimed at either breaking the deadlock and producing an acceptable FTA or slowing down the talks to buy time for other alternatives. They ultimately developed a proposal for a "European Economic Cooperation Union" ("Union

Européenne de Coopération Economique"). This plan called for successive stages of sweeping economic harmonization, each followed by tariff cuts if all the members unanimously agreed that sufficient convergence had occurred. Detailed sector by sector studies and agricultural arrangements would be required. The new "Union" would also have to follow several years behind the Common Market.[63] Essentially a summary of long-held French positions, the proposal was antithetical to the very idea of a British-style FTA. It was never formally presented to the OEEC because France's five partners in the Common Market rejected most of its premises. When word of its contents leaked out, some OEEC members described it as a declaration of economic war. The Austrians went so far as to state that it would lead to "a trade war between the Six and the rest of free Europe, the formation of blocs, the disappearance of the European payments union and the hegemony of the German economy within a community where it would be favored over British competition."[64]

The isolated French fell back on the alternative of purely pragmatic, bilateral arrangements between the Six and the eleven other OEEC members. French diplomats denied that the Common Market constituted the threat portrayed by the British and offered practical negotiations to alleviate any trade dislocations that might occur. Above all they denied the necessity of a multilateral–free trade solution to maintain the unity of Western Europe.[65] Throughout the Maudling negotiations, the harried French warned their Common Market partners and the other OEEC countries against pressuring them into accepting an unfavorable accord. The Quai d'Orsay threatened to activate the Common Market's escape clauses, which would effectively terminate it: "Anything that led to the isolation of France, whether political or economic . . . could only provoke the strongest distrust and would constitute a grave threat to the Treaty of Rome."[66]

It was never clear how much of the French position was the result of outright opposition to the British free trade plan and how much resulted from fear and unwillingness to make a tough decision on the FTA. As French cabinets changed with alarming frequency and each government became more difficult to form than the last, none was willing to take responsibility for a firm decision. Moreover, no government could be certain that the National Assembly would not repeat the EDC fiasco and reject an FTA treaty.[67] Because no government was strong enough to break off the talks, the foreign ministry, largely opposed to the FTA, had the unhappy task of stalling the Maudling negotiations with endless quibbling over technical issues. The French seemed incapable of any decisive action on the FTA, whether for or against.

It was in this strained diplomatic environment that yet another French government collapsed in mid-April 1958 after a vote of no confidence by the National Assembly on its Algerian policy, provoking the prolonged crisis that even-

tually returned de Gaulle to power. To the great frustration of the British, all negotiations on the FTA were suspended until July. In addition to the myriad problems facing him when he took office, de Gaulle was confronted with a decision
on the free trade area.

The Return of de Gaulle and the End
of the FTA, June–December 1958

During the six months following de Gaulle's return to power in June, the discussions on the FTA, which had dragged on for over two years, finally reached a
decisive, albeit unsuccessful, conclusion. De Gaulle did not alter the fundamentals of France's position, but he brought much stronger guidance to its policy
and a willingness to make difficult decisions. Prior to his return to office, de
Gaulle had been aware only of the general outline of the British free trade proposals. He was critical of the plan, fearing its economic impact on France and
viewing it as a British attempt to take advantage of Europe without joining it.[68]
In June and July the Quai d'Orsay briefed de Gaulle on the details of the debate
and counseled him on how to proceed: "Although we have already made considerable use of stalling tactics, it would still seem inopportune to rush things,"
and "Our top priority must be a common position among the Six, the essential
precondition of any progress in the negotiations."[69] Such an approach would
seek to reduce France's isolation and protect the Common Market.

De Gaulle approved this strategy at a special cabinet meeting on 17 July.[70] In
working out a common position for the Six, France undercut Germany's aspirations to act as a mediator. Paris offered a number of concessions. It agreed that
the Common Market and the FTA could move at the same pace (to avoid discrimination) and that an FTA accord could spell out the ultimate goals of the
association. Nevertheless, France's demands for unilateral escape clauses, unanimous decision making, a sectoral approach, and a certain amount of harmonization of tariffs and economic policy remained unchanged. The foreign ministry also set to work preparing a backup plan to reduce tariff discrimination
between the Six and Non-Six should the British prove intransigent and the negotiations fail.[71]

Even as they nominally promoted compromises to bring the FTA about, the
French still supported a leisurely, pragmatic approach to European trade relations, preferring bilateral negotiations between the Common Market and individual nonmember countries over further futile efforts to construct a grand free
trade system. With a stable government behind them, French diplomats hinted
that Paris opposed a free trade area in principle, that the French economy could
not handle the additional burdens, and that the risks the FTA posed for the

Common Market were too great. De Gaulle himself flatly told Macmillan that "the setup of free trade without any precautions could cause serious problems for [France]" and that Paris "could not tear up the Treaty of Rome."[72] Although these objections were not new, the British were startled by the candor of the French admissions. Paris also reminded its partners that it would not negotiate under threats or pressure, denied the significance of January 1959, the date of the Six's first tariff cuts, and insisted that all the technical points must be resolved.[73] France rejected the charge that the debate over the FTA could be reduced to a simple Franco-British conflict, claiming that what was at stake were two different conceptions of Western Europe. Even if France accepted British claims that they did not seek to damage the Common Market, the foreign ministry insisted that "the free trade zone must be envisioned not with regard to [the promises of] the Britain of today or the future, but in terms of the common denominators of all the OEEC countries that did not join the Common Market."[74]

With de Gaulle in power, France became even more suspicious of Britain's motives for the FTA. The foreign ministry now argued that the British sought to outmaneuver France and dominate Europe. It anticipated the failure of the talks and expected that London would retaliate against France and the Common Market. In order to contain the damage, the Quai d'Orsay sought a way to end the talks without provoking a crisis.[75] When the limited French concessions on the FTA had produced no real progress by late October, French diplomats concluded that the issue had come to a head, that their "partners [were] trying to hit the ball into [the French] court" and force them to cave in or end the talks.[76] At a cabinet meeting on 12 November, de Gaulle chose the latter course. The French government announced that it rejected the FTA and that the Maudling talks must cease.[77] Over the years, the British would become all too familiar with such unilateral pronouncements by de Gaulle.

Even as he pronounced his first "*non*" to the British, de Gaulle covered France's flanks in two important ways. First, to ensure German support he met Adenauer at Bad Kreuznach in late November. In return for Bonn's acceptance of his veto of the FTA, de Gaulle pledged to carry out the Treaty of Rome in full, alleviating one of the major concerns created in Germany by his return to power.[78] As an additional gesture, de Gaulle proposed that the Commission study a future association with the rest of the OEEC and report to the Six in the spring.[79] His promise to implement the Common Market in full, combined with his rejection of the FTA, left the Germans little choice but to acquiesce, since the former organization had always been their higher priority. Second, as we saw in Chapter 1, in order to counter charges of discrimination, the French proposed to extend the Six's internal tariff cuts planned for January 1959, not only to all OEEC members, but to all members of the GATT.[80] In so doing, the French demonstrated a conciliatory side and bought time for further discussion. They also made the point that they opposed any preferential European settlement, an important gesture to win American sympathy and further bury the idea of a purely European FTA. At the same time, de Gaulle and his foreign minister, Couve de Murville, underscored the Six's privileges by refusing to share the expanded trade quotas of the Common Market with nonmember countries. De Gaulle insisted that the British were wrong to view the start of "the Common Market as a sort of ultimatum" and argued that the Six must maintain some preferences toward one another in return for the burdens they had accepted.[81] Thus, despite French assurances of goodwill, some (largely symbolic) discrimination between the Six and the rest of the OEEC would come into effect in January 1959.[82]

Because of de Gaulle's well-known aversion to supranational integration, many in Germany had initially hoped, or feared, that he might support the FTA in addition to, or in place of, the Common Market.[83] The foreign ministry, facing continued pressure from the ministry of economics and the BDI in favor of the FTA, redoubled its efforts to maintain a common position for the Six.[84] German policy still emphasized the political and economic development of the Common Market, but favored an FTA accord for the sake of European unity.[85] Despite Germany's desire to avoid a choice, by late October when the imminent failure of the Maudling talks had become apparent, Bonn realized that it could not have the best of both worlds. It recognized that French fears of the FTA had reduced de Gaulle's reservations about the Common Market, and Adenauer sensed an opportunity to push the latter forward. Overruling Erhard's protests, Adenauer and the Auswärtiges Amt insisted that France presented Germany a much better overall package than had the British. Other than the maintenance of existing economic ties, Britain had little to offer, while cooperation with France advanced European unity. Some in the foreign ministry privately welcomed the French veto because it preserved the Common Market and spared Germany a divisive decision over ending the deadlocked FTA negotiations. Germany's need for French support in the Berlin crisis reinforced its decision to align with Paris, but the choice of France over Britain had predated Khrushchev's new moves against West Berlin.[86] Soviet pressures were not the root cause of Franco-German cooperation, but they did underscore the necessity of a close partnership across the Rhine on issues of European organization.

Thus when Adenauer met de Gaulle at Bad Kreuznach, the German government was prepared to accept the end of the FTA talks for the sake of maintaining the Franco-German rapprochement and strengthening the Common Market. After its initial doubts, Bonn wished to keep de Gaulle in power and prevent a return to the instability that had preceded him. As a foreign ministry official explained it to the Americans:

A stable and politically and economically strong France is most important for the Federal Republic. [I]t is essential that France, with its strategically vital location, remain a vigorous and effective member of NATO. Any hope of West Germany and the Western powers being able eventually to deal successfully with the Russians on the reunification question would be destroyed if France should become drastically weakened, or if France's active participation in and support of NATO should cease. For this reason the Federal Republic always has in mind the situation of France when considering foreign policy problems which could affect France. Specifically a major consideration now in connection with the Free Trade area dispute is the necessity of avoiding any action which could weaken the position of General de Gaulle. The consequence of this basic approach is such that even if the chancellor should think that Great Britain is one hundred percent right in its position on the Free Trade Area, and that to support the British viewpoint on the FTA would be useful for West Germany both economically and in some respects politically, he would still feel that the Federal Republic must not take a position on the FTA at variance with that of de Gaulle because of the danger that to do so might dangerously weaken de Gaulle's position in France.[87]

Nevertheless, Adenauer still hoped for a closer British association with the continent and supported steps to reduce discrimination between the Six and the rest of Western Europe. To the consternation of the French, he continued to offer his services as a mediator with the British.[88]

With de Gaulle's return to power, the United States was confronted with far more serious problems than the free trade issue. Aware of the French leader's reservations on European integration, NATO, and the American presence in Europe, Washington saw no reason to provoke de Gaulle by intervening in the free trade dispute.[89] It preferred that the FTA discussions continue without pressure or threats.[90] The more time went by, the more the FTA seemed a mere British afterthought to the Common Market.[91] U.S. officials still hoped to associate the Six with the rest of Western Europe, but now recognized that French opposition precluded the creation of another organization.[92] America's worsening trade and payments balances with Western Europe provided another reason for Washington to distance itself from the FTA. By late 1958 some in the State Department feared that "if de Gaulle were to decide on a highly unpopular step such as an agreement on the FTA, it seemed likely he would require gains in other areas to which he could point as part of a package deal" at the expense of the interests of the United States and other third countries.[93] American policy emphasized more than ever the need for all European countries, regardless of their affiliation, to follow a liberal trade policy and negotiate general tariff reductions via the GATT.[94] Obviously any preferential European solution would not only damage American economic interests, but could have an adverse impact on Atlantic cooperation and on organizations such as NATO. It also raised the specter of newly rich and self-confident Europeans arranging their political relations without the United States.

After the French rejection of the FTA in November, American officials focused primarily on urging the leaders of all OEEC countries to remain calm, avoid provocative reactions, and pursue other means of economic association. The United States welcomed the French announcement that the Six intended to minimize discrimination, not only within the OEEC, but in the GATT as well. Because the Six seemed committed to a liberal trade policy, Washington shed no tears over the fate of the FTA.

Like the Germans and Americans, British leaders had been uncertain of de Gaulle's intentions toward the FTA and London hoped he might support it to stop the supranationalism of the Common Market.[95] Macmillan tried to educate de Gaulle on the free trade issue, claiming that all that was required was the political will to reach an accord before the end of the year. He also sought to dramatize the situation, claiming that "if there is no free trade area by the time the Treaty of Rome takes effect in January [1959], [he] feared a very strong reaction in Great Britain and political consequences that, for him personally, would be very bad." There would also be "a trade war that might mean the end of NATO."[96] When de Gaulle ignored these exhortations and French opposition to the FTA actually increased, the British raised the pressure, stating that any discrimination would destroy the OEEC and all other European organizations, forcing the British to form their own trade bloc among the countries left out of the Common Market and use it to wage economic war against the Six.[97]

When it became apparent that there would be no agreement by the end of the year, and when the French, backed by Germany, announced that the negotiations had reached a dead end, British fears of a hostile continent led by France reached a new peak. The ambassador in Paris, Sir Gladwyn Jebb, received no reassurances from de Gaulle.[98] In his diary, Macmillan railed that "the French are determined to exclude [the] United Kingdom. De Gaulle is bidding high for the hegemony of Europe."[99] On this point Macmillan went too far. Although de Gaulle would later make a conscious decision to exclude Britain from Europe, this was not his primary motive in 1958. He simply opposed the free trade area conceived by the British.

During the spring of 1958, British leaders believed they had the support of most of the seventeen OEEC members, as well as the United States, and reckoned that the isolated French would have to make concessions. Given this expectation, they were very disappointed late in the year when the support of the two countries they most needed, Germany and the United States, dissipated so rapidly. Dulles categorically rejected all British pleas for U.S. mediation.[100] Macmillan's hopes regarding Adenauer were frustrated by the Bad Kreuznach arrangements, and afterward he complained that "the Germans have really sold out to the French on every count."[101] Although the French had killed the FTA, the British blamed the Germans as willing accomplices, and relations between the two countries suffered.

With the FTA talks now ended, the British had to decide how to pursue the kind of Europe they still hoped to create, a cooperative, nonsupranational economic association of all Western European nations within a wider Atlantic security system. They maintained the FTA as an ultimate goal, but sought new methods to achieve it.[102] There were still lingering hopes in the cabinet that de Gaulle would eventually become disenchanted with the supranational Common Market, "kill the original conception of the Treaty of Rome," and turn back to Britain. There was also hope for revived cooperation with the United States. But the most active thinkers began considering the formation of a counter-bloc to the Six to bring them to terms and unite Europe precisely by formally dividing it.[103]

On 15 December 1958 the last FTA deliberations in the OEEC turned into an acrimonious debate between France and Britain filled with indignation, threats, and harsh accusations. Foreign Minister Couve de Murville complained that Britain, Switzerland, and others outside the Common Market threatened that "if they were discriminated against by the Six as of 1 January 1959, then they would defend their economic interests by reestablishing quantitative restrictions on imports from those countries responsible, namely France."[104] Two and a half years of formal and informal negotiations had failed to reconcile the two very different approaches to European organization that the French and British championed. If anything, the choices had become more stark, the conflict more intense. Prior to de Gaulle's return to power, the French had at least been willing to consider the FTA. For de Gaulle, however, whose long range plans called for the development of a continental political association under French leadership, Britain not only constituted a rival for leadership, but also stood far too close to the United States.[105] Although these were not his primary motives for ending the FTA negotiations, such attitudes made him less concerned than his predecessors about British links to the continent and more intent on forging closer ties with Germany. De Gaulle made this decision in spite of the fact that the British would have been only too happy to help him void the Common Market of supranationalism, while the Germans were among its most staunch defenders. In any case, whether viewed as a major danger and a cause of impending conflict (the British view) or as relatively insignificant and exaggerated for its value as a threat (the French view), the much-discussed "division of Europe" had come about.

Prophecy Fulfilled: The Formation of the EFTA and the Division of Western Europe, 1959–1960

In the wake of the FTA debacle the British had to find new means to prevent the Common Market from damaging their political and economic interests. Even before the French veto of the FTA scheme, Britain and others among the Non-Six had discussed the idea of forming their own free trade zone. Once the FTA had failed, the British moved swiftly. In the spring of 1959, the countries that became known as the "Outer Seven" or the "Seven"—Britain, Switzerland, Sweden, Norway, Denmark, Austria, and Portugal—began negotiations to form the European Free Trade Association (EFTA). Quickly sweeping aside all economic and technical problems, they initialed a treaty in Stockholm in November. After the formal signature in January, the national legislatures ratified the accord during the early months of 1960; it took effect in July. The Seven shaped the EFTA as a free trade area according to the original British conception. It had no common external tariff, demanded no burdensome social or financial harmonization, and included industrial goods only. The one British concession was a special agricultural arrangement with the Danes who, fearing the loss of their continental agricultural markets in any conflict with the Six, insisted on it before they would sign.[106]

Although the Scandinavians believed in the intrinsic benefits of the EFTA, which did unquestionably improve the conditions of trade among its members, the British and most of the others viewed it primarily as a means of dealing with the Six. The British admitted that the Seven had little in common other than the desire to overcome the split in Europe and that they were largely peripheral to the wider European economy. In the effort to bring the Six to terms, the new organization would serve a number of purposes. First, if the EFTA proved to be an economic success, it would disprove the claims of the French that the British free trade model would never work in the real world.[107] Second, it would demonstrate the strength of Britain's commitment to association with the continent.[108] Third, the EFTA could serve as a bridge between the Six and the Seven. Once the new group was constituted, negotiations for an all-European free trade area (still the primary goal of Britain and its partners) could proceed between two groups rather than among seventeen countries. The Foreign Office insisted to the French that "the seven were not a war machine to be used against the [European] community. To the contrary, their purpose was to ease [French] distrust by enabling themselves to negotiate with the Common Market [as a group] and giving up on dissolving it in negotiations among seventeen countries."[109] While critics of the EFTA portrayed it as a preferential trade area lacking any political value, its members argued that its political significance lay in the fact that it aimed at restoring the economic unity of Western Europe and adapting the continent to the development of the Common Market.[110]

The Seven also understood that the EFTA could prove useful on the tactical level. Macmillan felt that "the stakes in this affair are very high. . . . For if we cannot successfully organize the opposition group—Scandinavia, Denmark, Switzerland, Austria, etc.—then we shall undoubtedly be eaten up, one by one, by the Six."[111] The Seven could also use the EFTA as a means of exerting pressure on the Six, particularly Germany, to negotiate. Exports from the Six to the Seven would now face the same sort of discrimination as exports from the Seven to the Six. Because Germany conducted such a high proportion of its trade with the Seven, it would be disproportionately affected.[112] Finally, although British officials always publicly denied it was intended as a weapon, should a trade war develop between the Common Market and the other countries of Europe, the EFTA would clearly be a useful tool in the struggle.[113]

While occupied with the negotiations for the EFTA in 1959, the British refused to engage in any discussions with the Six, insisting that such talks must await the formation of the new group.[114] In an ironic twist of fate, if one recalls the circumstances of 1956–57, it was now the British who sought to build an economic bloc and refused negotiations with outsiders until it was complete. Although they still hoped to restore the unity of Western Europe, the British insisted on dealing with the Common Market from a position of strength. The Foreign Office also stated that future talks must have a stronger foundation than those that failed in 1958, since "it was better not to negotiate at all than to rush into a new failure that might have more grave consequences."[115]

Keeping with habit, British diplomats used the carrot and stick. They nominally acknowledged the existence of the Common Market and endorsed its goals of political integration and linking Germany to the West, but insisted on a formal tie between the Six and the Seven.[116] British diplomats wanted the Six to acknowledge that the Common Market had divided Western Europe into two rival groups. When the Commission proposed that both groups avoid conflict simply by following liberal policies in the GATT, the British found this insufficient to bridge the gap. London insisted on a multilateral agreement to end all discrimination in Western European trade and grew increasingly frustrated and strident. "If our cars have to pay higher tariffs on the German market than do French cars," Maudling reminded the Germans, "we will be discriminated against, Europe will be divided, we will be treated like Cuba, as if we did not even belong to Europe."[117] In conversations with U.S. leaders, Macmillan conjured up the dangers of a Europe dominated by France and Germany unless Britain could function as a counterweight to them.[118] London again predicted a trade war, the breakup of NATO, and the withdrawal of British troops from the continent.[119]

Because the British realized they could not overcome French opposition alone, they focused on gaining American and German support for an EFTA–Common Market deal. They sought to regain their position of early 1958, when it was France that was isolated and Britain had U.S. and German support. In August 1960, Macmillan made an appeal to Adenauer. Taking advantage of a temporary rift in the Franco-German relationship, he persuaded the chancellor to launch bilateral British-German talks on the Six-Seven dispute. However, in the technical meetings that followed, the Germans refused to separate themselves from France, particularly as long as London would not take a decisive step toward Europe.[120] In their approach to the United States, the British failed to convince Washington that the EFTA served European or Atlantic interests or that a Six-Seven bridge was necessary.

During the EFTA negotiations, the Americans hoped that the new organization signaled a British desire for rapprochement with the continent.[121] However, once the organization took shape, the United States rapidly turned against it and American officials ultimately viewed the EFTA as a step in the wrong direction, a purely preferential trading area that would discriminate against the United States and others. Because of the preferential agricultural deal between Britain and Denmark, the EFTA could not even qualify as a free trade area according to the GATT definition, which forbade purely preferential arrangements. Unlike the Common Market, the EFTA lacked any redeeming political (meaning supranational) dimension that might have led American officials to tolerate a certain amount of economic discrimination. The United States made it clear to the British that it disliked the EFTA, but would tolerate it as long as it could be adapted to meet the requirements of the GATT. Eisenhower felt that the EFTA was "designed as nothing but a counter-irritant to the Common Market."[122]

American leaders were alarmed by British talk of using the new organization as a bridge to the Common Market. Once the EFTA appeared on the horizon, America's main fear was of a deal between the Six and the Seven at the expense of the United States, other GATT members, and the developing world. American diplomats constantly warned the Six and the Seven that they "would be opposed to a special arrangement between the Common Market and the United Kingdom to the disadvantage of others, including ourselves."[123] Since any bridge would likely take the form of an all-European free trade zone, American rejection of the bridge signaled that it also opposed any revival of the FTA idea.[124] The speed and finality with which the United States turned against any European free trade arrangement after the November 1958 French veto shows how shallow and hesitant American support had been and that the veto had served U.S. interests.

American leaders continued to believe that the Common Market needed further time to develop and that the Seven exaggerated its adverse impact on their economies. The United States remained convinced that the Common Market would fuel economic growth and that this would enable the Six to follow a liberal trade policy.[125] Washington welcomed the support of the Commission when it called for global (GATT) solutions to the Six-Seven debate.[126] By late 1960 many U.S. policy makers concluded that the only long-term solution to the British dilemma was for the United Kingdom to accept the Treaty of Rome and join the Common Market.[127]

Just as U.S. officials feared that the formation of the EFTA and the crystallization of the Six-Seven split might threaten their country's economic interests and endanger Atlantic cooperation, German leaders feared that the organization posed new political and economic threats to their country. Because Germany carried out a (slightly) greater proportion of its external trade with the Seven than with its Common Market partners, it was vulnerable to economic pressures and inducements to sway the French to a Six-Seven solution.[128] Not surprisingly, those most alarmed by the creation of the EFTA were the old FTA supporters, Erhard and German industry. Erhard had hoped to forestall the EFTA by concluding an all-European settlement in 1959, but the British determination to build their bloc had doomed these hopes.[129] Once the EFTA had actually formed, Erhard and his supporters urged Adenauer to intercede with the French. Fritz Berg, the head of the BDI, besieged the chancellor with reminders of Germany's need for markets outside the Six, the value of all-European organizations such as the OEEC, and the necessity of linking the Six and the Seven.[130]

Adenauer and the Auswärtiges Amt took a more circumspect view. Foreign ministry officials minimized the EFTA's importance, claiming that the Common Market was strong enough to withstand any pressure. Even those who viewed the EFTA as an anti-German device believed that the Seven could not possibly replace all the goods they purchased from Germany and that "the [economic] position of the Common Market towards Denmark, Austria, and Switzerland would remain so strong that [it] would have the opportunity for bilateral settlements with each of them even if the EFTA came into existence."[131] The foreign ministry eventually chose to regard the EFTA as a genuine effort to form a bridge to the Common Market and as a means toward a wider European association, but remained dubious as to its effectiveness. Given French intransigence, the

Auswärtiges Amt advocated cautious, pragmatic steps rather than outright support or rejection of the EFTA .[132] By 1960, the foreign ministry had largely given up on any free trade area or all-European solution. With the constant French rejection of their compromise proposals, they could not function as mediators.[133] Instead, Germany focused on cooperation with the United States and liberal solutions in the GATT.[134]

The French reactions to the EFTA and the subsequent British efforts to promote a Six-Seven arrangement were, not surprisingly, almost uniformly negative. The London embassy dismissed the EFTA as a tactical maneuver doomed to failure: "The cohesion of the Seven is doubtful at best: geographically separated and lacking in economic equilibrium, the zone is dominated by Great Britain, which nevertheless hardly does more business with its partners than it does with the Six, while Austria and Switzerland have economies that are basically oriented towards the Six and Denmark has as much interest in retaining its share of the German market as it does in finding new outlets in Britain."[135] The French disparaged the significance of the Six-Seven split and suggested that the formation of the EFTA showed that the British had still not accepted the existence of the Common Market. They rejected any revival of the FTA, or even discussion of it, and refused to consider any all-European solution. As Bonn noted with dismay, given the fact that they carried out a much smaller portion of their trade with the Seven than did the Germans, the French could afford to take the EFTA and other British threats less seriously.[136] This fact, combined with de Gaulle's solid leadership and strong U.S. support, made an aloof French attitude possible.

French officials tended to regard the EFTA primarily as a means for the Seven to demonstrate their desire for an all-European arrangement and to pressure Germany and Benelux. Because the EFTA was the model for a giant free trade zone, the French did not regard it as a real shift in British policy or as a serious tool for negotiations. Since the EFTA only lessened Britain's negotiating freedom, France decided to withhold criticism as long as it conformed to the GATT rules.[137] Paris would maintain its focus on global trade liberalization, refuse to take any initiative with the Seven, and concentrate on maintaining the unity of the Six. The Quai d'Orsay was convinced that "until the permanency of the Common Market has been made clear by the implementation of the common external tariff, the British government will continue to attempt to torpedo the Treaty of Rome."[138]

Both because it served their interests and because it earned them American goodwill, the French consistently stated that only mutual liberalization via the GATT could solve the Six-Seven problem. Each time the Seven or France's partners raised the possibility of a purely European solution, Paris dismissed any such settlement as impossible and stated that the Americans would reject it out of hand.[139] Franco-American cooperation on issues of European organization continued to advance the interests of both countries. With memories of their isolation in the FTA talks still fresh, the French feared that any purely European arrangement or negotiations would lead forces both within and outside the Common Market to combine against them. Paris favored American involvement in any future negotiations to prevent such an outcome.[140] The French knew that the Seven hoped to use the EFTA to coerce Bonn to persuade them to accept a European arrangement, but correctly judged that the Germans would not do anything to jeopardize the Franco-German relationship and the Common Market.[141] The Quai d'Orsay agreed to discuss technical issues with members of the EFTA on a bilateral basis, but emphasized that such sectoral talks would take a very long time to lead to anything. On the other hand, "Article 237 of the Treaty of Rome allows for any European country to ask to become a member of the Common Market and [France] remain[ed] ready, as in the past, to welcome any such request for admission."[142] This argument seemed to offer both the only viable long-term solution to the trade disputes and a strong rejoinder to British claims that France sought to discriminate against other European countries.

By the end of 1960 the combined Franco-American rejection of any all-European free trade area or preferential European solution effectively doomed Britain's two main hopes when it formed the EFTA in 1959. Aware of this possibility, Britain still hesitated to make a major policy change. During 1960 it consolidated the EFTA and worked to achieve the FTA as an ultimate goal. However, by the end of the year London held little hope of solving the Six-Seven problem. The EFTA had proven a failure. No serious negotiations on an all-European arrangement had taken place for two years, and the French and Americans had successfully diverted discussions toward the GATT. Another British effort to come to terms with the Common Market had failed.

Conclusion

By late 1960 the Common Market and the form of integration it embodied, a customs union with social and economic harmonization, close political cooperation, and some degree of supranationalism, had triumphed over the alternative of a looser all-European association, represented by both the original British free trade area ideas and the EFTA. Throughout, the British and French had largely talked past one another. The British often spoke of economics but were more concerned with politics and assumed their interlocutors thought the same way. The French carefully balanced political and economic considerations in their formulation of policy, but in negotiations they focused on technical economic issues and would not allow political pressures to sweep them aside.

Like Britain's unsuccessful efforts to slow or stop the Common Market, the free trade setbacks contributed to a reevaluation of British policy toward Europe. Four and a half years of frustration in both areas taught London that it could no longer hope to defeat or replace the Common Market and supranational European integration from the outside. Its lingering attachment to ideas of "splendid isolation," fading Commonwealth ties, and the "special relationship" with the United States had left it on the outside of European integration, always a step behind the continental states. Although relations between France and Germany underwent periods of strain, their mutual commitment to political and economic cooperation would not allow Britain to divide them. American leaders had made obvious their opposition to the British stance toward Europe, and without U.S. support the British could not hope to force their views on the Franco-German tandem. The Common Market had become a fait accompli, and Britain could only hope to change it from within. This unpleasant conclusion led to the July–August 1961 British application for admission to the Common Market, thereby acknowledging defeat in the FTA struggle.

With the exception of its 1959–60 efforts to promote general European liberalization and prevent a preferential European solution to the Six-Seven conflict, the Eisenhower administration took a relatively hands-off approach toward the free trade disputes. Given America's Cold War interest in Western European unity and Atlantic harmony, it could not afford an openly partisan position, particularly as long as the FTA seemed to enjoy widespread support in Europe. The United States had always made clear its preference for supranationalism over the British cooperative alternatives, but had avoided taking sides on the technical issues and sought to promote compromise. However, once France torpedoed the FTA, the Americans felt they could safely make known their reservations and support Paris in preventing any revival of the idea. This shift, part of the wider concern of the Eisenhower administration in its last years to ensure that European integration did not damage U.S. interests, formed another part of the background to Kennedy's Atlantic Community.

Between 1956 and 1960 Germany's position on Britain's free trade ideas evolved from doubt when it seemed Britain sought to block the Treaty of Rome in 1956 and early 1957, to mild support for the FTA as a means of assuring continental unity in late 1957 and most of 1958, to acceptance of France's rejection of the FTA for the sake of larger German political interests at the end of 1958. Throughout, Bonn refused to jeopardize its relations with France and linkage with the West in exchange for a questionable British commitment to the continent. Whether under weak governments, as under the late Fourth Republic, or a strong one, under de Gaulle, France was simply a higher political priority than Britain. Soviet pressures on Germany reinforced the need for close ties with a strong France. Erhard and German economic interests contested this policy from the outset but were unable to divert the government from its focus on France and the Common Market. The debate in Germany was not over, but Adenauer and the foreign ministry had won another round.

Although the transition from the Fourth to the Fifth Republic marks a watershed in many aspects of French foreign policy, on the issue of Britain's alternatives to the Common Market, the elements of continuity eclipse those of change. On one level this fact should not surprise us, given the ostensibly technical nature of the issues at stake and the fact that the same foreign ministry officials conducted the complicated negotiations on the various British proposals from 1956 through 1960. At a higher level, while de Gaulle disagreed with the politicians of the Fourth Republic on much else, he shared their concerns regarding the impact of a free trade area on the French economy and their fears that the huge group might lead to the dissolution of the Common Market. De Gaulle had very different goals for the Common Market than his predecessors, but neither he nor they could allow the British to replace it with a larger, looser association. In many ways, it was precisely the British challenges to the Common Market that made the French realize its value. The existence of the Common Market prevented the British from isolating and pressuring France. The FTA episode demonstrated how Paris could use the Common Market to keep a close rein on its partners and prevent them from working with the British to organize European political and economic relations in ways inimical to French interests.

The four and a half years of debates over the British free trade proposals forced the Six, and the French and Germans in particular, to cooperate and work to reach common positions on difficult issues in a way that they would not likely have done without such a challenge to the nature and existence of the Common Market. The acrimonious and divisive years of negotiations demonstrated the political commitment of the Six to push the Common Market forward against opposition from much of the rest of Europe. The Six also withstood internal debates and divisions within individual member countries.

Did the British offer Western Europe a real alternative to the Common Market? The answer to this question must be mixed and tentative. Had the original FTA proposals of 1956–58 been implemented, a different kind of Europe could have been built around them. However, the FTA and the Common Market could not realistically have coexisted. One would have replaced the other. In all probability the wider FTA would have simply overwhelmed the political and economic cohesion of the smaller Common Market. Although the French were the first to realize this, the Americans and Germans eventually came to much the same conclusion, which was an important factor in their tacit approval of the French veto of the FTA. It is difficult to find many ways in which the free trade alternative would have been a better choice for Europe. With the Cold War still raging, it would have replaced the tighter German political and economic links to the West provided by the Common Market and blurred distinctions between neutral and NATO countries, lessening the contrasts between East and West and likely decreasing the appeal of European unity for the countries of Eastern Europe. It would have hampered future steps toward political unity and disillusioned the United States in its hopes for a strong European partner somewhere down the road. A successful FTA would not have constituted a real European commitment on the part of the United Kingdom and would only have slowed Britain's already dilatory reconsideration of its relations with the continent. Worse, an FTA built on the British model would likely have alienated France from all European integration efforts.

Given these probabilities, de Gaulle did Europe and the United States a service when he vetoed the FTA in November 1958. His decision enabled America and other doubters to make their real views known and cooperate with Paris to make the Six the solid core of Europe. From this point onward, British "alternatives" to the Common Market were illusions. The heterogeneous EFTA could not hope to compete with the larger and more solid economic union of the Six or the political ambitions of its members. Almost from the moment the EFTA was created it was more of a burden than an asset. Although the British were slow to realize it, their window of opportunity to replace or transform the Common Market from the outside had closed and they would now have to play by the rules of the Six. As leaders of all the major countries eventually realized, this meant that Britain had to reverse its policy of the last five years and seek membership in the Common Market.

CHAPTER THREE

ADENAUER, DE GAULLE, AND THE FORMATION OF THE FRANCO-GERMAN ENTENTE, 1958–1960

Take de Gaulle, for example. He saved his country [during World War II] but thereafter failed miserably when he served as head of government.
—Konrad Adenauer, 6 August 1957

The Personalities and Parameters of the Franco-German Relationship

After spending much of the interwar period warning his country of the dangers posed by Germany and trying to curtail its power in the immediate postwar period, de Gaulle, by the late 1950s, believed that Germany's defeat and division, plus the rise of the two superpowers, had eliminated it as a threat to France and, indeed, made it a vital ally.[1] Like previous French leaders of widely different political persuasions, from Aristide Briand in the 1920s, to Pierre Laval in the 1930s, Marshal Pétain during World War II, and Robert Schuman during the Fourth Republic, de Gaulle understood that a smaller, economically weaker France must come to terms with its powerful neighbor to the east if it were to be secure and regain a predominant role in Europe. De Gaulle was determined to succeed where his predecessors had failed and to maintain the upper hand in the relationship. In the third volume of his war memoirs, written in the mid-1950s, de Gaulle recorded a revealing episode from early 1945. He reported receiving a message from Heinrich Himmler, head of Hitler's ss and Gestapo in the last days of the Reich: "You have won," conceded Himmler, "but what will you do now? Submit yourself to the Anglo-Saxons? They will treat you like a satellite and you will lose all honor. Associate with the Soviets? They will force France to submit to their law and liquidate you personally. . . . In reality, the only way that could lead your people to greatness and independence is an entente with defeated Germany. Proclaim it immediately! Make contact without delay with those men in the Reich who still have de facto power and want to lead their country in a new direction. . . . They are ready and waiting for your offer. . . . If you can master the spirit of vengeance, if you seize this occasion that history offers you, you will be the greatest man of all time." The most interesting aspect of this incident is de Gaulle's commentary on it: "Apart from the flattery that this missive from the edge of the grave directed toward me, there is undoubtedly some truth in the picture it paints."[2]

According to de Gaulle's long-term blueprint, cooperation between France and Germany would enable Europe to marshal its military, political, and economic strength and render the American presence in Europe less necessary. As Europe became able to stand on its own, the United States would gradually pull back from the continent. This development would make the Kremlin more secure and more willing to negotiate an end to the Cold War in Europe directly with the Europeans. Soviet domination of Eastern Europe would gradually be lifted and both the continent and Germany would be reunified under the direction of France, the most powerful and most independent of the Western European states. "It went without saying that such a policy would only be possible under conditions of equilibrium, which in turn implied the union of Germany with France and Europe."[3] A Franco-German "union" could lead the other states of Western Europe and free France of the need for NATO and the United States. It would serve as the core of the independent European "Third Force" de Gaulle hoped to create. De Gaulle's version of disengagement differed in almost every way from that promoted by George Kennan and others in the 1950s. De Gaulle's focus was political and long term and gave the initiative to Europe, while Kennan's ideas emphasized military withdrawal, short-term action, and the predominant roles of the two superpowers. De Gaulle's version kept Germany closely linked with the West, while Kennan envisioned a neutral Germany.[4]

None of this meant that de Gaulle trusted either the Soviets or the Germans. He and his subordinates were deeply distrustful of the USSR, particularly its designs on Germany. Because Paris viewed Germany as the key factor in the European balance of power, the negative Soviet policy toward it threatened any European equilibrium.[5] De Gaulle believed that Soviet leaders sought to detach Germany from the West, neutralize it, and then gradually draw it into their orbit. This would destroy any hope that a new balance of power might overcome the division of the continent.[6] De Gaulle shared the belief of his predecessors and of many others that it was essential to bind Germany to the West once and for all. He trusted Adenauer's commitment, but feared what the chancellor's successors might do. If Germany could no longer threaten France directly, there were still the old delusions of grandeur, the lingering hopes for early reunification, and the neutralist temptations that could lead German leaders to damage French and European interests.[7] As de Gaulle noted to a skeptical

Macmillan, "Economically and politically it is important that the Germans be linked to us and that they not return to the *Drang nach Osten*."[8] De Gaulle often asked the rhetorical question, "If Germany turned eastward and communism advanced to the Rhine, what would happen to France?" His answer was always the same: France would either follow or become an American satellite.[9] From de Gaulle's perspective, a strong Common Market and close Franco-German relations constituted the best ways to bind Germany to its former enemies and promote French interests.[10]

De Gaulle had a number of other goals for the Franco-German relationship that he could not state as explicitly. First, it is clear that he always intended the relationship to be unequal. Germany was an associate in Europe rather than a true partner. Bolstered by such trappings as France's permanent UN security council seat, de Gaulle referred to France as a global power like Britain, the United States, and the USSR, while Germany was merely a regional or European power. Because of France's greater status, it deserved a role in global summits, participation in the top-level planning of the Atlantic alliance, and possession of nuclear weapons. All these things were formally or informally denied to the Germans. De Gaulle wanted both the symbols and the power of an elevated position in order to keep the Germans in check, but French diplomats informed Bonn that "it was in Europe's interest, and especially Germany's, [that France] be involved in global affairs and strategy; thanks to France, [Europe] would have a voice in such crucial deliberations."[11] Second, for de Gaulle, one of the main purposes of close relations with Germany and the development of the Common Market was to minimize British influence in Europe. He came to view Britain as an opponent of European consolidation, a surrogate for American influence, and a potential rival for leadership. Although he usually claimed that it was economic issues that divided Britain from Europe, de Gaulle admitted in moments of candor that "the things that separate us from [Britain] with regard to the Common Market are essentially political."[12] This was a major reversal of France's position of the late 1940s and much of the 1950s when its leaders had viewed British participation in Europe as the best means to control Germany and advance European unity. Finally, de Gaulle left his primary goal unstated, the establishment of French leadership of Western Europe in global affairs, for fear of offending Germany and his other partners. Because Germany needed France's support on East-West issues, it would have to mask its negativism toward France's designs, and the Benelux countries, outspoken in their opposition to French hegemony, would be hard-pressed to prevent it alone.

Due to his forceful nature as well as the constitution of the Fifth Republic, de Gaulle was free to develop his own foreign policy agenda.[13] His foreign minister, Maurice Couve de Murville, a quintessential career diplomat who had previously served as ambassador to the United States and Germany, became a loyal instrument of Gaullist diplomacy for the next ten years.[14] The French ambassador in Bonn was François Seydoux, whose father, Jacques, had been one of the primary architects of the short-lived Franco-German rapprochement in the 1920s. The younger Seydoux, a de Gaulle loyalist, strongly believed in this policy. The prime minister between 1959 and 1962, the nationalist Michel Debré, was known as "plus gaulliste que de Gaulle." Debré's biting comments about the United States and Germany often distressed the Quai d'Orsay, but this complete Gaullist had little influence over the formation of French foreign policy.[15] Although there were some dissenters from the Gaullist line in the foreign ministry, the president reduced its role by failing to consult its officials on important issues and dealing directly with foreign leaders. He used the foreign ministry primarily to negotiate details and implement broad decisions he had already made. Although de Gaulle was always more concerned with promoting French national interests than in the popularity of his foreign policy positions at home, he did seek to educate the French public and channel it toward support of his policies, including the Franco-German entente. In the late 1950s public opinion and many organizations in France remained skeptical about Germany's recovery and any Franco-German rapprochement, but de Gaulle worked carefully to bring his country around to a rational acceptance of both. His regular efforts to demonstrate Germany's subordinate position in the bilateral relationship also served to reassure domestic opinion.[16]

Most studies of de Gaulle's foreign policy and of the Franco-German relationship of the era have been done by biographers, political scientists, and former diplomats. None has used archival evidence to examine the French leader's interaction with his contemporaries from a multilateral perspective.[17] Many of these earlier studies either center on the debates over the Primat der Innen- or Aussenpolitik in de Gaulle's policy or critique the French leader's policies without providing a historical or comparative context. Although historians have recently begun to gain access to the archival materials, there is as yet no comprehensive, full-length study of how German, British, and American leaders responded to de Gaulle's version of the Franco-German rapprochement.[18] Most of the recent works focus exclusively on one country, one episode, or one period, most commonly the 1963 treaty of cooperation and its immediate genesis.

Like de Gaulle, Adenauer justified the close Franco-German relationship in classic Cold War terms: "Without a close tie between France and Germany the Russians would dominate everything," dividing and conquering Western Europe. He counseled jealous outsiders, such as Britain and Italy, that it was a positive development for Europe and the entire world.[19] Although his support of de Gaulle was not unqualified, Adenauer ultimately accepted many of de Gaulle's ideas and tolerated those that he opposed for the sake of the wider Franco-German relationship and a strong and reliable France. Adenauer's views were practical and flexible, as well as politically motivated. Although hoping for "real" (meaning supranational) European unity on a wide scale, he modified his stance to fit changing circumstances. For political reasons alone he chose the supranational Common Market over the looser British-sponsored Free Trade Area (FTA), which might have offered Germany greater economic gain.[20] This decision enabled him to work with de Gaulle to create a strong European economic and political community of states able to exert and defend their own interests. Over time Adenauer even moved toward de Gaulle's views on interstate cooperation and on a "little" Europe (the Six) for the foreseeable future.[21] Since he knew that U.S. leaders viewed the Franco-German relationship and integration as the two key factors making possible a strong Western Europe and a viable Atlantic community, Adenauer was also convinced that good Franco-German relations were necessary to maintain America's commitment to Europe.[22] Despite his pragmatism, Adenauer's view of the Franco-German relationship was not without a degree of idealism. He believed that the Franco-German conflict had produced most of Europe's misfortunes during the past eighty years and that he had an opportunity to change the course of history and take a decisive step "for Europe and for world peace." By replacing conflict with cooperation, the two countries could accomplish almost anything.[23]

Adenauer shared de Gaulle's doubts on the "Anglo-Saxon" powers. His concerns over their commitment to Europe reinforced his desire for a close relationship with France. Adenauer distrusted Britain's conciliatory policies toward the USSR in general and on Berlin in particular. He also disliked its aloofness from Western Europe and resented its attacks on the Common Market, which he attributed to "the fear of an overly close rapprochement between France and the Federal Republic."[24] However, unlike de Gaulle, Adenauer did not want to exclude the United Kingdom from continental affairs, at least not in the late 1950s, and he feared that an irrevocable split between Britain and the continent would weaken the West. As for the United States, Adenauer viewed it as the cornerstone of German security but feared that it might someday sacrifice German interests in order to lighten its political and military burden or to reach an accommodation with the USSR. He feared that even his old ally Eisenhower might, "at the end of his term, be seduced by the role of mediator."[25] Adenauer thus sought a close relationship with de Gaulle not only to contain French attacks on the U.S. role in Europe and prevent Paris from isolating the United Kingdom, but also as insurance against U.S. and British abandonment.

Adenauer's view of the Soviet Union paralleled de Gaulle's. The chancellor believed that the Soviets sought to separate Germany from Western Europe by whatever means available, including threats to West Berlin, efforts to force contacts between the Federal Republic and East German authorities, and maneuvers to remove Germany from the process of European integration.[26] Adenauer suspected that the Soviets had supported de Gaulle's return to power in the mistaken belief that he would "continue the same policy that he had followed ten or twelve years earlier: alignment with Russia against Germany."[27] Adenauer even adopted de Gaulle's language on the need for France and Germany to establish a real balance with the Soviets in Europe as a prerequisite for any reduction of Cold War tensions, noting that "when discussing the German question, one can never lose sight of the more general problem of the European equilibrium."[28]

As we have seen in previous chapters, Adenauer, unlike de Gaulle, did not have the luxury of a political system that would allow him unilateral decision making in foreign policy. Adenauer's policies were often criticized and opposed by his subordinates. Even the foreign ministry was not always tractable, and Adenauer once reportedly stated that he "had only three enemies: the Communists, the British and [his] own foreign office."[29] In order to shape policy as much as possible, Adenauer, like de Gaulle, bypassed the diplomats whenever he could, despite the fact that his foreign minister, Heinrich von Brentano, agreed on the essentials of his Franco-German and European policies and followed the chancellor's lead.[30]

Key foreign ministry figures such as Karl Carstens, the director of the ministry's Western European political section between 1958 and 1960 and one of the two State Secretaries thereafter, and Herbert Blankenhorn, ambassador to Paris and an Adenauer confidant, shared the chancellor's belief in the Franco-German combination along with his doubts on Britain. Carstens, Blankenhorn, and other foreign ministry officials regretted de Gaulle's rejection of all further supranationalism, but believed that Germany should push forward on whatever forms of cooperation the French president would accept. Initially, between 1958 and mid-1960, it was the Auswärtiges Amt that reassured Adenauer over de Gaulle and smoothed over the frequent tensions in Franco-German relations provoked by the French leader.[31] Carstens, in particular, consistently urged a constructive policy whereby Germany would cooperate with de Gaulle primarily for the sake of moving him in the right direction. It was nevertheless important to maintain independence from France. Carstens, referring to Frederick the Great's statement that "to be an ally of France is to be its slave," remarked, "We can have cooperation with France at any time [by accepting] uncritically France's goals and demands [as] our own."[32] Blankenhorn, who also had doubts about de Gaulle, nevertheless insisted that Germany could not be "thankful enough for the fact that de Gaulle and Adenauer understand each other," and that "[the] Franco-German alliance is one of the few guarantees we have that the Soviet attempt to divide and conquer Western Europe will fail."[33] Given the foreign ministry's positive but cautious stance toward de Gaulle, it is not surprising that later, when it feared Adenauer had fallen too far into the French leader's orbit, the ministry played the opposite role, braking the chancellor's moves toward France rather than encouraging them.

Just as Erhard had been Adenauer's main opponent on issues of European integration, he became the chief German critic of de Gaulle and of Adenauer's focus on relations with France. As in the economic arena, Erhard preferred a wider sphere for German policy and feared that Adenauer was overly willing to abandon Britain for the sake of de Gaulle.[34] The Adenauer-Erhard duel over relations with France between 1958 and 1960, involving politics as much as economic issues, was won by the chancellor but cast doubt on the post-Adenauer future. Adenauer repeatedly insisted that Erhard "simply did not possess the necessary political qualities to be chancellor."[35] Outside the government, Adenauer's policy received a mixed welcome. The Bundestag as a whole never shared his enthusiasm for a close entente with de Gaulle. The SPD in particular disliked the general from the outset, viewing him as an autocrat, and it never supported an exclusive Franco-German link. Before long, the party championed relations with Britain and the United States as a means to weaken the chancellor. After a period of initial concern and distaste for de Gaulle, the German public welcomed further steps in the Franco-German reconciliation and de Gaulle's desire for close cooperation with Germany, but never understood or supported his wider foreign policy goals. The public, media, and special interest groups all made relations with the United States a much higher priority, resisted any exclusive relationship with France, and feared de Gaulle's hegemonic ambitions. However, between 1958 and 1960 none of these concerns limited Adenauer's policy, as the chancellor himself remained very cautious on de Gaulle. It was only later, after 1960, when he pursued a more exclusive and unreserved policy toward France, that Adenauer met opposition both inside and outside his government.[36]

De Gaulle's Return to Power, 1958

During the final crisis of the Fourth Republic, in April and May 1958, and the first few months after de Gaulle's return to power, the Franco-German relationship underwent considerable tension over the new leader's intentions toward Germany and Western Europe. In April and May France appeared to be degenerating into anarchy, with the National Assembly long unable to form a government and the army in Algeria defying Paris and threatening a paratroop assault on the capital. When the appointment of de Gaulle as prime minister finally stabilized the situation, Bonn welcomed the return to order in France, but otherwise expressed mixed emotions. On the one hand, the instability and indecisiveness of the Fourth Republic had often been a source of frustration, but on the other hand Bonn had been confident in its European convictions and commitment to the Franco-German rapprochement. The Germans recalled de Gaulle's anti-German policies between 1944 and 1946, which had included plans to annex the Saar and Rhineland and a treaty of alliance with the USSR. Aware of de Gaulle's hostility to supranational integration, they feared that he might undermine the European policy Bonn had followed since 1949. Adenauer himself held a negative view of de Gaulle's political abilities.[37]

During the crisis of April and May 1958, most German leaders avoided public commentary, particularly once it appeared likely that de Gaulle might return to power. The foreign ministry, predicting that any outcome of the crisis would likely harm German interests, warned that Bonn would still need France in the future and could not simply abandon it because of de Gaulle.[38] Nevertheless, some critical views did leak out. Erhard announced that Germany would cut all economic support for any regime that seized power illegally. The economics minister compared the "ousting" of the preceding government with the destruction of the Weimar Republic and the "manner in which dictatorship came to Germany" in 1933.[39] Erhard's comments infuriated de Gaulle, poisoned their relations from the outset, and prompted the latter to reassure the Americans on his intentions toward Europe.[40] German defense minister Franz-Josef Strauss, although ultimately more favorable than Erhard to working with de Gaulle, made the Weimar comparison as well.[41] Adenauer remained more cautious but doubted that de Gaulle could take power without a coup. When de Gaulle declared on 19 May that he would only come to power by legal means, a relieved Adenauer concluded that the general had removed himself from the picture.[42]

After the National Assembly installed de Gaulle as prime minister, the German government made its first official statement. Bonn expressed hope for greater stability in France and emphasized that the many treaty ties binding the two countries would be the "basis of cooperation with [the] newly formed French government," a veiled warning to de Gaulle not to abrogate the NATO or Rome treaties or abandon European integration.[43] By late June Adenauer's public stance on de Gaulle had considerably improved. He lauded de Gaulle's role in the resistance and emphasized his more positive views toward Germany.[44] Beneath the surface, Germany's leaders remained much less optimistic.[45] The foreign ministry prepared for the worst: the abandonment of the Common Market and NATO and the possibility of unilateral French overtures to the USSR at the expense of Germany. De Gaulle, who was known for ignoring political and economic realities in his pursuit of "grandeur" and the interests of "Eternal

France," would probably remain in the Western camp, but would not allow anything to limit his foreign policy options. At best Germany could expect to be used by de Gaulle: "Like the British, [de Gaulle] seeks freedom of action and, just like [the British], he is interested in Germany primarily as a financial and technical helper."[46] The Auswärtiges Amt questioned how much de Gaulle's foreign policy views had changed since 1946 and doubted his commitment to a close Franco-German relationship. Germany faced a minor role in a Gaullist Europe, but had no choice other than to show great patience and try to restrain the worst Gaullist excesses.[47]

Despite all these concerns, the foreign ministry felt that Germany must move forward with de Gaulle's France as it had with the Fourth Republic.[48] Germany and the other Common Market members might overcome de Gaulle's opposition to supranationalism by promoting greater political coordination among the Six.[49] According to the Paris embassy, Bonn must work to counter provocative Gaullist moves and channel them in directions favorable to German interests, since "no western country can seek advantages for itself via selfish, Machiavellian maneuvering without weakening the free world vis-à-vis the communist bloc."[50]

De Gaulle and the Quai d'Orsay tried to reassure Bonn by immediately calling for a Franco-German summit. During the preparatory meetings that summer, top Auswärtiges Amt officials met their French counterparts and received assurances on the continuity of French foreign policy.[51] De Gaulle, although preoccupied with the Algerian conflict and with writing a new constitution, hoped to alleviate Adenauer's doubts, and Bonn ultimately agreed to a September summit.[52]

The core of the Franco-German relationship under de Gaulle and Adenauer was established at two key meetings, at Colombey-les-Deux-Eglises in September 1958 and Bad Kreuznach in November. Held in rural areas, out of the public eye, and in or near the homes of the two leaders, these encounters emphasized the personal nature of the relations between the two aged statesmen. The importance of the first meeting to de Gaulle is made clear by the fact that Adenauer was the only foreign leader ever invited to the home that served as his retreat from the burdens of the world.

Despite Adenauer's hope for a detailed discussion of key European issues, the first meeting was a very general "tour d'horizon," but it did reveal the closeness of the two leaders' basic views. The French sought to establish a core Paris-Bonn alignment that took precedence over specific issues. De Gaulle and Adenauer agreed that their countries had to cooperate in order to be taken seriously by the United States and the USSR. As Adenauer put it, "The existence of the superpowers is the reason why Europe must be unified and why the cooperation between France and Germany must be reinforced."[53] Neither had an alternative partner. Franco-German cooperation could lead to a more independent Western Europe and to the ultimate liberation of Eastern Europe from Soviet control. At Colombey, Adenauer and de Gaulle formed a strong personal bond, based on mutual interests that contrasted with their doubts over the British and American commitments to Europe. The bond was sealed by de Gaulle's assurance that France would carry out the European treaties it had signed.[54]

A longstanding cornerstone of Adenauer's policy had been his determination to establish "*Gleichberechtigung*" (equal treatment) of Germany among the nations of the West. Yet he proved willing to set this aside for the sake of good relations with de Gaulle. At the Colombey meeting, Adenauer made three key concessions that downgraded important German interests and accorded France a permanent position of superiority in their relationship. There would be no development of German nuclear weapons, no German pressure for border changes, and an indefinite postponement of reunification.[55] After this meeting, Adenauer also allowed, and occasionally encouraged, de Gaulle to act as the Franco-German spokesman and the representative of Western Europe in East-West meetings from which Germany was excluded. De Gaulle as spokesman was better than no spokesman at all. Some of Adenauer's advisers were even more enthusiastic about using France to block British or American demands and uphold European interests.[56]

Two months later at Bad Kreuznach, a city built on the ruins of a Roman fortress just over a hundred kilometers to the southeast of Bonn, the general statements made at Colombey were given concrete form. Bad Kreuznach was another symbolic meeting place, as the city had been sacked by the armies of Louis XIV in 1689. De Gaulle now declared that France, by virtue of its improving financial situation, would not require recourse to any of the escape clauses of the Treaty of Rome, which would have delayed its full implementation. He also announced that France would carry out its tariff reduction obligations in full on 1 January 1959, and that Bonn could count on total French firmness on German issues with the USSR. He insisted that "the more united and firm the West, the less far the Soviets will push things." In return, Adenauer "thanked General de Gaulle for not wanting to resort to using the escape clauses" and agreed to support France's rejection of further negotiations on the British-proposed Free Trade Area.[57] In effect, Adenauer chose France over Britain at Bad Kreuznach and ended the FTA.

Seen from Bonn, the choice of France over Britain appeared inescapable. Had Germany sided with the United Kingdom on the FTA, the French would have invoked the escape clauses in the Treaty of Rome, ending the Common Market, European integration, and the Franco-German relationship. A triumphant Britain would have taken advantage of its new economic opportunities on the continent while offering only tepid support on Berlin and reunification, no guarantee that its army would remain in Germany, and vague statements of the value of good relations with a "world power" such as Britain. The foreign ministry judged that the alignment with France offered many more advantages than dangers. If de Gaulle sought to use Germany and Europe to bolster his great power ambitions, he was also Germany's principal ally on East-West issues and building a strong Europe. As the foreign ministry saw it, "The way things look now in France, only de Gaulle can guarantee the active participation of France in the European unity effort."[58]

During the fall of 1958 two crises, one within NATO and the other between the West and the Soviet Union, produced opposite effects on Franco-German relations. The NATO crisis provoked by de Gaulle revived Adenauer's doubts, but the new Berlin crisis strengthened the chancellor's conviction that he had chosen correctly in opting for France over Britain. On 17 September, only days after his first meeting with Adenauer at Colombey, de Gaulle issued his famous memorandum to Macmillan and Eisenhower on the reorganization of NATO. He stated that France deemed necessary the creation of "an organization including the United States, Great Britain and France to deal with global political and strategic affairs."[59] In this directorate, the United States, Britain, and France would consult on all major world issues and make all the important decisions, making Germany and the other NATO countries second-class members of the alliance. Adenauer, despite his alarm and irritation at having received no warning at Colombey, limited his criticism for the sake of the wider Franco-German relationship. De Gaulle and his diplomats denied any intention of forming a formal directorate within NATO and claimed to be promoting European interests.[60] Adenauer remained dubious, and de Gaulle's tripartite ideas continued as an irritant in the Franco-German relationship well into 1960.

This episode set a pattern that typified the Franco-German relationship for several years. In carrying out his global agenda in which Germany constituted only one part, even if an important one, de Gaulle often took audacious steps that risked angering Adenauer. When the Germans expressed their displeasure, the French mollified them with assurances of their desire to strengthen the independence and interests of Western Europe as a whole and denials of any discrimination against Germany. German leaders would accept these assurances for the sake of wider Franco-German relations, and all would move smoothly until de Gaulle provoked the next crisis. Although the French were almost always the source of tensions, the Germans quickly learned to use them not only to restrain their western neighbor but also to demonstrate to the United States and Britain that they did not follow de Gaulle blindly.

Two months later, in November, the Berlin crisis provoked by Soviet premier

Nikita Khrushchev gave de Gaulle the opportunity to demonstrate solidarity with Adenauer and strengthen the Franco-German bond. As noted above, de Gaulle was a hardliner on Cold War issues pertaining to Germany, in part because he knew that if push came to shove, it would be the Americans who would have to provide the force to back up western positions. Throughout the Berlin crisis, which extended beyond the construction of the wall in August 1961 until 1963, de Gaulle's firm opposition to any concessions to the Soviets, in contrast with Britain and America's greater willingness to negotiate, made a strong impression on Adenauer. France alone could do little to protect West Berlin in the event of a military confrontation, but Adenauer felt that its firmness helped to prevent U.S. and British concessions to the Soviets. As Adenauer confronted pressures for compromise from London and Washington, Moscow and East Berlin, as well as the reform and revival of the SPD as a serious opposition force at home after 1958, he tended to oversimplify the positions of all three of his western allies. He interpreted British and American willingness to discuss issues with the Soviets as a surrender and viewed de Gaulle as his only reliable ally. However, the French leader also took advantage of the crisis to reinforce France's elevated position over Bonn, as it not only increased German dependency on French support, but constantly demonstrated France's special role as one of the four occupying powers.[61] Ironically, Soviet pressures intended to divide the Western camp ended up making a major contribution to the strengthening of the Franco-German entente.[62] By the late 1950s, France and Germany had many other reasons to settle their differences and cooperate and would have done so in the absence of Soviet pressures, but the Kremlin's actions undoubtedly contributed to the depth and speed of their rapprochement.

Cooperation and Distrust, 1959

Although most of the diplomacy of 1959 centered on Berlin and other East-West issues, de Gaulle and Adenauer continued their personal meetings and Franco-German relations grew closer. Still seeking to establish a broad consensus with Adenauer, de Gaulle stayed on the level of generalities, while the chancellor attempted to channel French policy in European and Atlantic directions. On 4 March the two leaders conferred in Paris, their first encounter in the capital of either country.

The chancellor remained a cautious partner. Alarmed by Britain's anger over the FTA failure and its reticence over defending Berlin, he noted that the British "have complained that their FTA is rejected yet they are asked to die for Berlin," suggesting that "we must convince them that they will receive some satisfaction when the time comes." De Gaulle and Debré rejected this linkage as a threat to the Common Market, the new Franco-German tie, and France's wider plans for Western Europe. They insisted that the British must "put political solidarity in the face of Soviet maneuvers ahead of economic questions."[63] To balance Britain's negativism, de Gaulle reassured the chancellor of his total support on Berlin and insisted they must stay together regardless of the fate of NATO or of U.S. and British concessions to the Soviets. De Gaulle flattered Adenauer as one of the founders of European unity and traced a glowing picture of their future relationship.[64]

The next crisis occurred shortly afterward. Using a press conference to demonstrate France's superior position, the "reliable" de Gaulle declared that Germany must accept its territorial losses from World War II and not "reopen the question of [its] present frontiers to the west, the east, the north and south." This went directly against Bonn's long-held position that nothing in the outcome of the war could be considered permanent until Germany was reunified and a formal peace settlement was signed. Adenauer and his entourage, although furious at de Gaulle's declaration, muted their reaction to maintain their ties with Paris. Adenauer knew that he had little choice. It was Macmillan, not de Gaulle, who had done the most to undermine Germany by plying the route to Moscow and urging Bonn to make concessions on Berlin. Realignment with the British was not an option.[65]

In the spring of 1959 German domestic politics created another tremor. After ten years in power, Adenauer knew that he could not remain chancellor indefinitely. Concerned about Europe's continuing instability, he sought the best means to ensure the continuity of his foreign policy after he left office. With the post of president open in early 1959, Adenauer briefly considered resigning and taking the ceremonial office, hoping that he could guide the policy of his Christian Democratic successor and also of any SPD government that might take power. When it became clear that his party would nominate Erhard to succeed him, Adenauer quickly abandoned the whole idea. He viewed the anti-French, pro-British, anti-Common Market, and pro-FTA Erhard as unfit to be chancellor. Not surprisingly, the French strongly encouraged Adenauer to stay on as long as possible. At a dinner in Bonn in early May, Debré subtly praised Adenauer and dismissed Erhard: "Do not believe, gentlemen, that economic problems rule the world. Great statesmen and political questions shape it far more decisively. It is on these that the fate of the world, our future and freedom depend."[66] Adenauer's support of the Franco-German tie, if not unqualified, was firm and consistent. By mid-1959 he supported Paris's call for NATO reform and accepted France as the speaker for Western Europe, all in an effort to restrain the superpowers from making major decisions over the heads of the Europeans.[67]

On 3 November de Gaulle triggered another brief crisis with a speech at the

École militaire calling for a purely national defense policy. The Germans saw a threat to the integrated NATO alliance and to America's commitment to Europe. Within less than a week SPD leaders in the Bundestag attacked de Gaulle for antagonizing Britain and the United States and criticized Adenauer's support for his policies. As usual, both French and German diplomats worked to smooth over the conflict. The Germans were becoming accustomed to downplaying Gaullist rhetoric. By now, Adenauer's opponents, Erhard and the SPD, recognized the futility of their protests and used them primarily to score domestic points. French diplomats argued that much of the uproar merely reflected the dismay of those in Germany who "look more readily towards London than Paris," at the strength of the Franco-German alignment, but they also saw no reason to strengthen such elements by offending Bonn over NATO or its unequal treatment.[68] German officials remained as wary as ever of the French president, but rather than attack him directly, the foreign ministry preferred that Germany direct its energy toward restraining France's hegemonic aspirations and persuading it to cease antagonizing the United States and Britain and show greater support for NATO, European integration, and crucial German issues, such as the border problem.[69]

Adenauer and the French leadership held another summit in Paris in December to patch up their latest disagreements and advance their cooperation. They still disagreed on a role for Britain on the continent, as Couve de Murville and Debré rejected Adenauer's appeals for flexibility. Each side also restated its familiar points on the role of the United States in Europe and the relative merits of NATO. While they could not agree on relations with other countries, they agreed on their own bilateral ties. Here the personal de Gaulle–Adenauer relationship was crucial. When Adenauer met with Couve de Murville and Debré, they disagreed on almost everything, but when he met de Gaulle, the two men found areas of agreement. De Gaulle restated his support for Germany and his resistance to any concessions to the Soviets. Once reassured on this and on de Gaulle's commitment to the Atlantic alliance, Adenauer became much less dogmatic on relations with Britain and the United States. In hopes of gaining greater influence on French policy, the chancellor called for increasing bilateral cooperation in as many areas as possible, to "guarantee the permanence of friendly Franco-German relations." De Gaulle agreed that greater cooperation was necessary to prepare for the day when "the Americans withdraw from the European continent," but preferred to keep any Franco-German special ties informal and focus on the Six for anything more substantial. This would change later. For now the two leaders agreed to study possibilities for both bilateral and wider cooperation, but it would be difficult to go beyond generalities as long as the areas of disagreement between Paris and Bonn remained so vast. Despite

Bonn's amiable public rhetoric, most German leaders were still irked by France's tripartite ambitions, and they remained more concerned with deflecting the French leader on NATO, the United States, and Britain than finding new means of cooperation with him.[70]

Before and after the Paris Summit, 1960

After the difficulties of late 1959, the approach of the East-West summit in Paris in May brought de Gaulle and Adenauer closer together than ever. Since they expected that the summit would address not only Khrushchev's demands on Berlin, but also most other issues relating to Germany, Adenauer and de Gaulle made a concerted effort to put forth a solid Franco-German front both in public and in conversations with other leaders. De Gaulle, who hoped to act as the representative of Europe at the summit, called for total Western firmness on all German issues in order to guarantee Bonn's full support for his larger ambitions. Adenauer, seeing no alternative, pinned his hopes on de Gaulle. By the time of the summit, the French believed they had won the Germans over to de Gaulle's version of a privileged, Paris-Bonn relationship to control Western Europe. Adenauer seemed to have accepted French leadership, the Common Market was coalescing, and Franco-German ties had frustrated successive British efforts to seize the initiative in European affairs. As Ambassador Seydoux put it in a telegram from Bonn, "Who would have believed just a few years ago that the day would come when Germany, on the eve of a possibly decisive [summit], would feel such confidence in France that it would welcome France speaking in its name?"[71]

When de Gaulle met with Khrushchev, Macmillan, and Eisenhower in rapid succession in March and April 1960, he championed Germany's interests but also tailored his comments to the particular concerns of his audience. For example, he informed Khrushchev that the Soviet Union was responsible for the Franco-German alliance. After World War II a weakened France "had sought to reestablish the equilibrium in Europe and for that it had been necessary to bring Germany over to the side of the West." The Franco-German relationship not only ensured balance with the Soviet camp, but enabled Paris to act independently of the United States, something the Soviets undoubtedly desired. If equilibrium were established in Europe, "France would no longer have need of America."[72] With Macmillan, de Gaulle argued that the Soviets sought to divide Paris and Bonn, that a strong Germany was an absolute necessity in the Cold War, and that the Common Market was essential to maintaining Bonn's adherence to the West. "If the Germans felt abandoned, they might be tempted to make a deal with the Russians, who could be counted on to lure them with all sorts of promises."[73] De Gaulle assured Eisenhower that France fully accepted Germany as part of the West and wished to build Europe in cooperation with it but "did not want it to recover too much of its strength" and was in no hurry to see German reunification.[74]

The Germans appeared to be satisfied with de Gaulle's advocacy, but French observers noted that Bonn remained apprehensive about the Paris summit, because it would also need British and American support if damaging concessions were to be avoided.[75] On 5 May, Adenauer expressed complete confidence in France, but reminded de Gaulle that "when [he] spoke for Europe he also defended the interests of Germany" and urged him to keep the Americans and British firm at the summit.[76] As a sign of their harmony, the two leaders met on the eve of the summit and agreed to reconvene immediately afterward to move Franco-German and European cooperation and unity forward.[77] When the summit failed, due to the Soviet reaction to the U-2 incident, Adenauer feared greater East-West tension, increased Soviet pressure on Germany, and more efforts by Britain and the United States to accommodate Moscow. He became more convinced than ever of the need for alignment with France and more willing to pursue closer political and military ties to "guarantee the durability of the [Franco-German] relationship once and for all."[78] De Gaulle now had an opportunity to advance his German agenda, but could do so only after another crisis.

Longstanding disputes still produced frictions between Paris and Bonn. The French and Germans still worked against each other regarding Britain's relations with the continent.[79] Erhard and Strauss continued to speak out against French economic and defense policies, and Paris knew that they remained the most likely successors to Adenauer.[80] Despite the confidence he projected on the surface, Adenauer himself remained frustrated at his inability to influence de Gaulle on any of their disagreements.[81] It never took much to turn such lingering irritants into a crisis, and the next one began, as usual, with French efforts to elevate their international status, even if only in symbolic and rhetorical ways. Adenauer, who feared that de Gaulle remained tempted to choose tripartism with Britain and the United States over cooperation with Germany, became apprehensive over the three-power meetings during and after the summit.[82] His suspicions were fueled by de Gaulle's emphasis on the unique status of Britain, the United States, France, and the USSR at the annual 14 July celebrations in Paris and by Debré's earlier statement to the National Assembly that "powers are divided more and more into two categories: those that possess the bomb and missiles and those that do not. Only the former have a right to speak on global affairs, since the latter are merely satellites."[83] Playing the insulted party, Adenauer protested the prime minister's comments as a threat to his entire policy of Franco-German cooperation and even considered rejecting de Gaulle's invitation to France to discuss new forms of unity.[84] Indeed, there was now a strange parallel between Adenauer and de Gaulle, both using rhetorical and symbolic gestures to influence the wider Franco-German relationship in a complex international environment. Both Adenauer's advisers and the French leadership realized that only a de Gaulle–Adenauer meeting could clear the air and urged the chancellor to go forward with the meeting.[85] Adenauer ultimately accepted, but when he went to France to meet de Gaulle, two years of cooperation between the two leaders had only partially reconciled the diverging goals and methods that separated them.[86]

On the Outside Looking In: The United States, Britain, and Franco-German Relations, 1958–1960

Ever since the formation of the Federal Republic in 1949, American leaders and public opinion had strongly supported reconciliation between France and Germany. Given American fears of German neutralism or alignment with the USSR, almost anything that further tied Germany to the West was likely to receive support in Washington. A Franco-German rapprochement would eliminate the conflict that many Americans viewed as a primary cause of the two world wars, facilitate the creation of a strong Western Europe by making possible European integration, bind both France and Germany to the West, and prevent the USSR from dividing the western half of the continent.[87] During the 1958 French government crisis, Secretary of State Dulles had feared the emergence of a popular front government that would reject NATO and European integration and halt France's rapprochement with Germany.[88] Thus, U.S. officials greeted de Gaulle with a measure of relief. Although concerned over his ultimate goals and his impact on Franco-German relations, they counted on his European partners, particularly the Germans, to restrain his more reckless tendencies. Eisenhower and Dulles actively encouraged a de Gaulle–Adenauer summit as soon as possible. Since they feared that the aloof de Gaulle would not take the initiative, Eisenhower hoped that Adenauer was "a big enough man" to do so.[89]

During the next two years, American leaders supported the growing personal ties between de Gaulle and Adenauer and dismissed any danger of an exclusive relationship that might damage U.S., British, or anyone else's interests. Washington simply stated that while no exclusive relationship, European directorate, or bloc in the alliance could be tolerated, it did not believe that anything of the sort would result from the de Gaulle–Adenauer tie.[90] Eisenhower accepted de Gaulle's September 1959 assertion that no matter how friendly the United States and Germany might become, a close connection between France and Germany would remain essential, because in the eyes of the Germans, "America is far away while France, like the USSR, is very near." De Gaulle also insisted that German ties to France had, even more than those with the United States, changed the mentality of the German people in establishing their loyalty to the West, and he urged Eisenhower to convince the British to cease attacking the Paris-Bonn relationship.[91]

Although the State Department and the National Security Council endorsed the de Gaulle–Adenauer bond, as did the American embassies in Paris and Bonn, there were some hints of danger for U.S. policy.[92] Eisenhower and Dulles were concerned over France's propensity and ability to bully Germany. Like Carstens, Dulles noted cynically that "it is, of course, much easier to be liked by the French if you do nothing they do not like."[93] The State Department, questioning de Gaulle's fidelity to the alliance and his acceptance of America's predominance, predicted that he might organize a continental bloc in NATO based on a Franco-German political, military, and economic alliance in order to increase France's world stature, and ultimately to create a neutralist European "Third Force."[94] Observers in Paris worried that de Gaulle intended to use the Franco-German relationship as a means of diverting the Common Market away from liberal economic policies and toward the creation of a protectionist economic bloc hostile to the interests of the United States and others.[95] Despite these concerns, the Americans refrained from voicing opposition to the emerging Franco-German relationship as long as the threats remained hypothetical. Washington could afford to take a hands-off policy since it felt confident that it could win any contest with Paris for Bonn's loyalty and count on the Germans to restrain de Gaulle.

British leaders had also long supported the reconciliation between Germany and France as a means of stabilizing Western Europe. They shared the doubts expressed in British opinion polls regarding France's reliability and Germany's alignment with the West, but understood that solid bilateral relations were preferable to disharmony and instability. After 1955, however, when European integration rapidly moved forward around a Franco-German core, London saw a threat to its political and economic interests. This threat was made manifest when Paris and Bonn pushed through the Common Market and Adenauer acquiesced in ending negotiations on the FTA. After 1958, British leaders viewed the Franco-German alignment primarily as a device to organize Western Europe without them. De Gaulle and Adenauer increasingly seemed to be the main obstacles to a successful British policy toward the continent.[96] Outright opposition was difficult, however, because of the seemingly strong U.S. support for the Franco-German relationship. Moreover, British officials hesitated to offend either Adenauer or de Gaulle. They were well aware of the suspicions held by continental statesmen of Britain's penchant for standing aside from, or working against, efforts at European unity and did not wish to reinforce them.[97] They thus paid lip service to the de Gaulle–Adenauer rapprochement for its value in containing Germany.[98]

Although Foreign Secretary Selwyn Lloyd defended the Paris-Bonn tie, Macmillan became increasingly hostile, complaining that "the Germans and French [had] made an unholy alliance against the British."[99] The prime minister not only feared that Adenauer would blindly follow de Gaulle down the neutralist path, but also that the Germans would dominate Western Europe after de Gaulle was gone. Convinced of a widespread Anglophobia in France and the futility of reversing it, Macmillan concentrated on cajoling and threatening the Germans. He viewed Bonn as the weak link in the bilateral entente and hoped to play on German fears of British abandonment. Thus began a long and unsuccessful British effort to change French policy by exerting pressure on Germany.[100] Believing the chancellor would not respond to gentle persuasion, the British mobilized opposition to Adenauer, repeatedly arguing that the privileged Franco-German tie was a danger to NATO because (in the words of Macmillan) "it would be difficult for Britain to keep its troops in Germany while engaged in an economic struggle against Germany and France."[101] Adenauer stubbornly resisted Britain's threats and cajoling, and the chancellor's opponents failed to reverse his conviction that London was unreliable. A frustrated Macmillan also failed to impress Paris, Washington, or his other Atlantic partners of the Franco-German menace to the United Kingdom or to NATO. It was Paris and Washington that gave Adenauer crucial support to withstand British pressure.

Conclusion

Between 1958 and 1960 de Gaulle began to implement his grand design, albeit in very general form, for reshaping Western Europe and the Atlantic alliance. This design contained at least two important contradictions relating to Germany. First, de Gaulle's ambition to make France Europe's speaker in a tripartite global directorate produced repeated crises with Bonn. Second, his plan to develop a European political grouping without any supranational arrangements challenged the entire German approach to European unity.

Despite their differences over Britain, the United States, NATO, and supranationalism, pragmatism brought de Gaulle and Adenauer together. For example, de Gaulle's dismissal of ideology as a factor in international relations contrasted sharply with Adenauer's conviction that communism was the driving force behind Soviet policy. Nevertheless, the two leaders were not far apart on the crucial question of how the West should deal with the USSR. Both believed in strength, unity, and firmness. Moreover, de Gaulle, despite his desire to explore improved relations with the countries of Eastern Europe, followed Adenauer's intransigent line of rejecting all dealings with East Germany.[102] This pragmatic approach and focus on broad common interests typified their relations in almost all other areas. The result was a superficial harmony that allowed crucial disagreements on details to fester. Paris worried about the long-term direction of Germany while Bonn feared that France favored some elements of the status quo, such as the division of Germany, and neglected or undermined others, such as the maintenance of NATO. This mix of agreement and disagreement, trust and distrust, produced a volatile relationship that underwent cycles of confidence and crisis. But by mid-1960 it became apparent that the de Gaulle—Adenauer personal relationship and common Franco-German interests were strong enough to weather such crises, and the two leaders moved beyond their efforts to lay the foundation for a close Franco-German entente and began to shape wider European developments.

Adenauer recognized de Gaulle's intention to place Germany in a position of inferiority as well as the long-term risks of a close alignment with France, especially the damaging of Germany's ties with America. In the short term, however, between 1958 and 1960, the German choice was not between France and the United States but between France and Britain, and this was a choice Adenauer was prepared to make. His decision was exclusively political and at this point he retained the authority to overrule all pro-British voices. In exchange for Germany's support on the rejection of the FTA and on limiting supranationalism, the French would continue to support the Common Market and other forms of European cooperation. They would also provide solid support in the Berlin crisis and most issues of importance to Germany. A strong and stable France would develop to protect Germany's flanks. By contrast, Britain—whose leaders resisted close ties with the continent and integration in almost any form, argued for greater flexibility on West Berlin and other German issues, tried to sabotage the Franco-German connection, and focused on their global interests—could offer little.

Although in retrospect the German decision seems inevitable, the closeness and stability of the early de Gaulle–Adenauer relationship should not be exaggerated. Indeed, as late as the July 1960 de Gaulle–Adenauer summit meeting in France, which marked the beginning of an important new stage, there were still acute strains in Franco-German relations. Every summit had been followed by a crisis and each crisis had necessitated another summit to solve it. Indeed, the German decision to go to France in July 1960 was expressly for the purpose of settling new sources of bitterness. The importance of these personal meetings reflected Adenauer and de Gaulle's high degrees of personal control of diplomacy, but they were tainted by the aversion of the two leaders to discussing and dealing forthrightly with their specific differences on European and Atlantic issues. In their frequent meetings, the two leaders focused on areas of agreement and on smoothing over discord. Between meetings, each returned to his personal agenda and the fundamental contradictions resurfaced. With the public airing of these issues and the crises that ensued, each leader kept the other on notice that the harmony of any particular summit did not fully reflect the Franco-German relationship and that the entente could not be taken for granted. The centrality of summit diplomacy to the Franco-German relationship limited the impact of the opposition to an exclusive bilateral tie, but it also kept support for such an arrangement shallow.

Yet on the symbolic level, the nascent Franco-German rapprochement would soon produce real optimism in Western Europe. It signaled that the conflicts of the past could be overcome, that through unity Europe could regain a voice in the world, and offered Europeans something to replace their lost (or soon to be lost) overseas empires. Two countries with a combined population of over one hundred million, the two largest Western European armies and economies, could provide a foundation for a wider unity that offered the prospect of escape from the burdensome Cold War choice of subjugation by the Soviet Union or dependence on the United States.

The period 1958 to 1960 was a time of preparation for all concerned with the Franco-German relationship. Despite the continuing tensions and contradictions, by mid-1960 de Gaulle was ready to move beyond the preparatory stage, make concrete proposals for greater cooperation, and use the Franco-German relationship to advance his vision of Europe and the Atlantic alliance. Despite periodic crises, Adenauer had signaled his willingness to follow the French lead on Europe. The United States and Britain had played opposite roles. While British leaders were almost uniformly negative, American policy makers had accepted and even endorsed the Franco-German relationship. The creation of this privileged bilateral relationship foreshadowed a new rivalry among the Atlantic powers in the early 1960s for Germany's allegiance and for a predominant role in Europe.

CHAPTER FOUR

THE ATLANTIC COMMUNITY AND

THE ROLE OF THE UNITED STATES

IN WESTERN EUROPE, 1959-1963

It is true that, in this "integrated" Europe, as they say, there would perhaps be no policy at all.... But then, perhaps this world would follow the lead of some outsider who did have a policy. There would perhaps be a federator, but the federator would not be European.
—Charles de Gaulle, 15 May 1962

European Integration and Atlantic Cooperation

From the late 1950s onward, the progress of European integration posed a dilemma for American leaders.[1] They had long supported the integration process as a means to make Western Europe a stronger and more valuable Cold War ally, yet they now began to fear that a more dynamic and self-sufficient continent might gradually go its own way and forsake not only American leadership, but perhaps the alliance with the United States as well. These growing fears of an independent European "Third Force" led Washington to develop, gradually and haphazardly, the idea of an "Atlantic Community" to contain and channel European unity and enable the United States to intervene more effectively in European affairs. American leaders hoped that a wider and looser Atlantic arrangement could surround the more closely integrated continental structures and prevent Western Europe from damaging or abandoning American political and economic interests. These ideas had their origins in the later Eisenhower years, when the deteriorating U.S. balance of payments and the return of the nationalist de Gaulle to power in France began to alarm State Department officials. However, it was President John F. Kennedy and his advisers who gathered all the nascent American ideas into a semi-coherent Atlantic "Grand Design" in 1961–62.

At the outset, an Atlantic Community seemed to have a fair chance of success. Each of America's three main European allies supported the creation of stronger transatlantic links in principle. Common democratic values, mutual interest in economic development, and the need for a strong political and military front against the Soviet bloc held the Atlantic countries together and encouraged the development of new means of cooperation. However, each country's leaders also hoped to use the American initiative to advance their own agendas and had their own ideas on how Atlantic political and economic relations should develop. The French, Germans, and British all transformed the concept of an Atlantic Community to suit their own needs. In the process, the idea became distorted from the original U.S. blueprint. The Americans and French ultimately promoted rival versions that reflected their wider struggle over the future shape of Western Europe and its relations with the United States. When the British and Germans focused on their own interests and refused to take sides, a complicated debate over Atlantic relations ensued, lasting through the Kennedy administration and frustrating all four participants.

The predominance of the Atlantic debate in the diplomatic relations of the four major NATO powers from 1961 to 1963 indicates the importance each attached to the idea. Most historians, however, have tended to dismiss or minimize the Atlantic Community. European and American writers have argued that the Kennedy administration never took the Atlantic cooperation idea seriously and simply sought to promote U.S. interests and maintain the protectorate status of Western Europe.[2] Most of these studies, in article form, are based exclusively on American sources and wrongly assume that the Europeans simply disregarded the idea. When the subject appears in the memoir literature, it is usually treated in a very cursory and superficial manner.[3] By contrast, this chapter argues that however questionable were the American conception and motives behind the Atlantic Community, its supporters and opponents in the United States and Europe took it very seriously, either as a real solution to European and American problems or as a real threat to their interests. A number of recent academic works have dealt with the subject more seriously. Focusing on the rivalry between de Gaulle and the Americans, the studies of Maurice Vaïsse, Georges Soutou, and Frédéric Bozo are concerned more with strategic-military aspects than in the details of the Atlantic Community.[4] Geir Lundestad and Pascaline Winand examine the Atlantic Community in the context of Washington's long-term support for European integration, but their books are based almost exclusively on American archives.[5] This chapter seeks to build on the newer historiography by examining the Atlantic Community from a truly multilateral perspective.

The Atlantic Community was a new way to maintain American leadership in a unifying Western Europe by making that leadership more flexible, less overt, and therefore more palatable to the Europeans. Unfortunately, the various aspects of the plan were developed haphazardly and never formed a coherent whole. The basic idea, first developed by President Dwight D. Eisenhower's advisers in the State Department, was to create mechanisms in various areas (economics, politics, and nuclear defense in particular) to enable the West to form common positions on important global issues. These included its policy toward the USSR, aid to the developing world, and the organization of Western economic relations. The United States would function as coordinator of a system in which a revived Western Europe would ease America's burden of hegemony and provide political and economic support for its Cold War policies all over the globe. Superficially this represented a shift in the Atlantic alliance from a primarily military arrangement dominated by the United States to a wider diplomatic and economic grouping composed of two nominally equal partners, or "twin pillars," America and a united Western Europe.

When Kennedy and his advisers took office, they hoped to use the Atlantic Community idea to end the post-Suez drift and disarray of the late 1950s in European and Atlantic relations. Kennedy understood the reasons why Truman and Eisenhower had supported European integration, but he was more concerned than his predecessors with the possibility that a united Europe might discriminate against the United States economically and abandon it politically. He thus intended the Atlantic Community to promote further European integration, but prevent the exclusion of the United States or the creation of an independent Third Force rival. From a more cynical perspective, this amounted to a "divide and conquer" strategy whereby Washington would encourage its major partners to compete among themselves to be its closest "Atlantic" ally and thereby thwart the formation of a separate European bloc. In Kennedy's plan, once the United States solidified its leadership, it could safely modernize the Atlantic alliance, centralizing military and nuclear control in Washington and limiting the Europeans to a conventional role, and subsequently negotiate with the USSR over the Europeans' heads. A 1963 State Department memo for Secretary of State Dean Rusk summed up this agenda: "If it is assumed that our policy of keeping ultimate authority for the United States on the final decisions of war and peace for the Western alliance is to be maintained, we may consider whether an increasingly united and prosperous Europe would indefinitely accept this state of things. . . . A United Europe pursuing policies such as, for example, de Gaulle's, would present us with a more formidable challenge than the present divided Europe."[6] In Kennedy's vision, the Atlantic Community would consolidate U.S. leadership, placate Europe by providing new American commitments, and serve as a smoke screen to cover the shift of American attention to other areas of the world, such as southeast Asia and Latin America, where the Cold War remained less stable.[7]

How exactly was the Atlantic Community to work? Existing and new Atlantic bodies were to function as umbrella organizations to contain the more limited (but also more tightly integrated) groupings developing in Europe. Within these wider Atlantic organizations, such as NATO for defense and political ties, the Organization for Economic Cooperation and Development (OECD) for economic coordination, and a Multi-Lateral Nuclear Force (MLF) for nuclear defense and strategy, small steering groups of the major Atlantic powers would be established. These groups would be restricted enough to ensure efficient consultation and implementation of common policies. The smaller European countries would have a nominally equal status with the larger powers in each organization, but the latter would control the steering groups.[8] In this new Atlantic partnership, any "special" U.S. relations that had previously existed with individual countries, most notably Britain, would be replaced by a "special relationship" with Western Europe as a whole. Thus even as they urged London to join Europe and help them build the Atlantic Community, American leaders sought to downgrade the unique British role in U.S. policy by means of the new Atlantic arrangements. Otherwise, the State Department feared, "The arrangements that embody the 'special' U.S.-U.K. relation serve as a psychological and technical brake on Britain's full integration within the European Community and diminish the sense of partnership between Continental Europe and the United States."[9]

British leaders well understood the mixed nature of the U.S. offer. The Atlantic Community was a challenge to their existing policies toward both Europe and the United States, but one that might be turned to their advantage. Since 1945 Britain had remained aloof from European integration and clung to the Commonwealth and its close ties to Washington. It viewed integration into Europe as a reduction in stature and preferred to maintain the trappings of a great power. However, the United Kingdom had also long employed "Atlantic" terminology to reaffirm its privileged American ties and slow continental integration. In 1957, in the wake of the Suez debacle, Prime Minister Harold Macmillan had offered to coordinate British and American global policies and resources, both as a way of acting as the most "Atlantic" of the European powers and to reassert Britain's status as a world power. Although they recognized the risks and resentment this created for them in Europe, the British tended to minimize them by blurring the differences between Atlantic cooperation and European integration.[10] In the early 1960s London hoped that the Americans had finally heeded its warnings on the dangers of European unification and were prepared to launch a joint effort to restrain it and secure the political and economic unity of the West.

Although unconcerned about the precise form of Atlantic partnership, Macmillan had a list of essential elements to protect British interests. In the economic sphere, London aimed at the long-term development of an Atlantic free trade area for its industrial goods. This would build on previous unsuccessful British efforts to divert supranational European integration into a simple European free trade area. In the political realm, Atlantic cooperation had to reinforce the American commitment to Europe and recognize Britain's special relationship with the United States. This did not preclude close U.S.-French or U.S.-German relationships, but Macmillan insisted that "there was no possibility of [London] agreeing to this at the cost of [its] relations with the Americans."[11] Nothing could be done to jeopardize Britain's unique role as the bridge across the Atlantic. Herein lay the fatal Atlantic contradiction between London and Washington, since the latter intended the Atlantic Community to reduce Britain to the status of one European power among many.

Germany proved an even stronger adherent of the Kennedy administration's Atlantic Community proposals than Britain. Its leaders had long sought expanded American ties to the continent and greater U.S. consultation of Western Europe on major decisions. Frustrated with its second-class status in the Atlantic alliance, Bonn viewed the Atlantic Community as a means to thwart Franco-British-American dominance and gain a status equal to Paris and London. By acting as the most "Atlantic" of the European countries, Bonn hoped to gain Washington's gratitude as well as palpable rewards.[12] While the Germans did not view European integration and the Atlantic Community as contradictory and hoped to avoid any choice between the two, Chancellor Adenauer was long accustomed to playing his Western allies off against one another to maximize the benefits for Germany, and the Atlantic Community provided one more opportunity to do so.[13] However, the Germans had to proceed with caution as they played this dangerous game. As French hostility to the Atlantic Community grew in the early 1960s, Bonn exhibited more restraint toward the idea and reinforced its relations with the continental countries.[14] When the debates on Atlantic cooperation led to an open conflict between France and the United States in 1962–63, the German leadership split between "Gaullists" and "Atlanticists."[15] However, even then the foreign ministry sought to turn the Franco-American split to Germany's advantage, noting, "The simultaneous use of the Franco-German Treaty [of cooperation, signed in January 1963] and the Nassau [MLF] offer, not to mention the management of our multilateral ties, will best advance German interests."[16]

Like the Germans, the French had long been frustrated at the absence of political coordination in the Atlantic alliance, but their panacea was a tripartite directorate. Developed well before 1958, the French intended tripartism to dissolve the British-American "special relationship" and block unilateral American actions.[17] After returning to power, de Gaulle promoted Franco-British-American coordination of Western political, economic, and defense policies all over the world, with Britain speaking for the Commonwealth and France representing Western Europe. To de Gaulle, who stressed the divergence of American and European interests, tripartism was the only realistic form of Atlantic partnership. It reflected French ambitions to regain great power status as the speaker for Europe and post-colonial Africa in Atlantic and world councils.[18]

De Gaulle's tripartite Atlantic vision, unlike the loose, largely informal ties of British-American collaboration, called for a highly organized system of cooperation. This stance reflected the general's mistrust of the United States and its potential to dominate or desert Western Europe. Looking back at the history of American relations with Europe in the twentieth century, de Gaulle concluded that the United States fluctuated between aloofness from Europe and its conflicts and hegemony to settle problems when they finally intruded on American interests. He sought to retain America's protection while preventing any form of direct or indirect influence or control. He suspected Kennedy of wishing to reduce Europe to an American satellite and thwart European efforts at power and independence. However, the French president recognized that his continental partners, including Germany, Italy, and Benelux, shared neither his assessment of the United States nor his passion for tripartism. In dealing with his European partners, he therefore had to attenuate his anti-Americanism, downplay his tripartite goals, and emphasize his firm commitment to Atlantic cooperation. In a September 1960 note on strategy to his prime minister, Michel Debré, de Gaulle stated that the Atlantic issue should be postponed. Given Germany's doubts on his plans, "the question of the recasting of the alliance could not be posed in a practical way until after the beginning of the political construction of Europe."[19] De Gaulle nevertheless worked against the Atlantic Community, first behind the scenes and later, after the failure of his own plans to organize Western Europe under French leadership, in the open. He argued that the Americans would ultimately support a strong and independent French-led Europe that would lessen their burdens, though they would fight it tooth and nail over the short term.[20]

From OEEC to OECD: Atlantic Partnership at the End of the Eisenhower Administration, 1959–1960

Between 1959 and 1960, in the midst of the contest between the Six and the Seven, the OEEC was transformed into the OECD and expanded to include the United States and Canada. This change, based not only on economic considerations, reflected wider American political thinking on future relations with Europe. The Eisenhower administration and the State Department feared that the Six and Seven might become inward-looking, discriminate against the United

States and other countries, and ignore the wider global responsibilities of the West. This rift would divide Europe and frustrate America's hopes for a strong European partner. If they established a preferential trade settlement, it could move the continent in the direction of economic autarky and political neutralism. Facing such threats, the United States needed a means to "redirect the emerging trade rivalries in Western Europe into constructive channels which [would] reinforce rather than weaken world-wide trade and avoid the present risk of serious harm to [U.S.] exports and those of other friendly countries outside Europe."[21] If the United States could find a way to retain its leadership, it could settle the Six-Seven problem, direct the strength of a recovered Europe to promote "Atlantic" interests around the world and ease the economic burdens of American hegemony.

The solution the State Department developed was to expand the OEEC to include the United States and Canada and to update it to meet new challenges. The Americans floated their ideas with the Europeans in December 1959, and negotiations took place between January and December 1960. The American tactics in the negotiations reflected their wider goals, and Washington largely obtained the conditions it sought. There would be no supranationalism to the group and each member would have a veto. However, because the State Department felt that "a rigid rejection of any participation in activities beyond those labeled consultative would be a political and psychological mistake," the organization was empowered to make decisions that would be binding on its members.[22] This seemed the best compromise between the need to lead the Europeans and retain American freedom of action. The OECD was to "contain" the Europeans, not the United States. Washington assumed that it would be able to guide the Europeans and that vetoes would be rare.

De Gaulle played a relatively minor role in French policy toward the establishment of the OECD. He passively accepted the creation of the new institution for the benefits it provided France. But he already distrusted America's "Atlantic" intentions and feared that the formation of the OECD was the beginning of a more elaborate campaign to cement American political and economic control of Europe and prevent France or any other country from taking independent action.[23] De Gaulle's passive policy enabled Paris to use the American initiative for its own purposes rather than reject it. Indeed, the French had already proposed new means of Atlantic economic coordination even before the Americans addressed the matter in December 1959. Paris shared America's belief in the need to coordinate Atlantic economic policy and aid to the developing world and to settle European economic disputes in a larger forum. However, de Gaulle's solution was tripartite economic coordination.[24] When Washington refused, Paris made the best of the situation. It accepted the OECD as a means of discarding the

British-dominated OEEC in which France had often been isolated and welcomed American participation in the new organization as a means of thwarting British policy toward the continent. The Quai d'Orsay noted, "For the first time the United States will participate fully and on an equal basis in discussions on trade policy in Europe and throughout the entire free world. To put it in other terms, it will no longer be possible to discuss European problems without the presence of the United States."[25] The French also realized that if the OECD took up the role of Atlantic economic coordination, it would prevent NATO, de Gaulle's "bête noire," from doing so.[26] In practice it might even be possible to move toward de facto tripartite leadership in the new organization. With this hope in mind, the French cooperated with the Americans to structure the organization so that decisions were taken unanimously but members could abstain from a vote (and not be bound by it) without blocking it. French negotiators felt that this arrangement best embodied the combination of flexibility, national sovereignty, and authority they hoped the new organization would reflect.[27]

London, although recognizing that OEEC reform would reduce its influence, sought to make the best of the situation. British leaders endorsed any means of expanding American ties to Europe. With their free trade proposals blocked and the EFTA scarcely affecting the Six, they hoped the Americans would become more directly involved in European economic affairs and champion their struggle against the Common Market. After years of frustration with Paris, this seemed a better choice than "running after the French."[28] The British cabinet hoped that a loose Atlantic political and economic organization would swamp the Six and restore Britain's role as the bridge between the continent and the United States. The OECD seemed like a good start and the American "desire to work more closely with Europe . . . to find a solution of a large number of the problems of the West" appeared promising.[29] Either the Common Market would dissolve into the larger Atlantic group or, at the very least, the United States and Canada would support the British in attempting to lower the tariffs of the Six as far as possible. In order to meet these goals, the British accepted the provisions on unanimous voting and abstention promoted by Washington and Paris.[30]

For Bonn, the creation of the OECD solved both foreign and domestic problems and illustrated how Atlantic arrangements could ease tensions in German policy. On one level it lessened the backlash created by Bonn's choice of Paris over London in the free trade negotiations by placating the British and offering a solution to the Six-Seven split. German leaders also welcomed greater American involvement with Europe and hoped that it would lead to the expansion of liberal tariff policies and the protection of wider German trade interests as the Common Market developed.[31] Bonn believed that the new organization would complement rather than threaten the unity of the Six. The foreign ministry instructed German negotiators to work for "the maintenance of the previous OEEC system of cooperation and the full participation of the USA and Canada, while preventing anything that would endanger European institutions [the Common Market]."[32] It also offered Germany, at last, an equal position with both France and Britain in a European organization, and it blocked tripartism in at least one sphere.[33] For this last reason, Bonn would have preferred that the organization have stronger decision-making and enforcement powers, but bowed to the combined weight of its partners.[34] On the domestic level, the OECD promised to ease the tensions between the Erhard and Adenauer camps on European integration. Each side interpreted the new organization as moving Europe in the direction it favored. Adenauer and the foreign ministry viewed it as ending the British threats to the Common Market and were certain that the United States would support the Six against any future British moves, while Erhard argued that it signaled the elevation of economic issues from the narrow purview of the Six to an Atlantic level favoring loose, free trade arrangements.[35]

The agreement of the four countries on the general goals and nature of the OECD enabled the negotiations to move rapidly, and the convention was signed in December 1960. In practice, however, the new organization failed to meet the larger ambitions any of the four held for it. The absence of any real coordinating mechanism, combined with the unanimous voting arrangements, the diverse national motives behind the organization's creation, and the growing strife over all Atlantic arrangements in the early 1960s, limited the OECD to a technical and advisory role that it has held ever since.[36] Nevertheless, it did meet the immediate American concerns over U.S. leadership in Europe that had spawned it and encouraged Washington to seek other Atlantic solutions to its European problems. Unfortunately, it proved to be one of the few successes (however limited) of the entire American Atlantic campaign and demonstrated the limits of what was possible.

The Formation of Kennedy's Atlantic "Grand Design," January 1961–May 1962

Although Kennedy's Atlantic vision had its origins in the late Eisenhower years, the new administration added many new ingredients. Under Kennedy, the White House and the State Department were the main champions of the Atlantic Community, with a more cautious Department of Defense trailing behind. Despite his often visionary public rhetoric, Kennedy was generally very pragmatic on Atlantic relations. He worried about America's balance of payments with Europe and its access to markets on the continent, managing the NATO alliance to present a common front toward the USSR, and securing European support for American policies around the world. It was the State Department, led by Undersecretary George Ball and a group of ardent Europeanists, who championed a more firm and ideological commitment to the Atlantic Community. The new government's goal for the Atlantic alliance was to ensure the unity and strength of the West and retain American leadership in the political, economic, conventional defense, and nuclear areas. The three main components of its plan were a loose Atlantic community based on NATO in the political and defense areas, a sweeping round of Atlantic tariff reductions in the economic sphere, and the MLF in the nuclear realm.[37]

In the summer of 1960 a State Department planning paper known as the Bowie Report foreshadowed the transition from the Eisenhower to the Kennedy administration in the area of Atlantic relations. Focusing primarily on the links among the United States, Britain, and the Six, the document explored ways of reducing America's economic burdens while maintaining its leadership of the Atlantic alliance. It advocated policy coordination as the best immediate approach, using NATO and the OECD to promote greater economic and political unity. By 1960, despite Eisenhower's support for the idea, the term "Third Force" carried increasingly negative and neutralist connotations in Washington. Thus, the report recommended a strong American guiding hand for trade liberalization and greater political consultation to discourage any such tendencies among America's European partners. Arguing that "a strong political and economic unit in Western Europe, in alliance with the U.S., would contribute decisively to the political cohesion, economic health, and military strength of the Atlantic Community as a whole," the paper emphasized the need for British entry into the Common Market, both to end the division of Western Europe and to guide the Six in an outward direction.[38]

Drawing on reevaluations such as the Bowie Report, the new Kennedy team accepted most of the Eisenhower legacy toward Europe, but modified it to reflect its own ambitions and concerns. Kennedy promoted the use of NATO for political consultation and believed in greater burden sharing, but he reemphasized America's support for European integration and placed greater emphasis on Western coordination of aid to the developing world. He hoped to convince his European allies to take a wider view of the world and accept greater responsibilities in it.[39] Some of the Kennedy team, particularly Ball, were unenthusiastic about the OECD: "I was convinced that we could create an effective machine for common transatlantic decision and action only by beginning afresh. Unhappily it was too late to create anything new. The failure to scrap what existed and make a fresh start condemned the expanded organization to a pedestrian role, but, while lamenting the bad timing, I had no option but to support the [organization]."[40]

The interdepartmental Acheson Report of early 1961, named for the former secretary of state who played a key role in its preparation, brought the initial Kennedy vision into focus. It proposed increased cooperation between the United States and its allies, but also insisted on strengthening America's Atlantic leadership, particularly in strategic-military affairs. Consultation was to change European policies, not those of the United States: "[The] purpose of such genuine—and often abrasive—consultation in NATO should be to bring about this change in perspective and policy by our allies, by convincing them of our understanding of their problems."[41] The report called for placing U.S. relations with all Western European countries on an equal basis. It promoted the new "flexible response" deterrent strategy whereby the United States alone would determine and execute the appropriate reaction to any communist provocation rather than launch "massive (nuclear) retaliation" and asserted American control of all the nuclear forces in the alliance. Those European countries possessing or developing their own nuclear forces, namely Britain and France, were to be eased toward giving them up and taking their place in new nuclear arrangements within NATO. At the same time, the plan posited that Britain must join the Common Market to give the latter a more Atlantic outlook and counter its French-led continental focus.[42] The goal was to create a more unified bulwark against the Soviet threat, put all America's European partners on an equal basis under U.S. leadership, and meet challenges and opportunities in the nonaligned world. The mix of cooperation and American leadership the plan embodied reflected Kennedy's global ambitions as well as his personal inclination to cooperate with the Europeans when possible and his insistence that the United States be able to act alone when necessary.[43]

During its first year and a half, the Kennedy administration was preoccupied by other issues, from Cuba to Berlin, and thus proceeded cautiously on reshaping Atlantic relations. It limited itself to sounding out its European partners on increased cooperation and coordination. America's promotional effort was directed primarily at France, the most likely opponent of its new Atlantic ideas. Kennedy met de Gaulle for the first and only time in late May and early June 1961. Before this encounter, Washington made careful plans to offer France a vision of global partnership. Kennedy hoped to placate de Gaulle's tripartite ambitions with an offer of informal consultation and regularly scheduled bilateral meetings rather than institutionalized arrangements.[44] The president's advisers suggested that Kennedy make clear to de Gaulle that the United States was willing "to deal with Europe as serious major allies" and that Washington recognized that "the Europe of 1961 is not the Europe of 1947."[45] Kennedy hoped to wean de Gaulle away from his Third Force inclinations and channel him in an Atlantic direction, but rejected concessions on either formal tripartism or support for the independent French nuclear program, since this would have undermined his whole Atlantic agenda.[46]

Despite the glamour of the young president and his wife's visit to the French capital, the French leader, not unexpectedly, gave a cold shoulder to Kennedy's proposals. Instead of gratitude for Kennedy's concessions, de Gaulle argued for a real tripartite arrangement, refuted Britain's ability and desire to become part of Europe ("The British may have the Commonwealth Preference System or a membership in the Common Market but they cannot have both"), criticized almost every aspect of NATO, and suggested that Kennedy's proposals would not amount to anything.[47] De Gaulle's negative stance reflected his decision, born of his failure to win Eisenhower over to his tripartite ideas, to proceed independently to organize Western Europe without the United States. He intended ultimately to use the weight of a European group to demand tripartism as his price for any new Atlantic arrangements.[48] Although Paris believed that Washington was still committed to some form of European integration, de Gaulle and the Quai d'Orsay distrusted the United States, and Kennedy personally, on most issues pertaining to Europe and the rest of the world. The French leadership was well aware of Kennedy's hostility to European nuclear forces in general and the French "force de dissuasion" (more popularly known as the "force de frappe") in particular. They saw little new in Kennedy's Atlantic ideas, but rather the same subordination of Western Europe to American leadership that they had resented for years. De Gaulle believed that Kennedy's Atlantic ideas represented a maneuver to unload U.S. burdens on the Europeans without according them any more decision-making power.[49] He suspected that the United States sought to extend the existing inequality in NATO and military affairs to every other field.[50]

The French leadership concluded that the Americans had concocted a hasty, superficial program reflecting their penchant for hegemony, excess idealism, grandiose plans, and a strident anti-communism. Even if Paris gave Washington the benefit of the doubt and assumed it did not harbor hegemonic intentions, an Atlantic Community, "by calling into question existing arrangements, [would] cause more problems than it would solve. Such hasty and poorly prepared initiatives must not be allowed to cause confusion and render the West even more vulnerable to the machinations of the Eastern bloc."[51] Despite their negative attitude, the French decided to postpone a confrontation with the new Kennedy administration. Their first priority was to promote their own plans for a European political group, thereby enabling them to deal with the United States as an equal.

Nevertheless, in 1961–62 French suspicions rose over the growing American influence in Europe and the reaction of their European partners. Even as the United States sought to eliminate the vestiges of its "special relationship" with Britain, Paris believed it remained as strong as ever and chafed at the discrimination this implied.[52] France interpreted American support for British efforts to join the Common Market as a shift from Washington's previous support for continental integration to a move to prevent European autonomy. Foreign Minister Couve de Murville stated bluntly, "The United States views the entry of Great Britain into the Common Market as a means of introducing itself into the organization."[53] Paris also blamed the United States for its partners' reservations concerning its proposal for a continental political confederation and for their unwillingness to build a "European [independent] Europe." It viewed U.S. Atlantic policy as designed to create competition for American favors, as a divide-and-conquer tactic under a camouflage of support for European and Atlantic unity.

Thus while the French still perceived the potential advantages of new Atlantic cooperative arrangements, they were unwilling to move ahead under unequal conditions. They recognized that Kennedy intended to use the new OECD as the economic arm of his Atlantic vision, but hoped to turn the tables and use it themselves to restrain U.S. exuberance for more new "cooperative" institutions and to exclude America and Britain from the purely European organizations they hoped to create for the continent.[54] Couve de Murville argued that "it was not the Americans' role to enter into the details of European affairs. They should distance themselves somewhat from Europe."[55] France's reserve was a safe response to stall for time. For the same reason, de Gaulle delayed a second meeting with Kennedy until his European confederation negotiations reached fruition.[56] Although the U.S.-French rivalry remained muted, it was already clear to leaders in both countries. Its outcome depended largely on the two other Atlantic powers, Germany and Britain, which attempted to exploit the conflict while avoiding a stark choice between the two rivals.

The Germans hoped that Kennedy would provide new energy to reaffirm European unity, strengthen NATO, and improve the coordination of Western economic policy and global interests.[57] They also hoped that the new administration would be more open than its predecessors to outside influence and that Bonn, now one of America's strongest allies, might carry more weight in Washington. Defense Minister Franz Josef Strauss promoted the Atlantic cooperation idea as a means to increase Germany's role in the alliance, and the foreign ministry wanted increased consultation and coordination with Washington on policies pertaining to Europe and the rest of the world.[58] Erhard also supported the Atlantic Community, hoping it might supplant the narrow Common Market with a larger free trade area for German exports.[59]

Adenauer, on the other hand, was highly skeptical toward both Kennedy and the Atlantic Community. Unlike de Gaulle, his first meeting with Kennedy went well, but the two leaders never established a strong personal bond and the chancellor never trusted the president to act resolutely on any issue.[60] Adenauer, like de Gaulle, resented the persistence of the British-American tie, which raised his doubts on both countries' commitment to Europe. As the leader of one of the world's most dynamic economies, he also resented the U.S. failure to consult Germany on issues of importance to it, but doubted that Kennedy's Atlantic proposals would change anything. Lacking faith in the continuity and stability of U.S. foreign policy, Adenauer was reluctant to embrace the American vision over France's opposition. He thus decided to accept any of Kennedy's proposals that advanced German interests, while adhering to de Gaulle's ideas for organizing Western Europe at the same time. With this double game, Adenauer not only kept his options open, but also played de Gaulle and Kennedy off against one another for Germany's support, a tactic he made full use of in 1962 and 1963 when the French and Americans moved into open conflict. He explained this approach to de Gaulle by arguing that as a result of Germany's division and the Soviet threat, "the federal republic had less freedom [to distance itself from the United States] than did France."[61]

Macmillan too hoped for a new vigor in America's European policy and for more support against de Gaulle's challenges. As Kennedy's Atlantic ideas became known, Macmillan sought to shape them to promote British interests.[62] His initial contacts with Kennedy were extremely positive and a strong mutual confidence developed between them, one that was notably absent in the prime minister's relations with either de Gaulle or Adenauer. Macmillan's concept of an Atlantic Community was embodied in a document drafted in the winter of 1960–61 entitled the "Grand Design." Its nominal purpose was to "organize the great forces of the Free World—USA, Britain, and Europe—economically, politically, and militarily in a coherent effort to withstand the Communist tide all over the world," and it called for Britain to reshape its relations with all its major allies, enter and direct the Common Market, remain America's privileged partner, and represent an expanded Western Europe with the United States.[63] Hoping to win Kennedy's support, Macmillan produced a British version of Atlantic cooperation that proposed greater NATO political consultation, the development of a NATO nuclear force based on the coordination of national forces, and the creation of an Atlantic assembly and an Atlantic free trade area. Britain would join the Common Market in order to establish its leadership and then dissolve it into the broader Atlantic arrangement. Macmillan sought to convince the Americans that an Atlantic Community would only be possible with Britain at the head of Europe, and he urged the United States to make concessions to de Gaulle on nuclear aid and tripartism to make it possible.

Like the Germans, the British sought to play both sides in the French-U.S. debate over Atlantic relations. They eagerly grasped Kennedy's ideas on a revived and expanded U.S.-European partnership, hoping the United Kingdom would dominate the European "pillar." But in their discussions with continental European leaders over their entry into the Common Market, they emphasized the need for European independence and equality with the United States. In 1962 Macmillan informed de Gaulle that he sought to build up Europe to establish a "double-headed alliance" and make the continent the equal of both superpowers, adding, "We hope to free ourselves from American tutelage."[64] By throwing a rhetorical sop to de Gaulle, London hoped to convince him that it shared his political goals and blur the differences that separated its plans from his own.

Atlantic Community as a Weapon: Kennedy versus de Gaulle, May 1962–November 1963

Whereas the Atlantic Community began as a way to strengthen and modernize America's relations with a uniting Europe and protect its interests on the continent, beginning in May 1962 it assumed another dimension. That month, after de Gaulle openly declared his opposition to the idea, it became a weapon in the Franco-U.S. contest over the future of European and Atlantic relations. In this struggle, Britain ultimately took the U.S. side and Germany was caught in between.

De Gaulle's shift from reserve to outright opposition was prompted by the failure of his efforts to organize a Western European political confederation. Although it was the Belgians and Dutch who rejected his proposals in April 1962, and although their refusal resulted in large part from unilateral last minute changes made by de Gaulle, the French leader blamed the British and the Americans for his setback. He was convinced that he could no longer procrastinate on Atlantic relations because Washington had manifested its potential to thwart his plans. When the secretary of defense, Robert McNamara, opposed independent national nuclear forces at a NATO meeting in Athens in early May, the French were certain that the United States had thrown down the gauntlet. De Gaulle interpreted Kennedy's reference to U.S. Atlantic "leadership" in a 17 May press conference as an admission of America's desire to dominate the alliance. The end of the Algerian war of independence in March also made it easier for France to take a more aggressive stance.[65] De Gaulle's new campaign against the Atlantic Community was both private and public. He counseled the U.S. ambassador that America should stay out of all European affairs, stating, "The alliance cannot be maintained if American policy remains that of excessive leadership."[66] At a press conference on 15 May, he launched a blistering attack on U.S. Atlantic policy, arguing that Western Europe must escape its state of dependence on outside powers.[67]

The U.S. government understood the seriousness of de Gaulle's attacks and decided to challenge him directly. Finally realizing that Paris could not be cajoled into accepting the Atlantic Community, Washington decided to proceed without France.[68] For the remainder of the Kennedy administration, the United States combated de Gaulle's challenges, even as the French leader kept raising the stakes and provoking it on an ever-increasing number of issues. Each side assumed the worst about the other. Washington concluded that de Gaulle sought to create a Third Force and bring Western Europe under French domination. It viewed the Atlantic Community as a tool to stop France, whose anti-American diplomacy seemed to threaten the entire U.S. position in Europe. But Washington felt confident in its ability to isolate de Gaulle. George Ball argued, "All de Gaulle can really do is to oppose the initiative of others by being negative. He cannot build the Europe he desires because his actions are conditioned by his overriding desire to build the predominance of France. As a result, he has nothing to offer the other European states."[69] Rather than engage in polemics, the United States would offer alternatives to Gaullist policies with greater appeal for Britain and the continent and pursue the Atlantic Community without France.

Nevertheless, the United States did not simply ignore de Gaulle. Washington responded privately and publicly to his challenge. The American ambassador in Paris, James Gavin, was instructed to inform de Gaulle that the United States had no intention of retreating from Europe and would insist on maintaining its influence there.[70] Kennedy, in a ringing Independence Day speech, reiterated his ideas on Atlantic interdependence, urging the Europeans to decide between de Gaulle's narrow, autarkic Europe and a global European-American partnership. To counter suspicions sowed by France, the Kennedy team reaffirmed the depth and strength of its commitment to Europe. In adapting the Atlantic Community for use against de Gaulle, Washington gave its proposals more solid form. They now included the establishment of a political and economic partnership between Western Europe and the United States, a Multilateral Nuclear Force (MLF), the creation of a wider Europe via expansion of the Common Market to include Britain, American trade liberalization legislation, and a round of GATT tariff reductions to check protectionism and isolationism on both sides of the Atlantic.[71] The struggle with France over these issues now formed the core of America's Atlantic agenda.

In the economic sphere, the American countervision to de Gaulle was based primarily on what became known as the "Kennedy Round" of tariff negotiations in the GATT. Originally intended to reduce impediments to trade in industrial goods between the United States and the Common Market, the new round was transformed into a struggle with de Gaulle. America's promotion of Atlantic and global economic cooperation was refocused to counter French protectionism within the Common Market and encourage the resistance of Germany and the rest of Western Europe to de Gaulle's effort to push the United States off the continent. From mid-1962 onward, American leaders promoted the GATT round as a test of the Western European countries, and especially France, of their ability to share the burdens and responsibilities of the West, as conceived by the United States. Washington feared that Paris might "try to use the U.S. desire for successful trade negotiations as a lever to extract concessions from Washington in other fields . . . [including] such political and military questions as atomic armament in the Atlantic alliance."[72] The stakes were to prevent such linkages, keep the Common Market open to external trade, and integrate it into the global trading order. To the satisfaction of Washington, Bonn obligingly urged France to participate in the GATT negotiations in exchange for progress in the internal development of the Common Market.

The other central aspect of the Atlantic Community after mid-1962 was the MLF.[73] Both the Eisenhower and Kennedy administrations had promoted greater military coordination and consultation within NATO and floated the idea of a European nuclear force under American control, but it was only the French challenge to Atlantic cooperation that brought the MLF to the forefront of American plans. The Kennedy administration, still hoping to eliminate all independent nuclear forces in Western Europe in order to ensure American leadership of the alliance in both peace and war, realized that the Europeans were alarmed by the flexible response doctrine. The new policy seemed to reduce Europe's protection by suggesting that the United States might not respond to a Soviet conventional attack with a nuclear reprisal or that a nuclear confrontation might be limited to the continent. The National Security Council argued that Washington had to calm these fears and offer the Europeans an incentive to align with the United States over de Gaulle and his *force de frappe.* "A European attempt to go it alone in the nuclear field could be as disruptive in the trans-Atlantic partnership as spreading national European attempts to go it alone could be in the European community."[74] Although the French would reject any alternative to national nuclear forces, Washington hoped to isolate them on the issue.

The U.S. plan to eliminate national nuclear forces was the main idea behind the December 1962 Nassau agreement with the British. The United States would provide the United Kingdom with Polaris missiles to modernize its nuclear force. In return, the British nuclear forces would be placed under NATO control except in cases of "supreme national emergency." Even though the British interpreted the accord very differently and even though the State Department had hoped to eliminate British nuclear autonomy entirely, American leaders believed that by allocating the British nuclear deterrent to NATO they had successfully brought it under control. They viewed this as the first step in transforming the special U.S.-U.K. nuclear relationship into a multilateral U.S.-Europe arrangement. Washington blurred the crucial difference between its idea of the Multi-*Lateral* Nuclear Force (MLF) and the British promotion of a Multi-*National* Nuclear Force (MNF). The former would create an integrated European nuclear force under American control with an American veto, while the latter would simply coordinate the British and American (and theoretically the French) nuclear forces within NATO. The Nassau accord, aimed in part at preventing any separate Franco-British nuclear arrangement, was predictably rejected by Paris when the United States offered it a similar arrangement.[75]

The MLF was an essentially political cause, championed by the State Department, deprecated by McNamara and the Department of Defense, and questioned by Kennedy himself. Alongside the wider effort to integrate all alliance nuclear forces under U.S. control, the basic MLF plan was for a small flotilla of surface vessels armed with medium range nuclear missiles to be manned by crews selected from the various participating countries and under the control of the American military commander in Europe (SACEUR). It was the use of surface vessels and the mixed-manning that provoked the most grave military doubts on the plan in the United States and elsewhere. Kennedy was sympathetic to national (particularly British) nuclear ambitions and feared that with its promotion of the MLF, the United States was attaching itself to something that few in Europe really supported. "[He] wondered whether the multilateral force could have any real attraction unless the United States was prepared to give up its veto, and at this point he saw no justification for relinquishing the veto."[76]

Kennedy was persuaded to promote the MLF primarily as a counter to de Gaulle. The more the French attacked the MLF, the more important it became in the eyes of U.S. leaders. The proponents of the MLF believed it would limit Germany's nuclear ambitions and prevent a Franco-German nuclear arrangement. But to succeed, it required the participation of most of Western Europe, without allowing any state to act independently. MLF supporters generally viewed the issues of national possession and independent control of nuclear weapons in

Western Europe as symbolic, and hoped to convince the Europeans to accept the trappings of nuclear participation, via the MLF, rather than insist on the reality of nuclear independence as de Gaulle did: "What these countries want is a self-respecting role in nuclear deterrence. At the moment, they conceive such a role to be one which includes a share in manning, ownership, and control of strategic delivery systems and warheads, but not one which necessarily excludes a United States veto."[77] Washington offered an additional incentive by suggesting that if the MLF were established and European integration continued, at some point down the road the United States might feel sufficient confidence in its European partners to give up its veto over the force.

As the Atlantic struggle intensified, most of de Gaulle and Kennedy's moves were intended to counter the actions of the other. Fiery press conferences by one led to public responses by the other. In January 1963 de Gaulle, alarmed by the Nassau accord and the evident progress of the MLF, used another press conference for a frontal attack on the entire Atlantic Community. He rejected the MLF, attacked American hegemony, and vetoed British membership in the Common Market, declaring, "In politics and in strategy, as in the economy, monopoly quite naturally appears to the person who holds it to be the best possible system."[78] He also sought to consolidate his hold on Germany with a spectacular bilateral cooperation treaty. All this marked a major setback for the Atlantic Community and led the United States to scale back its ambitions. Washington dropped all vague talk of new political and economic institutions and focused entirely on concrete measures, such as the GATT round and the MLF, to give Europe attractive alternatives to de Gaulle's vision. Kennedy also sought to outflank the French leader by appealing to the European public. That summer, the president made his last trip to Europe, visiting Germany, Britain, and Italy, but avoiding France. He and his advisers sought to display a stark contrast between America's fresh internationalism and de Gaulle's anachronistic view of a Europe of autarkic nation-states. One briefing paper for the trip noted, "In the long run, the most effective means of blocking de Gaulle's conquest of Europe will probably be the upsurge of democratic protest against his conception of a paternalist-authoritarian Europe. By encouraging progressive tendencies, we can help counter the Gaullist idea of Europe without seeming to challenge de Gaulle directly."[79]

This European trip was indeed a stunning success, particularly two of its episodes. First, in a major speech in Frankfurt, Kennedy gave a brilliant rendition of his Atlantic vision, reiterating America's solemn commitment to Europe and its support for a strong and united continent and stressing the interdependence between the Old World and the New. By emphasizing his support for supranational European unity, he encouraged de Gaulle's European opponents and subtly undercut all the French leader's pronouncements.[80] The even more famous episode was Kennedy's trip to West Berlin and his speech at the Berlin Wall. The powerful public reaction to his restatement of America's solidarity gave new strength to anti-Gaullist forces in Germany and marked a major setback for France, which had previously sought to trump the United States in its support for German positions on Berlin.

After de Gaulle turned openly against the Atlantic Community in May 1962, his critique was largely rhetorical. With his tripartite ideas long since rejected in both Europe and the United States and even his political confederation plans for Western Europe in ruins, he lacked the support to offer a viable Atlantic alternative. He now acted primarily as a spoiler and viewed all Atlantic initiatives from the United States as means to "*camoufler hégémonie*."[81] De Gaulle and the Quai d'Orsay remained convinced of the dangers of the Atlantic Community. They rightly suspected America of using it to reduce France and Britain to the level of other European countries, the better to control Western Europe as a whole.[82] This hostile outlook colored French interpretations of all the component parts, but did not prevent Paris from choosing carefully when and how to fight it. The foreign ministry viewed the "Kennedy Round" as a veiled American intrusion into the Common Market to eliminate its external tariffs and control its future development. It had feared that the United States promoted the membership of the United Kingdom in the Common Market because it "would guarantee the presence at the heart of the EEC of an extra and powerful champion of liberalism in international agricultural exchanges" during the GATT negotiations.[83] However, finding themselves isolated after their veto of British entry into the Common Market and unable to block the GATT negotiations, the French agreed to participate under certain conditions. The Common Market had to remain a distinct group and France's partners had to agree to its terms on internal developments in the organization.

Predictably, the French view of the MLF was also negative, but here Paris saw no reason to compromise. In 1960–61 the French already suspected America's vague plans for a European nuclear force, but awaited specific proposals. They still had faint hopes for consultation on nuclear planning and some form of U.S. aid for the French nuclear program.[84] During 1962, with McNamara's opposition to independent nuclear forces, their doubts grew. After Nassau, they viewed the MLF as a crude U.S. effort to control all nuclear forces in the alliance and believed that Britain had surrendered its nuclear independence. De Gaulle never seriously considered accepting a comparable arrangement for France and instead used Nassau as a pretext for his frontal attack on the whole Atlantic Community idea. He publicly deprecated the MLF as nothing more than an American effort to control Europe. The more the United States promoted the MLF, the more de Gaulle appreciated the political necessity of developing the *force de frappe.*

De Gaulle was disdainful of the evident British and German acceptance of the MLF. "Great Britain pretends that the Nassau accords maintain its independence. . . . As for the poor Germans, they are invited to pay the bill but will have no responsibilities. The financing is multilateral, but the decision making is unilateral. The Americans mock them, taking advantage of their passionate wish to appear to have access to nuclear weapons, which they perceive as a sort of rehabilitation, as a breakthrough."[85] Paris nevertheless did all it could to derail the MLF by turning Bonn and London against it. Because the French were aware of the appeal of the MLF in Germany, they feared that it would stoke German nuclear ambitions and lead to much greater influence for Bonn on U.S. policy. If a privileged Bonn-Washington tie came into being, France's hopes of leading Europe by controlling Germany would be doomed. Paris attempted to dampen German support for the MLF by portraying its *force de frappe* as the core of a future European nuclear force over which its partners could exert real influence, in contrast with the pseudo-influence offered by the MLF.[86] The French also kindled British doubts on the MLF, exploiting a weak link in the British-American Atlantic front. They attacked the MLF as a trick by which the United States would foist off some of its defense costs on the Europeans and give them the illusion of participation while keeping all real control in Washington. Paris had little interest in a Franco-British nuclear arrangement, since, after Nassau, it believed the United Kingdom was no longer independent in this area, but in 1963 it nevertheless made hints that such a deal might be possible, purely to weaken British support for the MLF.[87]

Bonn's support for the Atlantic Community persisted in 1962–63, despite internal differences over the mounting Franco-U.S. rivalry. Almost every high public official took sides. Erhard and the "Atlanticist" faction placed top priority on Germany's relations with the United States and on developing an Atlantic Community, while Adenauer and the German "Gaullists" hoped to avoid making a stark choice but generally favored the more independent Europe that de Gaulle sought to create.[88] In 1962–63, many long-time supporters of Franco-German reconciliation concluded that Adenauer had gone too far, with such steps as the bilateral Paris-Bonn treaty, and were transformed into ardent "Atlanticists" to counterbalance the chancellor, while opponents of Britain's previous efforts to subordinate the Common Market to wider arrangements came out against the seemingly similar U.S. proposals.[89] One reason why the Atlanticists pushed so hard for Britain's entry into the Common Market was their awareness that it was a key aspect of Washington's Atlantic agenda.[90] The Atlanticists were bolstered in late 1961 by the arrival of Gerhard Schroeder at the head of the foreign ministry.[91] Although Schroeder supported the French-sponsored political confederation negotiations of 1961–62 and the Franco-German treaty of 1963, he was far more independent of Adenauer than his predecessor, von Brentano, and closer to many of Erhard's positions on European and Atlantic unity.[92]

Germany was in an ideal position to use the Atlantic Community and the Franco-German entente to extract concessions from both Paris and Washington. Adenauer sought the best of both worlds but inclined more and more toward France. He supported the MLF and the GATT round for the concrete benefits they would bring Germany, but rejected British entry into the Common Market, which would move the group in an Atlantic and free trade direction. He was angered by new signs of American hegemony, such as Washington's secretive bilateral contacts with the Soviets. Although he confided his doubts on U.S. commitments and on the whole Atlantic concept to de Gaulle, Adenauer argued that the general "underestimated France's influence and his own personal influence" and should work, as the chancellor did, to channel the Americans rather than challenge them at every opportunity.[93]

The treatment of nuclear issues within the Atlantic alliance was a sensitive subject for Germany. Bonn was critical of the Nassau agreement because it had not been consulted and had been relegated to a third-class position behind France and Britain on nuclear issues. Adenauer feared that Nassau had created a de facto British-American nuclear directorate, while the Auswärtiges Amt disliked the provisions that allowed Britain to withdraw its nuclear forces from NATO control in times of emergency.[94] Nevertheless, the MLF still promised to reinforce Germany's Atlantic links, particularly its ties with the United States, strengthen European and Atlantic integration, provide for greater equality in the alliance, and give Germany real participation in nuclear decisions. Support for the MLF also served to counterbalance the German Gaullists and demonstrate Bonn's fidelity to the Americans. The Auswärtiges Amt was aware of the practical (military) shortcomings of the MLF, but preferred it to the *force de frappe*, which it rejected as a cover for French primacy ("*Vormachtstellung*") in Europe.[95] Better a strong and distant hegemon than a weak and nearby one.

In 1963 Bonn's dominant Atlanticists hoped to move quickly on the MLF and were flexible on most of the technical issues involved in its creation.[96] Because Atlantic cooperation was synonymous with close ties to the United States, German leaders preferred an "Atlantic" (American-led) MLF over either a purely European MLF or a French-led arrangement. A denuclearized country such as Germany was in a weak position compared to both Britain and France and it did not trust the intentions of either. It depended on the United States to establish and maintain a multilateral Atlantic nuclear force that was the only realistic way for

Bonn to attain some degree of parity with Paris and London. It even pressured the British to participate in the MLF by making it a test of their commitment to Europe and implied that German support for British admission to the Common Market would disappear if the United Kingdom abandoned the MLF.[97]

After January 1963, in the face of de Gaulle's attacks on Atlantic cooperation, Erhard, Schroeder, and their supporters renewed their push for the entire Atlantic Community program, including the MLF, the GATT round, bilateral German-American ties, a strengthened NATO, and increased European integration, all to thwart de Gaulle's moment of triumph.[98] With Adenauer's retirement imminent, his critics increasingly controlled German policy. Bonn's Atlanticist direction became clear in the German stance on the GATT tariff reduction negotiations proposed by the United States. The Germans had supported this plan from the outset as a means to protect their wider economic interests and keep the Common Market outward looking. After January 1963, the issue took on a new urgency. The Kennedy Round now seemed crucial to strengthening Atlantic cooperation and the unity of NATO, preventing a trade conflict between Britain and the Common Market, and blocking French domination of Western Europe.[99] The new Schroeder-Erhard tandem confronted France with an ultimatum: Germany would move forward on the internal development of the Common Market, but only in return for French assurances on the GATT round. The Atlanticists argued that "Atlantic partnership [could] lead to a political and economic integration that [would be] almost indissoluble. The Americans continue to support European unity; their ultimate goal is a partnership with a Europe equal to them in every way and able to speak with one voice. The idea of partnership is based on precisely the integration of Europe, for without the partnership a rivalry would inevitably ensue between the united Europe and the United States which would be dangerous for both sides and for the free world."[100] France, which had succeeded in blocking British membership in the Common Market and thwarting America's grandiose plans, now faced a newly determined, economically self-confident, increasingly Atlanticist "partner" in Bonn.[101]

The Franco-American conflict greatly complicated Britain's already troubled relations with Europe. The U.S. Atlantic agenda led Washington to support Britain's entry into the Common Market, but it also contributed to the hardening of de Gaulle's attitude toward the United Kingdom. In 1962 Macmillan was alarmed by American provocation of de Gaulle and sought to avoid too much identification with Washington's Atlantic plans, even though he still supported them. "McNamara's foolish speech about nuclear arms has enraged the French and put us in a difficulty. . . . So far as the Common Market is concerned, the Americans are (with the best intentions) doing our cause great harm. The more they tell the Germans, French, etc., that they (USA) want Britain to be in, the more they incline these countries to keep us out."[102] Between June and December 1962 Macmillan tried to convince de Gaulle of Britain's willingness to help France build a truly equal European pillar in the Atlantic alliance. Trying to find some ground between the French and American extremes, he proclaimed a philosophy of "independence and interdependence" in Atlantic relations. By this he meant that each country should maintain its sovereignty and capacity for independent action even as it acknowledged the need for cooperation with its political and economic partners in most cases.[103] When Macmillan's failure to convince de Gaulle became clear in January 1963, London finally recognized its inability to maintain a balance between the United States and France as the Germans did. British leaders now concluded that their best alternative was to promote whatever Atlantic cooperative arrangements they could alongside the United States. They joined the Americans and Germans in supporting the Kennedy round as a means of moving the Common Market in the right direction, keeping the door open for future British membership, and perhaps even preparing the way for an Atlantic free trade area.[104]

The nuclear issue was far more complicated for Great Britain, because it threatened a rift with both Washington and Bonn. At Nassau, Macmillan had attempted to balance Britain's need for American nuclear cooperation with his determination to maintain independent British control of its nuclear force. However, because this special nuclear relationship contradicted the general European pose he took with de Gaulle, Macmillan tried to separate the issue of British-American nuclear ties from that of the United Kingdom's relations with the continent. He believed that he could convince the Europeans that the Nassau arrangement did not compromise Britain's nuclear independence or create any obstacles to closer relations with the continent. In retrospect, Macmillan's confidence on this issue, particularly his blithe answers to the concerns of the Americans and his own cabinet on the matter, both of which anticipated de Gaulle's reaction, is surprising.[105] Macmillan interpreted his Nassau "victory" as signaling the maintenance of Britain's nuclear independence, precisely the opposite of the conclusion drawn by both de Gaulle and Adenauer. Macmillan was intentionally vague on the wording of the agreement and on the future MLF and MNF. He argued that the MNF portion showed that the United States had accepted European national nuclear forces, the opposite of the American goal and of the U.S. interpretation of the accords, as we have seen. Hoping to defuse European opposition to the privileged British-American relationship, he was confident that the United Kingdom could ease its way out of any MLF commitment in practice by emphasizing its MNF responsibilities. He portrayed the Nassau agreement as reflecting his "independence and interdependence" effort to square the European-Atlantic contradictions in his policy. In short, Macmillan claimed to see nothing in Nassau that damaged either his European pretensions or his stated belief in the "twin pillars" idea for the alliance. However, it is likely that Macmillan was disingenuous in his assertion that there would not be a sharp French reaction to Nassau. After his meetings with de Gaulle a few days earlier had made clear that the French opposed British entry into the Common Market under any circumstances, Macmillan may simply have figured that he no longer had anything to lose by the agreement.[106]

Also behind Macmillan's evasions was the fact that the British cabinet took a dim view of the MLF, considering it militarily worthless and a colossal waste of resources. One cabinet memorandum stated that the proposal could not possibly amount to anything unless France, Germany, and Italy were "too lacking in intelligence to understand the military weakness of the case."[107] However, after January 1963 Britain hesitated to antagonize the United States and Germany or to line up with the French. It sought a way out of the dilemma that would maintain control over its deterrent, but coordinate it with the other nuclear forces in the alliance. This fundamental difference with Paris, which insisted on complete nuclear autonomy, prevented a Franco-British nuclear arrangement, both before and after de Gaulle's Common Market veto. Despite its differences with Washington on nuclear relations, Britain remained unwilling to choose between European and Atlantic defense arrangements or to surrender its privileged nuclear ties with the United States. Yet it refused to line up entirely with Washington either. After France vetoed its Common Market application, London might have sought revenge by fully supporting the MLF. Instead, it decided to promote the MNF and protect its nominal independence even at the risk of alienating the Germans and the Americans.[108]

For Britain, the MLF represented many dangers. Its opponents, led by Defense Minister Peter Thorneycroft, argued that it was not only likely to be expensive and threaten Britain's independent nuclear force, but would also increase Germany's nuclear ambitions and potentially give Bonn some nuclear control in the future. Thorneycroft asserted that the MLF was of no military value, that it would needlessly increase tensions with the Soviets, and that the political problems that motivated it could be better solved by improving political and nuclear consultation in NATO. Yet Britain could not openly sabotage the MLF without sustaining major diplomatic damage. With the United Kingdom already excluded from the Common Market, Foreign Secretary Lord (Alec Douglas) Home argued against Britain's further isolating itself and allowing Germany to become America's primary European ally. Worse, if the MLF failed because of British abstention, France and Germany might form an exclusive nuclear relationship.[109] However, Home found himself isolated in the cabinet and the naysayers prevailed. By the late summer of 1963 the cabinet voted against MLF participation, but also decided against risking the political consequences of outright opposition. Britain would promote alternatives, such as the MNF, increased NATO nuclear consultation, and the Test Ban Treaty with the Soviets. These would not only demonstrate its European and Atlantic convictions and lessen East-West tensions, but further isolate de Gaulle, who opposed all of them.[110]

The deliberations of the British cabinet on the MLF reveal the incompatibility of its ambitions to retain privileged ties with the United States and also to lead Europe. Sounding very Gaullist, British leaders derided U.S. efforts to sell continued American nuclear control to the Germans under a cloak of cooperation and the Germans' willingness to go along.[111] The negative British stance effectively killed the MLF in 1963, even though this was not apparent at the time. British-American differences did not become public until 1964. Without British support the project could not go forward, because Italy had linked its participation to that of the United Kingdom. With all other major Western European countries (France, Britain, Italy) staying out, the MLF was transformed into a German-American arrangement, which the United States knew to be untenable and had sought to avoid all along.[112]

Conclusion

By the end of 1963 the Atlantic Community had largely ground to a halt. Common values and interests had proved strong enough to hold the alliance together and preserve existing institutions and a modicum of cooperation, but were insufficient to overcome divergent national goals and enable the construction of a new Atlantic architecture. While the MLF lingered on life support through 1964 and the GATT round ultimately succeeded in 1967, after years of difficult negotiations, the wider prospect of Atlantic partnership was blocked by the competing agendas of the four major Atlantic powers. An obvious culprit was France, but others had contributed to the failure. The Germans refused to choose between France and the United States, the British to accept the MLF, and the Americans either to maintain the special relationship with the United Kingdom or to accept real equality with Europe. The conflict between France and the United States was clearly paramount in the disappointing outcome of the Atlantic Community. Neither country had been willing to compromise in the creation of new Atlantic arrangements, even though this was indispensable to the success of any initiative from either side. Just as de Gaulle's anti-Americanism had alienated his European partners and doomed his plans for a European confederation, the Europeans, and particularly the Germans, had been cautious over embracing an Atlanticism that excluded France and privileged the "Anglo-Saxons."[113]

Out of inexperience, overconfidence, or a combination of both, Kennedy and his advisers miscalculated on the Atlantic Community. While they sought to strengthen Atlantic unity in part to meet Soviet challenges around the world, their primary motive was the fear that without strong U.S. leadership a uniting Europe might forsake America's interests and wider global responsibilities. The Kennedy administration feared that the United States might be excluded from Europe, but failed to offer the Europeans an equal partnership. The result of this choice was a concept of Atlantic Community that was less than the sum of its diverse and divisive parts. Improved political consultation in NATO, coordination of aid to the developing world, tariff reduction negotiations, and help in improving America's balance of payments were all worthy goals that most Europeans would likely (and ultimately did) support, but they did not change the fundamentally unequal nature of Atlantic relations. Above all, the American attitude toward nuclear issues demonstrated the clear limits of the "twin pillars" idea and doomed the Atlantic Community. By rejecting Western Europe's aspirations for independence, rightly or wrongly focused on the issue of nuclear autonomy, the United States sacrificed both British and French support and gave London and Paris the means to thwart Kennedy's vague but threatening vision.

De Gaulle was undoubtedly the main spoiler of the Atlantic Community, but he paid a heavy price in the failure of his plans for a Western European political group and his subsequent isolation from his partners. He failed because his Atlantic ideas were even less appealing to Europe than those of the United States. Despite the limits of their vision, American leaders genuinely believed that European unity and Atlantic cooperation were complementary and not mutually exclusive. It was de Gaulle's rejection of this basic idea that derailed his own grand design. He failed to realize that his plan to use the weight of Western Europe to force the United States to reshape Atlantic relations was a castle built on sand, since most of his European "allies" worked to undermine him at every turn. By 1963 his key partner, Germany, had grown less compliant and was clearly unwilling to follow his lead toward a Third Force. Although de Gaulle's suspicions of America's overweening ambitions were largely accurate, his excessive maneuvers to counter Washington and London failed to promote French leadership as a viable alternative. De Gaulle was undoubtedly correct to assert that the alliance would be stronger over the long term if it were based on two truly equal pillars, but his determination to lead one of those pillars off on a completely independent course ruined his argument.

Germany, despite its internal differences, emerged stronger from the Atlantic debate of the early 1960s. The Americans had renewed their commitment in the summer of 1963 with Kennedy's visit, and closer ties with the United States had always been the primary German goal for Atlantic cooperation. Bonn, unlike

Paris, accepted the American leadership that inevitably accompanied such U.S. commitments. When Erhard, now chancellor after Adenauer's retirement in October, met the new president, Lyndon B. Johnson, in December 1963, both sides emphasized their full support of the lingering Atlantic Community elements, the Kennedy round and the MLF, and foresaw even closer U.S.-German ties.[114]

For Britain, the Atlantic Community had produced mixed results. It had unmasked America's intention to end the special relationship and increased de Gaulle's hostility to both "Anglo-Saxon" countries, but also offered a renewed U.S. commitment to Europe and stimulated London to devise its own version of the twin pillars idea for the European audience. However, London always remained ambivalent over its role in the Atlantic equation. By the end of 1963 British leaders still claimed to support the Atlantic Community, but in practice it became a mantra to be recited to please the Americans, isolate de Gaulle, and open the door to Europe. If all went well it might be possible to do something more substantial in the distant future.

By late 1963 there were significant changes of leadership in three of the four major Atlantic countries. With Adenauer, Macmillan, and Kennedy gone, there was a marked decrease of interest in reorganizing European and Atlantic relations. Sir Alec Douglas Home in Britain and Ludwig Erhard in Germany were both committed to close cooperation with the United States, but this cooperation rested on traditional, largely bilateral, bases, rather than any sweeping new Atlantic foundation. Lyndon Johnson had little knowledge of, or interest in, Europe. With Germany and Britain on its side and de Gaulle as obstructionist as ever, Washington saw little reason to sustain Kennedy's ambitious, but flawed, initiative. Even de Gaulle, the sole survivor, took stock of his gains and losses and chose to pursue new, unilateral goals with the Soviet bloc and the nonaligned world. French ties with Germany were now uncertain at best, with the new Erhard government advertising its Atlantic convictions and the MLF threatening to lead to privileged German-American ties. At the same time, Britain was using Atlantic rhetoric to attack de Gaulle's policies at every turn. Washington, with Bonn and London bidding for its support, could ignore Paris at will. When de Gaulle withdrew France from the NATO military command (but not the Atlantic alliance) in 1966 and challenged the supremacy of the dollar in the international monetary system during the later years of his presidency, he was only drawing the conclusion of the failure of his European and Atlantic reorganization proposals and France's subsequent isolation. Between 1963 and 1969 de Gaulle and Johnson had very little contact, almost none of it over Europe. France and the United States, having taken the other's measure, awaited initiatives from the other side without realizing, or caring, that neither had any intention of resuming the Atlantic discussion.

CHAPTER FIVE

DE GAULLE AND THE RISE AND FALL

OF THE FOUCHET PLAN, 1958–1963

Politics embraces everything. In the beginning there was God, then nothing, then politics. Economics and defense depend on politics, but the inverse is not true.
—Charles de Gaulle, comments to Italian foreign minister Antonio Segni, 4 April 1962

The Gaullist Design

Between 1958 and 1963, Charles de Gaulle promoted the centerpiece of his European program, a plan to organize the Six into a political union that would make Europe an independent actor on the international stage.[1] This political union would be led by France and become the equal of the two superpowers. Although this effort ultimately failed, the goal of creating a more self-reliant, influential Europe seemed within reach in the early 1960s. Had it succeeded, the plan could have reshaped the entire Western European and Atlantic political landscape.

Because de Gaulle's conception was frequently altered and because he dropped his proposals completely after 1963, there is considerable debate on the significance of his plans. Some observers have argued that de Gaulle always preferred a bilateral relationship with Germany and used his efforts with the Six as a cover.[2] Others, including the present author, view the Fouchet plan, named after the chief French negotiator, as the ultimate expression of de Gaulle's vision and its failure as a major setback for the French leader.[3] The growing historiography centers on the roles of individual European countries, but there is no comprehensive multinational study of the Fouchet plan and little attention to the British and American roles.[4] This chapter will examine the goals, means, and development of de Gaulle's Western European agenda and its impact on his three main Atlantic allies.

There was no separation between de Gaulle's tripartite ideas for the Atlantic alliance and his efforts to organize political relations among the Six. He pursued both goals simultaneously as two sides of the same coin. From 1958 onward he viewed the Six as a vehicle that would enable France to attain equality with the

United States and Britain. The creation of a European "concert" of powers under French leadership would also serve as a counterweight to the USSR, enabling Western Europe to act independently of the United States, negotiate with the Soviets from a position of strength, and ultimately end the Cold War. This strong and independent Western Europe would not only serve as a magnet for the occupied eastern half of the continent, but also gradually modify and improve Soviet behavior, reducing Moscow's fears of NATO and the United States. The creation of this strong and united Europe would "depend less on a miracle based on some particular recipe than on the determination, the perseverance and the good faith that each country brings to the common effort."[5]

De Gaulle believed that cooperation among states had to be based on formal, but not supranational, arrangements. Others, especially American leaders, believed that a strong Western Europe required supranationalism, but de Gaulle was convinced of the opposite. He believed that supranationalism would lead to a weak Europe under American domination. Characterizing supranational institutions as obstacles to real unity and desiring a complete break with past methods of integration, he set out to reorganize the political relations of the Six and block any "independent" or federal force that might dictate policy. De Gaulle favored a confederation of independent states that delegated carefully delineated amounts of sovereignty as the commonality of their interests increased. This was to be a union of states, economies, policies, and governments, not a fusion of peoples, languages, or cultures. For the short term it would have no democratic elements, such as a directly elected assembly, that might give it the appearance of something more ambitious. The ultimate confederation de Gaulle envisioned would overcome Western Europe's centrifugal forces and create opportunities for more ambitious political steps (far) down the road.[6]

Although he disliked the earlier process of European integration, de Gaulle endorsed the grouping of the Six that had been established. His worldview, dominated by the roles of the major powers, excluded the pretensions of the smaller European states to any significant diplomatic role. He thus viewed Benelux and, to a lesser extent, Italy as useful partners and additional diplomatic weight, but as unable to challenge French leadership in Europe. Germany, on the other hand, posed a potential problem, but de Gaulle was convinced that France could both use and dominate the truncated German state and tie it firmly to the West. He described Britain as "a European country, but less so than others," insisted that the British sought to "divide and conquer" the Six, and opposed Britain's entry in order to block a dangerous rival that could rally resistance to his leadership.[7] Although France wavered over linking Britain's entry into the political union with entry into the Common Market, de Gaulle opposed a British presence in either organization and gave only vague indications that the United Kingdom might be able to join Europe someday.

De Gaulle's program of organizing Europe without Britain and against the United States had two fundamental flaws. First, by barring supranationalism, de Gaulle enabled the British to push to enter the political union negotiations and influence the debate among the Six. Second, even as he opposed American hegemony and proclaimed the need for an independent Europe based on cooperation among equal partners, de Gaulle used "American" methods with the smaller powers and provoked Belgian and Dutch opposition.

The French foreign policy apparatus generally accepted de Gaulle's ideas but was prepared to add more pragmatism and flexibility. Foreign Minister Couve de Murville and (from April 1962) Prime Minister Georges Pompidou softened de Gaulle's demands and offered concessions and assurances to France's partners on minor issues in order to obtain the essentials of his goals. Michel Debré, prime minister from January 1959 to April 1962 and even more disdainful of the smaller members of the Six than de Gaulle, argued that France should work for greater cooperation with Germany and Britain instead.[8] For the most part, de Gaulle's subordinates shrank from criticizing his design and negotiated compromises with the Five that seemed to meet his objectives. This lack of open discussion among the French leadership ultimately caused serious problems when the Quai d'Orsay negotiated terms that de Gaulle refused to accept.

De Gaulle's confederation program received a mixed reaction in the country. Public opinion supported his Third Force ideas, growing out of postwar neutralist tendencies as well as ambitions for a renewed world role and for a Europe independent of the United States. However, the centrist political parties that had predominated under the Fourth Republic, the SFIO (Socialists), MRP (Christian Democrats), and Independents, fought his efforts to replace the European communities and cast Europe adrift from the United States. Indeed, after an inflammatory de Gaulle press conference in May 1962, the domestic "European" and "Atlantic" opposition had enough votes to bring down the Pompidou government but refrained from doing so because of its own divisions and fears of instability. The tense situation prevailed until the elections of November 1962, when de Gaulle's party won a comfortable majority.[9]

Traditional historical accounts tend to oversimplify foreign reactions to the Fouchet plan. The Germans have been portrayed as unwilling French partners, led by Adenauer against the rest of the government. Britain and the United States are generally cast as the inveterate opponents who provoked the resistance of Belgium and the Netherlands that ultimately doomed de Gaulle's plan. Even recent works, based on archival documents of the major participants, focus on one country and treat the policies of the others in stereotyped terms.[10]

In fact, all three of France's Atlantic allies were initially well disposed toward de Gaulle's ideas in principle, in return for minimal reassurances on his intentions.

The Germans shared de Gaulle's belief in the need for greater political ties among the Six to protect the economic cooperation that had been achieved. However, Bonn did not support new political arrangements to replace existing ones. It envisaged the creation of new political links alongside the supranational economic institutions and the formation of close ties between the two, not the reduction of the European communities to mere technical organizations. This attitude reflected Bonn's wider caution toward de Gaulle. The Germans accepted the Gaullist fundamentals of establishing a European political organization that would play a greater role in the Atlantic alliance and in the world: "These very positive elements of French policy can and should be used to improve cooperation among the EEC countries and facilitate greater integration in the future."[11] French hints of a Third Force agenda and of de Gaulle's intention to dominate the Six worried Bonn less than Benelux and the Italians. It did not intend to follow France blindly or to allow de Gaulle to alter basic German policies, such as its close ties with the United States.

The role of the United States in the debate over political cooperation between 1958 and 1963 has been misunderstood and indeed largely ignored. Because of the contest over European and Atlantic relations between the United States and France in the early 1960s, most observers have assumed that the Americans opposed the Fouchet plan. The fact that Atlantic issues played such a decisive role in the plan's ultimate failure has reinforced this assumption. Many contemporaries asserted that American leaders not only hoped for failure, but also worked covertly to bring it about. In fact, although American leaders were concerned about the implications of political coordination among the Six, they never publicly opposed it nor encouraged opposition behind the scenes. To be sure, both the Eisenhower and Kennedy administrations were disturbed by the vagueness of de Gaulle's plans and warned against an independent bloc within NATO or the destruction of existing European community institutions. As Eisenhower put it to Adenauer, "If [de Gaulle's] proposals clearly will contribute to achieving the goals of integration, then I believe they are deserving of the support of other members of the Six. If, on the other hand, they would be likely to weaken the integration concept, a serious question would arise. Similarly dangerous, would be any Six-Nation bloc within NATO."[12] America thus questioned two key Gaullist goals, but its doubts were similar to those of all five of France's partners. Throughout, the United States made its general views known but stayed out of the European debates on details. Even during the fiercest moments of Franco-U.S. conflict in 1962–63, Washington did not oppose the political consolidation of Western Europe per se, but rather the domination of the Five by de Gaulle.

Because the political union was an issue on which American public opinion was ignorant and Congress uninterested, both the Eisenhower and Kennedy administrations had a relatively free hand.

As Britain's wider relations with Europe changed between 1958 and 1963, its attitude toward de Gaulle's political schemes evolved considerably. Although political union was never as important for the British as for the French and Germans, the British could not remain as aloof as the Americans. Prior to Britain's application to the Common Market (August 1961), the specter of greater political ties among the Six loomed as an additional threat to the unity of Western Europe. As the British began to inch toward participation in Europe, their view of political relations among the Six changed. Proponents of British entry into the Common Market argued that the progress of the political union meant that the United Kingdom must move rapidly in order to shape the political organization of the Six and avoid falling further behind. But London was notably unenthusiastic about political union, urging simply that it must be involved to prevent any damage to its interests. At different times, this same mentality led the British to promote the WEU as a superior forum for European political cooperation and to urge the transformation of the political union into a loose, flexible vehicle for British influence in Western Europe and beyond.

The Beginning of Political Cooperation, June 1958–December 1960

France's desire for greater political cooperation among the Six preceded de Gaulle's return to power. The Suez crisis convinced Paris of the value of unified Western European positions on major international issues. But except for vague proposals for more regular foreign minister meetings, Paris produced no concrete plan, preferring informal and flexible forms of political cooperation.[13] De Gaulle built on these ideas, but made French policy more ambitious. Within his first months in office, he and the Quai d'Orsay informed their partners that "while avoiding integration of the EDC variety, France intended to promote European cooperation and organize a sort of European Concert."[14] This arrangement would be based on organized political cooperation in the form of regular meetings of the foreign ministers of the Six. De Gaulle knew the Five were thinking along similar lines and hoped to seize the initiative. Even as he launched his tripartite proposal to London and Washington, he hoped to mobilize Europe's resources to force the British and Americans to end their de facto directorate over the Atlantic alliance.

In their initial conversations with other European leaders, de Gaulle and

Couve de Murville were careful to disguise the scope of their plans. In private, however, they already envisioned the Fouchet plan of 1961–62, including regular meetings of both foreign ministers and government leaders and "organic" coordinating bodies for foreign policy, culture, defense, and economics that would "make Europe a reality."[15] France had to move cautiously in order to avoid provoking the Five's fears on the future of NATO and the existing European communities. Indeed, in late 1958 and early 1959, France allowed the Five to take the lead in championing political cooperation, to dissipate their fears that de Gaulle would chart a unilateral course.[16] This enabled the French leader to portray steps toward his own goals as "concessions" to the Five.

In public, de Gaulle initially focused on cooperation among France, Germany, and Italy, but when his partners insisted on the participation of all the Six, he proposed regular meetings of the whole group of foreign ministers as a first step.[17] These meetings, normal and unthreatening to outsiders, would instill habits of cooperation among the Six that could be institutionalized later. Because he felt that the Six "must practice an organized cooperation and do away with the supranational fiction," de Gaulle rejected any formal link between the foreign ministers' meetings and the existing European institutions.[18] He insisted that the six representatives have the liberty to discuss any topic, even those normally reserved for NATO. On the other hand, he gave assurances that the foreign ministers' meetings would serve the interests of the European communities, rotate between capitals, and establish no institutional dimension. The French thus disguised their plan to create a formal secretariat in Paris and to replace Brussels as the European capital, just as they hid their purpose of excluding Britain from the discussions.[19]

The Five accepted these assurances, and a series of quarterly foreign ministers' meetings took place in 1960, but the results were disappointing. The six diplomatic representatives discussed a variety of important issues without making major decisions. Disagreements were rampant and the prospect of common positions, much less anything more ambitious, seemed as distant as ever. These disagreements, which prefigured the failure of the Fouchet plan, centered on British participation, the further development of supranational institutions, and links to NATO. Above all, the Five were opposed to institutionalizing the political contacts among the Six in any way.[20]

Despite this initial setback, de Gaulle proceeded more boldly with his scheme. Indeed, his ambitions grew in proportion to his struggles with the United States and Britain over the Atlantic alliance. By 1960, he felt he had a close ally in Adenauer, who continued to express his solidarity with the French leader. With the collapse of the East-West summit in May 1960 and the decline of U.S. leadership during the last months of the Eisenhower administration, de Gaulle was more determined than ever to step forward as the architect of a new Europe.[21]

At his meeting with Adenauer at the Chateau de Rambouillet at the end of July 1960, de Gaulle raised his plans to the next level. After stoking the chancellor's fears of abandonment by the British and Americans, he presented sweeping new proposals that would provide Germany with strong reassurances via intergovernmental cooperation in political, economic, cultural, and military affairs. De Gaulle's aim was both to create new organisms and usurp existing ones. Through regular meetings and summits among the Six, organic cooperation would develop. These meetings would be prepared by a political secretariat and by four commissions located in Paris and composed of high-level government functionaries from the Six. The commissions would function like that of the Common Market, but would not have an independent status. The present supranational European institutions, subordinated to Paris's new arrangements, would be reduced to technical bodies. De Gaulle insisted that "unless the 'communities' were put in their place, no [real] Europe would be possible." Once their political consolidation was complete, the Six would insist on the reorganization of the Atlantic alliance and the end of the integrated NATO military command. The European parliament, restricted in its functions, would be retained as a debating society. A referendum would be held in all six countries to provide a democratic veneer to all the changes.[22]

After presenting it to Adenauer, de Gaulle made this program public at a 5 September press conference, but he still left out its most radical elements. First, France hoped to have the entire European arrangement in place by the end of the year, before the new American president took office in January 1961, enabling the Six to press the new administration for immediate NATO reform. The wider audience was important, as the plan was intended to send signals to "a menacing Soviet Union and a United States that had failed to adapt to changing circumstances."[23] Second, within days of the Rambouillet meetings, the Quai d'Orsay had already begun drafting changes in the existing European treaties that would formally subordinate them to the new arrangements. These included the elimination of Euratom and the ECSC and the diminution of the Common Market to a series of economic arrangements under the direct control of the Six governments.[24] The French did not divulge their full plans in order to prevent resistance from the Five and to avoid giving the British an opening to demand a place in the new arrangements. British participation remained the greatest threat to the Gaullist design. While the French argument that Britain must participate fully or not at all in Europe carried considerable weight, there was always the danger that the British might call their bluff and apply to join both the

Common Market and the political union. To guard against this remote possibility, the French emphasized the preliminary nature of their political union proposals and hinted at more sweeping arrangements down the road, statements designed both to weaken the resistance of continental supporters of supranationalism and discourage British participation.[25] As the foreign ministry's planning papers make clear, the entire French plan was developed with an eye to developing a new model of European "confederation" while avoiding a supranational "federation." The ministry was convinced that "the Six states have surrendered as much [sovereignty] as they can to community institutions without ceasing to be states."[26] Finally, as both a fallback position and a building block for the wider plan, de Gaulle was prepared to go it alone with Germany.[27]

From its founding, Adenauer's Germany had been highly receptive to European political union.[28] Like their French counterparts during the Fourth Republic, the Germans had favored flexible arrangements and held vague ideas about how to proceed with political cooperation. They had fluctuated between using the Common Market and the WEU as the foundation for Europe's political union and the foreign ministry had suggested that "the goal of this [union] would be to energize the various unity efforts and develop a common policy on all political and economic questions affecting Europe."[29] After de Gaulle's return to power, the Germans hesitated to commit to the sweeping changes he proposed. Adenauer preferred regular meetings and exchanges of views to institutionalized reforms. An avowed partisan of the Franco-German bond, he believed he could use informal contacts to divert the French president from his dangerous tripartite schemes and ensure Franco-German collaboration on all major issues.[30] Adenauer's subordinates hoped that Germany could induce greater French acceptance of supranationalism and contain de Gaulle's efforts to dominate Western Europe.[31] Everyone in Bonn sought to retain Germany's ties with the United States and avoid outright confrontation with Britain as they cemented the solidarity of the Six.[32]

There were nevertheless important differences in Bonn over political unification. Adenauer, to whom Franco-German unity was paramount, supported the idea and was willing to move forward even without the "Four" (Italy and Benelux). The chancellor's growing anti-British tendencies plus his periodic differences with the United States further increased his support for de Gaulle. His foreign ministers, von Brentano (1955–61) and Schroeder (1961–63), were more cautious toward the political union idea. Schroeder, in particular, was determined to maintain good relations with the United States and Britain. Erhard, who, as usual, insisted on becoming involved, worked to limit the progress of political union until Britain's entry into Europe was assured. Indeed, most of the German government favored British involvement as additional insurance against any dangerous Gaullist plans for the political union.

Public and parliament played an important role in constraining Adenauer's enthusiasm. The German public and Bundestag never really understood or supported de Gaulle's efforts to redirect European unity and resisted any step that threatened Bonn's focus on NATO, the European communities, and the United States. Public opinion constituted an important asset for Erhard, Schroeder, and others in Bonn who wished to move cautiously on political union and resisted Adenauer's tendency to fall into de Gaulle's orbit. The combined pressure of all these forces frequently forced Adenauer to follow a more restrained policy than he would have preferred.[33]

By early 1960, after the outbreak of the Berlin crisis and the failed summit, Adenauer's inclination to support de Gaulle grew. American and British pressures for compromise on Berlin increased his doubts on both countries, as well as his enthusiasm for greater cooperation among the Six. The German foreign policy establishment welcomed the idea of regular foreign ministers' meetings to provide Western Europe greater weight vis-à-vis the USSR, the United States, and Britain. Bonn never intended to create a bloc in NATO or to break with Britain, but it feared that the United Kingdom would prevent anything substantive from happening if it joined the political union while remaining aloof from the Common Market.[34] Unlike the leaders of the smaller European states, the Germans felt confident in their ability to block a French bid for hegemony. The foreign ministry argued that "no country can achieve a dominant position against the will of the others," but felt Bonn must be vigilant over de Gaulle's more radical proposals and warn against any attack on NATO or the European communities.[35]

When de Gaulle presented his new proposals to Adenauer at Rambouillet, the German chancellor gave a positive response. After hearing de Gaulle's tirades against Britain, the United States, and NATO, he endorsed the French leader's plan. To be sure, the official French accounts indicate a more total acceptance than the German ones, which reveal a certain amount of skepticism and confusion. Ambassador Blankenhorn in Paris felt that de Gaulle was too "vague and unclear" on the relationship between his new confederation and "the Common Market and the Commission in Brussels on the one hand and NATO on the other."[36] Despite this divergence, and the subsequent Franco-German misunderstanding it produced, it is clear that Adenauer gave as positive a response as he could to de Gaulle's ideas. He was still confident not only of France's goodwill but also of his ability to modify the Gaullist vision and achieve progress toward a European confederation without damaging Germany's relations with the United States or Britain.[37]

After Rambouillet, the Auswärtiges Amt realized how far Adenauer had gone and immediately applied the brakes. On learning the specifics of the French proposals, much of the German leadership, media, and public awoke to the threat that de Gaulle sought to divide and destroy NATO, eliminate the European communities, move the capital from Brussels to Paris, and push the Americans and British out of Europe. Ambassador Blankenhorn noted that "it was immediately clear to me that we must fight these ideas with all our strength."[38] Even those less alarmed insisted on examining de Gaulle's sweeping proposals one by one. Almost immediately, the Auswärtiges Amt announced its opposition to the revision of the European treaties and the creation of any political secretariat in Paris. It preferred strengthening the European parliament to a referendum and believed that the Six must settle outstanding problems with Britain before they could move forward on any political arrangement.[39]

Adenauer now faced a variety of pressures to take a step back. The chancellor was forced to retreat, not only because of domestic opposition but also because of the heavy-handedness of de Gaulle, who after Rambouillet renewed his public attacks on NATO and the U.S. role in Europe. Washington urged Adenauer to protect the alliance and the European communities.[40] Germany thus initiated a series of technical meetings with Britain on the Six-Seven problem and declined to promote the French proposals with other European governments.[41] A more assertive Erhard insisted on taking part in any political negotiations to prevent a further division of Western Europe and control the direction of the Six.[42]

France, quickly disabused of the euphoria of the Rambouillet meeting, also had to backtrack. De Gaulle met the leaders of the other four Common Market members in August and September to discuss his proposals and address their concerns. In October he sent Couve de Murville and Debré to meet Adenauer again. In order to gain his partners' acceptance of even a single summit meeting of the Six, de Gaulle was forced to concede that there would be no treaty revision and that he did not "intend to demolish NATO" or burn bridges with Britain.[43] French negotiators, although frustrated with the Germans, opted for patience and flexibility. De Gaulle decided to focus on reaching a quick, pragmatic agreement and institutionalizing it later.[44] He had linked the Common Market with the political union to keep Britain out, but to placate his partners he held out the possibility of "associating" the United Kingdom with the union. De Gaulle eventually grew tired of justifying himself on Britain's exclusion. At one point, clearly exasperated, he informed the leaders of Luxembourg that it was the British who refused to be a real part of Europe and that "the English are the English. That's not our fault."[45] De Gaulle nominally dropped economics from the purview of the political union with the intention of restoring it later. Indeed, upon reflection, the Quai d'Orsay was cautious about the risks of treaty revision, which might cost France some of the economic benefits it had gained from the Treaty of Rome and allow Britain to intervene in European affairs again. By eliminating supranationalism, it would be impossible to keep Britain out and maintain U.S. approval and active support at the same time.[46] With de Gaulle's concessions in hand, the Five agreed to a summit at the end of the year.

The dilemma de Gaulle faced in late 1960 was that he sought to overthrow the entire existing Western European and Atlantic order, yet dared not state this openly for tactical reasons. In order to reassure his European partners, he was constantly forced to pay lip service to the very European and Atlantic organizations he was most eager to demolish. Yet without these reassurances, he would lose the Five's support and fail in his design. Given the extent of his partners' opposition, France had the tough task of selling an unwanted product to indispensable clients.

Despite the importance of the United States in the debates of the Six, American officials gave scant attention to European political union until the closing days of the Eisenhower administration. Before the Rambouillet meeting, the State Department generally favored increased cooperation among the Six, but had been unsure of the direction it might and ought to take. U.S. observers were wary of any changes that might create a bloc within the Atlantic alliance, and the United States opposed any weakening of the existing communities.[47] But Eisenhower had nevertheless indicated his support for regular foreign minister meetings ("We are on your side in this") as a means of furthering European integration and Germany's linkage with the West.[48]

Washington also paid little heed to the critics of de Gaulle's proposals, mainly the British and the Dutch. The American mission to NATO in Paris relayed Dutch concerns over de Gaulle's threat to the Atlantic defense organization, the existing communities, and the U.S. presence in Europe, but U.S. officials did nothing to encourage their opposition. Indeed, the Americans tried to blunt Dutch critiques and exhorted them to take a more positive stance. This approach did not reflect a blind faith in de Gaulle, but rather Washington's confidence that the Five would not permit anything that it could not accept.[49]

The first reports that reached Washington after the Rambouillet meeting raised no concerns. These reports suggested that "not much was said about European political coordination in Paris. Adenauer seems to be going slowly on it."[50] As more accurate and detailed information filtered out, the Eisenhower administration finally recognized that de Gaulle planned a major and potentially dangerous initiative.[51] However, Washington decided not to intervene directly, counting on Adenauer's hesitations and the anticipated resistance of the Five to channel de Gaulle's ideas in less dangerous directions. The United States encouraged this redirection by championing existing European and Atlantic institutions. Eisenhower reminded the chancellor of the importance of NATO, noting that "the U.S. has assigned its own forces to NATO on the assumption that they would participate in an integrated defense system. There would be little justification for their continued presence if there were no integrated system."[52] The United States would have to radically reevaluate its entire European policy if the Five followed de Gaulle down the path of destroying NATO. It had been the United States, Eisenhower reminded Adenauer, that had blocked de Gaulle's tripartite schemes in the alliance. U.S. officials also informed Paris of their opposition to French "leadership" of Western Europe and asserted America's right of involvement in European political affairs. The Quai d'Orsay denied any hegemonic pretensions, any plan to form a bloc in NATO, any linkage between the political union and French tripartite proposals, and any intention of attacking the European communities.[53]

These American interventions focused entirely on France's intentions and did not address the institutional details of the French proposals. On these, Washington left it to the Five to deal with de Gaulle as they saw fit. American policy makers remained flexible on issues of European integration and realized that de Gaulle's ideas offered new momentum. If Europe were to shift temporarily from supranationalism to interstate cooperation, such a detour was acceptable to Washington if it did not prejudice the final outcome, or harm the existing institutions.[54]

The British also received warnings from the Dutch in 1958–59, but they too initially made no response, even though the issue received more high level attention in London than in Washington. De Gaulle's ideas for political organization seemed vague and less significant than his apparent plan to exclude Britain from Europe.[55] By early 1960, the British were better informed and more concerned. The Macmillan government saw the exclusive meetings of the Six as a threat to the WEU, to British influence in Europe, and to the unity of the West. However, it hesitated to simply ask to participate, not only for fear of rejection by the Six, but also because such a request would provoke "the gravest suspicions among [Britain's] EFTA partners."[56] Hoping to influence the deliberations, the British government insisted that any regular foreign minister meetings be under WEU auspices. Britain also tried, unsuccessfully, to limit the discussions of the Six to economic issues. It relied less on the Germans, who seemed inclined to follow de Gaulle's lead, than on the Dutch, who needed little encouragement to oppose the French design.[57]

After Rambouillet, London foresaw a new round of battles with Paris over its exclusion from Europe. There was mounting suspicion of de Gaulle's motives and aims, and the Foreign Office knew that any result of the meeting was "unlikely to be very helpful from [the British] point of view." The British disliked de Gaulle's effort to link the political union to the Common Market, which they rightly viewed as an excuse to justify their exclusion.[58] They believed that the more progress he achieved with his European schemes, the more determined he would be to keep them out. Disappointed with America's mild responses, they also understood they were largely on their own.[59]

Once British officials concluded that they could not control the political activities of the Six from the outside, their main goal was to join any new arrangements. In 1960, some Foreign Office officials still vainly hoped to replace the French political union idea with a WEU alternative.[60] But as long as the Macmillan government, weakened by its wavering over whether to apply for admission to the Common Market, was outside Europe, it could only attack the political union as another weapon of exclusion and rely on the five to check France on its behalf. French linkage of the Common Market and political union forced Britain to consider applying for membership in both as a means of turning the tables.[61] In late 1960, the British were heartened by France's setbacks, by Germany's opposition, and by de Gaulle's isolation. They sent out feelers to the Five, asking for an invitation to join the political discussions and supporting any arrangements whereby the "political primacy of NATO was preserved."[62]

By the end of 1960, de Gaulle's blueprint had been considerably modified. Germany and most of France's other partners supported his cooperation idea, but with a more limited scope than he envisaged. France still had Washington's support, albeit as a new administration was about to be formed. Of the major powers, Britain stood alone in opposition, though it was a careful resistance. De Gaulle had persuaded the Five to give his ideas a hearing, but the results would depend on his flexibility and political acumen.

The Fouchet Plan, January 1961–April 1962

The first summit of the Six took place in February 1961 in Paris.[63] It was preceded by a meeting between de Gaulle and Adenauer at which the two leaders staked out a joint position to present to their four counterparts. De Gaulle took advantage of Adenauer's doubts on the new Kennedy administration, as well as an improved atmosphere in Franco-German relations, to win the chancellor over to his basic ideas once again. Even though de Gaulle described his plan as "based above all else on the entente between France and Germany," the two leaders planned the details of their presentation to their partners to avoid accusations of a Franco-German diktat.[64]

This joint proposal was similar to the Rambouillet scheme, but with the most disturbing aspects removed. The French sought an agreement in principle and to work out the details later.[65] Careful to allay his partners' fears, de Gaulle presented his views in a much more benign light than earlier. He dropped defense from the meeting's agenda, pledged France's commitment to the Atlantic alliance, and conceded that the existing communities would remain the forum for the economic cooperation of the Six. This left only the new areas of foreign policy and cultural cooperation to be discussed. De Gaulle also spoke of an expanded role for the European parliamentary assembly, which would be able to discuss all affairs under the purview of the new political union. Emphasizing Western Europe's potential to play a greater role in the world, he presented himself as a flexible and reasonable advocate of political coordination to achieve this goal. Without referring specifically to a treaty, de Gaulle focused on the holding of regular intergovernmental meetings.

Both de Gaulle and Adenauer justified Britain's exclusion until it joined the Common Market, but the French president hinted at this latter possibility to the Five in light of Britain's interest in the political union. De Gaulle also recommended that the Six not limit their cooperation. Although their initial focus would be foreign policy and cultural affairs, no subject would be formally forbidden. Indeed, he still intended to make cooperation on defense issues the heart of his political union once the Five had approved the union in principle. He was determined to expand the range of the previous foreign ministers' meetings of 1959–60 to active coordination of policies. Despite de Gaulle's flexibility and his concessions, the Dutch still refused to accept any formal arrangements. The Dutch were unmoved by de Gaulle's exhortation that, "assuming they wished to remain a part of Europe," they should accept regular political meetings of the Six. Ultimately they would "see that this [was] the correct path." As a result of the Dutch obstruction, a decision by the Six had to be postponed.[66]

Nevertheless, the French had achieved a modest success. They had made de Gaulle's political ideas the basis of future discussion among the Six and persuaded their partners to set up a study commission (known as the Fouchet commission) to present concrete proposals to the government leaders. But de Gaulle was pessimistic about the Dutch resistance, which cast a shadow over his whole program. He refused any further meetings of the leaders of the Six until the Five, especially the Dutch, had become more supportive.[67] In the meantime, he fell back on the alternative of an arrangement with Germany alone, since "close Franco-German cooperation mattered above all else."[68] Throughout the work of the Fouchet commission, this idea was always in the back of his mind.

By mid-1961 a compromise seemed possible. De Gaulle, in an effort to appear conciliatory but also to isolate the Dutch, agreed to drop defense issues from the official list of areas to be covered by the Fouchet plan.[69] In return his partners agreed to postpone the thorny issues of British participation and the links between the new political union and the existing communities. This compromise was reached at a summit of the government heads of the Six. Meeting in Bonn in July, they issued a declaration approving the idea of regular political consultation. A triumphant de Gaulle urged the Six to build a political union with the same vigor that they had created the Common Market.

Although the Bonn meeting allowed the work of the Fouchet commission to move forward, it smoothed over the fundamental differences between France and its partners rather than settling them. De Gaulle still insisted that the Six must be able to discuss any topic at their meetings. Although defense had been dropped as one of the official areas of cooperation, de Gaulle's partners acceded to his demand that it be discussed in Bonn: "If we wish to build 'Europe,' we must establish our own policies and in order to do that we must build our defense. When one has no defense, one has the policy of others."[70] Even though the Bonn Declaration mentioned British participation, the French still feared Britain's influence over the Five. The Dutch and the other four announced their hope for an eventual British presence in the political talks, even before the United Kingdom sought entry into the Common Market. With Britain exerting this much influence from the outside, Paris was certain it would dominate the group after it joined. The British application to the Common Market in August 1961 only reinforced the French determination to move quickly on the political union to prevent the United Kingdom from intervening.[71]

For Paris, the creation of the political union would now also serve to reinforce the solidarity of the Six at a time when the expansion of the Common Market might dilute it. The French feared that the Five might be distracted by the British application or call the Bonn compromise into question now that outside circumstances had changed. They maintained the linkage between the Common Market and political union in order to make British efforts to join both as complicated as possible. In the hope of presenting the British with a fait accompli in the political area, they asserted that the United Kingdom could not participate in the political union negotiations until it had actually joined the Common Market. Paris refused to consult all the potential Common Market members on the political union, treat Britain as a de facto addition to the Six, or permit anyone to take its entry for granted. The French argued that since their anti-supranational views were identical to those of the British, they could represent the concerns of both countries and provide London with periodic reports on the negotiations. Privately, the Quai d'Orsay feared that U.K. membership in the Common Market and the political union would dilute the former and render the latter meaningless. "It [London] would seek to substitute simple cooperation for economic integration and replace political cooperation with simple consultation."[72] Not only would it thwart de Gaulle's Third Force agenda, it would also serve as a rallying point for opposition to France among the Five.

There was one major dissenter from this anti-British policy. Prime Minister Michel Debré warned that for "as long as it is condemned to remain on the outside, Great Britain will not cease trying to force its way in and will cause trouble" at every opportunity. He also argued that collaboration among France, Britain, and Germany was indispensable to giving Europe any significant global influence. Rather than focus on the conflicting Six, he urged that France create a European "Big Three": "France, Great Britain, and Germany *are* Western Europe. All the other nations orbit these three." He also deprecated de Gaulle's fallback arrangement with Germany, which he claimed would encourage the rest of Western Europe to rally around Britain to resist it. Debré doubted that France could coerce its smaller partners down paths they opposed. Although sharing de Gaulle's hostility to supranationalism and to American predominance, he recognized the fatal flaws in de Gaulle's plans. Acknowledging that cooperation with Britain would be difficult to achieve, he nevertheless deemed it indispensable to strengthening Europe. This was the essential point on which he and de Gaulle disagreed, and on which the Fouchet plan would ultimately fail. The most de Gaulle would concede was that Britain could join someday when all three major European countries "resolved to organize themselves without the United States."[73]

By late 1961, the Fouchet commission and the foreign ministers of the Six came close to an accord on political union. A confident de Gaulle gave the Quai d'Orsay free rein in the negotiations, and French diplomats responded to the critiques of their partners.[74] In January 1962 the foreign ministry produced a draft agreement calling for institutionalized cooperation among the Six not only in foreign policy and culture, but also in defense. Having won their partners over to both the inclusion of defense and signing an actual treaty on political union, the French negotiators had agreed to include a reference to the predominant defense roles of NATO and the Atlantic alliance, the establishment of an independent secretary general, and a few minor supranational elements in the union of "peoples" to be built. In December the Six had also agreed on a direct linkage between participation in the Common Market and the political union. The Five viewed this agreement as a guarantee that Paris would permit the United Kingdom to join the political union as soon as it was admitted to the Common Market. By contrast, the French still hoped that such a linkage would make the British task more difficult and keep them out of both organizations.[75]

Just as France seemed on the verge of success, de Gaulle intervened. He produced his own draft treaty, which voided most of France's concessions to the Five on preserving the European communities, permitting small supranational steps forward, accepting Britain in the group, and maintaining the Atlantic alliance unchanged.[76] To the Five, it seemed that de Gaulle had thrown down the gauntlet to all their European and Atlantic policies. As if this were not provocative enough, de Gaulle also made his renewed challenge to the Five public in a television address on 5 February: "No doubt because we [France] are now displaying a determination, building up a force and unfolding a policy that are our own, this new course does not fail to run counter to the network of former conventions that assigned us the role of a so-called integrated nation, in other words, a backseat nation."[77]

It is not clear why de Gaulle chose this moment to sabotage his entire European program. Undoubtedly there was a lack of communication between him and the Quai d'Orsay. French diplomats had made concessions that de Gaulle would never tolerate. At the same time, de Gaulle now made demands on the Five that the Quai d'Orsay knew they would never accept. Some participants, both French and otherwise, have suggested that de Gaulle never really believed in the political union of the Six and provoked a failure in order to keep his hands free to move forward with Germany alone.[78] Georges-Henri Soutou presents a more convincing explanation, arguing that de Gaulle sought to overturn all the existing European and Atlantic communities and to use the Germans to accomplish this. Having recently coerced Bonn and his other partners into installing his own conceptions on the Common Agricultural Policy (CAP) in the Common Market, de Gaulle wrongly assumed that these pressure tactics would work in the political arena as well: "De Gaulle undoubtedly believed that in the wake of the adoption of the CAP thanks to the decisive support of [Germany] on 14 January, and thanks to his strong entente with Adenauer, the [Fouchet] text would be accepted, despite its revisions, by France's partners."[79]

With the Algerian conflict nearing its end, de Gaulle also felt he had a freer hand in Europe. He wanted to compel his partners not only to codify the subordination of the existing European communities to his plan, but to formally sign on to all his foreign policy objectives, and he believed that this was possible. De Gaulle did not want to become trapped by a watered-down version of his original scheme and was willing to gamble everything on an all-or-nothing approach. The fact that Franco-American relations were at a standstill by late 1961 contributed to his rash decision to force events in Europe. Indeed, French leaders used this fact to deflect blame for subsequent events and pin the failure of the Fouchet plan on the United States and Britain.[80]

The foreign ministry, shocked by de Gaulle's revisions, was forced to promote them with the Five. Not unexpectedly, they provoked a storm of protest and indignation. Ambassador Fouchet reported to the Quai d'Orsay that the draft had been "immediately and violently criticized by all our partners." They would not even use the document as a basis for discussion, and the Italian delegate had bluntly proposed that the Five write up their own document, "purely for the purpose of isolating you [the French]."[81] At this point, Fouchet had suspended the talks to prevent a formal rejection. De Gaulle, surprised by the vehemence of the attacks, backtracked on several, but not all, demands. During separate meetings with Adenauer and the Italians between February and April, he agreed to add a reference to the Atlantic alliance to the treaty, but only in the preamble, and to include a statement that the new political arrangements were not to damage the European communities. De Gaulle also conceded that any adherent to the Common Market would automatically join the political union.[82] However, he would not back down on the inclusion of economic and defense issues in the political union, nor consult the British or accept any specific mention of future revisions in a supranational direction.[83] At the same time, de Gaulle attempted to coerce the Five to accept his concessions, insisting that the Six must demonstrate the political will to reach an agreement and warning that failure on the political union would harm all existing European arrangements.[84]

Although successful with Germany, Italy, and Luxembourg, de Gaulle failed to move the Dutch and Belgians, who had lost all confidence in him. Some of his subordinates and perhaps de Gaulle himself mistakenly believed that the accord with Germany would be enough to force the others into line: "If the [German] government demonstrated a will equal to our own, if no one questioned it, we would easily achieve our goal. We should not be overly concerned with the mood swings of the Italians, the Dutch and the Belgians whenever France and Germany hold a summit. What our friends fear the most in such circumstances is an accord that would prevent the triumph of their own views."[85] At meetings of the foreign ministers of the Six in March and April 1962, Foreign Ministers Paul-Henri Spaak for Belgium and Joseph Luns for the Netherlands refused to move forward without British participation in the negotiations. De Gaulle had frightened the Dutch and Belgians by opposing everything they viewed as important: British entry into Europe and the maintenance of the Atlantic alliance and the European communities. Frightened by the specter of Franco-German hegemony, Spaak and Luns were prepared to terminate the whole political union idea for the foreseeable future and thus made demands they were certain de Gaulle would refuse, including immediate British participation and the insertion of significant doses of supranationalism.[86] In the wake of the ensuing deadlock at the meeting of 17 April, de Gaulle decided to end the negotiations.[87]

While it is clear in retrospect that it was ultimately Belgian and Dutch distrust of de Gaulle that led them to veto the Fouchet plan, at the time the French government blamed Britain and the United States for their actions. It is no coincidence that after the April debacle, France's positions hardened against both British entry into the Common Market and the Atlantic Community. Even without proof of specific British or American encouragement, the Belgian and Dutch insistence on maintaining Europe's ties with the "Anglo-Saxons" convinced de Gaulle that the latter were his natural enemies, whether they had intervened directly or not.[88]

Throughout 1961 and the first months of 1962, the Germans had worked loyally with the French on the Fouchet plan to present a common front, make progress, and diminish its most dangerous elements. Germany had its own goals in the reform process, which included the election of a European parliament by universal suffrage and the fusion of the executives of the three European communities to strengthen their supranationalism and efficiency.[89] The Franco-German entente continued to grow stronger during this period of mounting East-West tension, which included the construction of the Berlin Wall in August 1961 and a crisis in German-American relations (over recognition of East Germany) in the spring of 1962.[90] In such a tense international environment, Adenauer, who never trusted the Kennedy administration as he had Eisenhower and Dulles, moved ever closer to de Gaulle, seemingly his sole reliable ally.[91]

The debates in Bonn over the French plan found Adenauer in support, Erhard in opposition, and the foreign ministry in the middle trying to mediate. During the Fouchet negotiations, Adenauer dropped the distinction between cooperation and integration and inclined to follow de Gaulle without hesitation. Erhard still opposed the whole idea and viewed it as a distraction from the higher priority of bringing Britain into the Common Market. The Auswärtiges Amt sought key modifications, such as the assurance that Paris would not be the location for any new institutions, and asked for guarantees that NATO and the European communities not be damaged.[92] In 1961, it was reassured by de Gaulle's conciliatory stance, by the Bonn Declaration, and by the initial French Fouchet drafts. It found the latter acceptable, "insofar as they are treated only as a first step on the road of European political unity and do not hinder the ultimate federal unity we desire."[93] Indeed, one German official compared the Bonn Declaration to the 1955 Messina declaration that had signaled the first step toward the Common Market.[94]

Bonn remained complacent until de Gaulle's dramatic revisions in January 1962.[95] Government and parliamentary leaders were shocked by France's efforts to dictate its European conceptions rather than compromise.[96] Even Adenauer criticized de Gaulle and urged France to restore the original agreement.[97] Schroeder, the new foreign minister, supported political union, but castigated de Gaulle's changes.[98] The foreign ministry tried to win the French over to new forms of democratic supranationalism, but with no success. However, de Gaulle's limited concessions were enough for Adenauer, whose optimism had been restored by late March 1962.[99] In their calls for compromise, the Germans failed to recognize the firmness of Dutch and Belgian resistance and their fears of a Franco-German directorate within the Six.[100] Focusing on the big picture, the foreign ministry argued that "every setback for European unity amounts to a victory for the Soviets. It gives the Soviet Union new hopes of playing the European countries off against one another and leads to a harder Soviet stance toward the West."[101]

During the Fouchet negotiations, Germany held no rigid position on British participation. Bonn agreed with the French that Britain could not be formally involved in the negotiations without joining the Common Market. Except for Adenauer, the Germans considered this a positive linkage. The foreign ministry expected that Britain would cease its obstruction and accept the basic institutions of the Six once it joined the Common Market. In the meantime, Bonn was prepared to use the WEU as the forum for semi-formal talks with the British, thus supporting Paris and London at the same time.[102]

During the first half of 1961 the British remained ambivalent on the political union. They feared exclusion from any new institutions and questioned de Gaulle's intentions, but remained confident in Dutch resistance and did all they could to encourage it. They remained preoccupied by the Common Market itself and hoped that nothing would develop on the political front until they had formed a clear policy toward the economic group. The Foreign Office warned against "dickering with the European political set-up before Kennedy has had a chance to take a hand."[103]

After Britain made its decision to apply to the Common Market, its desire to join the political negotiations increased, especially since the Bonn Declaration signaled that these were finally advancing. To be sure, the political union negotiations were not as important as the Common Market itself. London was far more concerned about the elaboration of the CAP than de Gaulle's confederation, but the Foreign Office noted that "if the success of the [Common Market] negotiations [were] not to be prejudiced, [Britain] must obviously be enabled to participate in the development of EEC policies on [all] fundamental questions."[104] During the debates among the Six over political organization, British diplomats had two main concerns over participation. The first was the fear of exclusion by de Gaulle. The second was the response of the British Parliament and public, which might refuse to add new political commitments to the economic demands of the Six. As it turned out, British public opinion ignored the political union and remained focused on the application to the Common Market. The Macmillan government would have preferred that the Six set aside the issue of political organization until Britain's relations with the Common Market were settled. But since most of the Six were determined to move forward, Britain supported the Bonn Declaration, to indicate interest in European unity.

In private, however, British policy makers were concerned whether this linkage would help or hurt their application to the Common Market, and they awaited an offer from the Six to join the talks.[105] At the same time, the Foreign Office began to study the technical issues involved in de Gaulle's proposals. It opposed a formal political secretariat, but also rejected any extension of supranationalism and preferred that all defense issues be left to NATO. Finding itself disagreeing with both sides, Britain kept its opinions on the divisive technical issues to itself.[106]

Despite their lack of enthusiasm, the British found ways to integrate the idea of greater European political cooperation into their wider plans. They recognized that it would further stabilize Germany. It would also serve their ambitions to lead a stronger Europe in an Atlantic partnership with the United States. In addition London hoped that some role for the European neutrals could be found, both to link them with the West and to make the political union more diffuse.[107] It recognized that careful linkage of the political union and the Common Market could be made to serve British interests. By encouraging the Five's resistance to the political union so long as they were left out, the British hoped to gain leverage on de Gaulle to persuade him to accept the United Kingdom in both the political union and the Common Market.[108]

When the first Fouchet draft was discussed in the fall of 1961, London still hoped any decision would be delayed until it joined the Common Market. Publicly the British declared their support for progress on political union, but also urged the Six to expedite the Common Market negotiations. Britain still counted primarily on Dutch aid and was reassured by Dutch promises that "any proposals put forward for developments on the lines of General de Gaulle's *Europe des patries* must be acceptable to Britain."[109]

When de Gaulle hardened his position, Britain judged that he had overplayed his hand. Some British officials concluded that European cooperation might be impossible as long as de Gaulle remained in power, and that it was best to remain aloof from the technical debates of the Six. Whether or not Britain actually sabotaged the Fouchet plan, it is clear that it benefited from its demise. On 10 April 1962, one week before the plan's burial, Edward Heath, the British government's main negotiator with the Six, told the WEU assembly that full British participation in continental affairs was necessary in order for European institutions to work properly. Heath implied that Britain's absence had led to the deadlock among the Six and proclaimed its readiness to participate fully in the talks.[110] One week later Spaak and Luns announced that Britain must participate in any further negotiations, a demand that France refused and that brought the political negotiations to a close. The British, who insisted that they had not intended to derail the talks and merely wanted to establish a "sensible relationship between the political and the economic negotiations," had known that Heath's speech would sharpen the disagreements among the Six. They had been prepared to exploit the situation to promote Britain's application to the Common Market. Heath informed the Dutch ambassador that "the advantage of the disagreement between the Six over holding over signature of the Treaty of Political Union until we could join the E.E.C. was that those who were strongly in favor of having a European Political Community would see that a pre-condition of this was that terms must be agreed for British accession on the economic side."[111] Some Britons even took credit for the negative outcome, which confirmed their importance as a counterweight to Franco-German hegemony.[112]

Unlike Britain, the United States neither welcomed nor profited from the failures of the Six. Neither the Kennedy administration nor the State Department had opposed de Gaulle's proposals. Both were satisfied with the progress of 1961 and refuted Dutch criticisms.[113] Washington remained confident that the Five would protect the foundations of European and Atlantic relations. The United States had encouraged the Dutch to stay in the talks and rein in Gaullist excesses. Washington thus responded positively to the Bonn Declaration, which indicated that moderate voices were being heard.[114] American officials did not press for British participation and, in fact, felt that the "British [were] not yet prepared for serious negotiations leading to an acceptable accommodation with the Six, nor [were] they prepared to use the WEU as a vehicle for political consultation."[115] Once London applied to the Common Market, Washington joined France in urging the Six to move quickly on political union and consolidate European institutions before they expanded.[116] Washington believed that the United Kingdom was not needed to contain the French and feared that British participation might prevent the Six from accomplishing anything substantive in the political sphere.

Until the end of 1961, the U.S. government supported the Fouchet draft and even lauded de Gaulle. Although Washington took a dim view of his long-term aims, France's present policies seemed flexible and unobjectionable.[117] However, when de Gaulle issued his revisions, U.S. observers became concerned, fearing he intended to create a bloc within NATO, force the United States to accept tripartism, or lead Western Europe in a neutralist direction. These were the same concerns that were beginning to surface as a result of de Gaulle's hostility to the Atlantic Community.[118] America's confidence in the ability of the Five to stand up to de Gaulle began to waver, since it was clear to the State Department that Benelux would accept a treaty "along the lines of the French proposals [if it] were the price demanded by the French for U.K. entry into the Economic Communities."[119] On the eve of the deadlock of 17 April 1962, Washington was deluged with alarmist reports about de Gaulle from the Belgians and Dutch, as well as from American embassies in Western Europe.[120] On the other hand, the Italians, Germans, and French tried to persuade the Americans of the benefits of the political union proposal. The Italians suggested that the United States bring the Dutch and Belgians around, and the French portrayed the deadlock as a "grave setback" and a British-inspired threat to the Common Market that would lead to "unpleasant consequences."[121] The State Department encouraged the Europeans to seek their own solutions providing the maximum unity within the broader framework of existing European and Atlantic institutions.[122]

Nevertheless, U.S. observers were unsettled by the deadlock, which they believed to be a menace to Western Europe. Privately, they feared a revival of French and German nationalism. Suddenly they gained a new appreciation for British participation to stabilize the Six, but still relied on the Five to champion the British cause. De Gaulle's behavior on the political union also contributed to the negative reappraisal of his foreign policy occurring in Washington and the ensuing Franco-American conflict. In early May, Secretary of State Dean Rusk warned against de Gaulle's pretensions at hegemony and urged the Kennedy administration to join the Five against him. "[The] French today are making proposals in [the] field of European integration which are being vigorously opposed by other members of [the] Six. These French proposals run counter to [the] concept of integration which [the] U.S. has long supported."[123]

De Gaulle's failure proved damaging to himself and to France, but it was not inevitable. He squandered his initial advantages: the isolation of the Dutch, the support of the United States, the acceptance of his other partners, and the uncertainty of the United Kingdom. However, his sabotage of the Fouchet treaty in January 1962 cost him the goodwill and confidence of virtually all his European and Atlantic allies. With the exception of Adenauer, none would ever trust him again. He revived Dutch opposition, gave Britain the ability to influence the Six, and raised Washington's ire. Now he had little choice but to shift toward a purely Franco-German arrangement, since no one else would follow him.

The Aftermath, May 1962–December 1963

Even though, in retrospect, April 1962 marks the end of the formal negotiations for a political union among the Six, it was not clear at the time that the issue was dead. Most of the participants and interested observers believed that the negotiations could be resumed and brought to a successful conclusion in short order. Even those who had frustrated de Gaulle's plans felt that the political union effort could be safely revived once Britain was in the Common Market.

De Gaulle shared none of this optimism. He was convinced that the idea was doomed, because his continental partners lacked the "political will" to create an independent Europe. De Gaulle, like Macmillan, used this phrase as a code word whose real meaning was that others should make all the compromises necessary to reach an agreement. Determined to maintain his principles, at a press conference in May de Gaulle launched a major attack on supranationalism, America's meddling in Europe, and the obstruction of his European partners. He accused the latter of hypocrisy in demanding both British participation and supranationalism, since "everyone knew that [Britain], a strong state committed to its own preservation, would never consent to dissolve itself in some utopian construct."[124] During the summer, the Italians and Belgians offered compromises, but de Gaulle rejected them. France would concede nothing on supranationalism nor engage in futile negotiations. De Gaulle refused to trade acceptance of Britain's application to the Common Market for progress on the political union and would "neither re-launch nor withdraw the project that [he] had proposed to his partners."[125]

De Gaulle now preferred to focus on a purely bilateral arrangement with Germany. As a sop to Adenauer, who continued to support a wider political union, he offered to hold another meeting of the Six, but only to sign a treaty. He insisted that some new political arrangement was necessary so that Europe "would not remain at the mercy of the United Kingdom and the United States." He stoked Adenauer's concerns over the divisions among the Six and the complications posed by expansion of the Common Market. This was not a difficult task. Adenauer bitterly blamed the Dutch for the political union failure: "Holland wrecked [the political union] intentionally. . . . For that we can thank our 'ally' Luns!"[126] The French arguments won Adenauer over to a bilateral Franco-German arrangement.

Although the specter of a Franco-German bloc alarmed the rest of the Six, it did not revive de Gaulle's political union. Italy joined the Dutch and Belgians in demanding Britain's participation in any political arrangement and abandonment of any effort to create a political union before Britain joined the Common Market. The Italians complained that "we wanted to work together and build a house for six, but two of our partners have seized the land for themselves and begun building for two." They informed the French that "you have launched a torpedo in the waters of Europe and it has hit its target."[127] The French, convinced of a British-led conspiracy, dropped political union once and for all and worked to keep the United Kingdom out of Europe at all costs.[128] In January 1963, de Gaulle's veto of Britain's Common Market application and the conclusion of a bilateral treaty with Germany ended any prospects of a political organization for the Six for years to come.

During the remainder of 1963, the French focused exclusively on progress in the existing European institutions, including the implementation of the CAP and the fusion of the three communities. After the high hopes of the two previous years, these steps demonstrated de Gaulle's willingness to make small gains while reserving grandiose political and defense designs for the future when the other Europeans were prepared to accept his views. After Erhard replaced Adenauer in late 1963, Bonn tried briefly to revive discussion of the political union. The new chancellor's vague proposals, only cautiously supported by the Auswärtiges Amt, elicited skepticism in France, which doubted that Erhard's Atlanticism and the resistance of the other Europeans to France's European conceptions had disappeared. According to the Quai d'Orsay, Erhard's proposals could not lead to anything more than "the simple resumption of political consultations among the Six."[129]

Erhard's proposals were the result of Germany's disappointment with the political union deadlock. In early 1962 Adenauer and Schroeder had strongly supported efforts at compromise.[130] The foreign ministry, unhappy at the prospect of an exclusive Franco-German relationship as the only alternative, sought a solution that would prevent this and include Britain.[131] When this proved impossible, Adenauer concluded that no compromise was possible and explored a purely Franco-German arrangement.[132] While the chancellor wholly embraced this solution, Schroeder and the foreign ministry viewed it as at best a stopgap measure to fill the void until the wider European political union became possible. The Auswärtiges Amt continued to study ways to revive the latter, including moving forward without the Dutch and Belgians, "whose delaying tactics did not correspond with the common interest," and hoped for progress once Britain was in the Common Market.[133]

Upon de Gaulle's veto of Britain's Common Market application, most German leaders realized hopes for the political union were doomed. As the foreign ministry put it, "The political union can be written into the history books. A bilateral Franco-German treaty of friendship and cooperation can no longer be viewed as the trailblazer for such a union."[134] During most of 1963, as the domestic environment heated up over the Franco-German treaty and Adenauer's succession, and as international debates centered on larger issues such as the future of the Common Market and Atlantic alliance, the German government dropped all efforts to revive political union.[135]

Little changed after Erhard took office in October 1963. A longtime critic of de Gaulle, the Common Market, and political union, the new chancellor felt obligated to signal his commitment to continuity in German foreign policy. He thus resurrected the idea of political cooperation, if only for domestic consumption. Germany, which lacked the ideas to overcome the obstacles among the Six, quickly buried its modest initiative in the face of rejection from all sides.

Erhard and Schroeder devoted themselves to such concrete issues as the Kennedy round in the GATT, the fusion of the executives of the communities, and the development of the CAP, reserving political union for the future.[136]

The United States maintained its support of European political union after April 1962, but grew increasingly suspicious of de Gaulle's uncompromising stance toward the Five and Britain.[137] After de Gaulle's veto in January 1963, Washington concluded that France's main aim was to exclude the United States and Britain from Europe and that the political union was a dead issue. During the mutual recriminations that followed the veto, the United States not only denied French-inspired rumors that it had used the Dutch and Belgians to sabotage the Fouchet negotiations, but held de Gaulle solely responsible for their failure.[138]

Because American leaders now assumed the worst about de Gaulle, they feared any revival of his proposals. During the summer of 1963 rumors circulated that he might counter the effects of Kennedy's European trip by reviving the political union and forcing the Five to choose between the Common Market and the "Anglo-Saxons." Ball and Rusk saw doctrinaire neutralist designs behind all de Gaulle's plans and "no real possibility of political unity in any significant sense" resulting from them since such unity was "clearly inconsistent with the General's emphasis on nationalism."[139] Washington was also skeptical of Erhard's halfhearted proposals in late 1963, expecting little progress on European political unity until de Gaulle left the scene.[140]

Britain's position between the collapse of the Fouchet plan and the failure of its application to the Common Market was the most delicate of all. Ideally, London might have liked to simply drop the political union complication, but Macmillan decided to use the deadlock to promote the British Common Market application. Hoping to leverage the United Kingdom into Europe without paying a major political or economic price, the prime minister spent the second half of 1962 trying to convince de Gaulle of Britain's value to his political plans. Macmillan portrayed Britain as a fellow opponent of supranationalism and the key to persuading the Five to accept de Gaulle's political union. At the same time, Macmillan downplayed his opposition to supranationalism with the Five, trying to convince them of Britain's European credentials, while working to "ensure that the Dutch continue[d] to block progress on political union until the outcome of the Brussels [Common Market] negotiations [was] assured."[141]

Although the political union provided extra leverage, it also increased Britain's vulnerability, since de Gaulle still had the upper hand. London failed to recognize that the French president could always drop the political union or use it to force Britain to choose between Europe and the United States. Nevertheless,

Macmillan continued to cajole de Gaulle with assurances of support. He also talked of organizing a European nuclear deterrent based on the French and British forces and of greater independence for Western Europe from the United States. De Gaulle, however, threw cold water on Macmillan's superficial European enthusiasm at every turn and went so far as to blame him for the failure of the political union: "We always talk of Europe but nothing ever results. That is mostly because of you, because the little countries insist on waiting for you."[142]

However, the British dared not allow the support of the Five to make them complacent. De Gaulle's steps toward a bilateral Franco-German axis to control Western Europe appeared an even more serious threat to Britain than a political union of the Six. With the de Gaulle–Adenauer summit meetings of mid-1962, Foreign Office officials feared "the mystic sense of communion which seems to envelop these two when they get together and which has so bedeviled our interests in the past."[143] After the Macmillan–de Gaulle meeting in December, there were hints of the consequences of Britain's strategy and that the French leader would abandon the political union rather than allow Britain to use it to force its way into Europe.

De Gaulle's veto forced Britain to reevaluate all its European policies. British diplomats recognized the link between the failure of de Gaulle's European schemes in April 1962 and his veto of their entry into Europe in January 1963, but gave little consideration to how their own behavior had contributed to the debacle.[144] There was a brief temptation to avenge Britain's setback by offering to organize a political grouping between Britain and the Five. This idea was quickly dropped, because the cabinet doubted that the Five would risk destroying the Common Market and because it rejected the concessions to supranationalism that a credible offer would require. Nor would the United States be pleased by a new British challenge to the Common Market. Macmillan knew that one way or another, the British bluff would be called almost immediately.[145]

Britain, far more than the United States, now considered de Gaulle a menace to Europe. As Sir Pierson Dixon, the ambassador to Paris put it, "De Gaulle is our adversary and we should therefore take him on and try to do him down."[146] This appraisal was a major factor behind the post-veto British decision to stay the course in their European policy. The United Kingdom would continue to act as European as possible and maintain political contact with the Five to check new French initiatives.[147] The renewed British emphasis on political consultations in the WEU and in NATO in 1963 was intended to provide the Five an alternative to de Gaulle's siren song. Britain opposed any revival of political union until its own place in Europe was resolved.[148] By the end of 1963 London felt secure that political union was a dead issue and its author, de Gaulle, successfully isolated. One British diplomat dismissed de Gaulle's "independent" France as a

"Switzerland with worldwide interests and influence."[149] The Foreign Office nevertheless remained on guard. During Erhard's brief initiative it rallied Belgian and Dutch resistance and scolded the Germans.[150]

Conclusion

Although the form evolved considerably between 1958 and 1963, the essence of de Gaulle's plans for Europe remained constant. He planned to build a foundation of intergovernmental cooperation in the four areas of foreign policy, economic affairs, defense, and culture. De Gaulle also insisted that his European organization, based in Paris, would stand above the Common Market and the other European communities, as well as NATO. With Germany as his key ally, de Gaulle was always prepared to move forward with Bonn alone should his wider efforts fail. After 1963, de Gaulle never abandoned his long-term goal for Western Europe, but he increasingly turned to unilateral efforts to assert French freedom of action. Barring major changes, he could only achieve his political union by either accepting Britain or making supranational concessions to the Five. If these were his only choices, he preferred to do nothing.

De Gaulle was always determined to limit his European political plans to the Six. Because France's postwar experiences with cooperation in wider international groupings, most notably NATO and the UN General Assembly, had been negative, de Gaulle wanted to avoid large organizations and wide, diverse groups that France could not dominate. Macmillan had offered a helpful partnership in containing supranationalism in Europe, but de Gaulle chose to exclude Britain, with its considerable influence among the Five, and go it alone. This split between the two European powers with the greatest international status and the strongest commitment to shifting Europe away from supranationalism ended up frustrating the ambitions of both.

De Gaulle's various plans for a political grouping of the Six failed because he was never willing to resolve their internal contradictions. He paid lip service to European integration to persuade the Five to allow him to eviscerate the European communities. He wanted to build a nonsupranational Europe yet sought to keep out the British, staunch defenders of an intergovernmental foundation for Western Europe. He decried American hegemony yet behaved in a hegemonic fashion toward his smaller European partners. He directed his European proposals against the influence of the United States, yet tried to implement his plans with five partners committed to the maintenance of American influence. These devastating contradictions were muted during the period (up to January 1962) in which de Gaulle remained willing to compromise to achieve his goals.

Thereafter, the French president's showing of his real hand and his subsequent intransigence gradually pushed Britain, the United States, and all of the Five into some degree of opposition to his plans. This development destroyed the atmosphere of mutual confidence that was necessary for any European political progress. By the end of 1963 most of the other members of the Atlantic alliance viewed de Gaulle as a threat to their interests, while he viewed all his potential European partners as mere tools of the United States, unwilling to practice a real foreign policy.

Another reason for the failure of de Gaulle's European political plans was that their negative aspects came to outweigh the positive ones. Initially his ideas had widespread appeal since it seemed they would expand European cooperation to new areas, including foreign policy, culture, and defense, and were not aimed against anything or anyone. Over time, however, it became clear that all of de Gaulle's proposals were intended to subordinate or absorb the existing European communities. The anti-British and anti-American aspects also grew in tandem with de Gaulle's frustrations at the influence of these two countries among the Five. As the negative aspects came to the forefront, de Gaulle's partners feared that he sought hegemony over them. They concluded that he went both too far in his attacks on the Americans, British, and Atlantic alliance and not far enough in his purely nominal support for the European communities and his determination to limit European unity to cooperative means. While de Gaulle initially made many positive contributions to Europe, including restoring stability to France, enabling it to implement its Common Market commitments, and blocking British efforts to dissolve the economic community, over time his unilateralism and his hostility to Britain and the United States made him more of a hindrance than a benefit to the cause of European unity. His hegemonic pretensions and reliance on Germany provoked strong fears in the smaller members of the European community, the echoes of which are evident in the reservations of many European countries toward the Paris-Bonn axis even today.

De Gaulle's legalism worked against him as well. He proved unwilling to accept the substance of his goals alone and insisted on formalized arrangements to enshrine them. Rather than work to convince the Five of his conceptions in practice, he sought to force them to accept things in writing that went against the core of their domestic and foreign policies. When they refused, he ended up with nothing. After the April 1962 debacle even the previous, practical forms of cooperation that the Six had established, most notably quarterly meetings of foreign ministers, went on hiatus. Throughout the rest of 1962 and 1963 only one such meeting was held, with no tangible results.

Germany, despite constant infighting on the details, put forth a relatively consistent policy toward European political organization from beginning to end. Bonn supported greater political ties among the Six for all the familiar reasons related to linking Germany to the West. Unlike de Gaulle, the Germans saw no contradiction between European unity and their wider Atlantic commitments. As long as its ties with the United States were not endangered, Bonn would go quite far to meet Paris on political union. Unlike the leaders of the smaller Western European countries, the Germans did not fear that the political union meant French hegemony. France could not force its will on Germany, much less on Germany and four other countries. Bonn thus followed a flexible approach and acted as mediator between the French and their shifting array of opponents. However, French provocation had a polarizing effect on the German government. In 1962–63 Adenauer inclined ever closer to de Gaulle, while Schroeder and the foreign ministry became distrustful of the French agenda. With Schroeder and Erhard ascendant at the end of 1963, Bonn still favored a political union, but questioned its short-term prospects and preferred to focus on more pressing matters.

American government observers realized, relatively early on, that de Gaulle's political plans for Europe were aimed at reducing their influence on the continent and in the Atlantic alliance. They were never particularly disturbed by any of the specific means de Gaulle proposed to organize the cooperation of the Six. Their concern was always his motives, but they found it difficult to challenge him directly on the political union and were always on the sidelines of the issue. Initially, however, between 1958 and early 1962, both Eisenhower and Kennedy felt confident that the Five would force de Gaulle to make concessions to protect the crucial American concerns in the whole debate: NATO, the European communities, and European (especially German) links with the United States. As long as greater European unity did not produce an anti-U.S. bloc, it would not contradict Kennedy's Atlantic Community program. Because the Kennedy administration counted on the Five to contain de Gaulle while advancing European unity, it tended to view the issue of British participation in the political union as peripheral at best and a nuisance at worst. After April 1962, however, the Americans realized that British involvement would be useful as another brake on de Gaulle's Third Force plans, even though the inclusion of Britain would add weight to any future European demands for a more equal relationship with the United States. As de Gaulle's program became more openly aimed against both America and Britain, this seemed a small price to pay to block the French leader and ensure that he did not lead Germany in dangerous directions. While de Gaulle envisioned the political union as a means to free Europe from what he viewed as excessive American influence, U.S. leaders hoped to use his own creation to restrain him and put "Atlantic" pressure on him, first via the

Five and later by means of the Five and the British together. When de Gaulle chose to abandon the whole project rather than accept this outcome, the United States regretted the failure for Western Europe but welcomed the setback for de Gaulle.

Not surprisingly, it was the British who were most alienated by de Gaulle during the whole political union episode. From the very beginning in 1958–59, the British had been convinced that de Gaulle's political schemes served primarily, if not exclusively, the cause of French domination of Western Europe at the expense of Britain and the United States. The course of events only reinforced these convictions. Once the Macmillan government decided to join the European communities, it accepted the basic means of political organization de Gaulle proposed, but it never trusted his intentions. Like the Americans, the British counted on the Five to stand up to de Gaulle, but unlike the Americans, they took the precaution of openly encouraging the Dutch and Belgians to block de Gaulle until he allowed them to join. The growth of British fears was also reflected in the gradual shift from asking for consultation to demanding full participation in any political negotiations. When de Gaulle's schemes were thwarted in 1962–63, London saw him switching to a purely destructive and obstructionist policy, blocking both the expansion and the development of the European communities. Some British observers hoped that de Gaulle would take this negative policy so far that he would destroy the communities and cast the Five adrift, allowing Britain to pick up the pieces. Others feared that de Gaulle would try to revive his European schemes and the Five might follow along. By now all viewed de Gaulle in an entirely negative light and were prepared to fight any efforts at a political union of the Six tooth and nail.

Although one reason to build the political union had been to confront the Soviet Union with a more united Western Europe, fears of the USSR played a relatively minor role during the negotiations. Indeed, the fact that de Gaulle, Luns, and Spaak consistently practiced brinkmanship on the union and ultimately allowed it to collapse rather than to compromise suggests that they viewed the intra-European debates as more important than augmenting the common front toward the East. When the negotiations collapsed, all sides proclaimed it a victory for the Soviets, but this was largely rhetoric. As long as NATO, the Common Market, and other Euro-Atlantic institutions survived, it would be difficult for the Soviets to draw any significant advantage from the failure of the political union. The real negative consequences of the setback lay elsewhere.

For the French and Germans the goal of greater political cooperation among the Six had been a central issue throughout the period 1958–63, but for the British and Americans it was always somewhat peripheral. At the outset the Americans viewed it as a possible step forward for Western Europe, but as only one possibility among many. Later, when both the British and Americans had come out openly against de Gaulle's European vision, the issue of political union was only one symptom of a larger problem. Except for Germany, de Gaulle's European and Atlantic allies were largely unaffected by the outcome of the political union episode, since none had made it the foundation of their European policy. For de Gaulle, however, the political union had been central. In theory, it offered a counter to British and American plans for Western Europe and a way to frustrate "Anglo-Saxon" dominance. Its failure thus paralleled that of the Kennedy administration's Atlantic Community and added to the wider European-Atlantic deadlock that the Franco-American rivalry produced in the early 1960s. If the failure of the Atlantic Community idea frustrated the establishment of a long term equilibrium between the United States and Western Europe, the failure of the political union had equally unfortunate long-term consequences, as its ambitions have never been matched in subsequent efforts to organize and coordinate the political relations of Western Europe.

CHAPTER SIX

BRITAIN'S APPLICATION TO THE

COMMON MARKET, 1961-1963

The Cross of Lorraine we can bear without too much burden, the double cross I find less tolerable.—Sir Harold Caccia, permanent undersecretary at the British Foreign Office, 1962

Prelude, July 1960–July 1961

In July 1961 the United Kingdom reversed the policy it had followed since 1955 and applied for membership in the Common Market. The subsequent entry negotiations between late 1961 and early 1963 became another episode in the ongoing struggle over the political and economic shape of Western Europe. Each of the Atlantic powers used the negotiations to advance its European agenda and viewed the technical problems as subordinate to the larger political issues at stake.

By 1961, the Macmillan government had decided it could only influence Western Europe from the inside since successive efforts to do so from the outside had failed. London, however, still overestimated its bargaining position, mistakenly believing it was negotiating from a position of equality, and thought it could transform the Common Market via its admission. Britain had changed its tactics, but its goal remained the same. France remained its main opponent and ultimately prevented the United Kingdom from joining. The United States welcomed the British shift, but because of its commitment to supranationalism insisted that the United Kingdom accept the Common Market unchanged. In Germany, the British application led to political infighting, with Adenauer almost alone in opposition and the majority committed to Britain's entry. The failure of the negotiations over British entry was more serious than that of any previous British overture to Europe, shaking the entire unity movement and creating a rift in the Atlantic community for years.

The historiography on the British application has grown dramatically in recent years as the government documents of most of the countries involved have become available for research. This literature tends to focus on either the technical negotiations or the larger political and diplomatic issues.[1] Much of the work on the latter subject takes a national approach to an international topic, and many authors have attempted to explain the international causes and consequences of the failure of the British application by examining the documents of one country alone while treating the others involved in a superficial manner.[2] This chapter attempts to correct this tendency of the diplomatic-centered historiography while making use of works dealing with the technical aspects of the negotiations.

In 1960, after its failure to prevent the Six from accelerating the implementation of the Common External Tariff (CET), Britain finally recognized that the Common Market was likely to last and could not be controlled from the outside. Although London began exploring ways of mitigating its political and economic exclusion from Europe, its initial efforts were half-hearted and insufficient. In July 1960 Britain offered to join Euratom and the European Coal and Steel Community but received a cool response from the Six, who insisted it must join all the European communities or none. During the summer an interministerial group commissioned earlier by Prime Minister Macmillan agreed that Britain needed a bolder policy.[3]

The report, dominated by the views of the Foreign Office, weighed the consequences of joining or remaining aloof from the Common Market and came down strongly in favor of entry. It acknowledged the high price, but argued that it was worth paying. The United Kingdom would have to make major concessions to adapt its system of agricultural price supports to that of the continent and would have to dissolve its privileged economic ties with the Commonwealth and the EFTA. Since these concessions would be necessary even to attain a loose "association" with the Six, the United Kingdom might as well obtain the benefits of full membership, which included the opening of vast new markets for its goods, reinvigorating its economy, and increasing Britain's political and economic weight on the continent and in the world: "From the political standpoint at any rate, the consequences to the United Kingdom of a somewhat isolated position whose diminishing relative strength would sap our will even to attempt to maintain an independent effective role in world politics is unacceptable."[4] The interministerial report urged a prompt application before the Six established more supranational institutions, leaped ahead economically, and left Britain behind. The Foreign Office concluded that Britain's preferred alternatives, an Atlantic community and a free trade area, were not attainable over the short term. There now seemed to be no real choices between "joining the community on the best terms we can get and [remaining in] a semi-isolated position."[5] Nonetheless, Whitehall, hoping to overcome opposition in the cabinet, proposed that the United Kingdom demand various technical concessions from the Six and refuse to relinquish its political ties to the Commonwealth and the United States.

In its brief in favor of membership, the Foreign Office stressed the political benefits, especially the restraining of neutralist or Third Force tendencies on the continent. It emphasized U.S. support for Britain's entry and the possibility of maintaining the special relationship as the leader of the Common Market. By promoting membership or association for the rest of the EFTA, Britain could gain the backing to thwart Franco-German dominance, contain supranationalism, and obtain predominant influence in Europe. But if Britain remained aloof, France and Germany would control an ever stronger continental bloc and they would replace the United Kingdom as America's main partner, while an ever-weaker Britain would be less appealing to the Commonwealth and the EFTA. With Britain's foreign exchange shifting away from the Commonwealth and toward Europe anyway and the remnants of empire moving toward independence, greater ties with Europe offered economic development and a new world role to replace a fading one.[6]

Because the majority of the cabinet was unready for such a bold step, the report was set aside. The cabinet objected to severing economic ties with the Commonwealth, insisted on a mass of special conditions, and still hoped for an alternative that would allow the United Kingdom to preserve all its global interests. Macmillan personally favored full entry, but had to move carefully to bring the cabinet along. Rather than apply for membership, the cabinet decided to explore negotiations between the Six and the Seven and delay a direct British approach to the Common Market until the prospects were more advantageous.[7] The Foreign Office responded with renewed arguments in favor of membership, minimizing the risks and exaggerating the potential benefits to sway the timid politicians. It feared that Britain would not be able to make any progress with the Six until it was ready to make "some far reaching and conspicuous decisions about going into Europe."[8]

In August 1960 Macmillan took advantage of the temporary rift between de Gaulle and Adenauer, resulting from their misunderstandings of the Rambouillet meeting, to convince the German chancellor to accept technical economic meetings between British and German officials to discuss an arrangement between the Six and the Seven.[9] During these discussions, Britain tested the Six's willingness to make concessions, but the Germans hesitated to make commitments without the French. The Foreign Office viewed the whole effort as a useless exercise. Much of the cabinet, however, still believed that France could be isolated, and Macmillan wanted to test all the options with the Germans, including a merger of the Six with the EFTA, some limited form of British membership in the Common Market that excluded agriculture and maintained ties with the Commonwealth, or an entry that transformed the Common Market into a British-dominated entity.[10]

After the technical discussions with the Germans stagnated, Macmillan and his advisers devised a new foreign policy strategy to solve all their problems, the aforementioned "Grand Design." As noted in Chapter 4, Macmillan developed the Grand Design primarily to gain support from the new Kennedy administration and maintain the special relationship, but it also dealt with Britain's role in Europe, arguing that it must join the Common Market as soon as possible to become the leader of the group. Once de Gaulle's opposition was overcome, France would become the United Kingdom's principal ally in the fight to contain supranationalism: "Difficult as de Gaulle is, his view of the proper *political* structure (Confederation not Federation) is [near] to ours." The main question was how to win de Gaulle's support, whether to play on France's fears of Germany and Soviet Russia or to make concessions on nuclear cooperation and tripartism. Macmillan and his advisers were remarkably confident of their ability to convince de Gaulle, the United States, and Germany if necessary. Macmillan would simply inform Kennedy that "only if he can help me to do a deal with de Gaulle, can we keep Britain in Europe and relieve the United States of some of their burden."[11]

Not unexpectedly, the ambitious new strategy reaped few results. At their meeting at the end of January 1961, Macmillan induced de Gaulle to agree to technical meetings between French and British officials similar to the British-German talks. Macmillan also floated the proposal, devised by Edward Heath, the Lord Privy Seal and Britain's main negotiator with Europe, of a customs union between Britain and the Six limited to industrial goods and with special provisions for the EFTA and the Commonwealth. De Gaulle conceded that there could be "no Europe without England," but the French leader insisted that Britain would have to choose between Europe and its broader interests and rejected anything short of full entry. Despite this setback, Macmillan retained his hope that Britain could join the Common Market and still protect its wider interests.[12]

During the next months, Macmillan's "Grand Design" received further jolts. The Germans rebuffed his ideas on expanding and diluting the Common Market and voiding it of supranationalism, and they refused to pressure the French on the technical issues unless Britain applied for full membership.[13] The Kennedy administration rejected any concessions to France on tripartism and nuclear issues and also insisted on a full British membership that was not designed to weaken the community.[14] The Franco-British discussions were equally frustrating, with the French refusing any accommodation on the technical issues. Vindicated, the Foreign Office insisted that a formal Common Market application demonstrating "real enthusiasm about the European Economic Community" and a "definite affirmation of our desire to be a full member of it" was the only signal to which Bonn, Washington, and Paris would respond.[15]

By the spring of 1961, the cabinet had not yet decided. After the failure of his customs union idea, Heath suggested that the Germans, French, and Italians might show more flexibility toward the Commonwealth and the EFTA if Britain applied for full admission. However, this optimism was belied by the cabinet discussions, which emphasized the vast list of conditions the British would attach to any application, and by Britain's unsatisfactory contacts with the Six, particularly de Gaulle's continuing truculence. Macmillan rightly informed a group of Tory MPs that "the French and Germans had the paramount influence in the Six and they, therefore, had to be brought along. He was quite sure that it would be a great mistake to embark on formal negotiation until a private basis for a political agreement had been reached," yet he proceeded to launch the British application in the absence of such an agreement.[16] Macmillan and the Foreign Office believed that Paris expected a British application and would make the best of it.[17]

By July 1961, more and more British leaders and officials had concluded that a Common Market application was the only solution to their relations with Western Europe. A new interministerial report argued that the obstacles to this or any other arrangement with the Common Market could be overcome. The study envisioned a compromise whereby the British and continental economic systems would move toward one another and each side would make major changes. The British would give up the EFTA, but only when the entry negotiations were completed. This conditional British entry into, and the transformation of, the Common Market would end the division of Western Europe. However, the report warned that major British concessions on agriculture and the Commonwealth would be necessary and suggested that the United Kingdom limit its demands for special conditions to those issues that were truly essential.[18] Macmillan, on the other hand, was convinced that "many of the paper provisions will prove to be less onerous in practice than they are in theory" and felt that major changes would not be necessary.[19]

The cabinet made the decision to apply for membership on 21 July. Macmillan's presentation, deliberately vague, was based on Cold War imperatives and emphasized the special conditions the British hoped to attain. This approach, aimed at soothing the cabinet, parliament, and public, contradicted the advice of the Foreign Office and foreign sources that Britain must make a positive, unequivocal application without a long list of special demands. Otherwise it would not, in the words of the Foreign Office, "command the support which we would hope to win in five of the six countries, with some sections of French opinion and in the United States."[20] But Macmillan sought the best of both worlds, to convince critics that British entry was inevitable, yet assure them that their concerns would be met. He wanted to play up the significance of the British decision and make it appear a fait accompli with the EFTA, the Commonwealth, and the domestic agriculture lobby, yet at the same time play "hard to get" with the Six and emphasize that the United Kingdom would only join the Common Market if it received the proper conditions from them. This risky, dual approach would hamper the British application from beginning to end. Macmillan informed Heath that the government must balance the need to "carry the House with us" and to "show reasonable enthusiasm towards the Europeans." According to Macmillan, the outcome of the talks would depend solely on "whether de Gaulle (becoming more and more Napoleonic and self-centered) really wants us in or not" and "whether even if de Gaulle wants to settle we can work out terms which seem reasonably fair to all concerned."[21]

The French were slow to recognize the extent of the change occurring in London. Since 1955, they had denied responsibility for Britain's exclusion from Europe and accused the United Kingdom of isolating itself by refusing to choose Europe over the United States and the Commonwealth. After his return to power, de Gaulle did nothing to bridge the gap separating the United Kingdom and the Six and claimed that it was up to the British to take the initiative to find solutions. The more the French linked the Common Market with all the other European communities and with their future plans for the political union, the more isolated Britain became. This was a deliberate policy, aimed at excluding Britain without antagonizing the Five, who generally supported British participation in Europe. Until the middle of 1961, the French did not anticipate that the British might call their bluff and ask for immediate entry into all the European organizations. The Quai d'Orsay still viewed Britain as "a country whose reactions to Europe are more negative than positive and that sought to brake or paralyze the movement toward economic unity."[22] It had disliked the bilateral British-German contacts on the Common Market and sought to restrain the Germans by insinuating that Britain's interest in Europe was purely opportunistic and that no progress was possible until London decided on full membership. At the same time, to avoid isolation, the French had conducted private discussions with the British and maintained a common front with the United States against a Six-Seven deal.[23]

The French recognized that British policy had shifted somewhat in 1960. Rather than thwart the Common Market, the British appeared to be reconciled to the new conditions on the continent. But Paris did not expect any new initiatives because most British leaders remained hostile to the group. It regarded Britain's overtures, such as the July 1960 offer to join only the ECSC and Euratom, as tricks devised by Macmillan to placate pro-Europe forces in the United Kingdom and stir up difficulties among the Six. The French recognized that the United Kingdom now respected the political and economic weight of the Common Market and accepted at least some of its technical aspects, but they still doubted Britain's adherence to its political goals, which it would undermine at every opportunity.

Although sensing that Britain had abandoned its outsider strategy, Paris was slow to recognize that its new approach might take the form of an application for membership. The French believed that the British would never abandon their "three circles" and that they simply sought new ways to paralyze the Common Market. The foreign ministry did not think that Britain "could risk, yet again, unwittingly reinforcing the Six by making an offer that might look like a simple move to dissolve [the community]."[24] The French thus responded coolly to London's proposal of an industrial customs union, derided Britain's weakness and partial initiatives, and announced that, barring major changes, Britain's presence in Europe had politically undesirable connotations. Paris perceived no benefit in making concessions to the United Kingdom even if it applied for full membership, because the British appeared incapable of becoming real Europeans.[25]

De Gaulle also countered British efforts to isolate and pressure France. He discouraged Adenauer's proposals to improve relations between Britain and the Six and thereby facilitate progress on the political union. In May 1961 de Gaulle convinced the chancellor of the potential dangers of Britain's entry, which would enlarge, dilute, and transform the Common Market. He argued that Britain "was an island, while we are a continent." Any attempt to "absorb" Britain would thus "go against nature."[26] At his meetings with Kennedy in May and June, he criticized Britain's relations with the continent and showed an implacable resistance to further association negotiations.[27]

In July, despite signals from London and elsewhere, the French were unprepared for a British move on the Common Market. As a precaution, Paris had warned London not to set any conditions.[28] The French did not believe that Britain was ready to make the concessions to join fully but feared long, politically risky negotiations if the United Kingdom tried to enter without transforming itself. Paris was also alarmed at hints from German officials that they would insist only that Britain subscribe to the "essentials" of the Treaty of Rome. It feared that Erhard and his supporters would use any negotiations with the British to resume their campaign to dilute the Common Market into a free trade area. France thus accelerated the work toward political union and strengthened its ties with Bonn to block any challenges from Britain.[29]

Most German leaders still desired British participation in the Common Market. They supported the United Kingdom's liberal trade policies, wanted to maintain Germany's contacts outside the Six, and, above all, feared a permanent division of Western Europe.[30] Although the German public remained more concerned with Atlantic issues than Britain's relations with Europe and hesitated to endanger relations with France for the sake of the United Kingdom, the elite remained strongly pro-British and urged Adenauer to improve relations. Although some worried about the precise nature of Britain's ultimate economic ties with the continent, industry leaders, agricultural interests, and the media all generally supported efforts to overcome the Six-Seven split. If Adenauer lined up with de Gaulle and turned against Britain, he would be isolated at home.[31]

The foreign ministry believed that London was moving in the right direction, but it was frustrated at the slowness of Britain's realignment and shared the French insistence that the United Kingdom must join fully or not at all.[32] British hesitancy made the bilateral discussions on economic issues a fruitless exercise, during which the Germans were careful to avoid alienating the French or damaging the Common Market. The Auswärtiges Amt also maintained a hard line because it knew the ministry of economics remained all too ready for concessions to the British. Indeed, shortly after negotiations began on Britain's admission, Erhard's ministry argued that "whenever possible a rapid conclusion of the negotiations should be ensured by interim solutions and special protocols."[33] Erhard and his supporters hoped to weaken French influence by bringing Britain into Europe immediately, but Adenauer and the foreign ministry maintained the upper hand.[34] Nevertheless, even the foreign ministry feared that the French opposed British entry in principle, regardless of what concessions London might make.[35] Adenauer, on the other hand, became increasingly distrustful of British policy, a result of de Gaulle's influence, his own fears that expansion of the Common Market meant inevitable dilution, and his distrust of British attitudes on Berlin in particular and relations with the USSR in general.[36]

The Kennedy administration inherited its predecessor's doubts over Britain's role in Europe, but also its desire for the Common Market to be as large as possible without damaging its cohesion. Britain's relations with the continent continued to receive attention at the highest levels in Washington, with the consensus that it must join fully or not at all. The Kennedy administration, which saw ways to make British entry serve U.S. policy, soon made it a foundation of the Atlantic Community. Without intervening directly, the United States sought to ease Britain into Europe. Washington recognized that the United Kingdom had been a divisive force in Europe and hoped to end this situation without damaging the Common Market. It hoped that British entry would lead to lower European trade barriers, improve the chances of political union, and end the infighting among the NATO countries. According to Secretary of State Rusk,

Adenauer could be counted on to "insist that the arrangements be such as to assure the maximum political integration," which would be crucial to ensure political stability in Europe when the United States had to "face the reality of a post-Adenauer government [and] the ever present possibility of a post–de Gaulle France."[37]

The Kennedy team sought to convince the British that they had no choice but to join Europe. They urged London to forego all special arrangements and prepare for a future U.S.-European special tie.[38] They also insisted on excluding the EFTA neutrals and the Commonwealth countries from the Common Market and joined the French and Germans in urging a full commitment to the Treaty of Rome and all its political ramifications.[39] Kennedy questioned whether "the weights and balances [would] be right without [Britain's] influence at the center" and counted on London to stabilize the Six, provide a counterweight to the Bonn-Paris tandem, and influence Europe to support American policies.[40] In a series of blunt conversations in the spring of 1961, the Americans informed the British of all this, reiterating that London should focus solely on its own (complete) entry into the Common Market and set aside all wider issues until it was safely inside. Only an all-out effort held any prospect for success.[41]

The Application and the Brussels Negotiations, August 1961–January 1963

The cabinet's decision in July 1961 had to be sold to a wary British and European public.[42] In his announcement to the House of Commons, Macmillan described the challenges and opportunities Britain faced and declared that he wished to "initiate negotiations to see if satisfactory arrangements can be made to meet the special interests of the United Kingdom, of the Commonwealth and of the European Free Trade Association." He asserted that Britain could contain supranationalism and find a way to integrate the Commonwealth and the Common Market, portraying membership in Europe as offering many benefits and minimal costs. Toward the Six, he expressed British enthusiasm and flexibility. Toward the EFTA and the Commonwealth, he exuded certainty that the negotiations would be successful and without major risk to them. Instead of a written proposal listing its conditions, London issued general pronouncements, for fear of impeding the negotiations from the outset. Macmillan also made it clear that the application was a Tory project, reflective of the party's progressive mindset and in contrast with a "backward" Labour's emphasis on the Commonwealth and protectionism.[43]

The British expected the negotiations to proceed very quickly and hoped to join all the activities of the Six in short order.[44] London nevertheless hesitated to demand immediate participation in such delicate areas as the negotiations on the political union and the CAP, which might complicate its application.[45] Indeed, the British government, fearing domestic opposition, was reluctant to accept any additional commitments beyond those of the Treaty of Rome.[46]

Britain's old Atlantic goals were temporarily set aside. London still hoped to create a broad European political community, led by an Atlanticist United Kingdom and Germany, functioning as a full partner of the United States in the OECD, NATO, and an Atlantic free trade area. Due to the widespread fears over the dilution of the Common Market, the British prudently kept their ambitions under wraps during the Brussels negotiations. They knew they would need the support of Europeanists, such as Jean Monnet and his Action Committee for the United States of Europe, to overcome the resistance of de Gaulle and doubts of Adenauer. As the British embassy in Brussels phrased it, while de Gaulle's France was "neither practicing, nor believing" when it came to the European "religion," the French could be expected to use it as "a stick to beat embarrassing applicants and, in particular, [Britain]."[47] Having absorbed the lessons of the FTA episode, the British also preferred not to lead the talks themselves, hoping that if France proved hostile, others would defend them, allowing the United Kingdom to appear flexible and reasonable.[48] Once it had entered Europe, Britain intended to recoup many of the concessions made in the entry negotiations and promote its wider Atlantic agenda.[49]

After the opening session in Paris in October 1961, the negotiations began a month later in Brussels. The British delegation, led by Heath and the ambassador to Paris, Sir Pierson Dixon, preferred the Belgian capital to Paris because of its symbolic as well as practical connotations. Heath's opening speech set out Britain's conditions for joining the Common Market. Essentially, the United Kingdom accepted the original Treaty of Rome, but argued that its mechanisms and details must be "adapted" to the needs of an expanded community. Heath took pains to assure his audience of Britain's desire for full membership, its value as a partner in the integration movement, and its wish to place no impediments in their way. Britain's chief delegate presented its three major conditions, the maintenance of its political and economic ties with the Commonwealth, mutual concessions on agriculture, and entry or association for the other members of the EFTA, but also emphasized its cooperative approach to the negotiations. Although expressing confidence that they would find a means to reconcile these conditions with the future security of the Common Market, Heath declared that the United Kingdom would not choose between them. He attempted to convince the Six to subordinate technical problems to a larger "political" perspective (the now-familiar codeword to suggest that others should make the necessary compromises) and divert the negotiations from the steps

Britain would be required to make to concessions by both sides to develop a "new equilibrium" between them.[50]

However, Heath and Macmillan failed to convince their partners. Macmillan argued that "if our friends in Europe will meet us reasonably, we shall be successful," but failed to persuade the Six to meet the United Kingdom halfway.[51] From the outset, Paris disliked the conditional nature of Britain's application and insisted on focusing on Britain's special conditions and the changes the United Kingdom would have to make, which impeded the rapid progress London had sought. After years of explaining that the British must join the Common Market fully or not at all, the French were mystified by the mass of conditions the United Kingdom attached to its application. French diplomats feared that either the application was insincere, and designed to fail and to place the blame on the Six, specifically on France, or that the British intended to achieve all their demands and destroy the Common Market from within: "To the extent that the admission of England, its Scandinavian clients, and others would give a global dimension to what was originally conceived as a regional organization, this would require addressing the interests of the United States, which in turn would lead to a vague Atlantic community wherein London would, once again, be the privileged interlocutor of Washington."[52] The French did not believe that the British were prepared to restructure their economy and foreign policy in order to join the Common Market or that they had abandoned the hope of transforming it. The Macmillan government might have staked its future on the application, but it had shown neither the will nor the power to accept France's demands.

Technical issues aside, Paris was still uncertain over the political implications of British entry into the Common Market. There would be some positive results, such as the addition of Britain's political and military weight to the European communities. France would also acquire a staunch ally against supranationalism. On the other hand, British entry had even greater disadvantages. It would push the Common Market in a free trade direction, decrease France's relative weight in the group, and undermine its Third Force plans, increasing American influence in Europe, allowing Britain and Germany to combine against French interests, and ending any chance of French hegemony. A Franco-British rivalry would replace the present Franco-German entente, blocs would form within the community, and French plans for a political union would fall by the wayside. "The community of the Six was organized as a sort of de facto fief for French influence," noted de Gaulle's advisers, but if Britain joined, France "would face constant competition. . . . Not only would [its] voice not always be heard, but it would often be drowned out by the lure of the sirens from across the channel."[53]

The French government thus decided privately on a negative stance toward the British application from the outset and would make no concessions to ease the United Kingdom into Europe. Yet at the same time, it dared not simply veto the application, for fear of the reactions of the Five and the impact of such a unilateral move on the development of the community. Paris faced the bleak prospect that either successful or failed negotiations endangered its interests. The moment was especially problematic because important measures such as the CAP remained to be worked out and could be influenced by the British. Because the French had always claimed that the door to the Common Market was open, they decided not to block the negotiations, but instead to insist that the United Kingdom adhere to the letter of the Treaty of Rome. According to the Quai d'Orsay, the French goal would be to ensure that "the talks failed because of some problem other than British admission per se." The British must be confronted with a choice between failure and so many concessions that they would be "isolated from their own clientele in the Commonwealth." Paris would make the negotiations long and difficult, not only to ascertain Britain's intentions and confront it with impossible choices, but also to buy time for the Six to consolidate the Common Market to face either success or failure.[54] The foreign ministry hoped to use agriculture to sabotage the negotiations, estimating that the gulf between the CAP and Britain's agricultural system would convince the Five to rethink their support for expanding the Common Market. The French warned London and their partners that without a settlement on agriculture, the National Assembly would reject Britain's admission.[55]

As noted previously with regard to the political union, one of the few French dissenters from de Gaulle's anti-British European policy was Michel Debré, prime minister from January 1959 to April 1962. While acknowledging the difficulties involved, Debré was convinced that British participation in Europe was essential to countering the USSR and making Europe independent of the United States. He thus advocated a policy of firmness on the essentials to ensure that Britain did not transform the Common Market and flexibility on the details to make British entry possible. Unfortunately for the British, Debré's influence was limited, and in April 1962 he was replaced by Georges Pompidou, who was much less inclined to oppose de Gaulle's will in foreign affairs.[56]

In setting up the negotiations, the French put forth a number of demands to protect their interests. They favored a rotating leadership, refused a single representative for the Six, out of fear that their interests would be sacrificed, and wanted the negotiations to be conducted in Paris. They also demanded a detailed written proposal to give them the chance to pin the British down from the outset on all the contested technical issues. When the Five and the British resisted a written report and preferred Brussels to Paris, the French conceded on these lesser issues, but they remained intransigent on the more important ones, the rotating presidency and the stipulation that each of the Six speak for itself in the negotiations. All six governments would represent their interests independently of the Commission and would have to coordinate their positions in advance of every meeting with the British. The Quai d'Orsay regarded this as a vital precaution against the strong and ingrained "tendency of the Five to agree" with London on everything.[57]

France's strategy throughout the negotiations was to question whether Britain could adapt to the Common Market. It insisted that the United Kingdom be granted no exemptions from either the Treaty of Rome or any subsequent arrangements concluded among the Six. All transitional arrangements must end by the 1970 deadline for full implementation of the Treaty. Moreover, Britain would have to enter alone. There would be no permanent guarantees for the Commonwealth, which would endanger the CAP and the CET. De Gaulle feared that Britain wanted to "involve the entire world" in the Common Market and claimed that while "France did not refuse entry to Britain, it must be Britain alone."[58] Britain would have to abandon the EFTA, whose members could negotiate their own terms with the Six.[59] After the failure of its political union effort in April 1962, France was even more intent on blocking British efforts to associate the EFTA with the Common Market, which would likely destroy any possibility of European political consolidation.[60]

Bonn's reaction to the British application was very different, reflecting its evaluation of the political significance of British entry. Despite the fact that they agreed with the French on many of the technical issues, Germany's leaders welcomed the British application as proof of the rightness of the European course they had followed ever since the Messina conference in 1955. The Germans, unlike the French, were unafraid of expanding the Common Market as long as its political and economic cohesion was maintained. Most in Bonn believed in Britain's sincerity despite their concern over its special conditions and its reticence on supranationalism. The Germans viewed Heath's opening statement in October 1961 as a positive sign and did their utmost to ensure success, for example by supporting inclusion of the Commission in the negotiations and by opting for Brussels over Paris.[61]

For Bonn, the benefits of British entry outweighed the risks. The Germans anticipated new markets, an important new ally on community issues, and a stronger Western Europe able to stand up to the USSR and act as a real partner of the United States. Bonn also recognized that the failure of the negotiations would benefit the Soviets, produce economic stagnation and political conflict in Western Europe, and conceivably bring a Labour government to power in London. The German foreign ministry assumed that Labour would be even softer toward the USSR than the Conservatives had been, whereas it hoped that entry into the Common Market would help bring Macmillan into line on dealing with the communists. Failure of the negotiations would "have serious consequences for the unity of both Europe and the free world."[62] The Auswärtiges Amt thus worked both to protect the integrity of the Common Market and exhibit the necessary flexibility to enable Britain to join the Six.

The German negotiators supported the French on most of the technical issues, even though they would have preferred to be more flexible had not the need to form a common front among the Six limited their autonomy. They agreed that the entry conditions must not endanger the community. However, they trusted Heath and believed that the negotiations could succeed quickly if the Six established a common position that the British could accept. Bonn expected Britain to make most of the concessions and was committed to maintaining the "essentials" of the Treaty of Rome, but it did not rule out minor modifications. The foreign ministry argued that there were no problems "that could not be solved if the political will for full British membership were present."[63] The Germans did adhere to the French argument that the development of the Common Market and the wider relations among the Six must not be slowed by the Brussels negotiations.[64] They insisted that Britain's demands for special conditions must be restricted to transitional arrangements and that there be no permanent exemptions from the Treaty of Rome. They also preferred to focus on the United Kingdom alone and deal with other countries afterward. The EFTA neutrals would have to take their chances in the GATT or the OECD. Only those Commonwealth members whose level of development was comparable to the French overseas territories and former colonies already linked to the Common Market could have special ties with Europe. The Germans supported France and the United States in insisting that the United Kingdom phase out all its special economic ties with the rest. The Germans hoped that Britain, if allowed to maintain limited economic ties with some Commonwealth countries within a European forum, as the French did with their former colonies in Africa, would accept the rules of the Common Market without having to make a stark choice between Europe and the Commonwealth.[65]

The ministry of economics disagreed with many of the positions of the Auswärtiges Amt, which led the German delegation in Brussels. Because Erhard and his subordinates had long favored the creation of a large and loose free trade area, they favored the broadest possible expansion of the Common Market, including the neutrals. Erhard supported the British demands to work out an arrangement with all the EFTA countries before the United Kingdom joined the Six and his ministry advocated sweeping technical concessions in order to guarantee that the negotiations succeeded.[66] Erhard, who emphasized the political advantages of British entry, especially the strengthening of Western Europe and dealing a setback to the USSR, urged the Six to make the requisite economic sacrifices. He was also convinced that the Commonwealth need not be dismantled.[67] Because Erhard viewed Britain as a crucial ally in his struggle for a more open, less French-dominated Europe, he supported the British argument that the negotiations must balance the needs of the community with those of the countries seeking to join it.[68] The Auswärtiges Amt and the ministry of economics remained divided through most of the Brussels negotiations.

In Washington, the conditional British application raised concerns. Kennedy supported British entry, but worried that the "economic effect on the United States" might be "very serious."[69] On the other hand, George Ball emphasized that "detailed State Department study has shown that the net effect of European economic integration will be to expand rather than diminish United States industrial exports." Similarly, "the net effect of British adherence to the Common Market should be favorable to [U.S.] industrial trade." Although the CAP would be more likely to damage U.S. exports than the industrial CET, the United States could expect Britain to move the CAP in a less protectionist direction once it was inside the Common Market. The reservations of the American public, business, Congress, and other government departments regarding the Common Market centered on European protectionism, and Britain could be expected to make the group more open. Ball also reassured Kennedy that the United States could prevent Britain from extending its Commonwealth preferences to Europe, which was the "principal danger to United States trading interests involved in the British move to adhere to the Common Market." The United States would tolerate nothing more than a transitional Common Market–Commonwealth arrangement. Finally, Ball suggested that the round of impending GATT tariff reductions would solve any specific economic problems created by Britain's Common Market admission and serve as another means to promote trade liberalization.[70]

Nevertheless, Ball and other American policy makers were alarmed over the special conditions attached to the British application. Ball hoped that Washington could use the OECD, as well as discreet bilateral contacts with London and the Six, to make U.S. views known to all and protect American interests behind the scenes. He was confident that the United States could ease the British away from their unrealizable ambitions, pressuring them to be more flexible but also supporting them in the negotiations. It was clear after the Kennedy–de Gaulle meetings in May–June 1961 that France would be the chief obstacle, and Britain would need U.S. support to rally the Five to pressure de Gaulle to change his mind. The United States assured the Five that Britain was strongly committed to Common Market entry and urged them to help reconcile the British and French positions.[71] An internal State Department memorandum listed the results the

United States expected from the negotiations: a low CET, no maintenance or extension of Commonwealth preferences, no new discrimination, no steps toward a European free trade area, no neutral or anti-supranational countries in the Common Market, and no purely economic "association" with the Common Market for any country. Ball summed up these ideas: "Our efforts must be directed at assuring [the success of the negotiations] while at the same time assuring that our economic interests, which are consistent with those of the Free World as a whole, are protected."[72] The Americans hoped that the British would accept the Treaty of Rome unchanged and that in return the Six would offer Britain generous transition arrangements.[73]

While the Americans constantly sought to make their goals as clear as they could to the Brussels participants, the French worked to make their own political views on the British application as opaque as possible. De Gaulle's strategy was to prolong the negotiations and to keep foreign leaders guessing. Generally regarded as the stumbling block to any agreement, the French proceeded as if the outcome were wide open. De Gaulle made no secret of his doubts concerning Britain's desire and ability to join Europe, but did not disclose the conclusions he drew. At a press conference in September 1961, the French leader seemed cautiously supportive of the British application. He noted that the Six "have wanted other countries, and in particular Great Britain, to join the Treaty of Rome, to assume the obligations involved in it and, I think, to obtain the advantages deriving therefrom."[74] However, at every opportunity de Gaulle stressed the mass of technical difficulties to be resolved. His basic formula was that Britain could join Europe "someday," but only "on the same conditions" as all the existing members.[75] Privately, he hoped and believed that this event would be many years away. He was convinced that the British sought to bring the entire Commonwealth into the Common Market and transform it into a loose global arrangement under joint British-American leadership.[76]

The British, realizing that de Gaulle's views were crucial to the outcome of the negotiations, tried to develop arguments to move him. Macmillan then floated these ideas with the French leader during their bilateral meetings, which were held at approximately six-month intervals throughout the negotiations. The British knew from previous experience that France's technical negotiators could only be moved by orders from de Gaulle.[77] They carefully monitored the French reaction to Heath's opening statement in Brussels and to the special conditions they sought. They observed the initial disarray in the Quai d'Orsay, which seemed unsure how to handle the negotiations, and concluded that this explained France's reluctance to make any significant concessions. Some British observers hoped that de Gaulle would maintain an open mind, while others suspected that he had ordered the Quai d'Orsay to stall in Brussels in order to delay Britain's entry so that France would have more time to shape the community.[78] In either case, the British were aware of de Gaulle's two primary concerns, the economic impact on France and the effects on French leadership in Europe, and they knew how difficult it would be to sway him. Officials in the Quai d'Orsay informed the British that they "recognized that it [the community] would not be quite the same animal when [Britain] entered. What they feared was that it would not be an animal of the same species."[79] These French diplomats warned the British that they must convince de Gaulle that the United Kingdom had no intention of transforming the community and that Britain could be a part of both the Commonwealth and the community without damaging the latter. The British concluded that if their efforts to persuade de Gaulle failed, they would have to avoid "giving the French any obvious opportunities for obstruction" and force the technical discussions along until they progressed so far that de Gaulle would find it impossible to "put the whole machine into reverse."[80] Both sides felt that time was on their side. The British were wrong.

In their first meeting, in November 1961, Macmillan tried to sway de Gaulle by portraying Britain as a potential partner in all his European plans, including containing Germany, blocking supranationalism, and building a strong Western European bloc to balance both the Soviets and the Americans. He insisted that "when it comes to economics, a deal is always possible" and that it would be "an advantage for Europe to be able to extend its influence to more of Africa and to the Commonwealth." Macmillan assured de Gaulle that Britain's special conditions could be met without damaging the Common Market. On the other hand, Macmillan hinted at dark consequences if the talks failed: "If Europe wishes to rebuild Charlemagne's empire, then it can defend itself. [Britain] will turn to the United States and the Commonwealth." De Gaulle, as always, questioned the ability of the United Kingdom to accept the system built by the Six and insisted that all the technical issues must be hammered out. He would not allow Britain to slide into Europe on the cheap. De Gaulle already began to prepare the British for failure by stating that such an outcome would be no particular tragedy and that interim solutions to European trade problems could be found until such time as Britain had really changed enough to join the Common Market without reservation. The Quai d'Orsay had coached de Gaulle to keep Macmillan guessing on his ultimate intentions as long as possible since it would be dangerous for French interests if Macmillan received a clearly positive or negative impression.[81]

As a result of de Gaulle's deliberate ambiguity, Macmillan overestimated the French leader's goodwill toward Britain. He believed that de Gaulle needed only to be convinced that British membership was technically possible and would create a positive "new equilibrium" in the European community.[82] This was a common British misapprehension, that de Gaulle and the French accepted

Britain's entry in the abstract but were apprehensive and inflexible over the technical arrangements.[83] Throughout most of 1962 many British leaders cherished the illusion that de Gaulle remained neutral on their application and could be swayed by pressure or inducements from Britain or the Five. The difficulty was how to do this, since the Foreign Office considered de Gaulle "in many ways a throwback to Louis XIV [toward whom] no ordinary approach would be any good."[84] British optimism gradually dissipated as the realization grew that de Gaulle was actually dragging out the negotiations to force the United Kingdom to take the blame for their failure.[85] The British government was determined to stay the course and hoped to compel the French either to acquiesce or openly veto the application and incur all the blame. As late as autumn 1962, British leaders, still believing that de Gaulle would not risk a veto, continued to insist on their determination to join the Six and that the negotiations would succeed. The Foreign Office was prepared to inform the French that Britain "would [become] thoroughly nasty if there is any sign of the final stages of the negotiations being unnecessarily dragged out."[86]

The British considered France's condition that they must fully accept the Treaty of Rome without any changes to be a smoke screen. As Macmillan put it, "This [insistence on total British acceptance of the Treaty of Rome] is the parrot phrase of the French. But it is a fraudulent phrase and they know it. The price of wheat, the facilities for foreigners, including the Commonwealth, to import foodstuffs, 'deficiency payments' in British agriculture, tariffs on raw materials and other points on which the French are obstinate are not in the Treaty of Rome."[87] London reaffirmed its adherence to the treaty and accused Paris of demanding that the community recognize the primacy of French national interests, elevating these to the level of principle and refusing to make any concessions whatsoever.[88] But the British watched helplessly as the Six continued to reach purportedly common positions that reflected the intransigent French stance.

Throughout the negotiations, British leaders considered alternative means to enter the Common Market and avoid difficult concessions. As far back as Macmillan's "Grand Design" in January 1961, they had hoped to bribe the French with tripartite or nuclear concessions. The prospects of U.S. acceptance of such a deal, however, were never good and they became worse as Franco-U.S. relations deteriorated in 1962.[89] Moreover, it seemed that de Gaulle would not rise to the bait in any case, not only because he opposed such a deal in principle, but also because he was gradually abandoning tripartism and focusing entirely on his independent nuclear program.[90]

Britain's situation grew bleaker when Adenauer joined de Gaulle's opposition. By mid-1962 the chancellor had become frustrated by Britain's role in the derailment of the political union, concerned that Britain's special demands would dilute the Common Market, and angered by London's wider European and East-West policies, particularly its willingness to make concessions to the Soviets on Berlin.[91] All this gradually dissipated the lingering goodwill Adenauer had once held, particularly during the free trade area negotiations, for British entry into Europe. De Gaulle's Anglophobia also played a part. As Franco-German ties grew closer, the chancellor increasingly accepted de Gaulle's view of the United Kingdom as a divisive, external force in European affairs. Beginning in the summer of 1962 Adenauer made a number of public statements against the British application that raised apprehension in London and a furor in Germany.[92]

Although he continued to pay lip service to Britain's value to Europe, by August Adenauer was firmly against the conditional application. He accused the British of seeking to bring in the entire Commonwealth and demanding a privileged status in the Common Market. He rejected the assurances of the Auswärtiges Amt that the negotiations were progressing and dismissed its charges that France was at fault for their slowness. Although denying that he had made a final decision, the chancellor made it clear that Germany's national interests depended, above all, on maintaining the Paris-Bonn relationship. British entry would not only disrupt this partnership and weaken European political and economic unity, but might drive France to seek an entente with the USSR. Following the Gaullist line, Adenauer conjured up the menace of a horde of new members, including Japan, which would swamp the Common Market. Referring to the pound's weakness, he claimed that the Six would have to waste their own resources to prop up the British currency and economy. He also warned that even if Macmillan succeeded in bringing Britain in, the next Labour government would probably withdraw. Finally, he raised the alarm that his own government might fall if it conceded too much to the United Kingdom.[93]

Outwardly, the German government continued to support British entry, but it was now divided, and Adenauer worked actively against a successful outcome in Brussels. The Auswärtiges Amt, which resisted the chancellor's negativism, increased its efforts to make the negotiations succeed. During the autumn of 1962 Adenauer questioned whether Britain's parliamentary system and legal practices were compatible with a lasting commitment to the Common Market or anything else, claiming that he feared Parliament would retain the power to "renounce the Rome treaty and to reject community regulations" at any time.[94] When the Auswärtiges Amt and ministry of economics strongly disagreed, a full-blown struggle over the direction of German policy developed. "Germany's interests must be our top priority," argued Adenauer, "ahead of the interests of the EEC in its current form and ahead of British interests," ignoring the fact that the debate in Bonn was precisely about the definition of Germany's interests.[95] Schroeder minimized all the technical difficulties that ostensibly worried the chancellor, but could not overcome his hostility to the United Kingdom.[96] Adenauer's opponents urged London to maintain its course, tried to convince de Gaulle of the futility of his and Adenauer's negativism, and rallied support in Germany and Europe for British entry. As Adenauer fell ever more into de Gaulle's orbit, his critics became convinced that British entry was also necessary to restore balance to German policy.[97]

The British had counted on the Germans, even more than the Americans, since it was "they who [would] have to put pressure on the French," and they gave Bonn numerous assurances that they would play a full part in Europe and that their special needs would not endanger the Common Market.[98] They were soon disappointed. Although the Germans expressed their goodwill and London was convinced that it was genuine on the part of all save Adenauer, a divided Bonn provided minimal concrete support.[99] Between July and October 1962 Macmillan appealed directly to Adenauer with a combination of promises, threats, and even flattery: "I have felt that you agreed with me that Britain's participation represents as it were the other half of the pattern of European Unity with which your name will ever be associated."[100] When this effort failed and the chancellor turned openly against them, the British tried to rally support from the Auswärtiges Amt, the Bundestag, and the German public.[101] In late 1962, London's key allies were Erhard and Schroeder, and it still hoped to isolate Adenauer and pressure de Gaulle.[102]

The British also found the Americans unhelpful. They had kept Washington informed on the Brussels negotiations in the hope that the United States would support them on the key technical issues and that the Six would follow the American lead.[103] The British tried to convince the Americans on the Commonwealth and the EFTA and that the French were seeking to "keep [Britain] out of the Empire of Charlemagne," but failed to move Washington or persuade the Kennedy administration to pressure the Six, and especially de Gaulle, for concessions.[104] Macmillan was baffled by America's refusal to support the British technical positions for the sake of the larger European and Atlantic goals the two countries shared, but he never entirely gave up. Even at the very end of the negotiations, when de Gaulle's opposition became open, the British counted on the United States to prevent a French veto.

The American position changed little during the fifteen months of negotiations in Brussels. The United States observed developments and privately reminded the participants of its interests, but rarely intervened directly. Because the United States intended to conduct negotiations with the enlarged Common Market in a round of GATT tariff reductions after the Brussels talks were complete, the longer the negotiations dragged on, the more Washington saw its own plans for a wider Atlantic economic program falter. George Ball feared that "too long a delay would increase the political problems for the British government."[105] Yet despite this desire for speed, the United States would not simply ignore the technical issues as the British wished. The Americans opposed the admission of the EFTA neutrals, because they could not accept the political responsibilities of Common Market membership. Ball was convinced that any form of "association" for the neutrals would not only constitute blatant economic discrimination against third countries, but also "impair the effectiveness of the EEC as a step towards European unity," thereby defeating the entire American purpose for supporting European integration from the outset. The Americans understood that one of the reasons the British wanted the neutrals in was precisely to help them dilute the organization. This British-American debate was still unresolved in January 1963 when de Gaulle's veto made it moot.[106]

Throughout most of the Brussels negotiations the de facto Franco-American alliance that had existed on issues of European economic organization ever since the days of the British free trade proposals in the 1950s continued to serve the interests of both countries. Despite latent fears of a British-French deal, the Americans generally counted on the French to protect American political and economic interests by insisting on the integrity of the Treaty of Rome and preventing risky compromises that would either lead to new economic discrimination or damage the chances of European political integration. In return, Paris could count on the support of Washington on all the major issues of principle in Brussels.[107] However, as the negotiations progressed, American observers began to fear that de Gaulle opposed British entry into the Common Market under any circumstances and would not allow it to come about.[108] Frustrated British officials informed the Americans that they believed political motives, not economic or legalistic orthodoxy, lay behind the inflexible French negotiating positions.[109]

By the spring of 1962 Kennedy and Rusk suspected that the French were indeed using technical arguments to cloak their political opposition to Britain, but were uncertain how to deal with this potentially fatal obstacle.[110] In time, the United States became certain that the French were sabotaging the negotiations while avoiding the blame for their failure. As noted in earlier chapters, it was in mid-1962 that U.S. leaders became truly alarmed at de Gaulle's European and Atlantic policies and began to consider ways to counter him. However, Washington found it difficult to challenge de Gaulle on this particular issue because it supported many of the French technical positions. Moreover, the Americans correctly judged that de Gaulle "probably regards with some suspicion our motives in urging U.K. inclusion in Europe" and that any overt U.S. pressure to facilitate British entry might backfire and make the French leader even more stubborn.[111] The United States thus limited itself to verbal support, with Ball and Kennedy arguing that Britain, which was "an element of disintegration" outside the Common Market, was prepared "to reverse four hundred years of policy towards the continent" and would become an element of cohesion on the inside and increase the stature of the group in the eyes of the Soviets.[112]

The United States was also reluctant to single out the French as the villains because it knew that the British too were deliberately inflexible. The Americans knew that Britain might try to enter Europe at little political or economic cost via some sort of political-military-nuclear deal with the French that would endanger American interests, the cohesiveness of the Common Market, and Germany's adherence to the West. Thus the United States could not wholeheartedly support the British or attack the French, who, regardless of their motives, were the main defenders of the Common Market.[113] Instead, the Americans attempted to convince the Five, particularly the Germans, not to go along with any Gaullist efforts to exclude Britain from Europe for political reasons.[114] In the autumn of 1962 both Rusk and National Security Adviser McGeorge Bundy attempted to counter Adenauer's doubts and fears on Britain, which had a remarkable similarity to de Gaulle's. Bundy reported, "I did what I could, but the chancellor obviously believes that juvenile Americans simply do not understand Europe." The Americans could only take solace from the fact that "the chancellor [was] almost alone in [his] suspicions" of Britain.[115] Washington hoped that if de Gaulle and Adenauer remained isolated, they might be forced to relent if the British dropped their special conditions and the technical negotiations in Brussels succeeded.[116]

Throughout 1962 the British pushed for speed because they now knew time was working against them. In March Heath tried to expedite the negotiations by calling for an end to the preliminary discussions and setting an autumn deadline for an outline agreement that would enable the United Kingdom to join in 1963.[117] A confident Heath assured the cabinet that Britain could capitalize on the deadlock among the Six on the French political union proposal.[118] However, this advantage failed to materialize, because de Gaulle lost interest in a political union and the Six were determined to maintain a common front in Brussels.[119] By the autumn Heath offered significant agricultural and Commonwealth concessions to speed the talks, but the Six still rejected the generous transitional arrangements that the British demanded.[120]

Domestic obstacles increasingly complicated the British government's task. To rally public support and prevent opposition, the government had emphasized the economic benefits of admission while downplaying the political aspects. Unfortunately, this tactic backfired. It prevented the government from rallying much public enthusiasm for the application, and the technical approach only gave its opponents concrete issues on which to attack it. Labour, which turned against the application in the latter half of 1962, seized on the loss of sovereignty and the loosening of Commonwealth ties.[121] A plurality in opinion polls favored the application throughout, but support decreased markedly from mid-1962 and the public increasingly favored a referendum on the issue before Britain joined. Poor performances by Tory candidates in by-elections and polls showing increasing support for Labour did not help matters. Parliamentary debates showed sharp differences both between the parties and within them. Most unions, media, and business organizations, save farming groups, were either neutral or supportive, but from mid-1962 all grew increasingly concerned on the terms of entry. Despite all this, Macmillan remained convinced that the public and Parliament would follow along if the talks were successful, and during the autumn conferences of the Commonwealth leaders and the Conservative party, he nominally retained his freedom to negotiate as he saw fit. At the same time, however, the worsening domestic front forced the British delegation to push even harder on many of its special demands.[122]

As Britain's domestic situation deteriorated and his own conflict with the United States escalated, de Gaulle became convinced of the necessity of blocking Britain's entry at all costs. He perceived America's support of the United Kingdom as a dangerous intrusion in Europe and British admission as the end of all his plans for Europe and NATO. Despite all the disagreements between Washington and London, he believed in a British-American conspiracy whereby the United Kingdom would recoup in the GATT round any economic concessions it might make in Brussels.[123] In return the British would ensure that the Common Market followed U.S. policies. If Britain became a member of the Common Market, "it would be a whole new world and there would be no more European Community."[124] De Gaulle's entire diplomacy would be ruined.

From mid-1962 de Gaulle moved against the British application on several fronts. First, he made a concerted effort to ensure Adenauer's support. In their meetings in 1962 he and the chancellor agreed that Britain could only join the Common Market on the same basis as the Six and could not be allowed to transform it by maintaining its Commonwealth ties. Adenauer simply dismissed the present British application: "If this country [Britain] presents a serious request for admission then it will be seriously examined." De Gaulle played on the chancellor's fears of a mass of new members and of an unwieldy Common Market unable to agree on anything.[125] However, during a trip to Germany in September, de Gaulle was made aware of the growing opposition to his, and Adenauer's, policy.[126] The Auswärtiges Amt informed the French that Adenauer's voice was no longer decisive on the Brussels negotiations and hinted that Germany might now link progress on internal Common Market developments with movement in the negotiations with Britain. The French also knew that the British were doing all they could to provoke German fears of a failure and stir opposition to Adenauer.[127] De Gaulle's desire to ensure that Germany sided with him in the end was one of the key factors behind the Franco-German treaty he signed with Adenauer in January 1963.[128]

De Gaulle also did all he could to encourage the British to abandon their application. The Quai d'Orsay still preferred that de Gaulle not state bluntly that France opposed British membership, since this would "lead to a premature crisis harmful to [French] interests," but at his two meetings with Macmillan in 1962 the French leader nevertheless hardened his tone to discourage the prime minister.[129] Having failed over the political union, he no longer had much to lose by provoking the Five. Prior to the first Franco-British summit of the year in June, de Gaulle informed Ambassador Dixon that he did not believe Britain capable of joining the Six. He portrayed Britain's special relationship with the United States as an overwhelming obstacle and stated that France would negotiate hard on every technical issue in order to defend the integrity of the Common Market.[130] This conversation, combined with six futile months of negotiations in Brussels, finally made the British aware of the extent of de Gaulle's obstruction and convinced them that Macmillan must apply new forms of persuasion. The Foreign Office debated whether de Gaulle's opposition served "to ensure that France is the dominating power in the new Europe" or to promote "the complete independence of Europe from the United States," but in either case, his doubts were now clear.[131]

De Gaulle and Macmillan met at the Chateau de Champs, outside Paris. Macmillan immediately went on the offensive. He stated that Britain accepted the Treaty of Rome and the Common Market in full and possessed the will and ability to adapt to them. He asserted that Britain's special conditions could be safely met by the Six and that Europe needed ties with the Commonwealth to increase its influence in the world. He promoted the "new equilibrium" idea for the European community, suggested that this equilibrium would make the political union possible, and promised that France and Britain could limit supranationalism and make Europe into an equal partner of the United States and a force able to stand up to the USSR. De Gaulle was impressed by Macmillan's obvious commitment to Common Market entry. He assured the prime minister that "if your admission proves feasible, we will not oppose it," but dismissed the prime minister's vision of a "new equilibrium" for the European community, stressed all the negative consequences of Britain's entry, and offered no concessions whatsoever. Macmillan could only reply lamely, "After all we have done, it is hard to be told that we are not needed."[132] The British failed to draw the appropriate conclusions, that de Gaulle opposed their admission under any circumstances, but they did realize that the French would prolong the negotiations to buy time for France to consolidate its hold on the Six and gain maximum British concessions. London still believed that de Gaulle would not dare to veto the British application and that the Five could pressure him to make concessions.[133]

De Gaulle, on the other hand, was even more convinced of the dangers of the British application based on Macmillan's clear determination to make the negotiations succeed. He feared that his strategy of burying the negotiations in technical details might not suffice to make the British withdraw. It seemed to the Quai d'Orsay that Macmillan and his government, who had so far triumphed over their domestic opponents, might yet be able to exploit the arcane Brussels negotiations to "take control of the long-term direction of the Common Market even before they join it." As more and more time elapsed, the French were not at all confident that they could maintain control over the Five in the face of a severe test engineered by London.[134]

At a special high-level planning session at the end of July 1962, the French government considered its options. Some officials suggested minor technical concessions to the British to maintain the unity of the Six, but the foreign ministry and Prime Minister Pompidou argued that it was in the French interest "that the [British] affair not succeed." Yet France "would not want to take responsibility for the rupture of negotiations. The best thing would be to ensure that they became lost in the sand. Then, down the road, some solution preferable to British entry into the Common Market could probably be found, perhaps in the form of association." De Gaulle agreed that the talks should be ended as soon as possible without France taking the blame: "If the negotiations must end in a failure, it would be best that we not be its sole authors." Despite the risks of last-minute British concessions, he ordered France's envoys to work actively to sabotage the deliberations via stringent demands. To mask the French tactics, Couve de Murville continued to assure foreign leaders that if the technical negotiations succeeded, then France would be obligated to allow the British to join the Common Market.[135]

By late 1962, deliberate French obstruction, combined with Britain's insistence on flexible agricultural conditions and long-term assurances for the Commonwealth, had brought the Brussels negotiations to a standstill. With the meetings limited to technical issues, other major topics, such as the arrangements with the EFTA or the necessary changes in the Brussels institutions, were set aside. Yet despite the deadlock, the Five seemed more committed than ever to British entry. Indeed, de Gaulle's moves to cement the Franco-German entente had only made Italy and Benelux more determined to bring in Britain. The division among the Six reinforced de Gaulle's suspicions of Britain's natural inclination to divide and conquer the continent by any means.[136] Sensing an impending crisis, the French sought to torpedo the negotiations without damaging their interests. The Quai d'Orsay hoped to take advantage of the growing countercurrent against the Common Market in the United Kingdom to force the British government to abandon its application.[137] Paris could confront London with the choice between conceding to the Six in Brussels and facing difficulties at home, or holding fast and causing the negotiations to fail. With another bilateral summit in December, de Gaulle planned to be more negative than ever and force Macmillan to give up. Fresh from his successes in parliamentary elections in November and in his referendum on the direct election of the president, which Ambassador Dixon felt gave him "what amounts to dictatorial powers," de Gaulle's domestic position was stronger than ever and he could afford to be increasingly blunt.[138]

At this summit, Macmillan decided to focus on the big issues and argue that the uncertainty in Western Europe must end before the Soviets posed another threat. He argued that success in the negotiations would give Europe a voice in global affairs and open up a vast field of potential Franco-British cooperation, whereas failure would lead the United Kingdom to reconsider its entire foreign policy. Success would restore progress to all areas of European development, including the political union, while failure would lead to general stagnation. The British also planned to make clear to de Gaulle that "association" was not an option: "No plan of this sort could of course meet our political objectives nor . . . is it likely that any form of association short of full membership could meet our economic needs."[139]

Despite such arguments, renewed hints at possible Franco-British nuclear cooperation, and Macmillan's talk of "independence and interdependence" for Europe in its relations with the United States, the British made no headway with de Gaulle. The French leader still rejected any package deal, deemed Britain incapable of joining the Common Market without transforming it, and announced that this was why the negotiations had stagnated. Also, de Gaulle finally admitted that he opposed Britain's entry because it would bring French dominance of Western Europe to an end: "At the heart of the Common Market, France carried considerable weight. If Great Britain entered, followed rapidly by the Norwegians, the Danes, [and] the Irish, who knows what would become of the Common Market and Europe itself?" A shocked Macmillan finally recognized that de Gaulle's opposition was a matter of principle.[140]

Faced with a French veto, London appealed to the Americans and the Five to pressure de Gaulle, doing all it could to isolate France in the hope of salvaging the negotiations.[141] A few days after the Franco-British summit, Macmillan met Kennedy at Nassau. Macmillan dismissed the French reaction to a new British-

American nuclear arrangement as unimportant ("the outcome of the Common Market negotiations would not be affected by decisions about nuclear delivery systems") and announced that the real issue in Brussels was whether the French were willing to give up their autarkic plans for Europe.[142] With no real chance of Common Market entry, Britain sought to shore up its relations with the United States.

The British, unprepared for failure in the Brussels negotiations, also explored alternative strategies. If the meetings collapsed, they wished both to ensure that they did so over an "international" issue such as the Commonwealth rather than a "domestic" one such as British agriculture. This would allow them to blame the French for the failure because they had endangered the Commonwealth and with it the entire free world. But the United Kingdom could not take a hostile stance toward the Common Market per se without alienating the United States and helping de Gaulle to push Western Europe in a Third Force direction. Instead, the British would focus their policy on the United States, the OECD, and GATT, maintaining close relations with the Five, and aiming for future entry into the Common Market. They would strengthen their ties with the Commonwealth and the EFTA, although neither offered a long-term solution to Britain's problems.[143]

Neither Washington nor Bonn was aware that failure was imminent. The German delegation in Brussels reported that the French had turned the talks into a Franco-British contest, with Germany and the Four forced to act as mediators, but the Auswärtiges Amt did not anticipate a de Gaulle veto and continued to study ways to overcome his obstruction and Adenauer's objections. Adenauer remained the odd man out in Bonn, totally devoted to the Franco-German entente, refusing to pressure the French to be more forthcoming, and warning his subordinates against forming "any front against the French delegation."[144]

Washington also continued to operate on the assumption that the Brussels negotiations would ultimately succeed. Despite de Gaulle's warnings and Adenauer's open opposition, the United States did not believe the two would risk the political consequences of a veto.[145] Kennedy and his advisers believed that the British would ultimately show the necessary flexibility to solve the technical issues. The State Department noted that "although it is clear that de Gaulle and many senior French officials are not enthusiastic about British entry, there is no indication that this will translate itself into [a] special effort to block British entry" and that "Adenauer's personal distrust of British intentions appears to be isolated."[146] The Americans encouraged Schroeder's resistance to Adenauer and acted cautiously at Nassau to avoid provoking de Gaulle. Ball warned that failure would bring an unreliable Labour government to power in Britain, alienate the United Kingdom from the continent, make the Common

Market more inward-looking, strain NATO, and endanger America's entire Atlantic agenda.[147] But the United States had no real fallback position. If the Brussels talks failed, then it would simply promote other portions of its Atlantic agenda.[148]

The Veto and After, January–December 1963

In late December or early January de Gaulle decided to end the Brussels negotiations. Having consolidated his domestic base, he wished once and for all to halt the British application before London and Washington pressured the Five to force France to surrender. The Nassau agreement confirmed de Gaulle's belief in British dependency on the United States and allowed Paris to claim that London had demonstrated its extra-European priorities once again. However, contrary to the myth promoted by the French, Nassau was not the cause of de Gaulle's veto but only offered the pretext to announce the decision he had already made.[149] With the technical negotiations stalled, de Gaulle seized the initiative to end them before the Five could start them moving again. On the eve of Adenauer's trip to Paris to sign the Franco-German cooperation agreement, de Gaulle hoped to confront Bonn with a choice between accepting his dictates on Britain or risking the entire Franco-German rapprochement.[150]

Taking advantage of his semiannual press conference on 14 January, de Gaulle announced that the Brussels negotiations must end. Britain was an insular, maritime, island country whose economy, particularly its agricultural and industrial interests, "differed profoundly from those of the other states of the continent." This was the reason why the United Kingdom had promoted alternatives to the existing community and why fifteen months of negotiations had produced so little progress. Britain was incapable of accepting the Treaty of Rome without altering it beyond all recognition and transforming the Common Market into a "colossal Atlantic Community under American dependence and leadership." Perhaps someday the United Kingdom would be willing and able to join the Six in creating a politically independent, economically self-sufficient Western Europe, but for now it would have to settle for some form of economic association "to safeguard trade."[151] It soon became apparent that an "association" between Britain and the Six meant nothing, because the French continued to insist that the only real options for Britain were full membership or total exclusion.[152] In Brussels the French delegation demanded an end to the talks.[153]

Britain's leaders were more surprised by de Gaulle's methods than the content of his remarks. Only days earlier Couve de Murville had assured Heath that if the technical negotiations succeeded then France would allow Britain to join the Common Market. Couve de Murville had even added that "he did not expect General de Gaulle at his press conference on Monday to make statements which might have the effect of bringing the Brussels negotiations to a halt."[154] London concluded that de Gaulle's strong domestic position, his confidence in the support of Adenauer, his ability to pressure the Five, and his desire to end the negotiations before any more progress was made had led him to conclude that now was the proper time to bring the Brussels conference to an end.[155] Nassau was merely a pretext.[156] When Couve de Murville tried to blame the "psychological" impact of Nassau for the press conference, the sarcastic Dixon reported back to London that he "thought it would be going a little far to suggest that the General should see a psychiatrist."[157] London rebutted de Gaulle's charges and hoped to ignore the press conference and push on with the Brussels negotiations. If the talks ended, the British intended to blame de Gaulle and to isolate him from the Five.[158] The British still counted on Adenauer to stand by them, if not out of conviction then because of domestic and American pressure.[159] To bolster the Five's resistance to France, they argued that the majority of the Common Market faced a choice between a large, open, multilateral Europe and de Gaulle's "rigid and old-fashioned" plans for a narrow, restrictive arrangement dominated by Paris.[160]

The French, who had expected that de Gaulle's announcement would suffice to end the talks, were disagreeably surprised when the British and the Five insisted they continue. De Gaulle's veto caused little difficulty at home, but it produced a mass of diplomatic problems. French public opinion had supported British entry, but after de Gaulle's veto it shifted to support him, as it did on many foreign policy issues. Even in the parliament and the media, most criticism was directed at de Gaulle's unilateral methods rather than his conclusions. The country as a whole accepted his argument that Britain was not ready to be part of Europe.[161] Unfortunately, things were not so simple on the international level. In Brussels, the German delegation, which had long resisted Adenauer's dictates, refuted all de Gaulle's charges and demanded further meetings.[162] Couve de Murville found himself isolated and forced to accept another round of ministerial meetings at the end of the month.[163] Thus, when Adenauer came to Paris, de Gaulle had stirred up a hornets' nest and weakened both Adenauer's domestic position and the Franco-German entente, all without ending the Brussels talks.[164]

De Gaulle won Adenauer over to his veto, but not the Auswärtiges Amt or Germany as a whole. Repeating his well-known objections, de Gaulle could easily convince Adenauer of the futility of further negotiations and the risks of admitting a Britain still closely tied to the United States.[165] To placate Bonn and smooth over his veto, de Gaulle proposed that the Commission conduct a review of the negotiations and examine the political and economic implications of British entry. This supposed compromise was a farce, however, as French diplomats confirmed when they feared that the Germans might take it seriously: "During the Paris meetings [with Adenauer], General de Gaulle agreed to an 'evaluation' [of the Brussels talks], but at no time to the establishment of any mechanism that would permit British entry."[166] The Auswärtiges Amt, disappointed with Adenauer's docility, viewed the failure of the Brussels negotiations as an unmitigated disaster. If de Gaulle's veto stood, it would revive the old Six-Seven conflict, loosen Europe's links with Britain, increase France's hegemonic pretensions, and encourage the Soviet Union. It seemed clear that de Gaulle sought to "separate and isolate the Federal Republic from its partners." His veto would likely bring an unreliable Labour government to power, sharply divide the Six, endanger Franco-German relations, and doom all hopes for a European political union and an Atlantic community.[167]

In Brussels in late January, France and its opponents disputed what was to happen next. The German delegation, holding firm against Adenauer, joined the Four and Britain in an effort to continue the negotiations. Schroeder, supported by Erhard, went openly against Adenauer's preference to end the negotiations quietly via de Gaulle's sham compromise. The French, facing a firm front, which was backed discreetly by Washington, failed to divert the talks to a long, inconclusive study by the Commission. Schroeder led the charge, in part to convince the British and Americans that Germany would not blindly follow French orders now that the Franco-German treaty had been signed.[168] While France wanted the negotiations suspended indefinitely and set no timetable for the Commission's study, Britain and the Five insisted on a quick investigation that would propose solutions to Britain and the Six and form the basis for further negotiations and British admission. When agreement proved impossible, the conference ended, since the French refused to negotiate further. An isolated France clearly bore the blame for the impasse.[169]

The United States had to adjust its European policy to the new situation. Contrary to American expectations, de Gaulle had revealed his political agenda and acknowledged that France would not accept Britain in Europe. A bitter George Ball compared de Gaulle's comments on European self-sufficiency in his press conference to the response of the Manchu Emperor Chien Lung when King George III sent an emissary to open British-Chinese trade relations: "The Celestial Empire possesses all things in prolific abundance and lacks no product within its borders. There is therefore no need to import the manufactures of outside barbarians in exchange for our own products."[170] Washington concluded that France had sabotaged the negotiations in order to eliminate the British challenge to its hegemony in Europe. It now saw de Gaulle's attacks on Britain as attacks on the United States. In the wake of de Gaulle's veto, Washington reviewed the whole range of its European and Atlantic policies but changed little. Secretary of State Rusk set the tone almost at once when he argued that the United States should, on the one hand, disregard negative French actions as much as it could and urge everyone else to act as independently of Paris as possible. On the other hand, Washington "should avoid fighting the French in those areas where they are cooperating" and "not block every line of policy we are now following toward France."[171]

This conclusion could not mask American disappointment at the defeat of Britain's application. Lingering hopes that the Five would stand up to de Gaulle and force him to reverse himself or that Adenauer's opponents in Germany could use the Franco-German treaty to force the chancellor to persuade de Gaulle to lift his veto had proven illusory.[172] The Kennedy administration rejected as counterproductive vague ideas circulating in Washington and among the Five on linking Britain's admission to the Common Market with other issues in order to force the French either to be reasonable or suffer total isolation. Ultimately Kennedy and Rusk realized the weakness of the American position and made the best of the situation. The United States would make sure the European deadlock did not become worse, ensure that Germany did not line up with France, and take no extreme actions to help the British.[173] The United States would consider ideas "around which 'good' Europeans could rally in opposition to de Gaulle" and promote its own Atlantic agenda, ensuring a positive European stance toward the GATT round and coordinating Western European economic policies to America's benefit. Without any master plan, Washington hoped for a pragmatic solution to Britain's entry in the indefinite future, since it was "unlikely that the British will be admitted to the Common Market as long as de Gaulle rules France."[174]

The infighting among the Six continued after the end of the Brussels negotiations. The French blamed Schroeder for betraying Adenauer's promises and the Auswärtiges Amt faulted de Gaulle.[175] Germany's diplomats accused Paris of issuing a political veto that had nothing to do with Britain's ability to enter the Common Market. In the process, de Gaulle had undermined the solidarity of the Six and the unity of the West. With the support of domestic opinion, the Auswärtiges Amt could now override Adenauer. The German foreign ministry was determined to maintain close relations with the United Kingdom until its entry into Europe became feasible, that is, when de Gaulle and his veto were removed from the equation. On the other hand, despite his comment to Heath that "I consider your failure to be my own," Schroeder resisted suggestions that Germany retaliate by obstructing further development of the Common Market, preferring to minimize the damage and prepare for Britain's ultimate admission instead.[176] The Auswärtiges Amt announced that it intended to consult the United Kingdom on all community issues. Such consultation was crucial to placate the Americans, the British, and the Four on the Franco-German treaty and facilitate its ratification by the Bundestag.[177] The foreign ministry wanted to maintain Britain's movement toward Europe and prevent a retreat into isolation, and it dismissed the idea of British "association" as an alternative.[178] Schroeder would now link issues of importance to the French, notably the CAP, with issues of importance to Germany, notably restoring contacts with the United Kingdom.[179]

Schroeder had strong support in the cabinet. The ministry of economics resented the fact that Paris had (ostensibly) rejected Britain as unfit for membership in the Common Market because of its special conditions, while it was France that had demanded and received a mass of special conditions, some transitional and some permanent, in the Treaty of Rome. Erhard challenged Adenauer with public attacks on de Gaulle. He suggested a British-German treaty to counter the Franco-German one and that the Five arrange their political and economic ties with the United Kingdom without France. When Adenauer protested, Erhard insisted, "The international trust I have built up in fifteen years of work for the creation of a peaceful, multilateral [European] order in cooperation with the U.S.A. is an asset for German policy, not a liability."[180] Germany's new defense minister, Kai-Uwe von Hassel, joined the list of Adenauer's critics advocating stronger British ties with Germany and the continent.[181]

Despite France's ostensible victory, the Quai d'Orsay anticipated possible reprisals by Britain or the Five. Some officials feared that the Five might either bring all the activities of the Common Market to a halt or leave the organization in favor of some arrangement with the United Kingdom. Rumors of plots circulated, suggesting that Britain would turn a willing Five against de Gaulle and the Franco-German treaty. The alarmed French ambassador in The Hague reported that "articles comparable to the very worst that appear in the British press can be found in Dutch newspapers every single day."[182] The Italians hinted darkly that if France did not reconsider its position on Britain, then Italy "would most likely have to reconsider its participation in the Common Market."[183] But when Schroeder hinted at linkage between German ratification of the bilateral treaty and French concessions on Britain, de Gaulle called the German bluff, correctly judging that Bonn would not endanger the treaty or the European communities for the sake of Britain.[184] Paris was relieved to learn that neither the Five nor the British had the desire or the determination to destroy the Common Market, even though they showed no intention of abandoning the goal of British entry.

The French concluded that the British, although shocked by de Gaulle's veto, had assumed no responsibility for the outcome. They did not expect the United Kingdom to launch any new European initiatives because of the upcoming 1964 elections. French diplomats insisted that while Britain was moving toward Europe, it remained unready to drop its conditions. After the "unhappy Brussels experience," things would be worse: "We are likely to see a long struggle for influence between Great Britain and France and the outcome is only likely to be in our favor if we make a supreme effort to maintain the cohesion of the Six."[185]

Like Bonn and Washington, London decided on a moderate response to de Gaulle's exclusion, generally avoiding recriminations and reprisals.[186] The British were disappointed with Adenauer's lack of support, concluding that American pressure on the chancellor had been too little, too late.[187] The Foreign Office derived consolation from the fact that de Gaulle's "domineering, dictatorial treatment" and his desire "to see the Common Market as a closely protected play-ground for [France]" had finally exposed his unbridled ambitions and the fact that he clearly bore the onus for the failure of the negotiations.[188] The British would now work closely with the United States, the Five, and the EFTA to resist the French leader. London hoped to cooperate with Washington on all European policy and all responses to de Gaulle, but it also intended to act more independent of the United States in NATO and elsewhere to prove its European credentials to the Five. The British rejected all proposals for association with the Common Market, which would necessitate more haggling with the French and still fall short of their political goals.[189] They expected little to happen until the French president left office. When that day came, Britain could join the Six and Western Europe could begin moving again.[190]

De Gaulle, although angered by the firestorm of protests, would make no concessions whatsoever. He chastised the Five for endangering European unity and accused the United States of promoting Britain's entry to expand its own influence in Europe. He rejected further formal contacts between the Six and the United Kingdom, seeing only dangers in meetings "between six governments that disagree with one another and a seventh that seeks to take advantage of their discord."[191] Paris also rejected the idea of a special status for the United Kingdom with the Common Market.[192] De Gaulle recognized that the Five wished to treat Britain as a virtual member and give it a voice in community affairs, which the French found both distasteful and dangerous. Aware that the Dutch and the Germans were maintaining close contacts with London, France refused every proposal for formal consultation between Britain and the Six and urged its partners to focus instead on internal issues, most notably the CAP and renewing arrangements with the French overseas territories and former colonies in Africa. The Quai d'Orsay feared that any concession on contacts would be interpreted among both the British and the Five as "proof that the bridges have not been burned, that negotiations continue, and that the United Kingdom could reasonably hope to join the Six in the near future."[193]

Although the Five hesitated to call the Common Market into question, they proved less compliant than France had expected and refused to let the consultation issue drop. Couve de Murville accused the Germans of playing up the matter simply as an excuse not to implement the CAP and wondered aloud "whether Bonn was really prepared to implement the Common Market or, on the contrary, if its intention was not to dilute it into something larger."[194] It was only in July that the problem was finally settled. To avoid another deadlock in the community, de Gaulle bypassed the lame-duck Adenauer and worked out a compromise with Erhard and Schroeder. The French agreed to quarterly ministerial meetings between Britain and the Six in the WEU on the condition that they not be used to revive the British application or to interfere with the internal affairs of the Six. The Germans agreed that there would be no discussion of technical economic issues unless the Six had worked out common positions in advance and, in return, the French accepted the occasional participation of the Commission. The Auswärtiges Amt had won this round, since there would be regular meetings, open discussion of all major issues, and a link to Brussels through the Commission.[195] With this victory, the Erhard-Schroeder team shifted to a long-term view of Britain's relations with the continent. Bonn would support a second U.K. application when the British felt the time was right and hoped that London would move toward Europe and avoid falling back on the United States and the Commonwealth in the meantime.[196]

The Foreign Office welcomed the use of the WEU for maintaining contacts, especially because France had no veto in the organization and because it would be an "even more serious step for France to frustrate the normal operation of WEU than for her to block United Kingdom admission to the EEC."[197] London planned to use the WEU meetings to shadow the economic and political consultations of the Six. But, however much they appreciated the efforts of the Five on their behalf and valued the WEU, the British understood that the real battles with de Gaulle would now occur within NATO and the GATT.[198] Britain's policy toward Western Europe became one of "wait and see." London knew that although de Gaulle had seriously alienated his partners, Britain would be unable to gain any immediate benefits. Until French policy changed, London would use the Americans and the Five to maintain pressure on Paris.[199]

American leaders, although dubious on its impact, supported the use of the WEU as one more means to maintain pressure on de Gaulle. Washington noted that "British entry into the Common Market, while important and desirable, has never been the first object of our policy in Europe, nor even a matter in which we could expect to have decisive influence."[200] The United States rapidly shifted its efforts to issues where its influence could be applied more directly and where some progress was still possible, particularly the GATT round. It encouraged the renewal of British-American ties as well as a stronger British role in Europe, whether in the WEU or the Multi-Lateral Nuclear Force (MLF). This would keep the European door open for Britain and prevent de Gaulle from moving the Common Market in an autarkic direction.[201]

Once the issue of contacts was finally resolved, the French followed a mixed policy toward Britain. They welcomed conciliatory gestures from London to reduce tensions among the Six and facilitate progress in the Common Market, but they rejected any ruses to reverse the Brussels outcome.[202] For example, when the British offered the lure of nuclear cooperation in return for lifting the veto, the French rejected the idea out of hand. Not only was Paris consistent in its insistence on the technical requirements of membership, but after Nassau it doubted Britain's independence to conduct any meaningful nuclear cooperation. This did not stop Paris from using the prospect of such a Franco-British nuclear force to undermine the MLF and separate the United Kingdom from the United States.[203] Similarly, Paris adopted a more positive view toward the GATT round as a means to weaken London's argument that Franco-British disagreements reflected conflicting desires for a closed versus an open Europe.[204]

Conclusion

In retrospect, London concluded that its application had little or no chance of success. The British realized that de Gaulle had opposed them throughout, but they failed to acknowledge that the half-hearted, technical, conditional nature of their application had greatly facilitated his sabotage.[205] Had the United Kingdom been willing and able to drop most or all of its conditions, admittedly an unlikely prospect, it would have been much more difficult, if not impossible, for de Gaulle to keep it out. The tenacity of the British adherence to their demands suggested that de Gaulle was not incorrect in his belief that the United Kingdom still had a long way to evolve toward the continent. In a final revealing reprise in late 1963, the British briefly hoped that they might yet enter Europe at minimal cost. During another bitter debate between France and the Five over the CAP, the Foreign Office and the cabinet entertained a brief hope that the Common Market would explode, allowing the United Kingdom to move into the void, lead the Five away from de Gaulle, and build the kind of loose, free-trade arrangement it had favored since the mid-1950s. When the Six managed to hold together, Britain acknowledged that it had to operate "on the assumption that the EEC will remain in being" and that coming to terms with the Common Market would be a long-term process.[206] The government insisted that there would be no second application without prior assurances from all of the Six.

Paris concluded that it had won a battle against the British effort to break up the Six, but believed that the long-term British goal of isolating France and leading a weak and diffuse Western Europe remained unchanged. Although Britain had beaten a strategic withdrawal, it could be counted on to sabotage progress among the Six, such as a revival of the political union initiative, and to promote the EFTA as a liberal and outward-looking institution to be contrasted with "autarkic" French policy. On closer inspection, even France's limited victory seems pyrrhic. De Gaulle's veto isolated France from Western Europe and doomed his vision of a Western European political and economic bloc independent of the United States. The victory had been won at the price of alienating Benelux and Italy and committing them wholeheartedly to eventual British entry, damaging Franco-German relations (and bringing a hostile Erhard to power), and angering the United States. Having burned its bridges with all its allies, France soon had no alternative but to extend its unilateral policy toward the Soviet bloc and the nonaligned world.

Washington's policy had supported the entry of its British ally into Europe to promote wider European unity and Atlantic cooperation, but without changing the basic supranational nature of the Common Market. The impact of American support for the British Common Market application and its effects on American interests were mixed. Washington and London never coordinated their goals well and this limited the degree to which the United States could support British admission. The Americans, along with the Five, wanted to build an Atlantic Community, based on a cohesive Common Market, which excluded any role for the neutrals and the Commonwealth. The British, who also supported Atlantic Community, intended to dilute the Common Market by adding the neutrals and the Commonwealth, and obtaining a privileged status that would allow them to maintain all their wider interests and avoid any exclusive commitment to Europe. Because of this contradiction, neither the United States nor the Five was willing to force the British application past de Gaulle's barrier. After the veto, Washington followed a more pragmatic policy, hoping that the trade negotiations beginning in 1964 would help heal the breach between the United Kingdom and the Common Market. Britain's admission would have to await de Gaulle's departure, but there was no reason European and Atlantic developments in other areas should halt as a result. The United States would now have to influence the Common Market directly, since the British could not serve as a proxy.

In Germany, the failed British application widened the fissures over European policy. Since 1955, Adenauer, Erhard, and the Auswärtiges Amt had debated the relative merits of an alignment with France or Britain, a European or an Atlantic focus, and the Common Market or a wider and looser arrangement. While the British application increased Adenauer's inclination toward the former, all the other German leaders became committed supporters of the United Kingdom and Atlantic cooperation to balance France and the Common Market. De Gaulle's veto ended any lingering hopes of replacing the Common Market with a wider free trade arrangement, but it also ended the Adenauer era and faced de Gaulle with committed opponents of his European schemes. The new German government realized that Britain's entry was a long-term prospect. It waited patiently but acted far more assertively toward France than had its predecessor.

For Britain, the events of 1963 reflected its slow turning toward Europe without making a clear decision to join. With each of its successive proposals to Europe between 1955 and 1963, London refused to choose between the continent and its wider interests. This hesitation allowed de Gaulle to block the British time and again and prevented the United Kingdom from obtaining sufficient support from others to overcome him. However, the effects of de Gaulle's vetoes changed over time. When de Gaulle rejected the FTA in 1958, no tears were shed outside Britain, but in 1963 the Americans were disappointed, the Germans and the Five disgruntled, and the French alarmed at the price of their victory. The Americans had made the mistake of counting on British entry into Europe as a pillar of their policy and paid the price. Their identification with the British application worked against the interests of both countries. Yet it was de Gaulle who foolishly sacrificed the de facto Franco-American partnership against British efforts to dilute the Common Market, which had served French interests since 1955. There is little doubt that de Gaulle was correct that Britain was not ready to be a full part of Europe. Had he worked to maintain U.S.-Six solidarity on demanding an unconditional British commitment to Europe and let the technical negotiations play themselves out instead of unilaterally terminating them, the Americans, Germans, and others could not, would not, have resisted. But because de Gaulle's real motive was not British shortcomings but French ambitions, he ended up isolating himself, destroying all his European plans, prolonging the negotiations, and increasing the support for Britain in Europe and the United States. He also allowed the British to escape a reexamination of their own policy and guaranteed that as soon as he left office (if not sooner), they would try again.

Finally, the failure of the British entry negotiations and the nature of that failure also had a decisive impact on the development of the European community itself. While the traditional view is that it was the 1965 "empty chair" episode in which de Gaulle sought to unilaterally block further supranationalism that ended the idealistic early days of the community, that end in fact came in 1963 with his veto of Britain's membership. While hard bargaining and trade-offs among competing national interests had been present from the outset, there had also been a degree of idealism and mutual sacrifice evident in the 1950s. But when de Gaulle broke this understanding in 1963 by focusing solely on France's national interests, his partners responded in kind and the horse trading that has since been a defining characteristic of the community came into being. De Gaulle's veto also froze the expansion and development of the community for nearly a decade. Until the British membership issue was resolved, no other countries could join the community. Similarly, since France would not compromise on Britain or supranationalism, its partners saw no reason to make concessions on French priorities such as the financing of the CAP. Only de Gaulle's resignation in 1969 would make it possible for a new generation of leaders to undo this tangle and begin moving the community forward on all fronts. This first effort to expand the community also left its mark on all subsequent negotiations with prospective new members, from the southern expansion of the 1980s to the applications of Central and Eastern European countries after the Cold War. To avoid a repeat of the British experience, applicants have insisted that the community accept their membership in principle in advance, while the French have continued to express their doubts on expansion by focusing on technical agricultural issues and questioning the readiness of candidate countries to make the sacrifices to join the community without reservation.

CHAPTER SEVEN

ADENAUER, DE GAULLE, AND THE

FRANCO-GERMAN TREATY OF 1963

[My] entire nature inclines me to work for a very close and lasting German-French friendship. [I] feel drawn to France because, as a Rhinelander, [I] come from an environment
that, like France itself, has its deepest historic roots in the Roman empire. The deep
changes in every aspect of the human existence, in art, education, and agriculture that
the Roman occupation on the Rhine brought with it produced people who feel linked to
the entire Latin world, whether they like it or not. From out of this old tradition developed political habits that differ fundamentally from those of North Germany and that
are characterized above all by a greater capacity for understanding other peoples and a
greater readiness for compromise. However, all of this does not mean that [I] am ready
to turn the Federal Republic into a French satellite state. France must learn to view us
as a partner and friend with equal rights and responsibilities.
—Konrad Adenauer, comments to Herbert Blankenhorn, 6 February 1961

The Franco-German Relationship
between July 1960 and April 1962

The entente between France and Germany, or, more precisely, between de
Gaulle and Adenauer, that had gradually developed after their first meetings in
1958 remained one of the key factors in European and Atlantic relations during
the five years that followed. As discussed in Chapter 3, the two leaders considered this special relationship the key to all Western European developments and
sought to use it to advance all their goals. There were setbacks between 1958 and
1960, but after the Rambouillet meeting in July 1960, Franco-German relations
solidified for the next two and a half years.

Between July 1960 and April 1962 the Franco-German relationship was eclipsed
by the negotiations for de Gaulle's political union. But de Gaulle viewed the bilateral entente as both the key to making the negotiations succeed and a fallback
option should they fail. He believed that if the French and Germans could reach
common positions on the central issues, their partners would follow along.

During the negotiations de Gaulle made concessions in those areas where the Germans insisted on them, but held firm when he believed Adenauer would follow his lead. He scaled back the political union in deference to German concerns over its impact on the Common Market and Atlantic alliance, but remained steadfast in his opposition to British involvement since he believed that Adenauer shared his views on the United Kingdom and felt confident that the chancellor could resist domestic pressures to alter this stance.

Above all, de Gaulle tried to gain Adenauer's adherence to his European and Atlantic conceptions and, since he knew that Adenauer could not remain chancellor much longer, de Gaulle also sought to assure the continuity of German policy after his departure.[1] Because his main rival was the United States, he fed Adenauer's doubts on its reliability. Despite their frequent denials, de Gaulle and his entourage viewed influence over Germany as a zero-sum game in which any advance for the United States constituted a setback for France, and vice versa. This was a highly delicate contest. On the one hand, de Gaulle used Bonn's fears and ambitions to gather support for his challenge to U.S. dominance, but on the other hand, he had to avoid the danger of arousing the ambitions of his powerful neighbor and frightening the rest of Europe. The Quai d'Orsay argued that France had to guard against anything that could "slowly move Germany back toward a nationalism that, even [if it were now] baptized 'European,' had always been bad for the continent."[2] Despite occasional cries of alarm from the foreign ministry, de Gaulle believed he could safely tutor the Germans in a long-term "independent" foreign policy consisting of partnership with France and aloofness from the United States. The Franco-German entente was also the key to keeping Britain out of Europe. The de Gaulle–Adenauer front thwarted London's demands for special conditions and its plans to transform the Common Market. Adenauer's support enabled de Gaulle to issue his veto without destroying the Six or the Paris-Bonn relationship.[3]

While Franco-German relations proceeded on an even keel in 1961–62, both countries engaged in disputes with the British and Americans. French relations with the "Anglo-Saxons" were strained by disputes over NATO, the Atlantic alliance, and the shape of Western Europe, while the Germans were frustrated by the willingness of the British and Americans to negotiate with the Soviets on Berlin and other important German issues.[4] De Gaulle and Adenauer's frustrations with their Atlantic partners reinforced their solidarity and their determination to remain together even if the political union failed.[5] Adenauer's subordinates supported the Franco-German entente as the engine of Europe, but, seeking to avoid an exclusive relationship, favored a political union that submerged the bilateral relationship in a larger forum. The Auswärtiges Amt went to great lengths to avoid the impression that France and Germany sought to dictate to their partners. Occasionally it even rescheduled meetings between Adenauer and de Gaulle to avoid provoking the Four with prior decisions.[6]

Although tensions and disagreements remained, relations between Paris and Bonn no longer underwent the cyclical pattern of distrust that had characterized them between 1958 and 1960. Bonn believed that it could restrain de Gaulle's wilder ambitions, as it had on the political union, and saw no reason to take sides in the French disputes with Britain and the United States. It preferred to influence the French leader than to confront him directly, which might provoke unilateral actions on his part. Bonn regretted that the Dutch and Belgians had torpedoed the political union and blamed them more than the French for the negative outcome. Although all save Adenauer still favored a political union of the Six over a bilateral Franco-German arrangement, German leaders were now forced to decide whether the latter was an acceptable alternative as long as the former was blocked.[7]

The United States, which had initially approved de Gaulle's plans for political union, still believed that Franco-German cooperation was a prerequisite for Western European unity and realized that any Franco-American contest over Germany could only damage the interests of all three countries. In Washington's view, the Germans exerted a positive influence on de Gaulle, and French policy toward Germany served the unity of the West against the USSR. Despite disagreements over details, Washington had been a silent partner in the Franco-German entente during the Eisenhower administration.[8] With Kennedy, changes occurred. Washington still viewed Germany as its single most important ally in Europe, but de Gaulle now seemed bent on transforming Europe and the Atlantic alliance, and Adenauer appeared overly inclined to follow him. The United States was on guard against the increasingly exclusive direction of the Franco-German entente as well as the policies of each government. The Kennedy administration mistrusted both partners, disliking de Gaulle's notions of a more independent Western Europe and fearing that "a post-Adenauer government [might] flirt . . . with the Kremlin out of nostalgia for a reunified Germany."[9] Thus the United States supported Britain's application to the Common Market, to balance the Paris-Bonn entente and to reassure the Four, restrain de Gaulle, and influence Germany in the post-Adenauer period.

American concerns over the Franco-German entente grew proportionally as the Franco-American relationship deteriorated in 1962 and U.S. distrust of de Gaulle increased. Were Germany to form an exclusive relationship with France, it would be endorsing de Gaulle's Third Force agenda and threatening the Atlantic alliance. Washington hoped that de Gaulle's provocative actions during the political union negotiations had swayed German leaders to act more independently. The State Department felt confident that Bonn recognized that its "ultimate security, as well as that of Western Europe, rest[ed] on close association with [the] U.S."[10] Thus, Washington was spared the need to intervene directly in Franco-German relations.

London was less alarmed over the Franco-German relationship than Washington, but it nevertheless intervened more directly to contain it. The British were far more interested in the political union and their application to the Common Market. Still, it was clear that the Paris-Bonn tie affected both, because Britain's only counterweight to a hostile de Gaulle was Germany. London thus viewed episodes of close Franco-German cooperation, such as the Rambouillet meeting in 1960, as menacing to its interests and was heartened by periods of Franco-German tensions. Like the Americans, the British counted on Adenauer to restrain de Gaulle, but made greater efforts to block an exclusive Franco-German relationship, for example by establishing regular British-German contacts on European political and economic issues in 1960–61.[11]

London concluded from the political union negotiations that the Germans would never abandon the French or their own ambitions for the Six for the sake of relations with Britain. Despite considerable British efforts to coordinate policy, the Germans were unresponsive. German support for de Gaulle's various European plans had provided an overwhelming trump card for the French leader. Out of frustration, Britain began to explore a tactic it would use more and more as time went on: undermining Adenauer's position at home. London found support not only in the opposition SPD, but also among many disgruntled diplomats and cabinet members disturbed by de Gaulle and his influence over the chancellor.[12]

By mid-1962 Franco-German relations had been relatively stable for nearly two years and broad areas of agreement had been found. However, the de Gaulle–Adenauer entente masked lingering disagreements that would have to be addressed if a formal bilateral political pact were to replace the failed political union. During the Fouchet negotiations Germany had played the role of mediator and downplayed its differences with de Gaulle over the future shape of Europe and the Atlantic alliance and relations with Britain and the United States. As Adenauer grew more isolated in Bonn, he and de Gaulle sought a means of ensuring continuity in German policy after he left office. Otherwise the nascent Franco-German entente would not outlast its authors.[13]

From the End of the Fouchet Plan to the Franco-German Treaty, April 1962–January 1963

With the failure of the Fouchet plan, de Gaulle was convinced he could persuade the Germans to accept a new political initiative for Western Europe. He felt confident that Adenauer was prepared to move forward with France alone. French leaders already realized Adenauer's support would be crucial to keeping the United Kingdom out of Europe, but were alarmed by the fact that the chancellor "found himself alone in his doubts on Great Britain."[14] The French had to find some way to strengthen Adenauer's domestic position and ensure that his French-centered policy remained dominant as long as possible. De Gaulle's solution to this dilemma was an exchange of "state" visits with the German leader, followed by a bilateral pact, to drive home the Franco-German reconciliation and entente to the people of both countries. The French hoped that these visits would foster the development of a European identity that, rather than replacing national allegiances, as many supranationalists advocated, would instead reinforce them.[15]

Bonn's response was mixed. Von Brentano, now serving as head of the Christian Democratic parliamentary group, advised the chancellor to revive the political union rather than sign a bilateral agreement.[16] From Paris, Ambassador Blankenhorn criticized de Gaulle's ongoing push for tripartism, feared that the French leader planned to exclude Britain from Europe, and predicted a drive for French hegemony on the continent. Blankenhorn worried that de Gaulle's proposals for a privileged Franco-German tie were merely a way to "extend [France's] isolation to the Federal Republic."[17] Foreign Minister Schroeder feared that Adenauer was abandoning Britain and the United States and worked to convince the chancellor that a total focus on relations with France would damage German interests. Adenauer, however, remained unmoved: "Now that the British, via their Dutch and Belgian proxies, have wrecked the political union, which was the primary goal of the entire European effort from the outset, all that remains is a France-Germany bloc, perhaps with participation of Italy and Luxembourg."[18] Not surprisingly, Adenauer agreed to a "state" visit to France in July.

Both the public and the private aspects of Adenauer's trip were significant. Although the reaction of the French public to the chancellor's extended tour of the country was not as warm as de Gaulle had hoped, it was sufficient to demonstrate support for Franco-German reconciliation and impress Adenauer. A joint mass at Rheims cathedral and a Franco-German military parade emphasized how far bilateral relations had progressed. In their private meetings, de Gaulle and Adenauer shared their doubts on British admission to the Common Market and agreed on closer coordination of their positions in the Brussels negotiations. They made one last token effort to move the political union forward, but agreed that if (and when) this effort failed, France and Germany would commence work on a bilateral political arrangement. The chancellor made it clear that he wanted a bilateral accord not only to stand up to the "Anglo-Saxons" and the Soviets, but to tie the hands of his successors and ensure continuity in German policy. The importance of making progress while Adenauer remained in office was driven home when discussions between Couve de Murville and Schroeder produced one disagreement after another.[19]

German leaders publicly portrayed Adenauer's trip as a demonstration of the solidity of Franco-German ties as the base of European unity.[20] However, behind the scenes there was less enthusiasm. While Adenauer prepared to move forward with France alone, the foreign ministry still hoped that Franco-German cooperation would lead to the revival of the political union instead. Rather than criticizing de Gaulle, the Auswärtiges Amt pinned its hopes on progress in the Brussels negotiations, which might also facilitate progress on the political union.[21]

Given Adenauer's weakening domestic position, Paris had to move quickly to cement the entente, which meant working almost exclusively with the chancellor. The French knew that it would be risky to base their whole German policy on Adenauer, but at the moment it seemed they had little choice.[22] De Gaulle planned a state visit to Germany in September to prepare Bonn to accelerate their bilateral relations by increasing cooperation in the core areas of foreign policy, defense, economics, and culture.[23] Placing particular emphasis on defense, the French hoped to win Germany over to a common military doctrine to wean it away from the United States. Regular ministerial level meetings and periodic bilateral summits would be the primary means of this cooperation. The French also envisaged regular Franco-German consultation in major international organizations and on major international issues, such as policy toward the Soviet bloc, aid to the developing world, and developments within the Common Market.[24]

The Germans had little advance warning of de Gaulle's new proposals and were uncertain how to respond. Even Adenauer's critics, sensitive to any moves toward a bilateral arrangement, welcomed the symbolic importance of de Gaulle's painstakingly prepared visit. The foreign ministry even gave a positive interpretation to the French leader's decision not to visit Berlin during his trip: "De Gaulle has clearly spoken out against a stop in Berlin. He feels that as head of state he cannot, during a trip to free Germany, make a stop in Berlin at the same time, since it remains under formal occupation."[25] The Auswärtiges Amt viewed the trip as a chance to demonstrate the support of the German public for Franco-German reconciliation and European unity.[26] To forestall any criticism, Adenauer informed the cabinet that the relationship with France was his overwhelming priority, the key to European integration and to blocking any Franco-Soviet condominium.[27]

During his visit, de Gaulle took pains to strengthen Adenauer's position and prepare the way for an exclusive Franco-German accord. His speeches, delivered in German for maximum effect, emphasized the greatness of Germany and Europe and the vast potential for Franco-German cooperation. During his private meetings with Adenauer, de Gaulle presented his proposals to increase Franco-German cooperation. Adenauer, angry at the Four for refusing to revive the political union negotiations, agreed that France and Germany should move forward with a "Gentlemen's agreement" on foreign policy coordination. De Gaulle suggested that since such an agreement already existed, it should be formalized to ensure that close Franco-German cooperation outlasted the two of them. The two leaders agreed to an exchange of letters that would bind their successors, but not require ratification by the Bundestag. The French would prepare specific proposals, the Germans would respond, and when agreement was reached, the exchange of letters would occur. De Gaulle also used the visit to test the German reaction to his anti-British policy. When virtually every German political or business leader responded negatively, de Gaulle realized more than ever that his sole supporter was Adenauer. To all his critics he simply replied that his trip had "brought the German people closer to France and thereby closer to the free world and led them away from other seductions."[28]

The French delivered their proposals in mid-September. They publicly claimed that the idea had spontaneously resulted from de Gaulle's trip, but detailed proposals had been worked out since late August.[29] Echoing the Fouchet plan, they consisted of cooperation in foreign policy, defense, financial-economic policy, and cultural-youth policy. The leaders of the two countries were to meet twice per year, the foreign ministers four times. The two governments were to consult each other on all major foreign policy decisions. They would systematize their military-defense cooperation, with the goal of common strategies in all areas. Coordination of all this was to be handled by the two foreign ministries, with the participation of other ministries as appropriate. The French were particularly concerned to ensure the maintenance of close Franco-German coordination in the Common Market, most notably on the issue of its expansion. This cooperation could keep Britain out or, in case the United Kingdom somehow managed to join, minimize its influence. Germany would be expected to follow the French lead on all other European issues as well, assuring informal French hegemony. French planning papers make clear that they intended to establish a de facto Franco-German directorate to run the Six, a clear result of their frustrations at the obstructionism of the smaller members during the Fouchet negotiations.[30]

The Germans accepted the basic French ideas but asked for time to formulate an official, detailed response. This period lasted nearly two months and French diplomats grew suspicious: "There is no doubt about the goodwill of the . . . Auswärtiges Amt, but [there are] so many indications of the desire of its chief

[Schroeder] to drag things out that a personal intervention by Adenauer appears necessary."[31] To urge Bonn along, Paris used the Cuban missile crisis in October as an example of America's unilateralism and of the need for Franco-German cooperation to give Europe a voice in world affairs.[32] In fact, a wary Auswärtiges Amt moved slowly to avoid any arrangement that threatened the Atlantic alliance or the European communities. It also sought to protect its own foreign policy role from subordination by Adenauer. Although favoring a positive response for the sake of moving Europe forward in the only way that presently seemed possible, German diplomats recognized that the French sought to split Germany from the United States and make it an accomplice of de Gaulle's "independent" diplomacy. After the Gaullist parliamentary victory of late November, Blankenhorn noted presciently: "I believe that we will now have to face a whole series of surprises, not the least of which will be in foreign policy, where [de Gaulle] will now attempt to bring his goals to fruition."[33] Given such concerns, the foreign ministry preferred to downplay political-military cooperation and focus on cultural relations, precisely the opposite of what de Gaulle and Adenauer intended. Nevertheless, reassured by the United States of its support for a bilateral agreement to advance European unity, Bonn went along with the proposals.[34]

The formal German reply accepted the basic French plan and even exceeded it by calling for exchanges of information, coordination of public positions, and common instructions to their embassies around the world on major international issues. However, in an intentionally discordant note, the German reply specifically mentioned cooperation within the Atlantic alliance as well. France and Germany were not to form an exclusive bloc, but to coordinate their policies within the wider alliance. The German reply also included the familiar caveat against damaging the European communities. The Germans' memo was silent on the specific means of cooperation, because they had not resolved this issue among themselves.[35] However, the two sides ultimately adopted the French formula of regular meetings and agreed that Adenauer would come to Paris in January to work out the final details and exchange the letters on cooperation. On orders from the chancellor, whose determination to move forward increased in proportion to the decline of his influence at home, the Germans made most of the concessions. They dropped any reference to the primacy of the Atlantic alliance and wider international cooperation. They nevertheless warned against provoking the United States and the Four and maintained their support for a wider political union.[36]

The French were satisfied with the German responses, despite the caution of the latter over strategic cooperation and their focus on such secondary issues as common instructions to French and German diplomats. The Germans had accepted the essentials: coordination in the Common Market, cooperation in international organizations, and harmonization of their policies on economic development, the USSR, and the developing world. The French also realized their enormous debt to Adenauer, who had overridden the objections of his subordinates.[37]

Once again in late 1962 and early 1963, de Gaulle saw himself in a position to determine the future course of Western Europe. With the Algerian war settled and his referendum on direct election of the president passed in late 1962, along with the parliamentary victory in November, he had a stronger domestic base than ever before. He had cemented a powerful partnership with Adenauer, who shared his distrust of Britain and had been given a green light by Washington to advance cooperation with France. Once again, an overconfident de Gaulle pushed his advantage too far. His press conference of 14 January was designed to slam the door on British participation in Europe, reduce American influence on the continent, and prepare the way for the Franco-German agreement and for their domination of Western Europe. By signing the Franco-German treaty a week after the press conference, Adenauer would be forced to tacitly support all de Gaulle's pronouncements.

Meanwhile in Bonn, German leaders were taking steps that would ultimately contribute to the downfall of de Gaulle's latest grand design. As late as 9 January, the Auswärtiges Amt still rejected any idea that the Franco-German accord constituted a treaty that would require the approval of the Bundestag because no new institutional arrangements were envisioned. The foreign ministry knew that the parliament had doubts on Adenauer's alignment with Paris and that Germany's other partners would be alarmed by a formal treaty. However, on 14 January, the same day as de Gaulle's press conference, the legal section of the foreign ministry concluded that the accord was ambitious enough to require parliamentary approval. The only alternative would be to water it down dramatically and term it a mere "declaration of intent."[38] After several days of debate, Adenauer and the foreign ministry ultimately decided to make the best of this unexpected twist and hope that the Franco-German agreement would be more durable in treaty form.[39]

The combination of de Gaulle's dramatic press conference and the German decision to shift the agreement to treaty form put Bonn in an awkward position. Washington and London were pressuring Adenauer to urge de Gaulle to lift his British veto. The press conference had turned the mood of the Bundestag sharply against France. A bilateral treaty would provoke the parliament and indicate Germany's approval of, and even subordination to, French policy. The foreign ministry made the prophetic comment that the "Bundestag could put the treaty on ice without rejecting it." However, the Auswärtiges Amt also understood the risks of a refusal to go to Paris and sign. Such a step would endanger a relationship that had taken years of painstaking efforts to develop and Germany "would gain nothing of substance in return for the break with France." As usual, Bonn decided that the way out of this dilemma was to emphasize the pro-German remarks in de Gaulle's press conference and to influence rather than confront him. Adenauer and the foreign ministry persuaded the leaders of a skeptical Bundestag that the chancellor would not follow de Gaulle blindly and could still plead for Britain in Paris. Schroeder also likely realized that the signature of a formal treaty and the subsequent need for ratification would provide him and the Bundestag with considerable leverage over Adenauer.[40]

The French never worried that Adenauer would refuse to come to Paris.[41] They readily agreed to conclude a formal treaty, which could work to their advantage by giving the agreement greater weight and compelling Adenauer's successors to carry it out.[42] In public, each side presented its own view of the treaty, but both agreed on its essential role of maintaining European unity against the Soviet threat. The French argued that the treaty would link Germany to the West and form the foundation for the future political organization of Europe when the Four came around and joined the agreement.[43] The Germans made similar arguments, but also emphasized that the treaty would allow them to influence the French in positive European and Atlantic directions.[44]

When de Gaulle and Adenauer finally met in Paris, their subordinates worked out the final details and the two leaders aired their worldviews and their plans for Europe. An overconfident de Gaulle dismissed Adenauer's concerns over American and European reactions to his press conference. He also admitted that the treaty's purpose was to create a Europe independent of the United States, one that would force Washington to reform NATO and move Europe ahead "by the coordinated efforts of the two countries." Their first task, he insisted, was to coordinate their positions on ending the British negotiations with the Common Market. He relented only marginally by agreeing to the farcical study by the Commission discussed in the previous chapter.

Despite these significant differences, the two leaders were in agreement on most points. Adenauer, defying the Auswärtiges Amt, echoed de Gaulle's criticisms of America and Britain. He complained that with the Kennedy administration "one never knows what will happen next" and that the British "enjoyed profiting from conflict on the European continent." The chancellor reassured de Gaulle of Germany's willingness to consult France on the MLF and praised France's own independent deterrent. De Gaulle, with his heavy emphasis on nuclear issues, argued for a European nuclear force (such as the *force de frappe*) providing real protection for France and Germany. Indeed, he kindled Adenauer's ambitions by suggesting that Germany would someday have its own nuclear weapons. An independently armed Europe, with a Franco-German core, would also one day negotiate an end to the Cold War with the Soviets. Compared with such grandiose designs, the issue of Britain's relations with the continent appeared trivial. To bolster Adenauer's doubts and support his argument that "whenever the Americans disagreed with the Europeans, the English would always side with the Americans," de Gaulle falsely claimed that the British had rejected his offer of a nuclear partnership in favor of the Nassau deal with the Americans.[45]

De Gaulle was able to reach this point with Adenauer by capitalizing on America's inattentiveness. Prior to Adenauer's trip to France in July 1962, the United States had only a few hints that Paris and Bonn might move forward without their partners. American officials had discounted the warnings of German diplomats, believing no German leader would abandon the United States, Britain, and NATO for an exclusive relationship with France. Except for Adenauer, the Americans perceived no significant German support for de Gaulle's agenda, and therefore saw no reason to intervene in the Franco-German relationship.[46] Adenauer's trip did not reduce America's complacency. U.S. diplomatic reports emphasized the lingering distrust between the two countries and concluded that shows of unity, such as Adenauer's visit, were more to reassure one another than harbingers of new agreements. The State Department saw no real chance that the Germans would "associate themselves with efforts to readjust the internal power balance of the Atlantic community in favor of other member countries, such as may be implicit in the hypernationalist accent of current French policy."[47] Riveted on the half-hearted de Gaulle–Adenauer attempt to revive the political union, Washington was unaware that the two leaders were already discussing a bilateral arrangement.

America also endorsed de Gaulle's return trip to Germany in September, despite some new worries. The French leader's negative comments on British entry into Europe while he was in Germany rang alarm bells in Washington, and State Department officials began to fear that the Franco-German relationship would overshadow not only a wider political union, but also the negotiations of the Six with Britain. Washington received disturbing reports from the British and Benelux on alleged French and German plans to exclude the United Kingdom and seize hegemony in Western Europe. A bitter Foreign Minister Spaak informed the Americans that France was not seeking to create a unified Europe, but rather "a Franco-German alliance which de Gaulle generously will permit Benelux countries to join as satellites." It became clear to Washington that de Gaulle's goal was to strengthen Adenauer against his domestic opponents and that his visit had increased the chancellor's determination to make the Franco-German relationship his top priority.[48]

Despite these concerns, the United States still refrained from any direct intervention, expecting the Germans to restrain de Gaulle. Adenauer personally reassured Washington that Germany would not pursue an exclusive relationship with the French and that his bilateral meetings with de Gaulle would "have a positive effect on our common interests."[49] Erhard made the same promise, adding that Germany would not allow the French to exclude Britain from the Common Market. Officials of the Auswärtiges Amt told the Americans that Germany could use its relationship with France to influence de Gaulle in positive directions. Even Paris assured Washington that the Franco-German relationship was not aimed against the United States or anyone else and denied any plans to injure NATO.[50]

Washington accepted the French and German assurances since it still viewed their bilateral tie as the key to European unity. With the political union among the Six stalled, here was an area where progress was possible. American observers mistakenly believed that both countries were creating a counterweight to Britain's imminent admission to the Common Market, which was precisely the sort of equilibrium the United States favored for Western Europe.[51] It was for this reason that Washington's reaction to France's actual proposals in the fall of 1962 was cautiously positive. They contained nothing objectionable and no treaty was foreseen. As long as the French proposals were directed at expanding existing cooperation rather than promoting sweeping new arrangements, they could be accepted. Rusk summed up the issue for Kennedy: "As long as we are not confronted with a closed French-German system (and there is at present no reason to assume that we are) we should welcome this development because intimate French-German relations are a *sine qua non* for greater European integration. General de Gaulle's spectacular visit to Germany has certainly been a great and lasting contribution to French-German cooperation."[52]

The United States was even more positive toward the German response. It was apparent that Adenauer had been curbed by the foreign ministry and America could exert further control by intervening in German domestic politics should the need arise. Washington was reassured by the German efforts to downplay high-level coordination, stress more routine forms of collaboration, and assert the importance of NATO. Ball agreed with Schroeder that "the foundation of European unity was Franco-German cooperation, but not a Franco-German axis."[53] Despite Adenauer's lack of balance over the Bonn-Paris relationship, Washington had no intention of forcing him to choose between France and the United States and rejected criticisms from the British and the Four.

The British view was far less enthusiastic. Since 1958 London had been convinced that neither de Gaulle nor Adenauer took the Four very seriously and was thus not surprised when, after the failure of the Fouchet plan, the two leaders moved toward a bilateral political arrangement. The Foreign Office feared a Gaullist plot to win Germany over to French policies and then use the Franco-German condominium to dominate Western Europe.[54] Despite his distrust of both de Gaulle and Adenauer, Macmillan was less certain. Like the Americans, he viewed the initial Franco-German steps in 1962 as a means of reviving the wider political union and described the Foreign Office theories as "interesting, but not convincing."[55]

After Adenauer's visit to France and de Gaulle's trip to Germany, a bleaker view emerged. British observers now rightly viewed the de Gaulle–Adenauer effort to revive the political union as a sham and realized that the two leaders were building public support for a bilateral arrangement.[56] As the Brussels negotiations dragged on, it seemed that de Gaulle was either preparing a counterweight to Britain's entry (the positive American view) or was gathering German support for Britain's exclusion. As their views darkened, the British pondered how to exploit Adenauer's isolation. The German ambassador indicated that Schroeder and Erhard, as well as the German public, could be counted on to keep the chancellor in line.[57] Aware of the delicacy of the situation and uncertain how best to intervene, Macmillan assured Adenauer of his support for Franco-German reconciliation. He praised the chancellor's trip to France as a step toward a political union that included Britain and all of the Six: "I was . . . very glad to see that you and President de Gaulle agreed about the importance of Britain's participation in order to strengthen Europe."[58] When it became clear that Adenauer shared France's opposition to Britain's admission to the Common Market, Ambassador Dixon predicted a bilateral treaty. In public, London took a cautious position, welcoming the Franco-German reconciliation, but rejecting an exclusive Franco-German relationship that threatened NATO or British and American ties with Europe.[59]

When the details became known, British observers viewed the French proposals to the Germans as the "Fouchet plan à deux," but remained divided over de Gaulle's ultimate goals.[60] Britain, like the United States, was less interested in the details than in the wider French and German intentions. There were mixed reports from Bonn and Paris about de Gaulle's designs, German resistance, and the omnipresent danger of Britain's exclusion from Europe. The ambassador in Bonn, Sir Christopher Steel, became increasingly frustrated by the de Gaulle–Adenauer duopoly ("these two aged Jesuitical devils") and argued that "the sooner we get rid of de Gaulle the better and . . . the same applies to Adenauer."[61] For the remainder of 1962 and the first weeks of 1963, the British response to

Franco-German relations fluctuated according to the latest developments between the two countries and the progress (or lack thereof) of the Brussels negotiations.[62] The Foreign Office still called for a wider European arrangement that would integrate Franco-German and British-German relations into a political union of the Six and Britain.[63] Thus both the British and the Americans were caught off balance in January 1963. In the context of de Gaulle's press conference, the Franco-German treaty extended relations farther and faster than either of them had anticipated or could accept.

The Treaty, the Bundestag Preamble, and Franco-German Relations in 1963

The three key factors that underlay American objections to the Franco-German treaty were its timing, the atmosphere in which it was signed, and the fact that it was a formal treaty rather than a set of protocols or exchange of notes as had been anticipated.[64] It was de Gaulle's press conference of 14 January that kindled all these American concerns. De Gaulle's rejection of British entry into the Common Market, the MLF, and America's leading role in Europe in one fell swoop destroyed whatever faith American leaders had retained in the French leader. When Adenauer signed a formal treaty of cooperation with de Gaulle a week later in what American observers viewed as a stridently anti-American and anti-British atmosphere in Paris, it seemed to many that the chancellor had surrendered to de Gaulle's entire Third Force program. The treaty provisions stating that "the two governments will consult, before all decisions, on all important foreign policy questions and, above all, on questions of common interest, with the goal of reaching, as much as possible, a common position" now took on sinister connotations.[65] Lacking any trust in de Gaulle, America also had its confidence in Germany shaken and was determined to intervene much more directly in Franco-German relations and in German domestic affairs than previously.[66]

Washington's task was made difficult by the fact that the actual provisions of the treaty were fairly benign and because it was very popular in France and Germany. It was the signers' motivations that concerned the United States and that had to be addressed. Kennedy initially wanted to "build sentiment in Bonn to carry out changes in the treaty" to indicate that it did not alter Germany's wider European or Atlantic policies.[67] Washington flooded Bonn with notes and objections complaining that Adenauer had surrendered to de Gaulle.[68] The Americans dismissed Adenauer's assertions that he could use the treaty to influence de Gaulle. American diplomats argued that "experience led us to doubt whether [Germany] could in practice influence de Gaulle; our concern was whether [the] center of gravity in policy had shifted to Paris."[69] In their view, Adenauer had never had any real impact on de Gaulle; influence in the relationship seemed one-way only. Washington warned the chancellor that he could go no further with de Gaulle without having to choose between France and the United States. Echoing the familiar British refrain, it also threatened to reevaluate its European and Atlantic policies if Germany did not clarify its position quickly.[70]

America's censure was swift and unequivocal. The former secretary of state, Dean Acheson, scolded the Germans for signing the treaty and hoped the Bundestag would reject it. General Lucius Clay, the hero of the Berlin airlift, stated that unless the treaty were changed, it would mean the end of NATO and of the Western defense of Berlin. John J. McCloy, the former U.S. high commissioner in Germany and Adenauer's unofficial political tutor in the early 1950s, argued that de Gaulle had twisted Franco-German reconciliation into a "power play" designed to "achieve French dominance in Europe" and that "the Soviets will exploit every opening General de Gaulle has given them." Other prominent American figures warned that the treaty endangered the Atlantic Community, European integration, and the American presence in Europe.[71]

In response, Adenauer and his subordinates tried to sell the treaty to Kennedy as a positive new step toward European and Atlantic unity that would allow Germany to influence France and work in favor of Britain's inclusion in Europe. The chancellor denied any link between the treaty and de Gaulle's press conference and also denied that Germany would follow de Gaulle's foreign policy. The pact was intended for bilateral consultation, not a European directorate or a bloc inside NATO.[72] The Germans refused to choose between France and the United States but denied any intention of endangering their country's European and Atlantic commitments. Adenauer blamed the British for the failure of the Brussels negotiations and refused to let the Franco-German treaty die with the British application. He used familiar Cold War logic to sway the Americans, portraying the Franco-German treaty as a "firewall against the Soviet Union" and a huge setback for its efforts to divide the West.[73]

In early February Schroeder sent his chief lieutenant, State Secretary Karl Carstens, to Washington to quiet the uproar. During his conversations with Kennedy and State Department officials, Carstens tried to reassure the Americans on German policy and to calm them on de Gaulle as well. Carstens reiterated Germany's commitment to British entry into Europe, its enthusiasm for the MLF, and its hopes for the strengthening of NATO. To convince the Americans that Germany viewed the Franco-German treaty from a wider European and Atlantic perspective, he agreed to work for a Bundestag resolution to accompany the treaty and place it in that context. Carstens succeeded in gaining U.S. understanding of the German motives behind the treaty but failed to alleviate American distrust of de Gaulle. Germany, now formally linked to France, was inevitably associated in America's eyes with de Gaulle's Third Force goals and would thus have to proceed with caution. As Carstens summed up, Germany "would have to deal with American dislike and distrust of de Gaulle for a long time to come."[74]

Looking for a way out, Bonn reminded the Americans that it had kept the United States informed at the highest levels of its plans for closer Franco-German relations from the summer of 1962 onward and could cite specific conversations in which George Ball and other American officials had expressed support for its efforts.[75] On the other hand, it blamed France for the accusations by the German media, the Bundestag, and the United States that Germany was following blindly in de Gaulle's wake. When the French ambassador protested any addition to the treaty, Carstens advised Paris to cease bullying Bonn. If forced to choose between France and the United States, Germany would inevitably choose the latter: "We will not skate out onto the thin ice where de Gaulle would obviously like to see us."[76]

Faced with strong criticism of the treaty from the British and Americans, the Four, and many at home, the German government did in fact decide to attach an explanatory statement when the treaty was ratified. Vice chancellor Erhard wanted a show of support for NATO and the existing European institutions, and hoped to weaken Adenauer in the bargain. Walter Hallstein, former state secretary of the foreign ministry and now head of the Commission, agreed that something must be done "to prevent the treaty from disrupting cooperation in NATO and the Common Market."[77] In the Bundestag, the SPD, FDP, and much of the CDU/CSU favored adding a resolution or preamble to the treaty. If Adenauer refused such an addition, the Bundestag might not ratify the treaty.[78] Polls suggested that the German public supported the treaty, but feared its impact on relations with Germany's other allies and would welcome a clarifying statement.[79] Even Schroeder, who disliked the precedent of the Bundestag's altering a treaty that the government had signed, accepted the additional text to clarify German policy and restrict Adenauer's room for maneuver.[80] The Auswärtiges Amt hoped to use the ratification debates to demonstrate Germany's independence from French influence and pressure Paris for concessions on Britain. Adenauer ultimately bowed to this overwhelming consensus, and the Bundestag added a preamble stating that the Franco-German treaty changed nothing in Germany's wider European and Atlantic policies. Germany remained committed to European integration, the entry of Britain into the Common Market, a liberal tariff policy, military integration into NATO, and the alliance with the United States. One German observer later stated that by adding the preamble, the Bundestag had "nullified the treaty at the same time as it ratified it."[81]

Paris, which had pushed the Germans too far, was angered by the hesitant and hostile reactions of the German media, parliament, and government. The embassy in Bonn had noticed danger signs immediately after de Gaulle's press conference and had warned Paris of the Bundestag's opposition to the treaty.[82] Thereafter, Ambassador Roland de Margerie detailed Germany's anger at the U.S. threats, but also Bonn's resentment of de Gaulle for its plight. He warned of the enormous pressure to reject or alter the treaty and doubted Adenauer's ability to resist.[83] Paris was disgruntled when high-level German leaders disparaged the treaty, called for changes, and publicly aired all the Franco-German differences in European and Atlantic policy. According to de Margerie, all this threatened to "reduce the political and psychological impact of the treaty."[84] French diplomats accused German critics of making false linkages between the treaty and other issues, such as the British application to the Common Market and French criticisms of NATO. France criticized the Auswärtiges Amt, the German financier and industrialist supporters of British participation in the Common Market, the Bundestag, which had devised the preamble, Erhard for his long-standing opposition to French European policy, and the SPD opposition, which the French accused of cynically attempting to act "plus atlantique que le roi."[85]

The end of the negotiations on Britain and the Common Market did nothing to ease the Franco-German tensions. Even Adenauer blamed de Gaulle's unconditional veto for all his domestic problems and complained that the Brussels talks should have been allowed to die a "natural death" as opposed to being "brutally strangled."[86] Led by Schroeder, Germany maintained its support for British entry, and the long debates between Schroeder and Couve de Murville on maintaining contacts with Britain further soured relations.[87] De Gaulle refused to make any concessions on Britain or any other issue to facilitate German ratification of the treaty or ease the pressure on Adenauer. The ongoing dispute over Britain convinced de Gaulle that much of the German leadership would never support his sweeping goals for the Franco-German treaty. As the Quai d'Orsay put it, he now decided to "close his eyes and wait until the end of the year to openly acknowledge the failure of Franco-German cooperation."[88]

In dealing with the preamble, the French took different attitudes in public and in private. In public they downplayed its significance by attaching a comparable statement to the French text of the treaty when the National Assembly voted on it. This tactic underlined de Gaulle's denial that he sought to separate Germany from the United States and his claim that the treaty promoted European unity and its ability to deal with the United States on an equal basis. The French government also stated that as long as the treaty was implemented as it was originally intended, then nothing had changed and the German preamble could be accepted.[89]

Despite this placid public pose, French leaders from de Gaulle on down were deeply disturbed by the preamble. However restrained they were with the Germans, for fear of making the situation worse, the French had suffered a great setback in their efforts to transform Western Europe into an effective Third Force. The German preamble was seen as an admission of dependency on the United States and of acceptance of American interference in German domestic politics. In the view of Ambassador de Margerie, it enabled Bonn to "offer France the homage of a near unanimous ratification while maintaining virtually intact its credit with Washington."[90] The United States did not have to block ratification of the treaty when it could simply dilute it and weaken Adenauer at the same time. The French now carefully weighed the impact of America's intervention on German domestic politics. They understood that Schroeder had tacitly supported the preamble, although he had signed the treaty along with Adenauer. They were also alarmed that Erhard, Adenauer's anticipated successor, and after April his designated replacement, supported the American interpretation of the treaty and preamble. Paris feared that Erhard and Washington had managed to redefine the accord as a symbol of reconciliation between the two countries, and nothing more.[91] Although Adenauer deprecated France's concerns, claiming that the preamble changed nothing and insisting that the treaty was binding on future German leaders, the French, and particularly de Gaulle, were not reassured.[92]

De Gaulle had turned many Germans who had once supported a very close Franco-German relationship into opponents of his entire foreign policy. Among the most notable was Ambassador Blankenhorn in Paris. As we have seen, in the late 1950s and early 1960s, Blankenhorn had supported closer Franco-German relations and encouraged a wavering Adenauer in this direction. However, after de Gaulle's press conference, Blankenhorn became convinced that the French leader sought to destroy NATO, isolate Germany from the United States and Britain, dominate Europe (with Germany as France's junior partner), and reach a status-quo deal with the USSR at the expense of German interests. His private notes became increasingly critical of Adenauer for leading Germany down the Gaullist path and he encouraged Schroeder and Erhard to resist the chancellor and de Gaulle at every opportunity: "History will view this phase of German foreign policy since 1961 as characterized by the weak leadership of a man who, because of his age, was simply no longer able to manage the complex, nuanced position of the Federal Republic on international issues or to make the right decisions. What we see here is simply bad foreign policy and the future, perhaps even the coming months, will make that very clear."[93]

Blankenhorn's views, although more extreme than those of the foreign ministry as a whole, were not exceptional. Bonn became increasingly negative on all France's goals, viewing its *force de frappe*, for example, as aimed more at securing hegemony in Europe and rivaling the United States than at deterring Soviet aggression.[94] Erhard and his ministry deplored the French leader's efforts to isolate Germany from its other allies and emphasized the dangers that de Gaulle's "obvious bid for hegemony" posed to Germany. Fortunately, France could never achieve its goals "without the support of the Federal Republic" and no such support would be forthcoming.[95] Although he did not publicly oppose the Franco-German treaty, Erhard championed the preamble.

French parliamentary approval of the treaty was less contentious than the Germans'. Although the constitution of the Fifth Republic enabled the president to sign and ratify most treaties, de Gaulle and the Quai d'Orsay decided to submit the Franco-German accord to the National Assembly and Senate for approval. They hoped that an overwhelming display of public and parliamentary support would demonstrate France's commitment to reconciliation and cooperation with Germany: "Because parliamentary approval is not required for the treaty to take effect, presenting it to the assemblies has a purely political significance."[96] However, the Conseil d'Etat, the body charged with upholding the constitution, advised the government that it would not be allowed to violate the constitution for purely symbolic purposes. A compromise was worked out, whereby the treaty was declared to be linked to the organization of Europe and could thus be submitted to the parliament for approval.[97] The government presented the treaty to the assembly as the preeminent tool to build Europe, via Franco-German solidarity. As noted above, there was also a preamble, attached by the government, to balance the Germans'. Unlike the German version, the French explanatory statement did nothing to undercut de Gaulle's aims and simply denied that the treaty was exclusive or that it called existing European and Atlantic arrangements into question.[98]

With ratification complete in both countries by June, the next test would be the implementation. But first, there was Kennedy's trip to Europe, which preceded by a week the first Franco-German summit called for in the treaty. The Auswärtiges Amt knew that the Americans viewed the treaty more as a symbolic affirmation of Franco-German ties than as the formal, binding arrangement envisaged by de Gaulle and Adenauer. Now that the extremes of Adenauer's policy had been corrected by the preamble, the foreign ministry wished to make clear to the Americans that it remained committed to the treaty, which offered considerable potential for cooperation and consultation over important issues.[99] Most Germans still hoped to avoid an irrevocable choice between France and the United States.

Publicly the French took an aloof stance toward Kennedy's trip to Germany. Privately, however, French diplomats discerned an "anti-French" tone to the president's speeches and viewed his trip as part of a wider American effort to void the significance of the treaty and "reassert American control over the European continent."[100] They were dismayed by the success of the trip for the Americans and all those Germans who favored close Atlantic relations. Kennedy's sweeping assurances on Berlin and other issues encouraged the Germans to keep France at a distance. Ambassador de Margerie summed up: "It is clear that, at least for a time, [the Kennedy trip] will have a profound impact on most of the German cabinet, particularly on Erhard, who was seen on television enthusiastically applauding. Only Adenauer remains immune to these seductions and blandishments, but his days are numbered and it is the Erhard–Schroeder–von Hassel trinity that we will have to deal with as of autumn."[101] De Gaulle's trip to Germany, following almost immediately after Kennedy's, had considerable damage to undo.

This trip, the first of the regular summit meetings called for in the treaty, had mixed results. The French hoped not only to demonstrate the strength of the treaty, even after the preamble, but also to make progress on the European communities, particularly the CAP. The lame duck Adenauer reiterated his support for the *force de frappe*, his determination to ensure that his successors maintained the bond with France, and his doubts on Britain, the United States, and the Atlantic Community. But the chancellor also tried to defuse the Franco-American tensions that had caused so many problems for Germany and still threatened the implementation of the treaty. After noting that Kennedy's visit had gone well and reinforced the American commitment to Europe, he attempted unsuccessfully to convince de Gaulle to reopen dialogue with Washington. The French leader simply replied that Kennedy demonstrated "a growing taste for leadership and hegemony."[102]

In his conversations with Erhard, de Gaulle found a much less tractable partner. Erhard, soon to be chancellor, emphasized that the Franco-German relationship would no longer be placed above German ties with Britain or the United States and that future negotiations in the Common Market would be on a quid pro quo basis. In a veiled barb at de Gaulle's methods, Erhard insisted that "a community can only be successful when each partner is ready to take into proper account the interests of its neighbor." Erhard and Schroeder rejected de Gaulle's efforts to make progress on the CAP the defining political test of the Franco-German treaty, and there was no agreement on Britain's place in Europe. De Gaulle questioned Erhard's commitment to the Franco-German treaty and repeatedly expressed his "amazement at [Erhard's] stubbornness" in demanding British and American involvement in European affairs.[103]

The first Franco-German summit was also weighed down by the withdrawal of the last remaining French naval units from the NATO military command in June. The Germans viewed this unilateral French move as a violation of the consultation requirements of the Franco-German treaty. It was particularly irritating that the French defense minister had been in Bonn the day it occurred, but had not bothered to inform the Germans.[104] De Gaulle's lame justification, that Germany had not consulted the French on its acceptance of the MLF in January, was easily rebutted by Adenauer, since this German decision had predated the signature of the treaty. Despite the predominance of these disagreements, not everyone was disappointed with the summit. Blankenhorn and many in Bonn welcomed the assertiveness with which Schroeder, Erhard, and even Adenauer had stood up to de Gaulle.[105]

The French viewed the Bonn meetings as neither a success nor a failure, but they left it to the Germans to improve relations. Since it was Bonn that had failed to live up to the treaty, Paris would take no initiatives. In another press conference at the end of July de Gaulle acknowledged that the meetings had not resolved the Paris-Bonn differences on European and Atlantic policy and insisted that the "full implementation of the Common Market" would be "the test case" of the Franco-German treaty.[106] He demanded progress on the CAP by year's end, provoking complaints from Bonn of coercion and lack of consultation. For the time being, the consultation provisions of the treaty had become a dead letter.[107]

During the last six months of 1963 there were more indications of the decline of the Franco-German entente and the difficulties that could be expected when a new government took office in Bonn. Even before Adenauer stepped down in October, the Auswärtiges Amt had become increasingly critical of French positions on European and Atlantic issues and studied ways to use the treaty to pursue purely German goals. The foreign ministry welcomed the fact that "thanks to the reaction of the German public, the efforts of leading German politicians and the reaction to Kennedy's trip through Germany, American fears [on the treaty] have been dramatically reduced."[108] Erhard announced that his priorities as chancellor would be Atlantic political and economic relations, and Schroeder chided the French for overestimating their ability to control Germany. In August the Germans broke with the French by signing the partial Test Ban Treaty, which Paris rejected as an attempt to enshrine U.S.-Soviet nuclear predominance.[109] Later that month the Germans signed a major accord on logistical arrangements in the Atlantic alliance with the Americans, without bothering to consult the French. German-American arms agreements continued to be signed, which precluded the arrangements the French had hoped would result from the Franco-German treaty.[110] Schroeder and Couve de Murville continued to conduct fruitless debates on the merits of military integration, the MLF, and cooperation with the United States.[111]

In public, French leaders attempted to put a positive face on all these disputes, but in fact they were exasperated. Couve de Murville attributed all the problems to the Americans, who had "force[d] Germany to choose between France and the United States."[112] Paris was also frustrated by Germany's blaming of France for the deadlocks on Britain and other Common Market issues. It was offended by the German linkage of the CAP and other community developments with French acceptance of a liberal stance in global tariff negotiations, because it implied distrust of France's assurances on the GATT round. The French themselves questioned German commitment to the CAP and the development of the Common Market.[113]

The last summit between de Gaulle and Adenauer in September 1963 had an air of unreality. Adenauer advocated greater cooperation and pledged continuity in German policy, but de Gaulle was pessimistic and unhelpful. The French leader complained about the divergence between the two countries and the lack of consultation. Adenauer blamed the Americans, the British, and the Four for damaging Franco-German relations and insisted that he had only gone along with the Atlantic Community and accepted the MLF "because he felt obligated for political reasons." De Gaulle was less interested in finding fault or rehashing previous disagreements than deploring Bonn's lack of "independence." The two leaders exchanged their familiar round of attacks on the United States and Britain, portrayed their own countries as the only two in Europe that mattered, and emphasized how much they could accomplish if they practiced real foreign policy and defense cooperation. This was more of a sentimental episode than a realistic discussion, because everything awaited Erhard's accession to office.[114]

As chancellor, Erhard accepted the Franco-German treaty, but would never give France the same support as Adenauer. Erhard planned to use the treaty to advance cooperation in Western Europe and to develop wider European and Atlantic relations under American leadership. He viewed the Six as a means to these wider ends and refused to drop the issue of Britain's role in Europe. The French had lost their docile junior partner, but they did not fear German pressure because they doubted the capability and cohesion of the new government.[115]

The first Erhard–de Gaulle summit took place in November. The new chancellor made Paris his first foreign destination to assure the people of both countries that he would not allow the Franco-German relationship to wither or abandon Adenauer's accomplishments. The meetings demonstrated both sides' willingness to compromise for the sake of maintaining positive relations, but also the differences in their basic conceptions. This time de Gaulle was unable to stir up German fears regarding America's commitment to Europe. Rather than join de Gaulle in a round of denunciations, Erhard rebutted him point for point and insisted that "only America's nuclear power could truly protect Germany in today's world" and that "it would be tragic if Germany were confronted with a choice between friendship with France and friendship with America." When it became clear that they disagreed on nearly every issue relating to the United States, NATO, and defense, they could only acknowledge their different geopolitical situations. There was greater harmony on the European community. When Erhard promoted the revival of the political union effort, de Gaulle was skeptical, but agreed that Franco-German political cooperation needed to be expanded to the other four members of the Common Market. They reached the outline of a compromise on the CAP and on the GATT round. But it was also obvious that de Gaulle focused on the Common Market, while Erhard emphasized wider political and economic relations between the Six and their Atlantic partners.[116]

Another public split occurred in December. France exaggerated the remaining differences on the CAP issues to pressure the Germans and provoke a crisis. Erhard and Schroeder were willing to compromise but not to surrender to pressure. The French acted in part out of frustration at the Germans' reluctance to fully implement the bilateral treaty. They also disliked Bonn's consultation with the United States on purely European issues such as the CAP, which they viewed as part of an effort to ensure "the Federal Republic a privileged position with regard to the other members of the alliance."[117] When the Germans made sufficient concessions to defuse the crisis before the end of the year, the French concluded that Erhard was at least committed to further progress in the European communities.

Throughout 1963, as their misgivings and suspicions grew, the Germans had resisted choosing between France on the one hand or Britain and the United States on the other. They wished to maintain good relations with all their Atlantic partners and acquire leverage to increase Germany's influence on issues such as the MLF. Moreover, the Germans regarded the French conflict with Britain and the United States as transitory. Indeed, by the fall of 1963 the Auswärtiges Amt interpreted French moves to improve their relations with the British as a means of applying pressure on Bonn by demonstrating that they had alternatives if the Germans failed to go along with their policies. "France has always been the 'Lieblingskind' of the USA in Europe. Even the current differences do not disturb the deeply rooted friendship that has survived numerous tests in the past."[118] France had been "allied" to the United States for almost two centuries and could restore good relations with relative ease. Germany, on the other hand, could not antagonize Washington without permanent damage to German-American relations and vital German interests.

In mid-1963 the Quai d'Orsay painted a gloomy picture of the state of Franco-German relations, blaming Germany for everything. The only positive developments were lower-level meetings on such issues as youth exchanges and on policy toward the developing world.[119] By autumn, the pattern of disagreement on major issues and cooperation on lesser ones was even clearer. The foreign ministry viewed this as the result of Germany's subservience to the United States, as well as the volatility of its domestic politics, which made almost every Franco-German issue the subject of strident debate. On the other hand, there had been real cooperation on contacts with Britain and effective coordination of their responses to East German efforts to gain diplomatic recognition by signing the Test Ban Treaty.[120] On the anniversary of the treaty the Quai d'Orsay was even more positive, emphasizing the regular meetings at all levels and the compromises reached on the CAP and other community issues. But on de Gaulle's major priorities, defense cooperation and political consultation, the balance was overwhelmingly negative. Both countries continued to inform one another of major foreign policy decisions rather than consult. Again, the Quai d'Orsay blamed the Germans, whose new government shrank before "independence," included far too many opponents of close cooperation, and used political and legal excuses to block the implementation of those parts of the treaty that it did not like. "In the dangerous situation in which they find themselves, the Germans cannot conceive of doing anything to displease the Americans. Instead of proclaiming the value of the extraordinary rapprochement that has taken place, they feel they have to apologize for it."[121]

The United States was greatly responsible for France's disappointments. American pressure had contributed to the Atlantic preamble. American leaders had encouraged the resistance of the SPD, the governing coalition, and members of the cabinet itself. Washington was gratified and relieved by their loyalty, by their support of the Atlantic alliance, and by the direction of post-Adenauer Germany. It had reduced the treaty to a simple statement of reconciliation and cooperation, contained de Gaulle, and reinforced Germany's alignment with the United States, without any major shift in American policies. As long as the treaty was carried out "in the spirit of the Bundestag resolution," the State Department would have no problems with it.[122] The selection of the Atlanticist Erhard as Adenauer's successor in April boded well for the future. Kennedy's trip to Germany had dealt another major blow to France's plan to separate Germany from the United States. The successful German-American negotiations in the late summer and fall of 1963 on logistical arrangements in NATO and on German purchases of American arms reinforced the solidarity between the two countries and curtailed Franco-German military cooperation.[123]

Whereas Washington's confidence in Bonn had been largely restored, it remained highly distrustful of French designs and encouraged Bonn in all its disagreements with Paris.[124] By the end of 1963, the United States advised Erhard against risky compromises with the French, since it would be better for Western

Europe to remain in a state of deadlock than to move in the negative directions the French favored.[125] The United States had regained its confidence that as long as it remained firm on key German interests and Atlantic cooperation, it need not worry overly about French influence in Bonn.[126]

Although the Americans led the outside resistance to de Gaulle and Adenauer in 1963, the British supported them throughout. However, Britain's concern over the Franco-German relationship still had a lower priority than did its wider relations with Western Europe. Thus London's futile warnings to Adenauer against an exclusive Franco-German relationship on the eve of the signature of the treaty had been accompanied by pleas for his support in the Brussels negotiations.[127] When these hopes were dashed and the British saw de Gaulle seeking to make "common cause with the Germans and capture the political initiative in Europe," they supported American moves both to dilute the treaty and stir up German opposition to Adenauer and made their own interventions in Bonn.[128] When the United States and the German opposition to Adenauer settled on the idea of a preamble, Britain welcomed it as proof that the Franco-German relationship was not to be exclusive and that Germany would not follow France blindly.[129]

With the preamble in place, the British anticipated few substantive results from the treaty. They never expected de Gaulle to carry out real consultation with the Germans on his foreign policy. Once the danger of a German surrender to French hegemony had been averted, London was not surprised by the tensions that surfaced in the latter half of 1963 and took pleasure in the French attacks on the United States and Britain for driving France and Germany apart. By the fall of 1963 Ambassador Dixon described the Franco-German treaty as a dead letter.[130] While most British observers did not go this far, the obvious divergences and the lack of consultation on major issues could only be welcomed in London. The Bonn embassy reported that German leaders now characterized the Franco-German tie as "friendship without illusions," while the Paris embassy noted that "literal interpretation of the Treaty would have required the French to consult the Germans in advance before General de Gaulle said half the things he said at his last press conference."[131] De Gaulle had clearly failed to force the Germans to alter their foreign policy.

Conclusion

Konrad Adenauer, almost alone in Germany, accepted a purely Franco-German relationship if that was all Germany could achieve. By 1962–63, under pressure from Khrushchev and East German leader Walter Ulbricht to negotiate with the

GDR, and facing growing challenges from both the opposition SPD and from within his own governing coalition at home after the construction of the Berlin Wall in August 1961, Adenauer oversimplified the positions of his three major allies in an effort to bring order to a chaotic domestic and international situation. Because Britain and the United States favored negotiations to reduce tensions in Europe while de Gaulle disdained any compromise reached by the superpowers, the chancellor convinced himself that the French leader was Bonn's only reliable ally, ignoring the fact that only America provided a credible defense to both Berlin and Germany. However, he failed to win over his subordinates to the idea of a purely bilateral arrangement that prejudiced Germany's relations with the Four, Britain, and the United States. When Adenauer presented them with a fait accompli by insisting on the signature of a Franco-German pact, Erhard and Schroeder promoted wider political and economic arrangements to void the Franco-German treaty of its exclusive dimensions, while using the treaty to engage in routine discussions and attempt to extract concessions from the French. The Germans, as well as the French, acknowledged the gulf between their respective European and Atlantic policies and used the treaty for the short term for negotiations on the European communities.

By the end of 1963 many observers believed that the Franco-German treaty was likely to become a historical footnote, at least in the original terms de Gaulle had conceived it. During the three-year Erhard government (1963–66), Franco-German cooperation remained stale and formulaic. Regularly scheduled meetings took place and maintained contact, but the solidarity and ambitions of the de Gaulle–Adenauer years fell by the wayside. Yet despite the failure of their larger goals, both sides had reason to be satisfied. The Quai d'Orsay believed that Bonn was permanently committed to Franco-German cooperation, the key to all progress in Europe. Even the more pessimistic felt that the treaty would one day bear fruit when the Germans dared to join France in an "independent" foreign policy.[132] The foundation for close cooperation could be revived when the political situation was more favorable and provide Europe a motor for action and autonomy. The fact that the treaty had provoked strong concerns on the part of both superpowers suggested the potential that the Franco-German tandem had to shake up the European status quo. While the Americans had pressured Bonn to attach the preamble, the Soviets had angrily criticized the treaty as a sign that "revanchist" Germany was finding allies and had denounced the 1944 treaty of alliance that de Gaulle had signed with Stalin precisely to control Germany. In any case, the course of subsequent events proved the French diplomats correct on the dormant potential of the treaty. Some improvements occurred under the German Grand Coalition (1966–69), but it was really only after de Gaulle stepped down in 1969 that Franco-German cooperation on the organization of Europe again blossomed, and the divisive issue of Britain was finally resolved. This cooperation, which continued throughout the 1970s, finally flourished in the 1980s under Helmut Kohl and François Mitterand in the way de Gaulle and Adenauer had envisaged, as a directorate to shape European relations.[133]

The containment of the Franco-German treaty represented a major victory for the United States, as it eliminated the dangers of an exclusive Franco-German axis and a Germany adrift, with or without France, for years to come. With Erhard in power, Washington had a partner committed to restraining France and focusing more on the United States and Britain. The Americans could hope that an isolated France, pressured by Germany, America, Britain, and the Four, would behave in a more realistic and flexible manner. America's perceptions of the German political elite had changed as well. Prior to the Kennedy administration and even into 1962, Washington had regarded Adenauer as the guarantor of German stability and linkage to the West. It had feared his departure and distrusted his CDU/CSU successors almost as much as the SPD opposition. All this changed in 1963 when Adenauer seemed to surrender to de Gaulle's Third Force agenda. The Americans were indebted to Erhard, Schroeder, and von Brentano, as well as to the SPD, for their resistance of Adenauer's total alignment with de Gaulle and for compelling the chancellor to accept the preamble. Thus when Adenauer stepped down in October 1963, the United States was far more confident in Germany's future leaders, both the new Christian Democrat–led government and the social democratic opposition that might take power at some point down the road. Without the crisis provoked by the Franco-German treaty, American leaders would have been far more alarmed by Adenauer's retirement. This outcome is especially ironic if one considers that it was the SPD under the nationalist Kurt Schumacher that had dubbed Adenauer the "chancellor of the allies" in the early 1950s.

London was also profoundly relieved. After years of fear and distrust of de Gaulle and Adenauer's intentions, British leaders could finally hope that the danger of an exclusive Franco-German relationship to exclude Britain from Europe had passed. Britain had long viewed Franco-German relations through the lens of its efforts to join the continent. The Franco-German tie had enabled de Gaulle to veto both the British free trade proposals in 1958 and their application to the Common Market in 1963. However, de Gaulle had failed in his effort to use the entente with Germany to reshape Europe according to his personal blueprint or to exclude Britain entirely. By late 1963, British observers believed that the French president had given up on his Franco-German and Western European organization schemes in favor of French unilateralism. Such unilateralism was unquestionably dangerous for Europe and the Atlantic alliance, but at least it would be France, and not the United Kingdom, which would be isolated. While its confidence in France remained rock bottom, Britain's faith in Germany had largely recovered from the shock of January 1963. With Erhard in office, Sir Alec Douglas Home's new Tory government, also established in October 1963, anticipated closer British-German cooperation as well as closer U.K. ties with Western Europe.

The development and denouement of the Franco-German treaty demonstrated the advantages and risks of a strong personal relationship between two leaders. The de Gaulle–Adenauer entente had added a permanent new dimension to the foreign policy of both countries. But it failed to alter Germany's basic diplomatic alignment, as de Gaulle had hoped, and it destroyed Adenauer's remaining influence when de Gaulle pushed Germany too far. As was his habit, de Gaulle sought to link issues to his advantage, in this case by pressuring the Germans to sign the agreement immediately after his peremptory veto of Britain's entry into the Common Market. However, in this instance it was he, and France, which suffered the consequences of linkage, when almost all the German leadership rebelled against Adenauer and reduced the significance of the treaty. Instead of swinging the Germans into place behind him, de Gaulle confronted them with a choice between France and the United States and reinforced Bonn's solidarity with the British and the Americans in a way that would block his European and Atlantic agendas for the remainder of his presidency and reduce him to an obstructionist element in both areas.

CONCLUSION

The Americans might be relieved to see a real Europe able to bear its responsibilities. That might be more likely to motivate them to defend Europe than if they are confronted with an incoherent and unreliable mass.—Charles de Gaulle, 30 July 1960

The creation of the Common Market between 1955 and 1957 opened a new phase in Western European and Atlantic relations. With Germany tightly linked to the West and the Soviet military threat somewhat alleviated, the Europeans had greater room for maneuver. While the mercurial Khrushchev provoked crises both in and outside Europe, his Soviet Union offered a less menacing visage to Europe than that of Stalin. Solid Western defenses were now in place in any case. The birth of the Common Market also came at a fortuitous moment economically. With recovery from the war largely complete and in the midst of a sustained economic boom, European leaders had the freedom and confidence to open their borders to trade. Such a commitment would have been impossible in the midst of economic uncertainty, either in the immediate aftermath of the war or in the more unstable environment produced by the oil crisis and the end of the boom in the 1970s. The fact that the community had its start during the era of European decolonization also propelled its development. With Britain, France, Belgium, and the Netherlands losing the empires that had guaranteed markets and resources and symbolized their world roles for centuries, they sought new means to ensure economic development and political influence. In a variety of ways and at different rates of speed, they turned away from the imperial past and toward a European future.

After the failure of the over-ambitious EDC in 1954, a period of relative pragmatism and flexibility followed in Europe. It was this willingness for compromise on all sides that made possible the creation of the Common Market. Once the Common Market came into being, it forced all the Atlantic countries to re-examine their European policies and consider how best to advance their interests in the new environment. Each country's leaders thereafter developed a variety of proposals to reorganize European and Atlantic relations, to adjust them not only to the existence of the Common Market, but also to wider changes in the world. The propagation of so many plans to update European and Atlantic relations and promote purely national interests at the same time led to a period of intense debate and renewed ambition in Western Europe. Because of the complexity and diversity of these proposals, their succession one after another produced ever-shifting alignments among the major Atlantic powers. In a few cases, the coalition of forces in favor of a given proposal was strong enough to implement it, but by the early 1960s most plans for change had become so divisive that there was rarely sufficient support for any new arrangement to overcome the entrenched opposition. Consequently, a period of deadlock and rancor in both European and Atlantic relations set in, lasting the rest of the decade.

This deadlock resulted primarily from the fact that by the early 1960s, the issues of European integration and Atlantic cooperation had become a strictly partisan affair. Throughout the 1950s there were sharp divisions on many issues of cooperation and integration, reflecting divergent national interests, but proposals for unity did not constitute attacks on individual Western countries. Even in the case of Germany, the main target of containment via the integration efforts of the early 1950s, all the other countries acknowledged Bonn's interests, including security, stability, acceptance in the West, and economic development, and sought to establish institutions that would promote these interests even as they placed limits on German sovereignty. This general consensus on keeping integration and cooperation a nonpartisan affair began to break down in the late 1950s when the British viewed the creation of the Common Market as a threat to their interests. The situation became worse when de Gaulle returned to power and began to use existing and planned institutions of integration as weapons to attack Britain and the United States and attempt to remove them from Europe. The mutual antipathy that de Gaulle's policy produced soon turned almost every proposal for new means of European or Atlantic cooperation into a divisive affair aimed against one country or another. De Gaulle attempted to use both the Franco-German entente and his proposed political union against Britain, the United States, NATO, and the supranational dimensions of the Common Market. In response, the Kennedy administration eventually turned its Atlantic Community into a plan aimed explicitly at isolating France and reducing its influence in Europe.

Once these and other proposals became openly partisan, the negative effects spread rapidly. The Franco-American conflict led Adenauer's opponents and successors in Germany to dilute an otherwise desirable treaty of cooperation with France in order to prove to the world that Bonn had not been captured by Paris. The partisan nature of European organization efforts in the early 1960s enabled the British to ignore the shortcomings of their application to the Common Market and blame de Gaulle exclusively for its failure. They and the Americans connived with the other countries of Western Europe to work against French influence and threatened to reevaluate their commitments to the continent if the Europeans lined up with Paris. As a result of their use for blatantly partisan purposes, many of the new proposals for cooperation and integration became more negative than positive and this often accounted for their ultimate failure. By 1962 de Gaulle's political union had shifted from an innovative means to provide the Six with greater cohesion in foreign policy and other areas into a crude attempt at French hegemony, and de Gaulle's smaller partners rejected it as a result. Similarly, the Atlantic Community failed in large part because American leaders ultimately interpreted it as a means to isolate France and cement American predominance in Europe rather than to make Europe a more equal partner of the United States.

The European-Atlantic stalemate of the 1960s also resulted from the contradictions produced by the shift to an overwhelming focus on purely national interests. These contradictions were difficult, if not impossible, to resolve and most have lasted to the present day. As each country defined its own interests as synonymous with European and Atlantic priorities, it created inconsistencies that led to deadlock. American leaders promoted Atlantic cooperation as a way to shift U.S.-European relations to a basis of equal partnership. Yet at the same time, most of the specific means of Atlantic cooperation promoted by the Americans were aimed at reducing the influence and autonomy of individual European countries and cementing American predominance or monopoly in important areas, such as alliance nuclear policy. This contradiction resulted from the ambivalence, which has outlasted the Cold War, that American leaders always felt when confronted with the prospect of an autonomous Western Europe. Likewise, de Gaulle promoted both the political union and the Franco-German entente as means to secure French hegemony in Europe and eliminate American influence on the continent, yet to achieve these goals he had to cooperate with five countries committed to maintaining the American presence in Europe, bringing Britain into a greater continental role, and preventing the dominance of any one country. He was never able to resolve these discrepancies. Even more than the opposition he provoked from the United States and other countries, it was these contradictions that frustrated his plans at every turn.

British policy suffered from fatal contradictions as well. From the outset, as a result of their isolation from the continent, British leaders were forced to pay lip service to integration to avoid further alienating the Six, yet they viewed it as a threat to their interests and sought to undermine it at the same time. They sought to control, limit, and even lead the European community, but always from a special position above the other Europeans, whether on the inside or the outside of the community. It was precisely this aloofness that prevented them from obtaining the European support to overcome French opposition to their entry under any circumstances. Although it was not so much a contradiction as the need to pursue good relations with two countries at odds with one another, the Germans faced this same sort of dilemma in their relations with France and the United States. The need to placate both Washington and Paris led to internal divisions in Bonn, forced it to follow a 'more hesitant policy on many issues than it would have otherwise, and produced a policy sympathetic to the United Kingdom but which offered little concrete action to bring Britain into Europe.

Despite these almost systemic problems of the 1960s, the phase of European and Atlantic cooperation that took place between 1955 and 1963 accomplished a great deal. The creation of the Common Market provided a solid foundation for all future cooperation and integration efforts. The ability of the institution to weather the variety of conflicts that its creation immediately produced demonstrated the commitment of all its members to the principle of European unity. The first effort ever to unify Europe by peaceful means demonstrated an impressive resiliency and became an increasingly robust community comprising an ever-wider array of functions.

The survival and development of the community were important for many reasons. After two world wars, the outbreak of the Cold War, and the traumas of decolonization, they offered Western Europeans a new role in the world and hope of regaining control over their own destinies. At the same time, the successful communities and the prosperity they helped to bring had a powerful resonance in Eastern Europe, whose peoples gradually came to see the European Community as a guarantor of democracy, prosperity, and human rights, and who aspired to escape Soviet control and become part of the West. The community showed the peoples of Eastern Europe that a real alternative system existed and gave focus to their aspirations. The allure of the community would eventually even extend to the Soviet Union itself, since the "Common European Home" that Mikhail Gorbachev aspired to join was really just the community that had grown up around the Common Market. In this way, the European Community played an important role in collapsing the Soviet bloc and bringing the Cold War to a peaceful end.

The same willingness for compromise that made the Common Market possible also led to the transformation of the European OEEC, which had exhausted its usefulness, into the Atlantic OECD. While the latter organization has never become the sweeping forum to coordinate global economic cooperation that many Americans and Europeans hoped it would, it has nevertheless remained a useful body for economic cooperation and study among the most industrialized countries of the world. Similarly, the Franco-German entente cemented by de Gaulle and Adenauer between 1958 and 1963, and in particular in the treaty of 1963, while rarely matching the ambitions of its authors, has remained the solid core of European cooperation efforts and the impetus to all major steps forward. Even the Franco-American rivalry should not be exaggerated. The de facto French-U.S. agreement to protect the Common Market helped to insulate it against years of British challenges and forced the United Kingdom to come to terms with Europe rather than vice versa.

It was also a significant accomplishment that despite all the Western infighting of the era, the common front toward the USSR was maintained and Moscow was unable to exploit the conflict among the Western powers. Indeed, on occasion Soviet actions served to remind the Atlantic powers of the things they had in common and the need to limit the damage of their internal rivalries. The Cuban missile crisis of October 1962 provides the ultimate example of this compartmentalization of Western disagreements. At a time when the Franco-American conflict had reached a sharp pitch in almost every area, de Gaulle nevertheless rallied to support Kennedy without hesitation and then, when the danger had passed, immediately returned to his efforts to reduce American influence in Europe. The infighting among the Western powers also demonstrates the degree to which episodes like the missile crisis were the exception to the rule by the early 1960s. The Atlantic powers would not have been able to focus so much on their political and economic reorganization and their own purely national interests a decade earlier when the Cold War remained at fever pitch. Even though in the early 1960s the era of détente was still years away, the infighting in the West demonstrates the extent to which the lessening of tensions with the USSR was already consciously or unconsciously acknowledged and exploited to pursue national interests in competition with one's nominal partners. While the Soviet threat was one of the more important factors in the beginning of European unity in the late 1940s and early 1950s, a decade later it played a more peripheral role.

Although the successes of 1955–63 were significant, the negative side of the balance sheet is also considerable and the deadlock of the early 1960s had important long-term consequences. De Gaulle's exclusion of Britain and the conflict this produced with the Five had the effect of freezing the development of the Common Market in most areas for a decade. Although implementation of tariff harmonization and the CAP continued, both the political development of the group and any expansion to include new members were put on hold until de Gaulle left office. The delay of Britain's entry for a decade widened the psychological gulf between the United Kingdom and the community and increased the awkwardness of Britain's relations when it ultimately joined. Britain's relations with the community have never been resolved to the satisfaction of either.

French influence in the community reached a high tide between 1955 and 1963 and declined thereafter in large part as a result of the battles between Paris and all its partners on both sides of the Atlantic. During the second half of the 1950s, the strength of the German desire for further integration placed France in a very strong position in the community. France could largely dictate the terms of the Treaty of Rome, veto the Free Trade Area with impunity, and obstruct cooperation in NATO without seriously jeopardizing its position. However, over time, as Paris repeatedly worked against the interests of its five continental partners, it gradually isolated itself and created a situation where its partners would no longer make concessions for the sake of goodwill or community interests. Indeed, after January 1963 they adopted an explicit quid pro quo policy in all their dealings with France. From this point onward French influence in the community declined precipitously. During the "Chaise vide" (empty chair) crisis of 1965–66 over supranationalism, control of the community budget, and a number of other issues, France was so isolated that it was only able to resist the will of its partners by leaving the French seat empty at all community meetings, thus threatening to destroy the Common Market, until the Five and the Commission gave in to its demands. The French had largely dissipated the community spirit that had led to the creation of the group in the first place and sped its development during its first few years. From the outset, the Common Market had been based on tough bargaining, but its early success had also resulted from a spirit of compromise for the sake of the larger goal of unity. From 1963 onward, the group would be characterized by the explicit tradeoffs among national interests that have typified it ever since.

The failure of de Gaulle's political union also cast a long shadow and has created a seemingly permanent problem for the community. The mechanisms for economic unity have always advanced much more quickly than those for the political guidance of the community. During the decades that have followed de Gaulle's proposals, innumerable plans for political unity have been proposed, debated, and forgotten. The debates over methods have changed little since de Gaulle's day, ranging from supranationalism, to purely cooperative efforts, to greater roles for "democratic" elements such as the European Parliament. The content of European political unity has also remained up in the air. Should it focus primarily on "external" issues such as defense and foreign policy or on "internal" ones by strengthening the Commission or easing the unanimity principle in the Council of Ministers? The failure of de Gaulle's political union was both a cause and a result of the intractability of these sensitive issues. Europe's political weakness remains to be overcome, but with resistance to the surrender of political sovereignty still strong in most countries, the methods proposed by de Gaulle must be considered in place of, or at least alongside, proposals for supranational solutions.

As for the United States, the failure of the Atlantic Community meant that American relations with Europe would remain based on NATO and the Atlantic alliance in the military sphere, but would not be institutionalized by any new political arrangements. The success of the Kennedy round in the GATT in 1967 meant that at least one aspect of the plan did ultimately succeed and reduce one American fear regarding the consolidation of Western Europe. But the renewed efforts of the Europeans in the 1970s for greater political cooperation and of the United States to define its political role in Europe signaled that most of the key issues in a long-term partnership of equals remained unresolved. Indeed, to this day, European and American leaders have never successfully defined the parameters of U.S.-European political relations or how Europe might take its proper place alongside the United States in promoting their common global interests. Because of the failure of the European Community to establish effective arrangements for political cooperation or bilateral relations with the United States, haphazard methods have had to suffice, and these have reinforced the predominant American role on the continent, even as direct U.S. involvement in European integration has decreased. The potential for conflict between the United States and a united Europe is evident in the one area where Europe has demonstrated an ability to speak with one voice in world affairs: economics. U.S.-European trade conflicts have become a seemingly permanent feature of the international landscape and constitute another factor giving American leaders pause when they consider the possible ramifications of European unity in other areas.

Another striking characteristic of the years between 1955 and 1963, particularly the latter half of the period, is the extent to which personal diplomacy by government leaders shaped the development of European and Atlantic relations. Kennedy, Macmillan, de Gaulle, and Adenauer all held very specific ideas about how to reorganize relations among the Atlantic powers, and the issue was of great importance to all of them. All four defined their national priorities as synonymous with European and Atlantic interests and sought to convince their skeptical partners. One obvious success of personal diplomacy, combined with a willingness for concessions, was the November 1956 Adenauer-Mollet summit that proved decisive for the creation of the Common Market. Yet this case was the exception rather than the rule. For the most part, rather than rein in his ambitions and compromise with his partners, each leader preferred to maintain his goals intact and attempt to persuade the others to change their minds via personal diplomacy alone. Although such an approach led to isolated successes, the long-term result in most cases was failure. The period thus provides an excellent example of the limitations of personal or summit diplomacy and the need for long-term lower level efforts at compromise to solve disputes among allies.

Macmillan, for example, counted on his summit meetings with Kennedy, de Gaulle, and Adenauer to ease Britain into Europe at minimal political and economic cost and to place it in a position of leadership in the European community. His personal relationship with Kennedy was instrumental in the Nassau deal of December 1962, but his refusal to make significant concessions either to de Gaulle or Adenauer prevented him from overcoming their resistance to British admission to the Common Market. Similarly, de Gaulle's persistent efforts to build a personal entente with Adenauer were decisive in the genesis of the Franco-German treaty, but the French leader's unwillingness to resolve the fundamental European and Atlantic policy differences between Paris and Bonn led both to the preamble to the treaty, which diluted most of what de Gaulle had hoped it would accomplish, and to the rapid downfall of Adenauer and his replacement by a new government opposed to French policy on almost every major issue. Summit diplomacy has its place, particularly in maintaining symbolic and personal contacts and demonstrating the political will to solve problems, but is no substitute for serious, patient, and flexible negotiation that acknowledges the national interests of the other side rather than attempting to bypass them.

This phase of intense personal diplomacy and strong interest of Atlantic leaders in new arrangements for cooperation and integration came to an end in late 1963 with changes of leadership in every country except France. While both Eisenhower and Kennedy had been actively engaged in relations with Europe throughout their administrations, Lyndon Johnson never had the same interest: Western Europe was one of his lower priorities. Between 1963 and 1969 he had relatively little contact with European leaders and when he did, topics outside of Europe, such as Vietnam, typically dominated. With the replacement of Adenauer by Erhard and Schroeder in October 1963, an era of German foreign policy came to an end. The new leadership maintained Adenauer's support for both Atlantic and European cooperation but was far less committed to further supranational development or to compromise with France, the two key factors that had previously defined German European policy. In London, Prime Minister Home continued Macmillan's basic policy of moving toward Europe, but with the elections that would eventually sweep the Tories out of office only a year away, he could not afford to take any new initiatives. The narrow range of options facing London became apparent after Labour took power in 1964 and decided on its own application to the Common Market, only to face another French veto in 1967.

Even de Gaulle, the lone remnant of the earlier period, turned away from Western Europe after 1963. With his efforts to transform the Atlantic alliance frustrated by the United States and his plans for reorganizing Western Europe blocked by Britain and the Five, and with no realistic prospects for change in either area, de Gaulle gradually turned to a unilateral foreign policy designed more to irritate the United States and demonstrate French freedom of action in the world than to lead to any constructive developments in European or Atlantic relations. Consciously or unconsciously, de Gaulle seems to have realized that there was no longer any prospect for new arrangements in the Western camp as long as he remained in power. As a result, he turned toward the developing world and the Soviet bloc in the hope that he could facilitate movement in both and that changes outside of Western Europe would eventually lead to movement there as well. By promoting improved relations with the East, de Gaulle hoped to break up the bipolar world and reduce American influence in Europe indirectly. De Gaulle's version of détente thus had its origins in his failures to reshape Western European and transatlantic relations.

Aside from these observations on the nature and development of European and Atlantic relations in the 1950s and 1960s, what judgments can be made about the individual policies of each of the four Atlantic powers? In general, the degree of continuity, both within the period of study and in the decades before and after, is striking. Although transitory factors such as the personalities of individual leaders clearly played important roles, the extent to which broad policy goals set during the 1950s and early 1960s have remained largely intact suggests that they resulted more from long-term national priorities and larger geostrategic factors than purely contingent causes. Although the Cold War was a crucial factor in the launching of European integration, it appears to have faded rapidly to the background thereafter. Instead, events in Western Europe during the period studied here appear to have set or reflected long-term patterns and goals. Many of these goals, such as the French effort to come to terms with Germany and the American attempt to stabilize Europe economically, dated back to the 1920s. The leaders studied here sought to avoid the mistakes of the interwar era, to adjust their countries and partnerships to changes occurring in the world around them, and to change the way their people viewed themselves and their place in the world. On the continent, leaders sought to foster a European identity to complement and strengthen national identifications, while in Britain, the government balked at such an unprecedented step and viewed it as a threat to national independence. In most cases the opposition parties that rejected the policies of the late 1950s and early 1960s ultimately came to accept them and built a national consensus around the results.

In the case of France, the Gaullist legacy is obvious in its continuing aloofness from NATO and its efforts to organize the European community into a coherent political force; but what is often overlooked is the extent to which de Gaulle's policies maintained the ambitions of the Fourth Republic. French leaders since the 1950s have promoted European cooperation, in a variety of forms, primarily as a vehicle for French economic development and political influence. After the

EDC debacle, the Cold War was rarely a decisive factor in their motivation. What de Gaulle accomplished was to set the parameters of foreign policy debate in France, making "independence" the defining characteristic of French action in the world. Foreign policy was to be the reserved domain of the president, whose top priorities would be the rhetoric of grandeur and the creation of a multipolar world with Europe as one of its axes and based on international cooperation, with France involved in all its major councils. Most of the major European and international bodies created since de Gaulle's day have been based on his model, from the European Council to the G-7. The power of de Gaulle's foreign policy prescriptions was most clearly shown in the 1980s when François Mitterrand, who had rejected most of them while in opposition, took up virtually the entire body of Gaullist theory and practice when he himself became president.

Since the 1950s French relations with each of their three major Atlantic partners have occupied a distinct place in the effort to carve out an independent world role. Cooperation with Germany has been the key to both progress in the European community and the ability of Paris to exert its will on Western Europe as a whole. The confidence of French governments in their ability to influence or control Germany has fluctuated over time. During periods of peak confidence, Paris has pushed the hardest to lessen British and American roles in Europe, as under de Gaulle. In contrast, when Paris has feared eclipse by Germany, it has been more willing to envisage continuing British and American roles. This occurred under the Fourth Republic, again when President Georges Pompidou accepted the United Kingdom into the European community in the early 1970s, in part due to fear of the German independence demonstrated by *Ostpolitik*, and during and after German reunification in 1990. French views on British participation in Europe have also changed relatively little over the decades since they lost their illusions on the interest of the United Kingdom in the continent in the mid-1950s. Paris has gradually accepted greater British participation in continental affairs but still takes advantage of British hesitations, most recently its refusal to participate in the common European currency, to ensure that all real initiative in the community remains in the hands of the Franco-German tandem. Finally, there is a high degree of continuity in French views on the role of the United States in Europe. The general pattern has been one in which periods of tension (Cold War or otherwise) temporarily increase French acceptance of a significant American role in European affairs and periods of détente lead to greater frustration with American hegemony. French efforts to organize Europe remain at least implicitly aimed at reducing U.S. influence over the long term, although they have generally been much less stridently anti-American than under de Gaulle.

The ambivalent British response to European integration that took shape in the 1950s has also remained largely unchanged, even after the end of the Cold War. Ever since 1955, British governments have been confronted time and again by efforts of the continental states to advance their unity as a means to promote their national interests. In almost every case, British leaders have questioned whether these continental steps toward unity advanced British interests as well. British calculations of their interests have been characterized by a complex mix of pragmatism and technical economic analysis on the one hand and visceral hostility to supranationalism and resistance of European "identity" politics on the other. Indeed, Britain has had only one leader who was a true enthusiast on European unity, Edward Heath, who led the unsuccessful entry negotiations between 1961 and 1963 and brought Britain into the community as prime minister in 1973. Although Heath's views on Europe would have been unremarkable in any continental country, in Britain they are exceptional.

In many cases the British answer to the question of Europe has been negative, although it has never been decisive enough to opt for a simple nonparticipation. Britain's tendency to oppose further unity while being unable to stop it has been accompanied by another pattern set during the late 1950s and early 1960s, excessively high expectations followed by disappointment and frustration.[1] When the Macmillan government finally decided to join the European community in 1961, it attempted to do so as a panacea for all the political and economic problems facing the country. The government also operated on the assumption that the United Kingdom could become part of Europe, take up a leadership position on the continent, and act as a bridge between Europe and the United States, all without any real concessions on its part to the political or economic interests of the continental states. When these excessive hopes were dashed, little real reevaluation of British policy occurred. Instead the British counted on the support of the United States and Germany, along with eventual political change in France, to bring them into the community down the road. This pattern of excessive ambition, accompanied by an unwillingness to make concessions to the interests of the continental states, by efforts to divert European unity in an Atlantic direction, and by frustration at the frequent setbacks these approaches have entailed, has changed very little over time. Europe has also remained a partisan issue in British politics ever since the days of Macmillan, with whatever party holds office generally acting relatively pro-European and the opposition playing the "Eurosceptic" card. Although the choice for Europe over the Commonwealth has now long since been made, Britain still seems to prefer the role of bridge between America and Europe over full participation in continental affairs and an equal position with the other large European states. For evidence of its continuing preference for free trade arrangements over supranational commitments, one need only compare the strong British support for the 1987 Single European Act, which sought to break down the last trade barriers within the European community, to its doubts and "opt-outs" on the Treaty of Maastricht, which set the foundations for the single currency, greater political unity, and unified social policies.

Although German policy toward European cooperation and unity has evolved a great deal, the essential goal of using Europe to advance German interests has not changed.[2] Governments of both left and right have employed steps toward unity as a vehicle to promote German interests without alarming their neighbors and as a means to reassure their Atlantic partners that the fundamental Western alignment of German policy has not changed, despite growing interest in contacts with the Eastern half of the continent. Examples include Willy Brandt's efforts to start the European community moving again after 1969 as a means to reassure the West regarding his *Ostpolitik*, and Helmut Kohl's acceptance of the euro as a means to reassure Europe, and especially France, on the direction of a reunited Germany. Adenauer's legacy also makes itself felt in an institutional sense, albeit an ironic one. When the chancellor split with most of the German establishment over relations with France and Britain, among other issues, in the early 1960s, the foreign ministry under Gerhard Schroeder became an effective rallying point for resistance. It is no coincidence that in every German government since 1966, the post of foreign minister has gone to the junior coalition party, precisely as a potential brake on the actions of the chancellor.

One change in German policy that is clear and that began to appear in the early 1960s is the extent to which the German public and government's support for supranationalism has shifted toward a preference for intergovernmental cooperation as Germany's political and economic power has grown and its political and military vulnerability has decreased. The extent of early German support for supranationalism clearly resulted from the Cold War and the vulnerability of the divided country. When the SPD resisted this trend during the first decade of the Federal Republic's existence, it was repeatedly punished by the voters as a danger to the stability of the country; by the late 1950s it had reversed its position. Supranationalism also served as a means to restrain an erratic France, both under the Fourth Republic and de Gaulle. Although German leaders still tend to conceive of greater unity as the best way to promote their country's interests, with the end of the Cold War and the decline of their fears about their western neighbors, Bonn's (now Berlin's) willingness to subordinate all its priorities to sweeping supranational integration has faded. While Adenauer felt that European unity was necessary to give his people a new, western identity, after fifty years of stability and linkage with the West, German leaders and public now seem as comfortable with a German identity as with a European one.

Despite this shift, Germany remains a much stronger supporter of supranational unity than either Britain or France.

While the legacy of Franco-German cooperation left by de Gaulle and Adenauer has remained strong and all German leaders have sought to establish a special relationship with their counterparts in Paris, the desire for a stronger British role on the continent has also remained constant, to relieve Germany of total dependence on the French. The German priority on transatlantic relations that so frustrated de Gaulle also appears to be a long-term policy that has survived the Cold War. This reflects a belief that Atlantic partnership protects and promotes Germany's political and economic interests both in Europe, now as the continent's largest power, and in the world.

In the case of the United States, the Cold War was clearly the crucial factor in early (1947–54) American support for European integration. Even in the subsequent period analyzed here, while the Cold War had receded somewhat to the background, it was always one of the essential reasons for which the United States promoted the consolidation of Western Europe. However, this support for integration rapidly took on a life of its own that has outlasted the original Cold War motivations. Fears regarding Soviet-communist encroachment on a weak and divided Western Europe were gradually complemented and then replaced by a general belief in the value of European unity as a means of promoting democracy and political stability, economic growth, and liberal trade policies in Europe as a whole. Particularly important throughout was the binding of Germany to the West, a goal that affected every aspect of American policy on Europe and U.S. relations with all other European countries. The United States often lined up with a France that sought to reduce its influence in Europe and against a Britain that wished to increase it precisely because the former offered a better anchor for Germany.

If the integration of Europe during the Cold War served to advance these goals for the Western half of the continent, after the end of the conflict it has served to extend them to Eastern Europe as well and insulate it from any hypothetical resurgence of Russian pressure or instability. However, despite this general belief in the value of European unity, America's ambivalence, which surfaced in the late 1950s, has remained a constant factor ever since. American leaders have consistently sought to make Europe a stronger and more self-sufficient partner, but they have generally hesitated to acknowledge the logical conclusions of such a policy: the diminution, or end, of American leadership in Europe. In many of the cases examined here, the United States was little more than an observer on the major issues of political and economic unification, a trend that has only increased with time. In this sense, the multipolar world of the post–Cold War era was already coming into existence. However, the United States has exhibited a mix of support and apprehension regarding such a development, reflecting the different approaches of Eisenhower and Kennedy to the problem. The former welcomed greater European strength and independence to ease the Cold War burden on the United States, while the latter feared that a strong Europe would abandon the Cold War entirely and become a rival of the United States or a pawn of the Soviet Union. These two alternative approaches have defined the essentials of the American debate on Europe ever since.

Because most Europeans have also hesitated to confront the implications of an equal relationship with the United States, a fact that de Gaulle constantly lamented, the result has been that both sides still talk of the creation of an equal partnership, just as they did in the early 1960s when discussing the ill-fated Atlantic Community, but neither side takes concrete steps to make a more equal relationship a reality. Europe resists taking on the burdens of an equal partnership, mainly higher defense spending and more sweeping and far-flung political commitments, while the United States refuses to give up its preference for unilateral action. If Europe did manage to establish some means to coordinate a common foreign and defense policy and demonstrate an ability to speak and act with one decisive voice, as it does on economic issues, the result would undoubtedly provoke alarm in Washington. Nevertheless, the author remains convinced that the United States would adjust to the situation relatively quickly, as long as the new Europe avoided de Gaulle's mistakes and made clear that it intended to remain a strong American partner. The United States quickly learned to take a united Europe seriously on economic affairs and would have to do the same on political and military ones. De Gaulle was correct when he said that a stronger and more independent Europe was in the long-term interest of the United States, but he was wrong to believe that such a Europe must be built on an anti-American foundation.

APPENDIX: CHRONOLOGY

1954
August: French National Assembly rejects EDC
October: WEU accords signed

1955
May: WEU accords take effect; West Germany joins NATO and regains sovereignty
June: Messina conference
July: Geneva East-West summit
November: Britain withdraws from the Brussels discussions

1956
January: French elections and formation of the Mollet government
April: Spaak report
May: Meeting of the Six at Venice and adoption of the Spaak report
July: OEEC proposes negotiation of a Free Trade Area
October–November: Franco-British military operations in Egypt
November: Adenauer-Mollet meeting
December–Spring 1957: Selwyn Lloyd's "Grand Design" proposals

1957
January: Eden resigns and Macmillan becomes prime minister
March: Signature of Rome treaties
May: Fall of Mollet government
October: British-American Declaration of Interdependence

1958
January: Treaties of Rome take effect
June: De Gaulle returns to power as the last prime minister of the Fourth Republic
September: First de Gaulle–Adenauer meeting (at Colombey); de Gaulle memo on tripartism sent to Macmillan and Eisenhower
November: French government ends negotiations on the FTA; de Gaulle–Adenauer meeting at Bad Kreuznach
December: Final OEEC meeting on FTA ends in failure; de Gaulle elected first president of the Fifth Republic

1959
January: The first tariff rapprochement occurs among the Six; de Gaulle takes office as president; formation of Debré government
March: De Gaulle press conference on Germany and Berlin
April: Herter takes over for Dulles as secretary of state
October: Macmillan government reelected

November: Signature of EFTA convention in Stockholm; agreement of the Six on regular political consultation meetings

December: Western summit in Paris

1960

January: Negotiations on OECD begin in Paris

May: Abortive East-West summit in Paris

July: De Gaulle–Adenauer meeting at Rambouillet; Home becomes foreign secretary

September: De Gaulle press conference on the organization of Europe

November: Election of Kennedy

December: Signature of OECD convention

1961

January: Acceleration of implementation of the Common Market; Kennedy takes office

February: De Gaulle–Adenauer meeting on political union; summit of the Six on political union in Paris

May–June: Kennedy visit to France

July: Summit of the Six on political union in Bonn and issuance of "Bonn Declaration"; British decision to apply for Common Market membership

August: Construction of Berlin Wall begins

September–November: CDU/CSU setback in West German elections; FDP joins cabinet and Schroeder becomes foreign minister

1962

January: Agreement of the Six on CAP outline; de Gaulle revision of draft political union treaty

February: De Gaulle–Adenauer meeting on political union in Baden Baden

April: De Gaulle meeting with Italian leaders on political union in Turin; Debré cabinet resigns; formation of Pompidou government; failure and end of negotiations on political union

May: NATO meeting in Athens; McNamara criticism of independent nuclear forces in alliance; de Gaulle press conference on organization of European and Atlantic relations

June: De Gaulle–Macmillan meeting at Chateau de Champs

July: Adenauer "state" visit to France; Kennedy speech on Atlantic Community in Philadelphia

September: De Gaulle state visit to West Germany

October: Cuban missile crisis; referendum in France on direct election of the president

November: Gaullist successes in French legislative elections

December: De Gaulle–Macmillan meeting at Rambouillet; Kennedy-Macmillan meeting at Nassau and Nassau agreement

1963

January: De Gaulle press conference rejecting MLF and British Common Market membership; Adenauer visit to Paris and signature of Franco-German Treaty; end of Brussels negotiations on British application to the Common Market

May: Bundestag ratification of the Franco-German treaty with preamble

June: French ratification of the Franco-German treaty; Kennedy visit to West Germany

July: De Gaulle–Adenauer meeting in Bonn; de Gaulle press conference insisting on CAP accord by end of year

August: Signature of partial Test Ban Treaty by United States, Britain, USSR

September: Final de Gaulle–Adenauer summit

October: Adenauer resignation; Erhard becomes chancellor; Macmillan resigns and Home becomes prime minister

November: First de Gaulle–Erhard summit in Paris; Kennedy assassinated in Dallas; Johnson becomes president

December: Signature of CAP accords in Brussels

1964

May: Opening of Kennedy round in GATT

1965

July–January 1966: "Chaise vide" crisis among Six

1966

March: French withdrawal from NATO

1967

May: Successful conclusion of Kennedy round in GATT

November: Second de Gaulle veto of British Common Market entry

1969

April: De Gaulle resignation; election of Pompidou follows in June

1973

January: Admission of Britain to Common Market

NOTES

Abbreviations

The following abbreviations are used throughout the notes.

AA
: Auswärtiges Amt

Akten
: *Akten zur Auswärtigen Politik der Bundesrepublik Deutschland 1963* (Bonn: Politisches Archiv des Auswärtigen Amtes, 1994)

Amérique
: Amérique, Ministère des Affaires Étrangères, Paris

B2
: Büro Staatssekretär, Politisches Archiv des Auswärtigen Amtes, Bonn

B24
: France, Politisches Archiv des Auswärtigen Amtes, Bonn

B32
: United States, Politisches Archiv des Auswärtigen Amtes, Bonn

B102
: Ministry of Economics Papers, Bundesarchiv Koblenz, Koblenz

B136
: Chancellor's Office Papers, Bundesarchiv Koblenz, Koblenz

BMWi
: Bundesministerium für Wirtschaft

CAB
: Cabinet Papers, Public Records Office, London

Cabinet Debré
: Debré Cabinet Papers, Archives des Services du Premier Ministre, Fontainebleau

Cabinet du Ministre
: Cabinet du Ministre, Ministère des Affaires Étrangères, Paris

CFEP Chair Records
: Council on Foreign Economic Policy Chair Records, Dwight D. Eisenhower Library, Abilene, Kansas

CFEP Policy Records
: Council on Foreign Economic Policy Records, Dwight D. Eisenhower Library, Abilene, Kansas

CM
: Maurice Couve de Murville Papers, Fondation Nationale des Sciences Politiques, Paris

D&M
: Charles de Gaulle, *Discours et messages*, 5 vols. (Paris: Plon, 1970–71)

DDF

Commission de Publication des Documents Diplomatiques Français, *Documents Diplomatiques Français* (Paris: Imprimerie Nationale, 1987–)

DE-CE

Coopération Économique, Ministère des Affaires Étrangères, Paris

Decimal File

Decimal Files, State Department Diplomatic Branch Papers (Record Group 59), National Archives, College Park, Maryland

DGESS

Institut Charles de Gaulle, *De Gaulle en son siècle*, 6 vols. (Paris: Plon, 1991–92)

Europe

Europe, Ministère des Affaires Étrangères, Paris

5AG1

Papers of the Presidents of the 5th Republic, Archives Nationales, Paris

FO

Foreign Office

FO371

Foreign Office Papers, Public Records Office, London

4AG

Papers of the Presidents of the 4th Republic, Archives Nationales, Paris

FRUS

Foreign Relations of the United States (Washington: Government Printing Office, 1861–)

INR

Bureau of Intelligence and Research, State Department, State Department Diplomatic Branch Papers (Record Group 59), National Archives, College Park, Maryland

JFD Papers

John Foster Dulles Papers, Dwight D. Eisenhower Library, Abilene, Kansas

LNC

Charles de Gaulle, *Lettres, notes et carnets*, 13 vols. (Paris: Plon, 1980–97)

Lot File

Lot Files, State Department Diplomatic Branch Papers (Record Group 59), National Archives, College Park, Maryland

MAE

Ministère des Affaires Étrangères, Quai d'Orsay

MB

Ministerbüro, Politisches Archiv des Auswärtigen Amtes, Bonn

NAUK

Office of Atlantic Political and Economic Affairs, Alpha-Numeric Files, U.K. Entry into EEC, State Department Diplomatic Branch Papers (Record Group 59), National Archives, College Park, Maryland

NIE

National Intelligence Estimate

NL1239

Heinrich von Brentano Papers, Bundesarchiv Koblenz, Koblenz

NL1254

Franz Etzel Papers, Bundesarchiv Koblenz, Koblenz

NL1266

Walter Hallstein Papers, Bundesarchiv Koblenz, Koblenz

NL1337

Karl Carstens Papers, Bundesarchiv Koblenz, Koblenz

NL1351

Herbert Blankenhorn Papers, Bundesarchiv Koblenz, Koblenz

NSAM

National Security Action Memorandum

NSC Special Assistant Papers

National Security Council Special Assistant Papers, Dwight D. Eisenhower Library, Abilene, Kansas

NSC Staff Papers

National Security Council Staff Papers, Dwight D. Eisenhower Library, Abilene, Kansas

NSF

National Security Files, John F. Kennedy Library, Boston, Massachusetts

OCB

Operations Coordinating Board, State Department

POF

President's Office Files, John F. Kennedy Library, Boston, Massachusetts

PPS

Policy Planning Staff, State Department

PREM11

Prime Minister's Office Papers, Public Records Office, London

Referat 200-IA2

European Economic Integration, Politisches Archiv des Auswärtigen Amtes, Bonn

Referat 201-IA1 and IA1

European Political Integration, Politisches Archiv des Auswärtigen Amtes, Bonn

Referat 304-IA5

Great Britain, Politisches Archiv des Auswärtigen Amtes, Bonn

Secrétariat Général

Secrétariat Général, Ministère des Affaires Étrangères, Paris

STBKAH

Konrad Adenauer Papers, Stiftung Bundeskanzler Adenauer Haus, Bonn

WBA

Willy Brandt Archive Papers, Archiv der Sozialen Demokratie, Bonn

WHCF/DDEL

White House Central Files, Dwight D. Eisenhower Library, Abilene, Kansas

Whitman File

Ann Whitman File, Dwight D. Eisenhower Library, Abilene, Kansas

WHONSAR
White House Office—Office of the Special Assistant for National Security Affairs
Records, Dwight D. Eisenhower Library, Abilene, Kansas
WHOSS
White House Office—Office of the Staff Secretary Records, Dwight D. Eisenhower
Library, Abilene, Kansas
Wormser Papers
Olivier Wormser Papers, Ministère des Affaires Étrangères, Paris

Introduction

1. Throughout this book "Germany" is used to refer to the Federal Republic of Germany (FRG, or West Germany). This is a choice made for convenience and not intended to imply any political statement. When the German Democratic Republic (GDR, or East Germany) appears, the text distinguishes clearly between the two German states. Similarly, "Europe" and "European integration" appear throughout the book, in almost every case referring to Western Europe alone. In 1947 the Soviet Union refused to allow the countries of Eastern Europe to take part in the Marshall Plan, and from this point until the end of the Cold War they were left out of the integration process. Two other terms used frequently are the "Six," referring to the original members of the European community (France, West Germany, Italy, and Benelux), and the "Five," referring to these same countries save France, which from the late 1950s onward frequently took positions at odds with those of its partners.

2. Milward, *The European Rescue of the Nation State*; Hogan, *The Marshall Plan*; Reynolds, *The Origins of the Cold War in Europe*; Lundestad, "*Empire" by Integration*. The term "sectoral integration" refers to proposals to unify specific economic "sectors," such as the production of coal and steel or the development of atomic energy. In the early days of European integration, such proposals were frequently contrasted with more ambitious ideas for comprehensive political, military, and economic communities.

3. On Soviet policy, see Zubok and Pleshakov, *Inside the Kremlin's Cold War*.

4. For a general discussion of American European policy, see Winand, *United States of Europe*.

5. For basic German policy goals as defined by Adenauer, see Schwarz, *Adenauer*.

6. For a good early summation of Britain's postwar European policy in its wider global context, see Northedge, *Descent from Power*.

7. On the elements of continuity and discontinuity between the Fourth Republic and de Gaulle, see Bossuat, *L'Europe des Français*.

8. Some representative examples: Camps, *Britain and the European Community*; Grosser, *La politique extérieure de la Ve république*; Kolodziej, *French International Policy*; Cerny, *The Politics of Grandeur*; Gordon, *A Certain Idea of France*; Couve de Murville, *Une politique étrangère 1958–1969*; Carstens, *Erinnerungen und Erfahrungen*; Blankenhorn, *Verständnis*; Maillard, *De Gaulle et l'Allemagne*; Peyrefitte, *C'était de Gaulle*; Schlesinger, *A Thousand Days*; Ball, *The Past Has Another Pattern*.

9. Bossuat, *L'Europe des Français*; Vaïsse, *La grandeur*; Kaiser, *Using Europe*; Winand, *United States of Europe*; Lee, *An Uneasy Partnership*; Conze, *Die gaullistische Heraus-*

forderung; Hanrieder, *Deutschland, Europa, Amerika*; Mayer, *Adenauer and Kennedy*; Soutou, *L'alliance incertaine*; Bozo, *Deux stratégies pour l'Europe*; Ambrose, *Eisenhower*; Lacouture, *De Gaulle*; Horne, *Harold Macmillan*; Schwarz, *Adenauer*; Ludlow, *Dealing with Britain*; Gerbet, *La construction de l'Europe*; Urwin, *The Community of Europe*; Trachtenberg, *A Constructed Peace*; Bange, *The EEC Crisis of 1963*; Pagedas, *Anglo-American Strategic Relations*.

10. For a good introduction to these debates, see Wurm, *Western Europe and Germany*.

Chapter One

1. Among others, see Bossuat, *L'Europe des Français*; Gerbet, *La construction de l'Europe* and *La France et l'intégration européenne*; Bitsch, *Histoire de la construction européenne*; Urwin, *The Community of Europe*; Lundestad, *"Empire" by Integration*; Duchêne, *Jean Monnet*; Gillingham, *Coal, Steel, and the Rebirth of Europe*; Nugent, *The Government and Politics of the European Union*; Ellwood, *Rebuilding Europe*; Brusse, *Tariffs, Trade and European Integration*.

2. Duchêne, *Jean Monnet*, 262–83.

3. Second Messina Session, 2 June 1955, Cabinet du Ministre—Pineau 1. See also Dulles to Bonn on embassy conversation with German foreign ministry officials, 1 July 1955, *FRUS* (1955–57), 4:307–8. The German policy statement presented at the Messina conference made most of these points.

4. Adenauer, *Teegespräche, 1959–1961*, 90.

5. Garton Ash, *In Europe's Name*, chap. 1; Blankenhorn, *Verständnis*, 47–50. Contemporary expressions of this policy are in Karl Carstens (head of the subsection for European questions in the AA at this point) to Ambassador Herbert Blankenhorn (Paris), 20 November 1958, NL1351/92b; Adenauer speech on European unity, 25 September 1956, B2/12; Undated comments of Carstens and von Brentano at a conference of German ambassadors in late 1955, NL1351/41a.

6. Adenauer, *Teegespräche, 1959–1961*, 134, 138; Schwarz, *Adenauer*, 285–86.

7. Von Brentano note to Adenauer, 3 September 1959, NL1337/646; von Brentano, *Sehr Verehrter Herr Bundeskanzler!*

8. Adenauer-Erhard debate, 15 February 1957, NL1337/643-5; Lee, *An Uneasy Partnership*, 159–63. Other revealing sessions in the German cabinet include 5 October 1956 and 10 January 1957, NL1337/643–5.

9. Immerman, *John Foster Dulles* and "Confessions of an Eisenhower Revisionist"; Preussen, *John Foster Dulles*.

10. Eisenhower comments to the NSC, 21 November 1955, *FRUS* (1955–57), 4:348–49; Eisenhower-Erhard conversation, 5 June 1959, Whitman File—International series, box 15.

11. Eisenhower comments to Max Kohnstamm, Louis Armand, and Francesco Giordani (European officials involved in the Common Market negotiations), 6 February 1957, *FRUS* (1955–57), 4:516–18.

12. Eisenhower-Dulles conversation, 1 May 1956, JFD Papers, box 4; Ambrose, *Eisenhower*, 49–50.

13. Eisenhower conversation with Franz Etzel (vice president of the ECSC and later German minister of finance), 6 February 1957, Whitman File—DDE Diary series, box 22.

14. Immerman, "Confessions of an Eisenhower Revisionist."

15. NSC meeting, 4 October 1956, Whitman File—NSC series, box 7.

16. Ibid.

17. Dulles-Eisenhower conversation, 26 December 1955, JFD Papers, box 3; Dulles to Eisenhower, 3 February 1956, Whitman File—International series, box 9.

18. Foreign Secretary Selwyn Lloyd minute to Macmillan, 13 December 1959, PREM11/2985. These ideas are also emphasized throughout Horne, *Harold Macmillan*, vol. 2; Northedge, *Descent from Power*; Dimbleby and Reynolds, *An Ocean Apart*.

19. Cabinet meeting, 4 March 1959, CAB128/33; Northedge, *Descent from Power*, chap. 5.

20. Burgess and Edwards, "The Six plus One."

21. Cabinet meeting, 30 June 1955, CAB128/29; cabinet meeting, 15 December 1959, CAB128/33.

22. Cabinet meeting, 23 December 1958, CAB128/32.

23. Cabinet meeting, 4 January 1956, CAB128/30; cabinet meetings, 5 November and 15 December 1959, CAB128/33.

24. Undated [early 1958] cabinet memorandum C. (58) 65, CAB129/95; Macmillan, *Riding the Storm*, 435.

25. De Gaulle–Macmillan conversations, 29–30 June 1958, *DDF*, 12:861–71; Macmillan, *Riding the Storm*, 434, 440.

26. DE-CE note, 22 December 1956, DE-CE (1945–60) 614; Bossuat, *L'Europe des Français*, 241–42.

27. Bossuat, "Le choix de la petite Europe."

28. Gallup, *The Gallup Poll*, vol. 2–3; Lundestad, *"Empire" by Integration*, 83–90.

29. Gallup, *The Gallup International Public Opinion Polls*, vol. 1.

30. Moon, *European Integration in British Politics*. See also the articles on various interest groups in Britain and their views on Europe in Baker and Seawright, *Britain for and against Europe*.

31. Bulmer and Patterson, *The Federal Republic of Germany and the European Community*, 108–22.

32. Noelle and Neumann, *The Germans*, 214–16.

33. Feld, *West Germany and the European Community*, 35–48.

34. Bossuat, *L'Europe des Français*, chap. 12, and "Le choix de la petite Europe."

35. Blankenhorn, *Verständnis*, 50.

36. Adenauer letter to Pinay, 13 April 1955, B2/101; Franz Etzel paper, 22 April 1955, B2/104; Carstens note, 24 November 1955, Referat 200-IA2/87; Bitsch, *Histoire de la construction européenne*, 107.

37. Jean François-Ponçet (Bonn) to Mendès-France, 29 November 1954, 4AG/28.

38. Pinay-Macmillan (foreign secretary at this point) conversation, 21 April 1955, *DDF*, 4 (Annex vol. 1): 21–29; Rimbaud, *Pinay*, 303.

39. MAE note for Prime Minister Faure, 7 April 1955, MAE note, 14 April 1955, DE-CE note, 18 April 1955, DE-CE (1945–60) 611.

40. Hallstein statement of the German position at Messina, 2 June 1955, Cabinet du Ministre—Pineau 1. On the divisions among the Germans on how best to proceed, see Bitsch, *Histoire de la construction européenne*, 107, and Schwarz, *Adenauer*, 287.

41. Hallstein statement at Messina, 2 June 1955, Cabinet du Ministre—Pineau 1; Hallstein note, 30 March 1955, B2/100.

42. Dulles-Erhard conversation, 7 June 1955, Dulles-Adenauer conversation, 14 June 1955, Dulles to Bonn, 1 July 1955, *FRUS* (1955–57), 4:291–92, 297, 307–8.

43. MAE to Stations on 21 April Pinay-Macmillan conversation, 25 April 1955, DE-CE (1945–60) 611.

44. MAE note on the Benelux proposals, 7 April 1955, *DDF*, 4:418–21; DE-CE note, 18 May 1955, DE-CE (1945–60) 611; Bossuat, *L'Europe des Français*, 272–73.

45. MAE note, late April–early May 1955, *DDF*, 4:546–51.

46. MAE note to Brussels delegation, 5 July 1955, *DDF*, 5:19–23; DE-CE note, 1 August 1955, DE-CE (1945–60) 612; Bossuat, *L'Europe des Français*, 266–67.

47. Pinay to Stations on Messina outcome, 10 June 1955, *DDF*, 4:756–58.

48. Adenauer-Dulles conversation, 14 June 1955, *FRUS* (1955–57), 4:297.

49. Dulles comments at NSC meeting, 6 October 1954, Whitman File—NSC series, box 6.

50. State Dept. to Rome on U.S. European policy, 30 May 1955, *FRUS* (1955–57), 4:290.

51. Dulles conversation with Harold Stassen (an Eisenhower adviser/assistant on disarmament and security matters), 7 June 1955, JFD Papers, box 11; Ambrose, *Eisenhower*, 404.

52. State Dept. planning paper on U.S. European policy, 18 August 1955, Lot File 66 D 70, box 97.

53. Dulles-Erhard conversation, 7 June 1955, and Dulles-Adenauer conversation, 14 June 1955, *FRUS* (1955–57), 4:291–92, 297; Winand, *United States of Europe*, chap. 3; Lundestad, "*Empire" by Integration*, 50. So dubious were the Americans that they initially put more stock in the success of a European atomic community (the ultimate Euratom) than in the chances of a common market.

54. Macmillan-Pinay conversation, 21 April 1955, *DDF*, 4 (Annex vol. 1): 21–29.

55. FO note on France, 13 April 1955, and Sir Gladwyn Jebb (Paris) to Eden, 1 April 1955, FO371/118115; Burgess and Edwards, "The Six plus One."

56. R. A. Butler (chancellor of the exchequer) memo for the cabinet, 29 June 1955, CAB129/76; cabinet meeting, 30 June 1955, CAB128/29.

57. FO to Stations, 17 November 1955, and unsigned note on Eden's views, 19 November 1955, PREM11/1333; Young, "The Parting of the Ways"; Horne, *Harold Macmillan*, 1:362–64.

58. AA note on the progress of the negotiations, 14 May 1956, B2/11.

59. Note on von Brentano-Spaak conversation, 14 November 1955, B2/106; Christian de Margerie (Bonn) to MAE on conversations of German leaders with Spaak, 15 November 1955, DE-CE (1945–60) 629.

60. Carstens, *Erinnerungen*, 214–15.

61. Erhard letter to von Brentano, 23 November 1955, NL1266/1457; AA note, 2 December 1955, NL1266/1457; AA note, 3 December 1955, Referat 200-IA2/87; von Brentano letter to Adenauer, 18 December 1955, NL1239/156.

62. AA note, 24 October 1956, Referat 200-IA2/110.

63. AA note on 29 September 1956 Adenauer meeting with French prime minister Guy Mollet, 1 October 1956, MB155.

64. Schwarz, *Adenauer*, 289.

65. Paris embassy to AA, 25 April 1956, B24/308.

66. AA note on disagreements with Erhard, undated [November 1956], B2/12.

67. Cabinet meeting, 5 October 1956, NL1337/643.

68. AA note on 6 October 1956 interministerial meeting, undated, Referat 200-IA2/89a.

69. Cabinet meeting, 9 May 1956, NL1337/642; AA note, 19 September 1956, B2/11.

70. Briefing note for Adenauer's meetings with Mollet in November 1956, undated, B2/12.

71. Erhard letter to Etzel, 16 November 1956, NL1254/85.

72. Von Brentano letter to Adenauer, 29 October 1956, AA note, undated [late October–early November 1956], NL1254/84; Etzel letter to Erhard, 3 December 1956, NL1254/84.

73. Von Brentano–Mollet conversation, 15 September 1956, MB155; Paris to AA, 3 October 1956, B24/309.

74. Adenauer had already made many of these points in a 25 September 1956 speech in Brussels calling for the creation of a European federation. The text of the speech is in B2/12. On his growing doubts about the United States in 1956, see Schwarz, *Adenauer*, 291–96.

75. Mollet-Adenauer meeting, 6 November 1956, *DDF*, 9:231–38; AA note on the meeting, 9 November 1956, MB156.

76. Pineau to Stations, 8 November 1956, *DDF*, 9:249–51; Text of Franco-German technical agreements, 6 November 1956, Europe (1944–60): Généralités 185; Bossuat, *L'Europe des Français*, 336.

77. Cabinet meeting, 10 January 1957, NL1337/644.

78. Euratom was designed to pool the civilian nuclear programs of the member countries. In practice it was quickly overshadowed by the Common Market and it was actually merged with the more successful economic community in 1967.

79. Carstens note, 18 July 1957, NL1266/1462.

80. Carstens note, 8 July 1957, NL1266/1462; von Brentano letters to Adenauer, 9 and 22 December 1957, NL1239/157.

81. Paris to State Dept. on Pineau conversation, 7 February 1956, *FRUS* (1955–57), 4:407–8; MAE note, 23 February 1956, and DE-CE note on the Spaak report, 17 April 1956, *DDF*, 7:272–73, 610–13; Bruno Riondel, "Maurice Faure et la négociation des Traités de Rome," in Girault and Bossuat, *Europe brisée, Europe retrouvée*, 347–64; Christian Tauch, "The Testimony of an Eyewitness: Christian Pineau," in Griffiths, *Socialist Parties and the Question of Europe in the 1950s*, 57–62.

82. Guillen, *La question allemande*, 64.

83. Note of the ministry for overseas territories to Pineau, 17 May 1956, Cabinet du Ministre—Pineau 2; DE-CE note, undated [January 1956], *DDF*, 7:121–23; interministerial meetings on European integration, 22–25 April 1955, DE-CE (1945–60) 611.

84. DE-CE note, 22 December 1956, DE-CE (1945–60) 614.

85. DE-CE note, 27 December 1955, DE-CE (1945–60) 612.

86. Alphand (Washington) to MAE, 24 January 1957, DE-CE (1945–60) 706; Christian de Margerie (Bonn) to MAE, 12 December 1955, Amérique (1952–63): Etats-Unis 379.

87. Christian de Margerie (Bonn) to MAE, 3 May 1956, Europe (1944–60): Généralités 184.

88. Pineau to Stations, 24 November 1956, *DDF*, 9:401–2; DE-CE note, 29 November 1956, DE-CE (1945–60) 614; Mollet letter to Adenauer, 11 January 1957, Cabinet du Ministre—Couve de Murville 69; Alphand (Washington) to MAE, 16 February 1957, Amérique (1952–63): Etats-Unis 333; MAE note, 19 December 1957, *DDF*, 11:938–42; Guillen, "L'Europe remède a l'impuissance française"; Lefebvre, *Guy Mollet*, 246–75; Bossuat, "Guy Mollet."

89. Pineau, *1956/Suez*, 86–87.

90. Mollet-Eden meeting, 27 September 1956, PREM11/1352.

91. Cabinet meeting, 26 September 1956, CAB128/30.

92. FO memo, 22 September 1956, FO meeting, 4 October 1956, and cabinet meeting, 1 October 1956, PREM11/1352; Adamthwaite, "Marianne et John Bull."

93. MAE note, 19 January 1957, *DDF*, 10:118–20.

94. MAE note, 28 November 1956, Amérique (1952–63): Etats-Unis 332.

95. Alphand (Washington) to MAE, 12 January 1957, DE-CE (1945–60) 706.

96. Mollet letter to Adenauer, 31 October 1956, Europe (1944–60): Allemagne 1259; Franco-German conversations, 6 November 1956, *DDF*, 9:231–38; Soutou, *L'alliance incertaine*, 46–47.

97. MAE briefing note for Mollet for the Adenauer meeting, 3 November 1956, Cabinet du Ministre—Pineau 13.

98. Eden comments at cabinet meeting, 9 February 1956, CAB128/30.

99. Dulles–Selwyn Lloyd conversation, 30 January 1956, and Peter Thorneycroft (president of the Board of Trade) letter to Macmillan (chancellor of the exchequer at this point), 18 February 1956, PREM11/1333.

100. FO note on Pineau conversation with FO officials, 3 January 1956, FO371/124443; FO note, 22 May 1956, FO371/124448.

101. Cabinet meeting, 13 November 1956, CAB128/30.

102. Vaïsse, *La grandeur*, 163–64.

103. Macmillan minute to Selwyn Lloyd, 3 June 1957, FO371/130972.

104. Briefing memo for January 1956 Eden-Eisenhower meeting, undated, PREM11/1334; FO paper on European issues, 2 July 1956, FO371/124443.

105. Jebb meeting with FO officials in London, 15 July 1957, FO371/130973; Jebb (Paris) to FO, 27 April 1957, FO371/130970.

106. See Dimbleby and Reynolds, *An Ocean Apart*, for analysis of Suez in the long-term context of British-American relations, particularly chaps. 11–12.

107. Selwyn Lloyd memo on France's European policy, 6 December 1957, and FO note, 18 December 1957, FO371/130636.

108. Paris to State Dept., 8 February 1957, Decimal File 440.002/1-257 (1955–59), box 1847.

109. Dulles-Spaak conversation, 17 December 1955, *FRUS* (1955–57), 4:369–71; Macmillan-Eisenhower meetings, 22 March 1957, *FRUS* (1955–57), 27:722–27. Britain's initial refusal to participate in the EDC had done much to discredit the plan in France, and its April 1954 pledge to assign one division to the project came too late to sway French opinion.

110. Paris embassy memo, 17 January 1956, *FRUS* (1955–57), 27:25–26; Ambrose, *Eisenhower*, 181–83.

111. NSC planning note on NSC 5721 (U.S. policy on France), 8 October 1957, NSC Staff Papers—Special Staff File, box 3.

112. NSC paper on U.S. policy toward France, 19 October 1957, *FRUS* (1955–57), 27:181.

113. Dulles conversation with German politicians, 18 February 1957, *FRUS* (1955–57), 4:525–26.

114. State Dept. to Stations on U.S. goals for the Common Market, 13 July 1956, *FRUS* (1955–57), 4:450–53; Winand, *United States of Europe*, 110–11.

115. CFEP report, 20 November 1956, NSC Staff Papers—CFEP series, box 7; Winand, *United States of Europe*, 114. The GATT was the international organization, established after World War II, which administered the General Agreement on Tariffs and Trade to set rules for, and facilitate the multilateral liberalization of, trade policy. In 1994 it was transformed into the current World Trade Organization (WTO) at the end of the Uruguay round of negotiations.

116. MAE notes, 19 March and 5 April 1957, Europe (1944–60): Généralités 186.

117. Vaïsse, *La grandeur*, 167; Bossuat, *L'Europe des Français*, 384–86, 398–99; Maillard, *De Gaulle et l'Europe*, 120–28.

118. Unsigned note on interministerial plans for French foreign policy approved by de Gaulle, 22 July 1958, Cabinet du Ministre—Couve de Murville 34. For detail on the military and NATO dimensions of de Gaulle's plans, see Bozo, *Deux stratégies pour l'Europe*.

119. MAE notes, 1 October 1958 and 14 August 1959, DE-CE (1961–66) 509.

120. DE-CE note, 12 September 1958, DE-CE (1945–60) 615.

121. Debré note to Couve de Murville, 15 March 1960, and de Gaulle note to Couve de Murville and Debré, 1 March 1960, CM7; Debré, *Gouverner*, 392.

122. Couve de Murville comments during Franco-Italian conversations, 19–20 March 1959, *DDF*, 14:395–98; Couve de Murville, *Une politique étrangère*, 292–99.

123. MAE note, 6 September 1958, Europe (1944–60): Allemagne 1260.

124. Von Brentano letter to Adenauer, 5 November 1957, NL1239/157.

125. AA note on French European policy, 5 March 1958, B24/311.

126. Schwarz, *Adenauer*, 439–40.

127. Carstens, *Erinnerungen*, 245.

128. AA note on European policy and de Gaulle, 19 June 1958, MB55.

129. AA note on French European policy, 20 November 1959, Referat 200-IA2/485.

130. Carstens (now state secretary) comments to Austrian ambassador, 14 September 1960, Referat 200-IA2/489.

131. AA note for Carstens, 25 November 1958, Referat 200-IA2/150; AA note for Carstens on the views of the German cabinet on the fusion issue, 10 June 1960, MB50.

132. AA paper, 27 October 1958, B24/293; Carstens, *Erinnerungen*, 245–47; Schwarz, *Adenauer*, 464–66; Lee, *An Uneasy Partnership*, 278–88; Adenauer, *Teegespräche 1959–1961*, 146–47.

133. British planning papers for the meetings between Macmillan and de Gaulle, undated, PREM11/2336; Macmillan–de Gaulle meetings, 29–30 June 1958, *DDF*, 12:861–86; Macmillan, *Riding the Storm*, 434, 450–55, 527.

134. Macmillan conversation with French ambassador Jean Chauvel, 20 June 1958, PREM11/2336; Horne, *Harold Macmillan*, 2:109–12.

135. FO note, 6 November 1959, FO371/145755; Macmillan, *Pointing the Way*, 55–56.

136. Christopher Steel (Bonn) to FO, 10 April 1958, PREM11/2341.

137. Derick Heathcoat Amory (chancellor of the exchequer) memo for the cabinet on the United States and Europe, 14 December 1959, CAB129/99; Macmillan, *Pointing the Way*, 59.

138. Dulles to Stations, 20 March 1958, *FRUS* (1958–60), 7 (pt. 1): 20–23; State Dept. planning paper, "U.S. Policy toward European and Atlantic Regionalism," 10 June 1960, Lot File 67 D 548, box 152.

139. NIE on Western Europe, 29 July 1958, *FRUS* (1958–60), 7 (pt. 1): 61–64.

140. State Dept. INR paper 8141, "Western European Interrelationships over the next five years," 17 December 1959, INR File 8141.

141. Briefing note for Eisenhower's August–September trip to Europe, 23 August 1959, Lot File 65 D 265, box 2; Unsigned briefing paper for the same trip, WHCF/DDEL— Confidential File, box 53; Ambrose, *Eisenhower*, 538–41.

142. State Dept. INR report, "A Critical Appraisal of Western Unity," 7 August 1959, Lot File 67 D 548, box 151; State Dept. planning paper, "U.S. Policy toward European and Atlantic Regionalism," 10 June 1960, Lot File 67 D 548, box 152; Winand, *United States of Europe*, 118, 130–31.

143. MAE to Bonn, 12 February 1960, DE-CE (1945–60) 802. This aspect was very important to the French.

144. Macmillan-Herter-Dillon conversation, 28 March 1960, *FRUS* (1958–60), 7 (pt. 1): 272–77. The editors of *FRUS* removed some of the more inflammatory comments of both the British and the Americans, but the uncensored version can be found in Lot File 64 D 199, box 15.

145. Macmillan, *Pointing the Way*, 313–16.

146. Macmillan letters to de Gaulle, 7 April and 10 May 1960, *DDF*, 17:434–35, 452–55; de Gaulle letter to Macmillan, 13 April 1960, *LNC*, 8:348–50.

147. Dillon–Olivier Wormser (head of the economic section at the Quai d'Orsay) conversation, 5 October 1959, *FRUS* (1958–60), 7 (pt. 1): 155–58; briefing paper for 14–17 March 1960 Adenauer visit to the United States, March 1960, WHCF/DDEL—Confidential File, box 80.

148. Dillon-Herter-Macmillan conversation, 28 March 1960, *FRUS* (1958–60), 7 (pt. 1): 272–77; Winand, *United States of Europe*, 120–21.

149. MAE note, 15 April 1960, *DDF*, 17:485–90; Chauvel (London) to MAE on conversation with Selwyn Lloyd, 28 March 1960, and MAE to Washington, 5 April 1960, DE-CE (1945–60) 764.

150. De Gaulle letter to Macmillan, 13 April 1960, *LNC*, 8:348–50.

151. Wormser to Bonn, 8 April 1960, and DE-CE note, 12 April 1960, DE-CE (1945–60) 616.

152. Note of the French permanent delegation in Brussels on the United States and the Common Market, 8 January 1960, DE-CE (1945–60) 615; briefing note for April 1960 de Gaulle visit to the United States, undated, Cabinet du Ministre—Couve de Murville 129; Vaïsse, *La grandeur*, 171.

153. AA note, 5 April 1960, B2/80; Adenauer, *Erinnerungen*, 4:46; Feld, *West Germany and the European Community*, 45–48.

154. Seydoux (Bonn) to MAE on conversation with von Brentano, 7 March 1960, DE-CE (1945–60) 630; von Brentano letter to Adenauer, 20 March 1960, NL1239/158.

155. Meeting of the foreign ministers of the Six, 23 November 1959, Europe (1944–60): Généralités 168; chancellor's office note, 20 November 1959, B136/1299.

156. AA note on Erhard's views, 9 March 1960, B2/73.

157. AA note, 5 April 1960, B2/75; Seydoux (Bonn) to MAE on the German position, 5 April 1960, and Seydoux (Bonn) to MAE on Carstens conversation, 23 April 1960, DE-CE (1945–60) 630; Dillon–von Brentano conversation, 12 April 1960, Lot 64 D 199, box 14.

158. Wormser to Bonn, 8 April 1960, DE-CE (1945–60) 616; Seydoux (Bonn) to MAE, 29 April 1960, DE-CE (1945–60) 630.

159. Couve de Murville to Stations, 14 May 1960, *DDF*, 17:625–28.

160. State Dept. study on recent European developments, 20 June 1960, NSC Staff Papers—NSC Registry series, box 13. See also Winand, *United States of Europe*, chap. 7, on the Kennedy administration's "inheritance" from its predecessor.

161. FO371/150361 and FO371/150362; interministerial report, 6 July 1960, CAB129/102; cabinet meeting, 13 July 1960, CAB128/34; Macmillan, *Pointing the Way*, 316–23. The failure of the May 1960 Paris East-West summit, and with it Macmillan's hopes for détente, also influenced his move toward Europe.

162. Chauvel (London) to MAE, 2 December 1960, *DDF*, 18:699–702. See, for example, the French attitude during a rough spot in Franco-German relations in late 1960 when Germany appeared to be aligning with Britain.

Chapter Two

1. Macmillan (Exchequer) and Thorneycroft (Board of Trade) note for the cabinet on the FTA, 6 November 1956, CAB128/84.

2. General studies and biographies that go into considerable detail on the Common Market make little or no mention of the FTA: Grosser, *Affaires extérieures* and *La politique extérieure de la Ve république*; George, *Politics and Policy in the European Community*; Lundestad, *"Empire" by Integration*; Ambrose, *Eisenhower*; Schwarz, *Adenauer*; Gerbet, *La construction de l'Europe*. Exceptions to the rule include Camps, *Britain and the European Community*; Urwin, *The Community of Europe*.

3. Greenwood, *Britain and European Cooperation*; Winand, *United States of Europe*; Lee, *An Uneasy Partnership*; Bossuat, *L'Europe des Français*; Kaiser, *Using Europe*; Bell, "Les attitudes de la Grande Bretagne"; Bossuat, "Le choix de la petite Europe"; Ellison, "Perfidious Albion?"; Frank, "France–Grande Bretagne"; Lynch, "De Gaulle's First Veto."

4. For examples, see Greenwood, *Britain and European Cooperation*, 70, on the British motivation for the FTA; Vaïsse, *La grandeur*, 162–69, on the role of the United States; Anne Deighton on the significance of the FTA (or lack thereof, in her view), "La Grande Bretagne et la Communauté économique européenne."

5. Kaiser, *Using Europe*, 88; Moon, *European Integration in British Politics*, 146–51, 174–78; George Wilkes and Dominic Wring, "The British Press and European Integration: 1948 to 1996," in Baker and Seawright, *Britain for and against Europe*, 185–205; Gallup, *The Gallup International Public Opinion Polls*, vol. 1.

6. Lundestad, *"Empire" by Integration*, 40–57; Winand, *United States of Europe*, 119; Gallup, *The Gallup Poll*, vols. 2 and 3.

7. Feld, *West Germany and the European Community*, 45–48, 145; Noelle and Neu-

mann, *The Germans*, 266, 271, 281; Bulmer and Paterson, *The Federal Republic of Germany*, 104–11.

8. Bossuat, "Le choix de la petite Europe" and *L'Europe des Français*, 401–33; Charlot, *Les Français et de Gaulle*.

9. Cabinet meeting, 13 November 1956, CAB128/30; Greenwood, *Britain and European Cooperation*, 61–63.

10. Macmillan-Thorneycroft note for the cabinet and additional cabinet notes Nos. 191–92, 9 July 1956, CAB129/82; Lee, *An Uneasy Partnership*, 125–27; Greenwood, *Britain and European Cooperation*, 68.

11. British note for the OEEC, 31 January 1957, DE-CE (1945–60) 761; Macmillan memo for the cabinet, 11 September 1956, CAB129/83; cabinet meeting, 14 September 1956, CAB128/30.

12. Eisenhower-Eden conversation, 30 January 1956, *FRUS* (1955–57), 27:620; cabinet meeting, 9 February 1956, CAB128/30; Macmillan note for the cabinet, 11 September 1956, CAB129/83.

13. Cabinet meetings, 18 September and 3 October 1956, CAB128/30; Chauvel (London) to MAE on the Macmillan press conference, 4 October 1956, *DDF*, 8:513–14.

14. FO briefing note for March 1957 U.S.-U.K. meetings, undated, FO371/130968; Selwyn Lloyd draft memo on the Grand Design for the cabinet, 29 January 1957, FO371/130966; Selwyn Lloyd–Dulles conversation, 22 March 1957, FO371/130969; British note on the Grand Design, 31 May 1957, Lot File 61 D 179, box 1; Kaiser, *Using Europe*, 96–100. Not everyone in the British cabinet was enthusiastic and many anticipated the negative American and European responses.

15. Chauvel (London) to MAE on British account of a conversation with Erhard, 2 April 1957, and Macmillan–Christian Pineau (French foreign minister) conversation, 9 April 1957, *DDF*, 10:427–32, 548–50.

16. Selwyn Lloyd–Chauvel conversation, 11 July 1957, *DDF*, 11:65–69; Macmillan, *Riding the Storm*, 436–37.

17. Cabinet meeting, 15 February 1957, NL1337/645; cabinet meeting, 5 October 1956, NL1337/643; Lee, *An Uneasy Partnership*, 128–29.

18. Washington to AA, 16 January 1957, B32/39.

19. Maurice Faure (French secretary of state for foreign affairs)–Adenauer conversation, 17 September 1956, and Couve de Murville (ambassador in Bonn at this point) to MAE on Adenauer conversation, 10 October 1956, *DDF*, 8:395–96, 553–54; cabinet meeting, 5 October 1956, NL1337/643; AA note on 4 April 1957 interministerial meeting on the FTA, 5 April 1957, Referat 200-IA2/457; Lee, *An Uneasy Partnership*, 60–69.

20. Carstens notes, 30 March and 6 April 1957, Referat 200-IA2/89a; AA notes, 11 and 15 April 1957, Referat 200-IA2/110; Hallstein to Stations, 16 May 1957, Referat 200-IA2/110; Adenauer–von Brentano–Dulles conversation, 4 May 1957, Lot File 64 D 199, box 6.

21. Pineau to Stations, 2 October 1956, *DDF*, 8:493–96; MAE note, 19 January 1957, *DDF*, 10:118–20.

22. MAE note on the FTA, 17 May 1957, DE-CE (1945–60) 751; DE-CE note, 22 December 1956, DE-CE (1945–60) 614; Bossuat, *L'Europe des Français*, 371. However, the note cited also stated that France should seek the largest possible FTA, while protecting French economic interests and the Common Market.

23. Pineau to Stations, 19 April 1957, *DDF*, 10:644–45.

24. Wormser conversation with a British treasury official, 16 April 1957, DE-CE (1945–60) 701.

25. MAE note, 19 January 1957, *DDF*, 10:118–20.

26. Maurice Faure–Erhard conversation, 16 September 1956, *DDF*, 8:584–87.

27. MAE notes, 25 January and 15 May 1957, DE-CE (1945–60) 751.

28. MAE note, 15 May 1957, DE-CE (1945–60) 741.

29. MAE notes, 25 January, 1 February, and 29 April 1957, DE-CE (1945–60) 751.

30. Chauvel (London) to MAE on conversation with Selwyn Lloyd and Macmillan, 28 December 1956, DE-CE (1945–60) 761; Pineau-Macmillan conversation, 9 March 1957, and Raymond Bousquet (Brussels) to Pineau, 6 May 1957, *DDF*, 10:427–32, 736–37; MAE note, 13 April 1957, DE-CE (1945–60) 636; MAE note, 25 April 1957, Europe (1944–60): Généralités 167; MAE note, 1 July 1957, DE-CE (1945–60) 741; Bossuat, *L'Europe des Français*, 361.

31. MAE note, 25 January 1957, DE-CE (1945–60) 751; Pineau to Stations, 24 November 1956, *DDF*, 9:401–2.

32. MAE notes, 18 January and 8 March 1957, DE-CE (1945–60) 740.

33. Pineau to London, 13 April 1957, *DDF*, 10:612–13.

34. MAE notes, 11 April and 15 May 1957, DE-CE (1945–60) 741.

35. London to State Dept., 2 August 1956, CFEP Policy Records, box 7; CFEP report, 15 November 1956, *FRUS* (1955–57), 4:482–86; NSC note, 19 November 1956, and CFEP note for the NSC, 23 November 1956, NSC Staff Papers—CFEP series, box 7; State Dept. to Stations, 28 November 1956, Decimal File 840.00 (1955–59), box 4387; Winand, *United States of Europe*, 111–12.

36. State Dept. note, undated [October 1956], Decimal File 440.002 (1955–59), box 1847; Eisenhower-Dulles conversation, 10 January 1957, Whitman File—Ann Whitman Diary series, box 8.

37. Position paper for January 1956 Eden visit to Washington, undated, Whitman File—International series, box 22; Dulles to London, 9 July 1957, Lot File 61 D 179, box 20.

38. Christian Herter (undersecretary of state) to Stations, 6 May 1957, and U.S. delegation to NATO (Paris) to State Dept., 20 February 1957, Lot File 61 D 179, box 1; Position paper for May 1957 Adenauer visit to Washington, undated, WHCF/DDEL—Confidential File, box 74; Dulles–von Brentano conversation, 4 May 1957, Whitman File—Dulles-Herter series, box 8; Winand, *United States of Europe*, 116.

39. Dulles–Selwyn Lloyd conversation, 22 March 1957, *FRUS* (1955–57), 27:725–27.

40. Selwyn Lloyd–Pineau conversation, 3 May 1957, and Steel (Bonn) to FO, 18 May 1957, PREM11/1829B; Macmillan conversation with French prime minister Maurice Bourgès-Manoury, 15 June 1957, FO371/130645; Macmillan letter to Eisenhower, 12 June 1957, Whitman File—International series, box 23; Macmillan, *Riding the Storm*, 433–37; Lee, *An Uneasy Partnership*, 171.

41. Maurice Faure–Thorneycroft (chancellor of the exchequer) conversation, 7 May 1957, DE-CE (1945–60) 751; Thorneycroft memo for the cabinet, 30 April 1957, CAB129/87.

42. Macmillan-Mollet conversation, 9 March 1957, PREM11/1831B; Adamthwaite, "Marianne et John Bull."

43. Maudling note for the cabinet (No. 218), 4 October 1957, CAB129/89; MAE to Sta-

tions on British views expressed at Maudling meetings, 25 October 1957, *DDF*, 11:589–91; Maudling memorandum for the cabinet, 4 February 1958, CAB128/32; Paris to AA on conversation with British embassy officials in Paris, 17 February 1958, Referat 200-IA2/351; Macmillan, *Riding the Storm*, 434–41.

44. Adenauer-Macmillan conversation, 18 April 1958, NL1351/87; Maudling note to Macmillan, 11 April 1958, PREM11/2314.

45. Selwyn Lloyd–Chauvel conversation, 24 April 1958, FO371/137268.

46. Macmillan-Adenauer conversation, 18 April 1958, NL1351/87.

47. Pineau to Chauvel (London), 22 March 1958, *DDF*, 12:381–82; Macmillan, *Riding the Storm*, 435.

48. Erhard comments at a meeting with Adenauer and British leaders, 18 April 1958, NL1351/87; Lee, *An Uneasy Partnership*, 159–60.

49. Carstens note, 8 July 1957, NL1266/1462; AA notes, 17 August and 1 October 1957, B24/292.

50. Macmillan-Adenauer meeting, 18 April 1958, NL1351/87.

51. AA notes, 24 and 29 July 1957, NL1266/1462; AA notes, 13 August and 1 October 1957, B24/292; AA note on 3 October Franco-German talks, 5 October 1957, Referat 200-IA2/351; chancellor's office position paper, 5 March 1958, B136/2597.

52. AA note for Carstens, 9 January 1958, Referat 200-IA2/149; chancellor's office note on the FTA talks, 21 February 1958, B136/2597.

53. Chancellor's office notes, 6 and 11 March 1958, B136/2597.

54. Chancellor's office position paper, 5 March 1958, B136/2597.

55. Faure-Erhard conversation, 20 February 1958, *DDF*, 12:216–19; Macmillan-Adenauer conversation, 18 April 1958, NL1351/87.

56. Dillon–Selwyn Lloyd conversation, 24 October 1957, *FRUS* (1955–57), 27:315; Erhard-Dulles conversation, 21 March 1958, Lot File 64 D 199, box 6; Dulles-Alphand conversation, 29 March 1958, *FRUS* (1958–60), 7 (pt. 1): 30–31.

57. Intelligence report, 17 October 1957, Whitman File—DDE Diary series, box 27; briefing paper for October 1957 Eisenhower-Macmillan meeting, undated, WHCF/DDEL—Confidential File, box 74; Washington to MAE, 17 May 1958, *DDF*, 12:626–29.

58. NSC paper, "U.S. Policy on France," 19 October 1957, *FRUS* (1955–57), 27:181–93.

59. Eisenhower-Dulles conversation, 22 October 1957, WHOSS—State Dept. series, box 2; Dulles note for Eisenhower, 21 October 1957, Dillon–Selwyn Lloyd conversation, 25 October 1957, *FRUS* (1955–57), 27:798, 833.

60. Herter to Paris on the FTA, 10 October 1957, *FRUS* (1955–57), 4:564–65; Herter to Stations, 13 February 1958, and Dulles to Stations, 20 March 1958, *FRUS* (1958–60), 7 (pt. 1): 14–16, 20–23.

61. MAE notes, 8 June, 4 October, and 16 November 1957, Brussels to MAE, 16 November 1957, DE-CE (1945–60) 752; Maurice Faure–Maudling conversations, 25–26 November 1957, Secrétariat Général 4; MAE note, 20 January 1958, DE-CE (1945–60) 742; Bossuat, "Le choix de la petite Europe."

62. MAE note, 17 February 1958, *DDF*, 12:191–92; MAE note, 20 January 1958, DE-CE (1945–60) 742.

63. Text of French proposal, 24 February 1958, DE-CE (1945–60) 753; Bossuat, *L'Europe des Français*, 373.

64. MAE note on conversations with the Germans and Belgians on the proposals, 3 March 1958, Pineau to François Seydoux (French ambassador to Vienna and later to Bonn), 8 March 1958, *DDF*, 12:264–66, 292–93.

65. Pineau–Selwyn Lloyd conversation, 21 January 1958, *DDF*, 12:70–73; MAE note, 28 April 1958, DE-CE (1945–60) 753; Bossuat, "Le choix de la petite Europe."

66. MAE note, 12 April 1958, Europe (1944–60): Généralités 193; MAE to Rome, 8 May 1958, *DDF*, 12:570–71.

67. Chauvel (London) to MAE on conversation with Maudling, 15 August 1957, *DDF*, 11:216; Pineau–Selwyn Lloyd conversation, 21 January 1958, *DDF*, 12:70–73; Bossuat, "Le choix de la petite Europe." Informing the British of this problem was also another convenient way to call for slowing down the negotiations.

68. Jebb (Paris) to FO on de Gaulle conversation, 24 March 1958, PREM11/2338; Maillard, *De Gaulle et l'Europe*, 132; Vaïsse, *La grandeur*, 162–67; Bossuat, *L'Europe des Français*, 383–86.

69. MAE note for de Gaulle on Macmillan visit, 27 June 1958, MAE note for de Gaulle on the FTA, 27 June 1958, DE-CE (1945–60) 753; MAE note for de Gaulle on the FTA, undated [July 1958] DE-CE (1945–60) 754.

70. Note on 17 July cabinet meeting, 18 July 1958, DE-CE (1945–60) 754.

71. MAE note, 10 July 1958, DE-CE (1945–60) 753; AA note on 21–22 July German conversations with the French, 13 August 1958, Referat 200-IA2/149; AA note on meeting of BMWi officials with Jean Rey (Belgian minister of economics) on the French positions, 19 July 1958, B136/2597.

72. De Gaulle–Macmillan conversations, 29–30 June 1958, *DDF*, 12:868–71; AA note on German conversations with Wormser and other French officials, 25 July 1958, B24/292; Macmillan–Couve de Murville conversation, 6 November 1958, FO371/137272.

73. Wormser conversation with FO economics official, 14 October 1958, DE-CE (1945–60) 762.

74. MAE note, undated [June 1958], and MAE note on June 1958 Macmillan visit to the United States, undated, 5AG1/169; State Dept. note on Livingston Merchant (assistant secretary of state for European Affairs) conversation with MAE official, 20 November 1958, Lot File 64 D 199, box 11; de Gaulle letter to Adenauer, 20 December 1958, *LNC*, 8:155.

75. MAE note, 12 July 1958, and Chauvel (London) to MAE, 21 October 1958, DE-CE (1945–60) 762; MAE note, 5 November 1958, DE-CE (1945–60) 744.

76. MAE note, 25 October 1958, DE-CE (1945–60) 754.

77. MAE note on 12 November 1958 cabinet meeting, undated, DE-CE (1945–60) 754; Seydoux (Bonn) to MAE, 25 November 1958, Europe (1944–60): Allemagne 1260; Couve de Murville, *Le monde en face*, 98–99; Bossuat, *L'Europe des Français*, 389–91; Vaïsse, *La grandeur*, 168–69.

78. De Gaulle–Adenauer conversations, 26 November 1958, *DDF*, 13:754–63; MAE note, 12 September 1958, and Seydoux (Bonn) to MAE, 25 November 1958, Europe (1944–60): Allemagne 1260; de Gaulle draft letter to Adenauer, undated [November 1958], Secrétariat Général 6; MAE note on an interministerial meeting under de Gaulle's leadership, 18 November 1958, DE-CE (1945–60) 754. There had previously been some fear among the Five that the unstable French financial situation would require Paris to activate some of the escape clauses in the Treaty of Rome as soon as it took effect, re-

gardless of how de Gaulle personally might feel about the treaty. The German preparatory documents for the meeting are in NL1351/94.

79. Seydoux (Bonn) to MAE on the Bad Kreuznach discussions, 28 November 1958, *DDF*, 13:776–79; de Gaulle–Erhard conversation, 15 December 1958, 5AG1/160.

80. MAE note, 14 November 1958, DE-CE (1945–60) 754.

81. De Gaulle–Erhard conversation, 15 December 1958, 5AG1/160.

82. De Gaulle–Selwyn Lloyd conversation, 17 December 1958, Secrétariat Général 6; MAE note on Franco-German meeting in Bonn, 9 January 1959, DE-CE (1945–60) 757.

83. Carstens note, 7 June 1958, B24/292; von Brentano letter to Adenauer, 8 July 1958, NL1239/157; AA note on conversation with Antoine Pinay (minister of finances and economics in the de Gaulle government), 24 July 1958, MB157.

84. Chancellor's office notes, 23 September and 29 October 1958, B136/2597.

85. Carstens to Stations, 30 October 1958, Referat 200-IA2/150.

86. AA paper, 27 October 1958, B24/293; Schwarz, *Adenauer*, 464–66; Lee, *An Uneasy Partnership*, 131–35, 148.

87. Bonn to State Dept. on embassy conversation with AA officials, 26 November 1958, Decimal File 651.62a (1955–59); Carstens, *Erinnerungen*, 246; Lee, *An Uneasy Partnership*, 148.

88. Adenauer letter to Macmillan, 12 December 1958, Referat 200-IA2/150; de Gaulle letter to Adenauer, 20 December 1958, *LNC*, 8:155.

89. State Dept. paper, "Policy Considerations toward a de Gaulle Government," 27 May 1958, *FRUS* (1958–60), 7 (pt. 2): 17–20; State Dept. briefing paper for Dulles, 5 June 1958, Lot File 61 D 30, box 1; Dulles to Stations, 12 July 1958, *FRUS* (1958–60), 7 (pt. 1): 47–49; Bozo, *Deux stratégies*, 21–43.

90. Dulles memorandum on British tactics, 10 June 1958, Decimal File 840.00 (1955–59), box 4389; briefing note for June 1958 Macmillan visit, undated, WHCF/DDEL—Confidential File, box 76; Dillon to Brussels, 25 July 1958, *FRUS* (1958–60), 7 (pt. 1): 56–58; Intelligence report, 28 July 1958, Whitman File—DDE Diary series, box 34.

91. CFEP note for Dillon, 8 April 1958, CFEP Policy Records—Chronological file, box 2; Alphand (Washington) to MAE, 21 November 1958, *DDF*, 13:726–27.

92. State Dept. background paper for Dulles's meeting with de Gaulle, 2 July 1958, Lot File 61 D 30, box 1.

93. John H. Whitney (U.S. ambassador in London) to State Dept., 3 November 1958, and State Dept. note for Dulles, 4 November 1958, Decimal File 641.51 (1955–59).

94. John Tuthill (minister for economic affairs at the Paris embassy)–Jean Monnet conversation, 12 November 1958, *FRUS* (1958–60), 7 (pt. 1): 72–76.

95. Macmillan-Chauvel conversation, 20 June 1958, PREM11/2336; Macmillan comments to the cabinet, 1 July 1958, CAB128/32.

96. FO briefing note for June 1958 Macmillan meetings with de Gaulle, undated, FO371/137276; Macmillan–de Gaulle conversations, 29–30 June 1958, *DDF*, 12:868–71; Macmillan letter to de Gaulle, 19 July 1958, 5AG1/173; Chauvel (London) to MAE on conversation with Macmillan, 15 October 1958, *DDF*, 13:518–21; Macmillan, *Riding the Storm*, 445–50.

97. Macmillan note to Selwyn Lloyd and Heathcoat Amory, 24 June 1958, PREM11/2315.

98. De Gaulle–Gladwyn Jebb conversation, 12 December 1958, *DDF*, 13:854–55.

99. Macmillan comments on FO analysis of the European situation, 12 December 1958, PREM11/2696; Macmillan, *Riding the Storm*, 455.

100. Whitney (London) to State Dept., 3 July 1958, Decimal File 641.51 (1955–59); Dulles-Eisenhower conversation, 3 July 1958, *FRUS* (1958–60), 7 (pt. 2): 50–52; Lee, *An Uneasy Partnership*, 280.

101. Macmillan, *Riding the Storm*, 573; cabinet meeting, 10 December 1958, CAB128/32.

102. Cabinet sessions, 18 November and 18 December 1958, CAB128/32.

103. Cabinet session, 23 December 1958, CAB128/32.

104. Couve de Murville to Stations on the OEEC meeting, 17 December 1958, *DDF*, 12:888–93; Macmillan, *Pointing the Way*, 49.

105. Peyrefitte, *C'était de Gaulle*, 1:23–29; Bossuat *L'Europe des Français*, 394; Vaïsse, *La grandeur*, 162–69.

106. Report by John Coulson (an assistant of Maudling's in the FTA and EFTA negotiations) on the EFTA treaty, November 1959, CAB129/99; Macmillan, *Pointing the Way*, 51–53.

107. MAE note on the goals of the Seven, undated [late 1959], DE-CE (1945–60) 749; AA note on the Seven, 2 June 1959, Referat 200-IA2/353, AA. This goal was recognized by both the French and the Germans.

108. Heathcoat Amory–Dillon conversation, 8 December 1959, *FRUS* (1958–60), 7 (pt. 1): 173–86.

109. Chauvel (London) to MAE on conversation with British officials, 15 October 1959, DE-CE (1945–60) 763; Selwyn Lloyd–Dillon conversation, 8 December 1959, PREM11/2870; Hans Heinrich von Herwarth (German ambassador to London)–David Eccles (British minister of commerce) conversation, 3 June 1959, Referat 200-IA2/353.

110. Macmillan-Dillon conversation, 9 December 1959, PREM11/2870; W. Randolph Burgess (chief of the U.S. mission to NATO and the European regional organizations in Paris) to State Dept. on Dillon conversation with EFTA officials, 13 December 1959, *FRUS* (1958–60), 7 (pt. 1): 202–3.

111. Macmillan, *Pointing the Way*, 52–53; notes on British meetings on future foreign policy, undated [November 1959], PREM11/2679; Whitney (London) to State Dept. on conversation with Coulson, 25 February 1959, *FRUS* (1958–60), 7 (pt. 1): 102–4.

112. Macmillan minute to Selwyn Lloyd, 10 October 1959, prime minister's office note for Macmillan, 30 October 1959, PREM11/2985.

113. Kaiser, *Using Europe*, 101.

114. FO briefing papers for the planned 1959 visit of French prime minister Michel Debré to London, undated [spring 1959], FO371/145622.

115. Chauvel (London) to MAE on conversation with British officials, 15 October 1959, DE-CE (1945–60) 763; Heathcoat Amory–Chauvel conversation, 25 October 1960, FO371/153916.

116. Cabinet meeting, 20 February 1959, CAB129/96; de Gaulle–Couve de Murville–Selwyn Lloyd conversation, 12 November 1959, *DDF*, 16:566–68; Dillon–Maudling–Selwyn Lloyd–Heathcoat Amory conversation, 8 December 1959, *FRUS* (1958–60), 7 (pt. 1): 176–84; Macmillan–de Gaulle conversations, 12–13 March 1960, PREM11/2997; Macmillan–de Gaulle conversation, 5 April 1960, PREM11/2978.

117. Carstens note on conversation with Maudling, 24 November 1959, Referat 200-IA2/354.

118. Dillon-Herter-Macmillan conversation, 28 March 1960, Lot File 64 D 199, box 15.

119. Whitney (London) to State Dept., 24 March 1960, *FRUS* (1958–60), 7 (pt. 1): 263.

120. Macmillan-Adenauer meeting, 10 August 1960, PREM11/2993; Carstens note, 7 November 1960, B2/73; Carstens, *Erinnerungen,* 277.

121. Intelligence report, 2–6 July 1959, WHOSS—Alpha file, box 9; Herter–Selwyn Lloyd conversation, 1 September 1959, NSC Staff Papers—NSC Registry series, box 114; Eisenhower–de Gaulle conversation, 2 September 1959, Whitman File—International Meetings series, box 3.

122. Eisenhower-Dillon conversation, 26 April 1960, WHOSS—State Dept. series, box 4; Dillon-Wormser conversation, 5 October 1959, *FRUS* (1958–60) 7 (pt. 1): 155–58; Dillon conversation with Selwyn Lloyd, Maudling, and Heathcoat Amory, 8 December 1959, *FRUS* (1958–60), 7 (pt. 1): 176–84; State Dept. paper INR 8242, "Problems and Prospects of the European Free Trade Association," 24 March 1960, INR file 8242; Brief for Eisenhower for Macmillan visit, 26 March 1960, WHCF/DDEL—Confidential File, box 80.

123. Dillon-Erhard conversation, 4 June 1959, Lot File 64 D 199, box 12; Tuthill conversation with Quai d'Orsay officials, 19 June 1959, Decimal File 840.00 (1955–59), box 4394.

124. Briefing note for Eisenhower trip to Europe, 23 August 1959, CFEP Chair Records, box 4; Dillon to Eisenhower, 27 November 1959, WHOSS—International series, box 5; briefing note for Eisenhower for March 1960 Macmillan visit, undated, Whitman File—International series, box 25; conversation of State Dept. and British Treasury officials, 4 April 1960, Decimal File 840.00 (1955–59), box 2460.

125. Briefing paper for Eisenhower for March 1959 Macmillan visit, undated, Whitman File—International series, box 24; Eisenhower-Erhard conversation, 5 June 1959, WHOSS—International series, box 6; conversation of State Dept. and British Treasury officials, 4 April 1960, Decimal File 840.00 (1955–59), box 2460.

126. Dillon to Eisenhower, 19 August 1959, WHOSS—International series, box 14; AA note on conversation of German and American officials in Brussels, 15 October 1959, Referat 200-IA2/456.

127. Herter to Stations, 20 October 1960, *FRUS* (1958–60), 7 (pt. 1): 303–5.

128. Carstens note for Adenauer, 7 November 1959, MB67.

129. AA note, 22 June 1959, Referat 200-IA2/353; BMWi notes, 30 October and 5 December 1959, B136/2071; Adenauer, *Erinnerungen,* 4:518–23.

130. This extensive correspondence is found in B136/2553.

131. AA note on German conversations with State Dept. officials, 11 March 1959, Referat 200-IA2/457; AA notes, 18 June and 29 September 1959, Referat 200-IA2/353; Carstens note, 8 July 1959, NL1337/646; AA note, 15 July 1959, Referat 200-IA2/356.

132. AA meeting on the EFTA, 23 June 1959, Referat 200-IA2/353; AA note, 7 November 1959, B136/2054; Carstens, *Erinnerungen,* 246.

133. MAE note, 18 April 1959, DE-CE (1945–60) 758; AA note, 5 June 1959, B136/2598.

134. Chancellor's office note for Adenauer, 28 January 1959, B136/2598; von Brentano letter to Kurt Birrenbach (a CDU Bundestag member and foreign affairs specialist), 2 March 1959, MB67.

135. London embassy paper on the Six-Seven dispute, 11 March 1960, *DDF*, 17:260–63.

136. DE-CE note, 5 September 1958, Europe (1945–60); Allemagne 1260; Paris embassy note, 21 September 1959, Referat 200-IA2/353.

137. Chauvel (London) to MAE, 27 May 1959, DE-CE (1945–60) 763; Wormser note, 18 July 1959, DE-CE (1945–60) 748; MAE notes, 23 September and 12 October 1960, DE-CE (1945–60) 764; MAE note, undated [late 1959], DE-CE (1945–60) 749.

138. MAE notes, 31 March and 30 November 1960, DE-CE (1945–60) 747; MAE note, 27 October 1959, DE-CE (1961–66) 509; MAE note, 1 December 1959, DE-CE (1945–60) 746; London embassy paper on the Six-Seven dispute, 11 March 1960, *DDF*, 17:260–63.

139. Wormser to Washington, 17 April 1959, DE-CE (1945–60) 745; Franco-British-American summit meeting in Paris, 20 December 1959, *DDF*, 16:765–71.

140. MAE note, 11 September 1959, Europe (1944–60): Généralités 187.

141. Wormser note, 20 June 1959, DE-CE (1945–60) 748; Wormser note, 24 August 1959, DE-CE (1945–60) 747; MAE note, 12 October 1960, DE-CE (1961–66) 509; Chauvel (London) to MAE, 2 December 1960, DE-CE (1945–60) 764; Wormser to Bonn on Couve de Murville–Carstens conversation, 8 December 1960, DE-CE (1945–60) 755.

142. MAE notes, 6 September and 30 November 1960, DE-CE (1945–60) 747.

Chapter Three

1. Maillard, *De Gaulle et l'Allemagne* and *De Gaulle et l'Europe*; Peyrefitte, *C'était de Gaulle*, vol. 1; Peter Schunk, "De Gaulle und seine deutschen Nachbarn bis zur Begegnung mit Adenauer," in Loth and Picht, *De Gaulle, Deutschland und Europa*, 21–44; de Gaulle speech to the British Parliament, 7 April 1960, de Gaulle speech to the National Press Club in Washington, D.C., 23 April 1960, *D&M*, 3:179–82, 189–90. See also de Gaulle's interwar writings and his memoirs on the 1940–46 period: *La discorde chez l'ennemi*; *Le fil de l'épée*; *Vers l'armée de métier*; and *Mémoires de guerre*.

2. De Gaulle, *Mémoires de guerre*, 3:175–79.

3. De Gaulle comments to Theodor Heuss (former German president), 8 March 1960, de Gaulle–Khrushchev conversation, 23 March 1960, *DDF*, 17:243–45, 356–61; Couve de Murville–Selwyn Lloyd conversation, 12 November 1959, *DDF*, 16:557–59.

4. Mayers, *George Kennan*.

5. MAE note, 9 March 1959, Europe (1944–60): Crise de Berlin 1330; MAE note, 28 November 1959, Europe (1944–60): Crise de Berlin 1333.

6. MAE notes, 12 and 27 November 1958, Europe (1944–60): Crise de Berlin 1326.

7. De Gaulle–Selwyn Lloyd conversation, 12 November 1959, *DDF*, 16:566–68.

8. De Gaulle–Macmillan conversation, 21 December 1959, *DDF*, 16:780–82.

9. De Gaulle comments at Western summit meeting, 19 December 1959, *DDF*, 16:756.

10. De Gaulle–Macmillan conversation, 5 April 1960, *DDF*, 17:415–19.

11. Seydoux (Bonn) to MAE, 31 October and 1 November 1958, *DDF*, 13:610–12, 616–17; Bozo, *Deux stratégies*, 21–43.

12. De Gaulle–Eisenhower conversation, 2 September 1959, *DDF*, 16:284; de Gaulle–Macmillan meetings, 15–16 December 1962, 5AG1/170.

13. On this subject see Jolyon Howorth, "The President's Special Role in Foreign and

Defense Policy," in Hayward, *De Gaulle to Mitterand*, 150–89; Institut Charles de Gaulle, *De Gaulle et ses premiers ministres*.

14. Couve de Murville, *Le monde en face*, chaps. 1–2, *Une politique étrangère*, chap. 7.

15. Vaïsse, *La grandeur*, 227, 304–5; Debré, *Gouverner*, 422–26; Institut Charles de Gaulle, *De Gaulle et ses premiers ministres*, 255–85.

16. Bossuat, *L'Europe des Français*, 410–11; Vaïsse, *La grandeur*, 259–60; Charlot, *Les Français et de Gaulle*.

17. The following list is representative of this vast literature: Kolodziej, *French International Policy*; Cerny, *The Politics of Grandeur*; Gordon, *A Certain Idea of France*; Kocs, *Autonomy or Power?*; Peyrefitte, *C'était de Gaulle*; Schwarz, *Adenauer*; Lacouture, *De Gaulle*; Malraux, *Les chênes qu'on abat*; Couve de Murville, *Une politique étrangère* and *Le monde en face*; Debré, *Gouverner*; Hoffmann, *Decline or Renewal?*; Maillard, *De Gaulle et l'Allemagne* and *De Gaulle et l'Europe*; Kusterer, *Der Kanzler und der General*; Osterheld, *"Ich gehe nicht leichten Herzens."*

18. A representative sample: Bozo and Mélandri, "La France devant l'opinion américaine"; Mélandri, "Le Général de Gaulle, la construction européenne et l'Alliance atlantique"; Bozo, *Deux stratégies*; Buffet, "De Gaulle et Berlin," "La politique nucléaire de la France," and "The Berlin Crises"; Soutou, "Le Général de Gaulle, le Plan Fouchet et l'Europe," "Les problèmes de sécurité," and *L'alliance incertaine*; Vaïsse, "Aux origines du mémorandum," "Le Général de Gaulle et la défense de l'Europe," and *La grandeur*; Vaïsse, Mélandri, and Bozo, *La France et l'OTAN*; Institut Charles de Gaulle, *De Gaulle en son siècle*; Picht and Wessels, *Motor für Europa*; Conze, *Die gaullistische Herausforderung*.

19. Adenauer, *Teegespräche 1959–1961*, 26, 225; Hildebrand, *Integration und Souveränität*; Blankenhorn, *Verständnis*, 43–50.

20. Adenauer, *Teegespräche 1959–1961*, 146–47. See also chaps. 1–2.

21. Adenauer, *Teegespräche 1959–1961*, 275; Bonn to MAE on embassy conversation with Adenauer, 5 August 1958, *DDF*, 13:274; Lee, *An Uneasy Partnership*, 69–70.

22. Adenauer, *Erinnerungen*, 3:518.

23. Adenauer, *Teegespräche 1959–1961*, 26, 90.

24. Seydoux (Bonn) note on conversation with Adenauer, 25 November 1959, Debré–Couve de Murville–Adenauer conversation, 1 December 1959, *DDF*, 16:614–16, 646–50; Adenauer–Willy Brandt (SPD mayor of West Berlin) conversation, 5 April 1960, Berlin 70, WBA.

25. Seydoux (Bonn) note on Adenauer conversation, 15 October 1959, de Gaulle–Adenauer conversation, 2 December 1959, de Gaulle–Debré–Adenauer conversation, 20 December 1959, *DDF*, 16:452–53, 656–65, 773.

26. Seydoux (Bonn) note on Adenauer conversation, 21 January 1959, Europe (1944–60): Allemagne 1246.

27. Adenauer, *Teegespräche 1959–1961*, 39.

28. Western summit, 15 May 1960, *DDF*, 17:648–53; Adenauer, *Teegespräche 1959–1961*, 225.

29. Steel (Bonn) to FO, 27 June 1959, PREM11/2706.

30. Blankenhorn, *Verständnis*, 351; von Brentano letter to Adenauer, 10 April 1959, B41, STBKAH; Blankenhorn-Adenauer conversation, 7 October 1959, NL1351/98a.

31. Carstens policy paper, 5 April 1960, NL1337/649; Schwarz, *Adenauer*, 463.

32. Carstens paper on Franco-German relations at the beginning of the Fifth Republic, 30 December 1958, NL1351/97a; Carstens, *Erinnerungen*, 241–45.

33. Blankenhorn year-end report, 31 December 1959, NL1351/98a; Blankenhorn, *Verständnis*, 361, 381; Lee, *An Uneasy Partnership*, 33–34.

34. Dillon-Erhard conversation, 4 June 1959, *FRUS* (1958–60), 7 (pt. 1): 120–25.

35. Blankenhorn-Adenauer conversation on Erhard, 7 October 1959, NL1351/98a.

36. Bulmer and Paterson, *The Federal Republic of Germany*, 135–36; Noelle and Neumann, *The Germans*, 252, 271, 509–11, 524, 532, 535, 537; Feld, *West Germany and the European Community*, 45–48; Paul Noack, "Er kam und ging als Fremder: Charles de Gaulle in der westdeutschen Einschätzung zwischen 1958 und 1970," in Loth and Picht, *De Gaulle, Deutschland und Europa*, 83–94; Vaïsse, *La grandeur*, 225–62.

37. Adenauer, *Teegespräche 1955–1958*, 218; Schwarz, *Adenauer*, 440.

38. AA note on the French situation, 23 May 1958, MB55.

39. Bonn to State Dept on Erhard comments, 30 May 1958, Decimal File 751.00 (1955–59); Blankenhorn, *Verständnis*, 294–96.

40. Amory Houghton (U.S. ambassador in Paris) to State Dept., 27 May 1958, Decimal File 651.62a (1955–59).

41. Bonn to State Dept., 30 May 1958, Decimal File 751.00 (1955–59).

42. Adenauer, *Teegespräche 1955–1958*, 287–89.

43. Bonn to State Dept. on 2 June 1958 German statement, 3 June 1958, Decimal File 651.62a (1955–59).

44. Adenauer, *Teegespräche 1955–1958*, 294.

45. Schwarz, *Adenauer*, 441–43; Adenauer, *Erinnerungen*, 3:396–435.

46. AA note for ambassador Blankenhorn, 31 October 1958, B24/355.

47. Carstens list of questions for Adenauer to ask Couve de Murville, 7 June 1958, B24/292.

48. AA note on Franco-German relations, undated [mid-August 1958], B24/292.

49. AA note, undated [August 1958], B24/294.

50. Paris embassy note on possible de Gaulle foreign policies, 19 June 1958, MB55.

51. Meetings of AA and Quai d'Orsay officials, 12, 22, and 24 July 1958, MB157.

52. Maillard, *De Gaulle et l'Europe*, 135–64.

53. De Gaulle–Adenauer conversations, 14 September 1958, *DDF*, 13:341–45.

54. MAE note, 6 September 1958, DE-CE note, 12 September 1958, Europe (1944–60): Allemagne 1260; Seydoux (Bonn) to MAE, 22 September 1958, Cabinet du Ministre—Couve de Murville 69; AA note on Colombey, 2 October 1958, B24/285; Houghton (Paris) to State Dept., 17 September 1958, Decimal File 651.62a (1955–59); Adenauer, *Teegespräche 1959–1961*, 19, 26, 180; Schwarz, *Adenauer*, 451–56.

55. Maillard, *De Gaulle et l'Allemagne*, 155.

56. Blankenhorn, *Verständnis*, 379–81.

57. De Gaulle–Adenauer conversations, 26 November 1958, *DDF*, 13:754–63; Seydoux (Bonn) to MAE on conversation with Adenauer, 31 October 1958, *DDF*, 13:611–12; AA conversation with Couve de Murville, 19 November 1958, NL1351/94; AA note, 21 November 1958, B24/295; de Gaulle letter to Adenauer, 21 November 1958, *LNC*, 8:135–36; Maillard, *De Gaulle et l'Europe*, 135–90; Blankenhorn, *Verständnis*, 335–38; Schwarz, *Ade-*

nauer, 464–66; Bossuat, *L'Europe des Français*, 390–94. The French accounts of both the Colombey and Bad Kreuznach meetings are also in 5AG1/160.

58. AA note, 2 October 1958, B24/286; AA notes, 27 October 1958 and 8 January 1959, B24/293; Carstens note for Blankenhorn, 31 October 1958, B24/355.

59. De Gaulle memorandum, 17 September 1958, *DDF*, 13:377; Bozo, *Deux stratégies*, 21–43.

60. De Gaulle letter to Adenauer, 5 October 1958, *LNC*, 8:109–10; Seydoux (Bonn) to MAE on Adenauer comments to French officials, 28 October 1958, Seydoux (Bonn) to MAE on conversation with Adenauer, 31 October 1958, *DDF*, 13:590–91, 610–13; Paris embassy note on tripartism, 3 November 1958, AA–Couve de Murville conversation, 19 November 1958, NL1351/94; Blankenhorn, *Verständnis*, 324–28; Schwarz, *Adenauer*, 458–62.

61. Adenauer, *Erinnerungen*, 3:437–82; Buffet, "De Gaulle et Berlin," "La politique nucléaire de la France," and "The Berlin Crises"; Conze, "Hegemonie durch Integration."

62. Zubok and Pleshakov, *Inside the Kremlin's Cold War*, 194–209.

63. Adenauer-Debré conversation, 4 March 1959, *DDF*, 14:276.

64. De Gaulle–Adenauer conversation, 4 March 1959, *DDF*, 14:279; Schwarz, *Adenauer*, 496. The French accounts of the March 1959 meetings are also in 5AG1/160.

65. De Gaulle press conference, 25 March 1959, *D&M*, 3:82–94; Seydoux (Bonn) to MAE, 28 March 1959, Europe (1944–60): Allemagne 1241; Paris to AA, 20 April 1959, B24/270; Seydoux (Bonn) to MAE on conversation with Adenauer, 7 April 1959, Seydoux (Bonn) note on British-German relations, 13 April 1959, Europe (1944–60): Allemagne 1249; Paris to AA, 7 August 1959, B24/287; Maillard, *De Gaulle et l'Allemagne*, 169–73.

66. Adenauer, *Erinnerungen*, 3:499–541; Adenauer–Debré–Couve de Murville conversation, 6 May 1959, *DDF*, 14:612.

67. AA note for Adenauer, 7 August 1959, B136/3624; Gaston Palewski (French ambassador in Rome) to MAE, 26 August 1959, *DDF*, 16:230–31.

68. Seydoux (Bonn) to MAE, 11 November 1959, *DDF*, 16:547–49; Seydoux (Bonn) to MAE, 26 November 1959, MAE note, 27 November 1959, Europe (1944–60): Allemagne 1262.

69. AA note, 20 November 1959, B24/294.

70. Adenauer letter to de Gaulle, 30 October 1959, de Gaulle letter to Adenauer, 2 November 1959, 5AG1/165; Paris to AA, 2 November 1959, MB56; Adenauer–Debré–Couve de Murville conversations, 1 December 1959, de Gaulle–Adenauer conversations, 2 December 1959, *DDF*, 16:646–69; Blankenhorn–Quai d'Orsay conversation on the Franco-German summit, 8 December 1959, NL1351/97a; AA note on the de Gaulle–Adenauer meetings, 21 December 1959, B24/294; Blankenhorn year-end report, 31 December 1959, NL1351/98a; Adenauer, *Erinnerungen*, 4:15–21.

71. Seydoux (Bonn) note on German foreign policy, 21 March 1960, Europe (1944–60): Allemagne 1242; de Gaulle–Heuss conversation, 8 March 1960, *DDF*, 17:243–45 and NL1351/99.

72. De Gaulle–Khrushchev conversation, 24 March 1960, *DDF*, 17:357–63.

73. De Gaulle–Macmillan conversations, 13 March 1960, *DDF*, 17:264–67; "Points discussed with General de Gaulle at Rambouillet," 12–13 March 1960, PREM11/2997; de Gaulle–Macmillan conversations, 5–6 April 1960, *DDF*, 17:415–26. De Gaulle and Macmillan actually met twice in the spring of 1960, first in France and then in Britain.

74. De Gaulle–Eisenhower conversation, 22 April 1960, *DDF*, 17:513–25. The American account is in *FRUS* (1958–60), 7 (pt. 2): 343–46.

75. Seydoux (Bonn) note, 11 May 1960, Europe (1944–60): Allemagne 1242.

76. Adenauer letter to de Gaulle, 5 May 1960, NL1351/100; Seydoux (Bonn) note, 5 May 1960, Seydoux (Bonn) note on conversation with Adenauer, 12 May 1960, Europe (1944–60): Allemagne 1263.

77. De Gaulle–Adenauer conversation, 14 May 1960, *DDF*, 17:638–42; Adenauer, *Erinnerungen*, 4:42–47.

78. Blankenhorn account of Adenauer–Jean Monnet conversation, 14 June 1960, NL1351/101; Adenauer, *Erinnerungen*, 4:50; Blankenhorn, *Verständnis*, 367–70; Adenauer, *Teegespräche 1959–1961*, 241. For details on the U2 incident and Khrushchev's decision to abort the summit, see Zubok and Pleshakov, *Inside the Kremlin's Cold War*, 202–6.

79. MAE note for Couve de Murville, 5 July 1960, Europe (1944–60): Généralités 170.

80. Washington embassy note on Strauss's comments while in the United States, 2 July 1960, Europe (1944–60): Allemagne 1247.

81. Adenauer, *Erinnerungen*, 4:54–59.

82. Accounts of these tripartite meetings are scattered through *DDF*, vol. 17.

83. Blankenhorn note, 14 July 1960, Blankenhorn-Carstens-Adenauer conversation, 21 July 1960, and AA note for Blankenhorn, 26 July 1960, NL1351/102.

84. Blankenhorn-Debré conversation, 26 July 1960, NL1351/102.

85. Blankenhorn-Carstens-Adenauer conversation, 21 July 1960, Blankenhorn–Couve de Murville conversation, 27 July 1960, NL1351/102; Schwarz, *Adenauer*, 562–64; Blankenhorn, *Verständnis*, 371–82; Adenauer, *Teegespräche 1959–1961*, 306–7; Kusterer, *Der Kanzler und der General*, 131–32.

86. Berndt von Staden, "Charles de Gaulle und die Aussenpolitik der Bundesrepublik Deutschland," and Ingo Kolboom, "Charles de Gaulle und ein deutsch-französisches Misverständnis über Nation und Europa," in Loth and Picht, *De Gaulle, Deutschland und Europa*, 121–33, 135–50.

87. Schwartz, *America's Germany*; Lundestad, *"Empire" by Integration*, 13–28; Dulles–Couve de Murville conversation, 7 February 1959, JFD Papers—General Correspondence & Memoranda series, box 1; Conze, "Hegemonie durch Integration." American efforts to promote Franco-German reconciliation for the sake of European stability had their roots in the interwar era.

88. Dulles to David Bruce (ambassador in Bonn), 2 April 1958, *FRUS* (1958–60), 7 (pt. 2): 4–5.

89. State Dept. note for Christian Herter (undersecretary of state at this point), 27 May 1958, *FRUS* (1958–60), 7 (pt. 2): 17–20; Dulles-Eisenhower conversation on de Gaulle's return, 25 July 1958, WHOSS—State Dept. series, box 3; State Dept. (OCB) report on Germany, 3 September 1958, NSC Special Assistant Papers—Policy Papers subseries, box 23; State Dept. note on Germany, 3 September 1958, *FRUS* (1958–60), 9:652.

90. State Dept. (OCB) plan for France, 28 February 1958, State Dept. (OCB) plan for Germany, 17 September 1958, Lot File 61 D 385, box 18; de Gaulle–Dulles conversation, 5 July 1958, *DDF*, 13:22 and *FRUS* (1958–60), 7 (pt. 2): 57; Eisenhower–de Gaulle conversation, 2 September 1959, *FRUS* (1958–60), 7 (pt. 2): 255–68, and *DDF*, 16:275–96; de Gaulle–Eisenhower conversation, 19 December 1959, *DDF*, 16:757–61.

91. Eisenhower–de Gaulle conversation, 2 September 1959, *FRUS* (1958–60), 7 (pt. 2): 255–68, and *DDF*, 16:275–96; briefing paper for September 1959 Eisenhower trip to London, undated, Whitman File—International Meetings series, box 3.

92. NSC meeting, 6 February 1958, NSC No. 5803, 7 February 1958, NSC meeting, 1 April 1960, *FRUS* (1958–60), 9:628–61, 680; NSC No. 5910, 4 November 1959, *FRUS* (1958–60), 7 (pt. 2): 296–310; Interim operations plan for France, 24 April 1959, Operations plan for France, 13 April 1960, Lot File 61 D 385, box 18; Bonn embassy note on Franco-German relations since the return of de Gaulle, 18 September 1959, Decimal File 651.62a (1955–59); Paris embassy note on Franco-German relations, 20 May 1960, Decimal File 651.62a (1960–63); State Dept. paper for Adenauer visit, 10 March 1960, WHCF/DDEL—Confidential File, box 80.

93. Dulles letter to Livingston Merchant (ambassador to Canada at this point), 10 June 1958, Decimal File 611.51 (1955–59); Eisenhower-Erhard conversation, 5 June 1959, WHOSS—International series, box 6; briefing paper for August 1959 Eisenhower visit to Bonn, undated, Whitman File—International Meetings series, box 3.

94. State Dept. (PPS) intelligence report, "France and the Western Alliance," 14 August 1959, Lot File 67 D 548, box 136.

95. John Tuthill (counselor for economic affairs at the Paris embassy), comments to Jean Monnet, 12 November 1958, *FRUS* (1958–60), 7 (pt. 1): 72–76; Conze, *Die gaullistische Herausforderung*, 158–61.

96. Memorandum C.(58)65, undated [March 1958], CAB129/92; Kaiser, *Using Europe*, 96; Lee, *An Uneasy Partnership*, 169–72.

97. Steel (Bonn) to FO, 10 April 1958, PREM11/2341.

98. Macmillan–de Gaulle conversations, 29–30 June 1958, *DDF*, 12:868–71, and PREM11/2326; Selwyn Lloyd–Couve de Murville, Selwyn Lloyd–Debré, and Selwyn Lloyd–de Gaulle conversations, 12 November 1959, de Gaulle–Macmillan conversation, 21 December 1959, *DDF*, 16:551–58, 780–82; Macmillan and Selwyn Lloyd comments at a British policy planning meeting, 29 November 1959, PREM11/2679; Selwyn Lloyd note for Macmillan, 31 December 1959, "Points discussed with General de Gaulle at Rambouillet," 12–13 March 1960, PREM11/2997.

99. Macmillan, *Riding the Storm*, 452, 574, *Pointing the Way*, 55–56, 97; cabinet meeting, 10 December 1958, CAB128/32; cabinet meeting, 15 December 1959, CAB128/33; Macmillan minute on 12 December 1958 FO note, 13 February 1959, PREM11/2696; meeting of Macmillan, Selwyn Lloyd, and Heathcoat Amory (chancellor of the exchequer), 22 November 1959, PREM11/2679; Selwyn Lloyd letter to Macmillan, 13 December 1959, PREM11/2985; Selwyn Lloyd letter to Macmillan, 31 December 1959, PREM11/2997; Horne, *Harold Macmillan*, 2:129–30.

100. Macmillan note to Selwyn Lloyd, 13 October 1959, PREM11/2985; FO note, 6 November 1959, Steel (Bonn) to FO, 15 December 1959, FO371/145755.

101. De Gaulle–Macmillan–Eisenhower conversation, 20 December 1959, *DDF*, 16:771 and *FRUS* (1958–60), 9:144–46; Steel (Bonn) to FO, 2 February 1960, FO371/154033; Macmillan-Herter-Dillon conversation, 28 March 1960, Lot File 64 D 199, box 15.

102. The French rejection of even the most minute contacts with the GDR becomes apparent in Europe (1944–60): République Démocratique Allemande 1.

Chapter Four

1. An earlier version of this chapter was published as Giauque, "Offers of Partnership or Bids for Hegemony?"

2. For representative examples, see Costigliola, "The Failed Design"; "The Pursuit of Atlantic Community"; "Kennedy, de Gaulle et le défi de la consultation entre alliés," in *DGESS*, 4:254–66; "Kennedy, de Gaulle and the Challenge of Consultation," in Paxton and Wahl, *De Gaulle and the United States*, 169–94; Artaud, "Le grand dessein"; Conze, "Hegemonie durch Integration."

3. Schlesinger, *A Thousand Days*; Ball, *The Past Has Another Pattern*; Sorensen, *Kennedy*; Bohlen, *Witness to History*; Schaetzel, *The Unhinged Alliance*; Adenauer, *Erinnerungen*; Blankenhorn, *Verständnis*; Osterheld, *"Ich gehe nicht leichten Herzens"*; Carstens, *Erinnerungen*; Kusterer, *Der Kanzler und der General*; de Gaulle, *Memoirs of Hope*; Peyrefitte, *C'était de Gaulle*; Couve de Murville, *Le monde en face* and *Une politique étrangère*; Debré, *Gouverner*; Maillard, *De Gaulle et l'Europe*; Macmillan, *At the End of the Day*; Dixon, *Double Diploma*; Rusk, *As I Saw It*.

4. Vaïsse, *La grandeur*; Soutou, *l'alliance incertaine*; Bozo, *Deux stratégies*.

5. Lundestad, *"Empire" by Integration*; Winand, *United States of Europe*; Mayer, *Adenauer and Kennedy*; Conze, *Die gaullistische Herausforderung*; Trachtenberg, *A Constructed Peace*; Risse-Kappen, *Cooperation among Democracies*; Bange, *The EEC Crisis of 1963*; Pagedas, *Anglo-American Strategic Relations*.

6. State Dept. Intelligence and Research memorandum for Rusk, 6 April 1963, NSF, box 72.

7. State Dept. paper, April 1958, WHONSAR—Briefing Notes subseries, box 8; State Dept. (OCB) paper, 22 April 1959, WHONSAR—Policy Papers subseries, box 22; State Dept. (PPS) paper, "U.S. policy toward European-Atlantic Regionalism," 10 June 1960, Lot File 67 D 548, box 152; Conze, "Hegemonie durch Integration."

8. Kennedy letter to Adenauer, 12 January 1963, POF, box 117.

9. State Dept. Paper, "The North Atlantic Region: Guidelines of U.S. Policy and Operations," September 1962, Lot File 69 D 121, box 221.

10. Planning papers for the March 1957 Eisenhower-Macmillan Bermuda meeting, undated, PREM11/1835; Macmillan note for the cabinet, 25 March 1957, PREM11/2043; Macmillan-Dulles conversation, 23 October 1957, PREM11/2329.

11. Macmillan, *Pointing the Way*, 112–14; briefing note for Macmillan, 28 November 1959, PREM11/2679.

12. Blankenhorn note, 31 December 1959, NL1351/98a.

13. Schröder, "Chancellor of the Allies?"

14. AA note, 17 July 1963, *Akten*, 2:761–67; Carstens, *Erinnerungen*, 262–64.

15. Hildebrand, "'Atlantiker' versus 'Gaullisten.'"

16. AA note, 9 April 1963, B2/127.

17. Prime minister's office note to MAE, 31 May 1957, Amérique (1952–63): Etats-Unis, 333.

18. De Gaulle–Adenauer meetings, 29–30 July 1960, DDF, 18:163–79; de Gaulle–Adenauer meeting, 9 February 1961, 5AG1/160.

19. De Gaulle note to Debré, 30 September 1960, LNC, 8:398–99.

20. De Gaulle comments to Ambassador James Gavin, 26 May 1962, 5AG1/201.

21. Herter letter to Eisenhower and attached draft proposal on OEEC reform, 24 No-

vember 1959, Whitman File—Dulles-Herter series, box 12; Lundestad, *"Empire" by Integration*, 75–94; Winand, *United States of Europe*, 109–37.

22. Dillon comments to NSC, 16 December 1959, Dillon letter to Eisenhower, 14 January 1960, Paris to State Dept., 10 February 1960, *FRUS* (1958–60), 7 (pt. 1): 218–20, 235–36, 243–46; Herter to Eisenhower, 28 February 1960, Whitman File—Dulles-Herter series, box 12.

23. MAE note, 30 December 1959, DE-CE (1945–60) 344; de Gaulle note to Couve de Murville, 8 January 1960, CM7; MAE note, 15 March 1959, DE-CE (1945–60) 755; Couve de Murville conversation with Italian leaders, 7 December 1959, 5AG1/178; MAE briefing note for de Gaulle trip to the United States in April 1960, undated, Cabinet du Ministre—Couve de Murville 129; MAE note, 26 August 1960, DE-CE (1961–66) 509.

24. State Dept.-Quai d'Orsay conversations, 5 October 1959, *FRUS* (1958–60), 7 (pt. 1): 155–58.

25. Wormser to stations, 22 December 1959, DE-CE (1945–60) 801; Couve de Murville comments to Dillon, 14 December 1959, *DDF*, 16:723–28; MAE instructions to French representatives on OEEC reform, 5 January 1960, *DDF*, 17:12–16.

26. De Gaulle–Adenauer conversations, 1–2 December 1959, *DDF*, 16:646–69; Wormser to the French mission to NATO (Paris), 4 January 1960, DE-CE (1945–60) 801.

27. Couve de Murville to Alphand (Washington), 5 January 1960, *DDF*, 18:17–18; MAE note on French goals, 15 February 1960, DE-CE (1945–60) 344; MAE note, 23 March 1960, Amérique (1952–63): Etats-Unis 336.

28. Macmillan comments to French ambassador Jean Chauvel, 4 November 1959, Selwyn Lloyd note for Macmillan, 8 November 1959, PREM11/2699.

29. Heathcoat Amory memo for the cabinet, 14 December 1959, CAB129/99; Selwyn Lloyd (now chancellor of the exchequer) memo for the cabinet, 6 December 1960, CAB129/103; prime minister's office note on OECD progress, 20 July 1960, PREM11/4228.

30. Jebb (Paris) note for Macmillan, 14 January 1960, FO note for Macmillan, 26 April 1960, PREM11/4228.

31. AA note, 15 October 1959, Referat 200-IA2/456; note for Adenauer's trip to the United States in March 1960, undated, B136/2050; von Brentano letter to Adenauer and dossier on economic issues for the January 1960 OEEC reorganization meetings in Paris, 16 December 1959, MB50.

32. AA note, 8 February 1960, Referat 200-IA2/383.

33. Ambassador Wilhelm Grewe (Washington) to AA, 29 December 1959, B2/80; AA note, 9 November 1960, Referat 200-IA2/385.

34. AA note, 6 January 1960, B2/80; AA note, 8 February 1960, Referat 200-IA2/383; AA note, 23 June 1960, Referat 200-IA2/384; AA note for the cabinet, 25 November 1960, Referat 200-IA2/385.

35. Carstens note, 27 November 1959, Referat 200-IA2/354; AA note, 23 February 1960, B32/105; Erhard note for Adenauer, 10 January 1961, B136/2553.

36. Lundestad, *"Empire" by Integration*, 71–75.

37. Schlesinger, *A Thousand Days*, 842–66; Winand, *United States of Europe*, 139–201; Bozo, *Deux stratégies*, 69–101.

38. Eisenhower-Bowie conversation, 19 August 1960, Whitman File—DDE Diary series, box 51. The text of the Bowie report is in WHOSS—Subject-Alpha series, box 6.

39. Kennedy speech to the North Atlantic Council, 15 February 1961, NSF, box 220.

40. Ball, *The Past Has Another Pattern*, 221; Kennedy comments to Italian ambassador Manlio Brosio, 11 April 1961, NSF, box 120; Schlesinger, *A Thousand Days*, 845.

41. NSC memo on the Acheson Report, 3 April 1961, Policy directive on its implementation, 20 April 1961, NSF, box 220; Schlesinger, *A Thousand Days*, 849–50. The text of the Acheson Report itself is in Lot File 67 D 548, box 153.

42. Ball conversation with Edward Heath (Lord Privy Seal and lead British negotiator on Europe), 6 January 1962, NSF, box 170; Ball, *The Past Has Another Pattern*, 208–22; Winand, *United States of Europe*, 265–94; Conze, "Hegemonie durch Integration"; Costigliola, "Kennedy, de Gaulle et le défi de la consultation entre alliés"; Lundestad, *"Empire" by Integration*, 62.

43. State Dept. (PPS) paper, "Long-range Possibilities for the North Atlantic Region," 19 May 1961, Lot File 67 D 548, box 153; Sorensen, *Kennedy*, 563.

44. Walt W. Rostow (NSC) note for Kennedy, 15 May 1961, NSF, box 70; State Dept. paper for Kennedy on de Gaulle's motivations, 18 May 1961, POF, box 116a.

45. Rostow note for National Security Adviser McGeorge Bundy, 25 May 1961, POF, box 116a.

46. NSC draft paper, "A new approach to France," 21 April 1961, NSF, box 70.

47. Kennedy–de Gaulle meetings, 31 May–2 June 1961, POF, box 116a and *DDF*, 19:669–710; Schlesinger, *A Thousand Days*, 357–58; Bozo, *Deux stratégies*, 75–77; Vaïsse, *La grandeur*, 143–45.

48. Washington to Paris, 15 December 1960, Hervé Alphand (Washington) to Paris, 28 February 1961, Alphand (Washington) to Paris, 17 May 1961, Amérique (1952–63): Etats-Unis 376; Paris to Washington, late January 1961, de Gaulle note, 13 June 1961, and de Gaulle letter to Kennedy, 11 January 1962, *LNC*, 9:29–34, 96, 191–94; Soutou, *L'alliance incertaine*, 186.

49. Peyrefitte, *C'était de Gaulle*, 1:150; Soutou, *L'alliance incertaine*, 213.

50. De Gaulle press conference, 11 April 1961, *D&M*, 3:299–300; Soutou, *L'alliance incertaine*, 184–86.

51. MAE note, 25 May 1961, Cabinet du Ministre—Couve de Murville 21.

52. Note from Prime Minister Debré to Couve de Murville, January 1961, CM7.

53. Couve de Murville to Alphand (Washington), 23 May 1962, CM7.

54. Couve de Murville–Herter conversation, 19 September 1960, *DDF*, 18:367–69; de Gaulle letter to Adenauer, 9 March 1961, 5AG1/165.

55. Couve de Murville to Alphand, 23 May 1962, CM7.

56. Alphand (Washington) to Couve de Murville, 2 February 1962, CM7.

57. AA note, 22 November 1960, Referat 304-IA5/181; Blankenhorn, *Verständnis*, 372–74.

58. AA paper on Kennedy's election, 8 November 1960, B136/3611; AA note, 15 February 1961, B32/124; von Brentano letter to Adenauer, 23 March 1961, NL1337/558; Blankenhorn paper on 1961 developments, 3 January 1962, NL1351/126b; Osterheld, "*Ich gehe nicht leichten Herzens*," 28–30; Schwarz, *Adenauer*, 629–40; Blankenhorn, *Verständnis*, 390–94.

59. Erhard comments to the foreign relations committee of the Bundesrat (the upper house of the German parliament), 16 December 1960, NL1337/648.

60. Mayer, *Adenauer and Kennedy*; AA note, 24 April 1961, B32/132; Adenauer letter to von Brentano, 31 May 1961, NL1239/158; Osterheld, "*Ich gehe nicht leichten Herzens,*" 30.

61. Adenauer–de Gaulle conversation, 22 January 1963, *Akten*, 1:140; Adenauer–de Gaulle meeting, 15 February 1962, 5AG1/161.

62. Macmillan minute to Foreign Secretary Home, 9 November 1960, FO note for Home, 9 December 1960, PREM11/3599; Macmillan, *Pointing the Way*, 308–13, 323–26; Horne, *Harold Macmillan*, 2:284.

63. Text of Macmillan's Grand Design, December 1960–January 1961, PREM11/3325; Macmillan letter to Kennedy, 28 April 1961, PREM11/3311; FO371/166972–3.

64. Macmillan–de Gaulle conversations, 2 June 1962, PREM11/3775; de Gaulle–Macmillan meeting, 15 December 1962, 5AG1/170; Macmillan conversation with French ambassador Jean Chauvel, 19 April 1962, PREM11/3792; briefing notes for June 1962 de Gaulle–Macmillan meetings, undated, PREM11/4258.

65. Couve de Murville to Alphand (Washington), 23 May 1962, CM7; Vaïsse, *La grandeur*, 147–52.

66. De Gaulle comments to Ambassador Gavin, 26 May 1962, 5AG1/201.

67. Text of the press conference, 15 May 1962, *D&M*, 3:402–17.

68. NSC note for Bundy on de Gaulle, 27 November 1962, NSF, box 71a.

69. NSC meeting, 2 April 1963, NSF, box 314; unsigned note "Thoughts on Reading the Morning Papers" on de Gaulle's intentions, 9 May 1962, NSF, box 71; State Dept. paper, "De Gaulle's foreign policy and basic differences with U.S. objectives," 23 January 1963, Lot File 65 D 265, box 5.

70. Rusk to Gavin (Paris), 18 May 1962, *FRUS* (1961–63), 13:704.

71. Kennedy speech in Philadelphia, 4 July 1962, *Public Papers of the Presidents: John F. Kennedy, 1962*, 537–39; briefing paper for Kennedy trip to Europe, undated [June 1963], Lot File 66 D 54, box 1; Winand, *United States of Europe*, 233–43.

72. CIA report on the impact of French economic policy on U.S. interests, 29 March 1963, NSF, box 72; State Dept. paper on Atlantic partnership and European integration, 29 October 1963, Lot File 66 D 54, box 1; Winand, *United States of Europe*, 173–90; Conze, "Hegemonie durch Integration"; Schlesinger, *A Thousand Days*, 846–48.

73. Heuser, *NATO, Britain, France and the FRG*; Schwartz, *NATO's Nuclear Dilemmas*; Steinbruner, *The Cybernetic Theory of Decision*; and Bluth, *Britain, Germany, and Western Nuclear Strategy*. These books provide an introduction to the MLF historiography.

74. NSC paper, "Post-Nassau Strategy," 2 January 1963, NSF, box 230; unsigned note, 9 February 1962, NSF, box 216.

75. Pre-Nassau paper on U.S. concerns on a Franco-British nuclear arrangement, NSF, box 226; Rusk note to Kennedy on the offer to the French, 24 December 1962, NSF, box 71a; Ball, *The Past Has Another Pattern*, 266–68; Schlesinger, *A Thousand Days*, 860–66; Bohlen, *Witness to History*, 500; Winand, *United States of Europe*, 295–329; Trachtenberg, *A Constructed Peace*, 367–79; Artaud, "Le grand dessein." On the French view of Nassau, see Bozo, *Deux stratégies*, 98–101; Peyrefitte, *C'était de Gaulle*, 1:334–52; Vaïsse, *La grandeur*, 154–57; Soutou, *L'alliance incertaine*, 235–37.

76. Kennedy comments to his top advisers at a meeting on the MLF, 18 February 1963, NSF, box 217; Lawrence Kaplan, "Les débats stratégiques," in Vaïsse, Mélandri, and Bozo,

eds., *La France et l'OTAN*, 307–22; Winand, *United States of Europe*, 203–43; Ball, *The Past Has Another Pattern*, 259–74; Sorensen, *Kennedy*, 567–68; Lundestad, *"Empire" by Integration*, 75–78; Schlesinger, *A Thousand Days*, 851–53, 871–75.

77. Livingston Merchant (Kennedy's special representative on the MLF) to Kennedy, 21 March 1963, Merchant to Rusk, 20 March 1963, NSF, box 217; Steering Group paper on the MLF, 7 February 1963, NSF, box 316.

78. De Gaulle press conference, 14 January 1963, 4:61–79; Conze, "Hegemonie durch Integration"; Bohlen, *Witness to History*, 502–3; Ball, *The Past Has Another Pattern*, 269–72.

79. Schlesinger to Kennedy on the purposes of his European trip, 10 April 1963, POF, box 65a; Ball to Kennedy on the European trip, 20 June 1963, *FRUS* (1961–63), 13:204–13.

80. Text of the Frankfurt speech, 25 June 1963, POF, box 45; State Dept. to Bohlen (Paris), 22 September 1963, NSF, box 72; Conze, "Hegemonie durch Integration"; Osterheld, *"Ich gehe nicht leichten Herzens,"* 231.

81. Peyrefitte, *C'était de Gaulle*, 1:282; Alphand-Kennedy conversation, 9 April 1963, Amérique (1952–63): Etats-Unis 339.

82. MAE note for de Gaulle, 24 November 1961, Wormser Papers, 48; Adlai Stevenson (U.S. representative to the United Nations) conversation with French prime minister Georges Pompidou, 27 March 1963, Amérique (1952–63): Etats-Unis 339.

83. MAE note, 10 December 1962, 5AG1/170; Couve de Murville–Ball conversation, 26 November 1962, 5AG1/201; de Gaulle conversation with Dutch foreign minister Joseph Luns, 16 March 1963, 5AG1/181.

84. MAE telegram to Washington, undated [late Jan. 1961], *LNC*, 9:29–34.

85. Peyrefitte, *C'était de Gaulle*, 1:418–19.

86. Roland de Margerie (Bonn) to Paris on German MLF motives, 4 October 1963, Europe (1961–65): Allemagne Z187; Couve de Murville–Kennedy conversation, 7 October 1963, Secrétariat Général 19.

87. Pierre Messmer–Peter Thorneycroft (French and British defense ministers) conversation, 18 July 1963, Secrétariat Général 19; Peyrefitte, *C'était de Gaulle*, 1:281, 334; Couve de Murville, *Une politique étrangère*, 47–119; Colette Barbier, "La France et la Force multilatérale (MLF)," in Vaïsse, Mélandri, and Bozo, eds., *La France et l'OTAN*, 285–305; Vaïsse, *La grandeur*, 154–57; Soutou, *L'alliance incertaine*, 278–81.

88. Hildebrand, "'Atlantiker' versus 'Gaullisten'"; AA note, 17 July 1963, *Akten*, 2:761–67.

89. Blankenhorn paper, 23 May 1962, NL1351/132a; AA note, 29 August 1962, NL1266/1883.

90. AA note on U.S. policy, 30 June 1962, B32/183.

91. No relation to the chancellor elected in 1998.

92. Adenauer–de Gaulle conversation, 22 January 1963, *Akten*, 1:143; Schwarz, *Adenauer*, 721–22.

93. Adenauer–de Gaulle conversations, 22 January 1963 and 4 July 1963, *Akten*, 1:137–48, 2:689–702; Mayer, *Adenauer and Kennedy*, 75–94; Schwarz, *Adenauer*, 770; Kusterer, *Der Kanzler und der General*, 293; Osterheld, *"Ich gehe nicht leichten Herzens,"* 148.

94. De Margerie (Bonn) to Paris on conversation with AA officials, 29 December 1962, Europe (1961–65): Allemagne Z189; Adenauer–Walter Dowling (U.S. ambassador to

Bonn) conversation, 24 January 1963, *Akten*, 1:173–79; Osterheld, "*Ich gehe nicht leichten Herzens,*" 168–69.

95. AA note for 14 Jan. 1963 Adenauer-Ball meeting, undated, *Akten*, 1:51–54; AA note, 9 April 1963, B2/127; Franco-German conversations, 9–10 May 1963, B24/473; Schroeder-Home conversation, 14 August 1963, *Akten*, 2:1020–23; Osterheld, "*Ich gehe nicht leichten Herzens,*" 177; Schwarz, *Adenauer*, 811–12; Carstens, *Erinnerungen*, 272–74.

96. AA note, 4 February 1963, B32/184; comments of the new Atlanticist defense minister Kai-Uwe von Hassel to his French counterpart, Messmer, 23 March 1963, NL1351/155a.

97. AA note on Schroeder's views, 20 October 1962, MB242; Schroeder-Home conversations, 21 May 1963, *Akten*, 1:585–89; Schroeder-Home conversations, 14 August 1963, *Akten*, 2:1020–23; AA note, 15 November 1963, *Akten*, 3:1439–43.

98. AA note, 11 February 1963, MB226; Osterheld, "*Ich gehe nicht leichten Herzens,*" 196, 201; Mayer, *Adenauer and Kennedy*, 90.

99. AA note, 11 March 1963, B2/128; AA briefing note for Adenauer on Common Market/GATT issues, undated [September 1963], B24/476.

100. AA note, 5 November 1963, Referat IA1/530.

101. Franco-German summit meeting, 5 July 1963, AA note, 17 July 1963, *Akten*, 2:718–28, 761–67.

102. Macmillan, *At the End of the Day*, 111, 123, 335; Horne, *Harold Macmillan*, 2:329–30.

103. Macmillan–de Gaulle conversations, 2–3 June 1962, PREM11/3775; Macmillan–de Gaulle conversations, 15–16 December 1962, PREM11/4230. For more on Macmillan's ideas on independence and interdependence as they applied to nuclear issues, see Clark, *Nuclear Diplomacy and the Special Relationship*.

104. FO notes, 11 and 15 January 1963, London to Stations, 28 February 1963, FO371/173302; briefing papers for December 1963 Home-Rusk meetings, undated, PREM11/4583.

105. Nassau meetings, 18–21 December 1962, PREM11/4229 and *FRUS* (1961–63), 13:1091–112; cabinet session held in Macmillan's absence, 21 December 1962, CAB128/30; Macmillan, *At the End of the Day*, 357–60, 469; Horne, *Harold Macmillan*, 2:437–43.

106. Macmillan–de Gaulle conversations, 15–16 December 1962, PREM11/4230.

107. Thorneycroft memorandum for the cabinet, 7 June 1963, PREM11/4589; Home-Rusk conversation, 28 June 1963, PREM11/4586.

108. Briefing paper for meetings with U.S. leaders on the MLF, undated [March 1963], PREM11/4587; FO briefing note for Macmillan for meetings with Kennedy, 19 June 1963, FO371/173345.

109. Cabinet meeting, 30 May 1963, CAB128/37.

110. Cabinet meetings, 25 June, 20 and 23 September 1963, CAB128/37.

111. Cabinet meeting, 25 March 1963, CAB128/37.

112. MLF steering group note, 7 February 1963, NSF, box 316.

113. Bozo, *Deux stratégies*, 103–9; Vaïsse, *La grandeur*, 161, 363–71; Schaetzel, *The Unhinged Alliance*, 43; Carstens, *Erinnerungen*, 274; Winand, *United States of Europe*, 351–66.

114. German-American summit, 28 December 1963, *Akten*, 3:1672–79, 1689–99, 1712–13, *FRUS* (1961–63), 13:242–48, and *FRUS* (1961–63), 14:655–58.

Chapter Five

1. A portion of this chapter was previously published as Giauque, "The United States and the Political Union of Western Europe."

2. Blankenhorn, *Verständnis*, 316–17; Debré, *Gouverner*, 442; Osterheld, "*Ich gehe nicht leichten Herzens*," 115–17; Burin des Roziers, *Retour aux sources*.

3. Soutou, *L'alliance incertaine*, 149–201, "Le Général de Gaulle, le Plan Fouchet et l'Europe," "Le Général de Gaulle et le Plan Fouchet d'union politique européenne," and "Le Général de Gaulle et le Plan Fouchet," in *DGESS*, 5:126–43.

4. See in particular the articles on the Fouchet plan in *Revue d'Allemagne* 29 (April–June 1997). It is interesting that in this otherwise excellent (and extensive) collection of articles there is not a single article on the American or Atlantic dimensions of the Fouchet episode. See also Vaïsse, *La grandeur*, 175–91, and "De Gaulle, l'Italie et le projet d'union politique européenne"; Gerbet, "The Fouchet Negotiations for Political Union and the British Application," in Wilkes, *Britain's Failure to Enter the European Community*, 135–43; and Maillard, *De Gaulle et l'Europe*, 191–233. The memoir literature and historiography on the United States either ignores the political union issue or provides a brief narrative of it as a counterpoint to U.S. policy without examining how the United States viewed the political union per se. See, for example, Lundestad, "*Empire*" *by Integration*; Mayer, *Adenauer and Kennedy*; Winand, *United States of Europe*. There is also little on the Fouchet plan in the British historiography, with the exception of Ludlow, "Le paradoxe Anglais."

5. MAE note, 16 November 1961, Europe (1961–65): Généralités 1955.

6. De Gaulle comments to the leaders of the Five, 11 February 1961, Europe (1961–65): Généralités 1961.

7. Ibid.; de Gaulle note for Couve de Murville, 1 August 1960, 5AG1/160; de Gaulle–Adenauer conversation, 5 July 1962, 5AG1/161; de Gaulle letter to Macmillan, 12 December 1961, *LNC*, 9:172–73.

8. Debré paper, 27 February 1961, CM7; Vaïsse, "Changement et continuité dans la politique européenne de la France," in Association Georges Pompidou, *Georges Pompidou et l'Europe*, 29–43; Geoffroy de Courcel, "Les rapports entre le président de la république et le premier ministre du début de 1959 aux premiers jours de 1962" and Pierre Racine, "Les rapports entre le président de la république et le premier ministre, janvier 1959–avril 1962," in Institut Charles de Gaulle, *De Gaulle et ses premiers ministres*, 23–51.

9. Charlot, *Les Français et de Gaulle*, 81–82; Vaïsse, *La grandeur*, 180, 188.

10. Couve de Murville, *Le monde en face*, 152–60; Artaud, "Le grand dessein"; Bozo, *Deux stratégies*, 88; Conze, "Hegemonie durch Integration"; Vaïsse, *La grandeur*, 175–91.

11. Carstens note on German European policy, 3 August 1959, MB50; Carstens paper on European policy, 5 April 1960, NL1337/649.

12. Eisenhower letter to Adenauer, 5 October 1960, Whitman File—International series, box 16; State Dept. memo, 25 September 1962, Lot File 65 D 265, box 4.

13. MAE to Bonn, 18 November 1956, Europe (1944–60): Généralités 167; DE-CE note, 21 February 1958, DE-CE (1945–60) 689; Bossuat, *L'Europe des Français*, 333–77.

14. MAE note, 6 September 1958, Europe (1944–60) 167.

15. De Gaulle note for the foreign ministry, 13 August 1958, *LNC*, 8:73.

16. Couve de Murville–von Brentano conversation, 3 March 1959, 5AG1/160; Soutou, "Le Général de Gaulle, le Plan Fouchet et l'Europe"; Vaïsse, *La grandeur*, 175–78.

17. MAE note, 5 September 1959, Europe (1944–60): Généralités 187.

18. De Gaulle–Giovanni Granchi (Italian president) conversation, 24 June 1959, *DDF*, 14:873–76.

19. MAE note on the French positions, 28 October 1959, Europe (1944–60): Généralités 187; Vaïsse, *La grandeur*, 177–78, and "De Gaulle, l'Italie et le projet d'union politique européenne."

20. The minutes of the various meetings in 1960 are in Europe (1944–60): Généralités 170.

21. Soutou, *L'alliance incertaine*, 154–58.

22. De Gaulle–Adenauer conversations, 29–30 July 1960, *DDF*, 19:163–79; de Gaulle note for Adenauer on political union, 30 July 1960, *LNC*, 8:382–83; Kusterer, *Der Kanzler und der General*, 139; German translation of de Gaulle's note, 30 July 1960, B136/6407.

23. MAE note, 26 July 1960, CM7.

24. Wormser note for Couve de Murville, 3 August 1960, CM7.

25. MAE note, 11 August 1960, Europe (1944–60): Généralités 169; Debré note to Couve de Murville, 31 August 1960, File 820478/1, Cabinet Debré.

26. MAE note, 24 June 1960, CM7. This note examined the historical development of Switzerland, the United States, and Germany from confederations to federations and sought ways to prevent this from happening to de Gaulle's political union.

27. De Gaulle note to Couve de Murville, 1 August 1960, *LNC*, 8:383–84; Kusterer, *Der Kanzler und der General*, 166–73; de Gaulle letter to Adenauer, 9 March 1961, *LNC*, 9:54–55; Schwarz, "Präsident de Gaulle, Bundeskanzler Adenauer und die Entstehung des Elysée Vertrags," in Loth and Picht, *De Gaulle, Deutschland und Europa*, 169–79.

28. Adenauer speech in Brussels, 25 September 1956, B2/12; AA note, 25 August 1959, Referat 201-IA1/369. In a major speech on the subject in Brussels on 25 September 1956, Adenauer proclaimed many of the ideas that de Gaulle would later promote.

29. AA notes, 15 September 1956 and 1 October 1956, MB155; AA note, 24 October 1956, Referat 200-IA2/100; AA note, 9 November 1956, MB156; Proposal for an all-European federation, 9 January 1957, NL1351/73; AA note on political cooperation among the Six, 9 August 1957, NL1266/1462.

30. Adenauer, *Teegespräche 1959–1961*, 111–12.

31. AA to stations, 18 September and 15 October 1959, Referat 201-IA1/369.

32. AA conversation with Couve de Murville, 19 November 1958, NL1351/94.

33. Noelle and Neumann, *The Germans*, 266, 281, 509–11, 520–21, 537; Schwarz, *Adenauer*, 571–73; Noack, "Er kam und ging als Fremder," and von Staden, "Charles de Gaulle und die Aussenpolitik der Bundesrepublik Deutschland," in Loth and Picht, *De Gaulle, Deutschland und Europa*, 83–94, 121–33.

34. Carstens note on conversation with British embassy official, 6 October 1959, Referat 201-IA1/369.

35. Carstens note on German European policy, 5 April 1960, NL1337/649; AA paper on German European policy, 7 August 1959, B136/6204; von Brentano letter to Adenauer, 3 September 1959, NL1337/646.

36. Blankenhorn note, 5 August 1960, NL1351/103.

37. Blankenhorn note on de Gaulle–Adenauer conversations, 29 July 1960, NL1351/102;

Soutou, *L'alliance incertaine*, 160–66, and "Les problèmes de sécurité"; Maillard, *De Gaulle et l'Allemagne*, 169–202, and *De Gaulle et l'Europe*, 191–233; Schwarz, *Adenauer*, 566–73; Bozo, *Deux stratégies*, 62–63; Blankenhorn, *Verständnis*, 383; Conze, *Die gaullistische Herausforderung*, 156–58; Bariéty, "Les entretiens de Gaulle–Adenauer de Juillet 1960 à Rambouillet."

38. Blankenhorn note, 5 August 1960, Blankenhorn note on conversation with Adenauer, 15 August 1960, NL1351/103.

39. Note of AA study group on the French proposals, 29 August 1960, Referat IA1/517; Schwarz, *Adenauer*, 573.

40. Adenauer letter to de Gaulle, 15 August 1960, NL1337/617; Schwarz, *Adenauer*, 576, 583.

41. AA note, 14 October 1960, B2/76; Lee, *An Uneasy Partnership*, 253; Schwarz, *Adenauer*, 575.

42. AA note on contacts with BMWi, 23 November 1960, Referat 201-IA1/372; Erhard letter to Adenauer, 28 November 1960, B136/6407.

43. De Gaulle conversation with Pierre Werner and Eugène Schaus (the prime minister and foreign minister of Luxembourg), 17 September 1960, *DDF*, 18:362–67; Schwarz, *Adenauer*, 586; Soutou, *L'alliance incertaine*, 170; Osterheld, "*Ich gehe nicht leichten Herzens,*" 7–8; Vaïsse, "De Gaulle, l'Italie et le projet d'union politique européenne"; Soutou, "Le Général de Gaulle, le Plan Fouchet et l'Europe." Accounts of all these meetings are in *DDF*, vol. 18.

44. De Gaulle note to Debré, 30 September 1960, *LNC*, 8:398–99.

45. De Gaulle conversation with Pierre Werner and Eugène Schaus (the prime minister and foreign minister of Luxembourg), 17 September 1960, *DDF*, 18:362–67.

46. Alphand (Washington) to MAE, 7 October 1960, Wormser to Couve de Murville, 8 August 1960, CM7.

47. Briefing paper on European political cooperation prepared for Eisenhower's September–October 1959 meetings with Italian government leaders, undated, WHCF/DDEL—Confidential File, box 78.

48. Eisenhower–Antonio Segni (Italian prime minister) conversation, 5 December 1959, Whitman File—International Meetings series, box 4; State Dept. to Brussels, 8 December 1960, Lot File 65 D 265, box 4.

49. Briefing note for Eisenhower for March 1960 Adenauer visit, undated, WHCF/DDEL—Confidential File, box 80. On the Dutch opposition to de Gaulle, see Bernard Bowman, "'Longing for London': The Netherlands and the Political Cooperation Initiative, 1959–62," in Deighton, *Building Postwar Europe*, 141–58.

50. Intelligence Reports on Rambouillet for Eisenhower, 10 August 1960, WHOSS—Subject-Alpha series, box 9.

51. Herter–Harold Caccia (British ambassador to Washington) conversation, 12 August 1960, WHOSS—International series, box 13; State Dept. to Paris, 22 August 1960, *FRUS* (1958–60), 7 (pt. 1): 294–95.

52. Eisenhower letter to Adenauer, 5 October 1960, Whitman File—International series, box 16; Conze, *Die gaullistische Herausforderung*, 158–61.

53. Herter–Couve de Murville conversation, 19 September 1960, *FRUS* (1958–60), 7 (pt. 1): 298–300.

54. Herter to Stations, 20 October 1960, *FRUS* (1958–60), 7 (pt. 1): 303–4.

55. Paris to FO on Dutch warnings, 7 November 1958, FO371/137272.

56. FO note, 13 April 1960, FO371/154493.

57. Cabinet policy planning session, 29 November 1959, PREM11/2679; The Hague to FO, 22 January 1960, FO371/154493; Macmillan, *Riding the Storm*, 431–59, 527.

58. Steel (Bonn) to FO, 27 July 1960, FO371/154038. See also FO371/154496.

59. Herter-Caccia conversation, 12 August 1960, WHOSS—International series, box 13; Caccia (Washington) to FO, 2 August 1960, FO371/154038.

60. FO note, 28 August 1960, FO371/150364.

61. Jebb (Paris) to FO, 5 August 1960, FO371/154038; Macmillan, *Pointing the Way*, 247–48, 316–20.

62. Steel (Bonn) to FO, 2 November 1960, FO371/154493.

63. De Gaulle letter to Adenauer, 3 December 1960, 5AG1/165; Kusterer, *Der Kanzler und der General*, 157–58. De Gaulle postponed the meeting from late 1960 due to the illness of Adenauer, reflecting his longstanding conviction that only an agreement between himself and the chancellor would make any progress possible.

64. De Gaulle–Adenauer meeting, 9 February 1961, 5AG1/160; Seydoux (Bonn) to MAE, 2 and 6 February 1961, Europe (1961–65): Allemagne Z220; Kusterer, *Der Kanzler und der General*, 158–66; Maillard, *De Gaulle et l'Europe*, 191–33; Soutou, "Les problèmes de sécurité."

65. MAE to The Hague, 16 February 1961, Europe (1961–65): Généralités 1961.

66. De Gaulle comments at the meeting of the Six, 10 February 1961, Europe (1961–65): Généralités 1961. The German account of the meeting is in B136/2055.

67. De Gaulle note to Couve de Murville and Debré, 27 April 1961, CM7.

68. De Gaulle letter to Adenauer, 9 March 1961, *LNC*, 9:54–55.

69. MAE note, 15 March 1961, Europe (1961–65): Généralités 1959; MAE note, 4 July 1961, Europe (1961–65): Généralités 1961.

70. 18 July 1961 Bonn meetings, Europe (1961–65): Généralités 1961.

71. Soutou, *L'alliance incertaine*, 187; Kusterer, *Der Kanzler und der General*, 173–80; Osterheld, "*Ich gehe nicht leichten Herzens*," 40–43; Vaïsse, "De Gaulle, l'Italie et le projet d'union politique européenne."

72. MAE note, 9 June 1961, Europe (1961–65): Grande Bretagne 1738; MAE notes, 26 August and 15 November 1961, Europe (1961–65): Grande Bretagne 1739.

73. Debré paper and de Gaulle comments on it, 27 February 1961, CM7; Debré, *Gouverner*, 428; Blankenhorn, *Verständnis*, 345–47.

74. On the lack of direction from above in the autumn of 1961, see files Europe (1961–65): Généralités 1955 and 1958, particularly the 20 September 1961 note from the European section of the ministry to the minister's office in file 1955.

75. French account of the foreign minister meeting, 15 December 1961, Europe (1961–65): Généralités 1961; MAE draft text delivered to de Gaulle, 15 January 1962, Europe (1961–65): Généralités 1958.

76. De Gaulle draft of Fouchet treaty, 17 January 1962, Europe (1961–65): Généralités 1958. Specifically, de Gaulle's draft formally included economic affairs in the plan for the first time since Rambouillet in July 1960, a clear threat to the European communities. In order to justify this backtracking, de Gaulle's draft stated that there would be no limits whatsoever to the topics discussed in the meetings of the six governments. De Gaulle's

draft also eliminated the minor nods to supranationalism that French negotiators had accepted, including the independent secretary general for the political organization, an expanded role for the European parliament, and its election on the basis of universal adult suffrage. These changes made it clearer than ever that de Gaulle intended the new political union to absorb the existing European institutions, a goal that he had shrewdly left unstated since the fall of 1960. De Gaulle's draft also dropped both the "revision clause" on future development of the political union in a democratic and supranational direction and the reference to the Atlantic alliance, both of which French negotiators had accepted in order to calm the fears of the Five on French intentions. On top of all these affronts to the Five, de Gaulle's draft even implied that admission of new members to the Common Market would not automatically lead to their admission to the political union, since a unanimous vote of the existing members would be required.

77. De Gaulle televised speech, 5 February 1962, *D&M*, 3:382–87; Seydoux (Bonn) to MAE on the German reaction to de Gaulle's televised speech, 7 February 1962, Europe (1961–65): Allemagne Z174.

78. Blankenhorn, *Verständnis*, 316–17; Debré, *Gouverner*, 442; Burin des Roziers, *Retour aux sources*, 57.

79. Soutou, "Le Général de Gaulle, le Plan Fouchet et l'Europe" and *L'alliance incertaine*, 188–97. For additional explanations of de Gaulle's motives, see Vaïsse, *La grandeur*, 184, and "De Gaulle, l'Italie et le projet d'union politique européenne"; Schwarz, "Präsident de Gaulle, Bundeskanzler Adenauer und die Entstehung des Elysée Vertrags," in Loth and Picht, *De Gaulle, Deutschland und Europa*, 169–79.

80. Couve de Murville, *Le monde en face*, 152–60; Fouchet, *Mémoires d'hier et de demain*, 193–204; Burin des Roziers, *Retour aux sources*, 47–64; Maillard, *De Gaulle et l'Europe*, 207–8; Debré, *Gouverner*, 440–41.

81. MAE note on 18 January meeting of the Fouchet group, 19 January 1962, DE-CE (1961–66) 401.

82. Seydoux (Bonn) to MAE, 13 March 1962, Europe (1961–65): Allemagne Z220. On the Italian role in the Fouchet plan see Vaïsse, "De Gaulle, l'Italie et le projet d'union politique européenne"; Schweizer, "Le gouvernement italien et le projet d'union politique de l'Europe," and Varsori, "La classe politique italienne et le couple franco-allemand."

83. Blankenhorn note on conversation with Couve de Murville, 7 February 1962, NL1351/128b.

84. De Gaulle–Adenauer conversations, 15 February 1962, 5AG1/161; de Gaulle–Segni conversations, 4 April 1962, Europe (1961–65): Généralités 1955; Blankenhorn note on conversation with de Gaulle, 10 April 1962, NL1351/130b; Schwarz, *Adenauer*, 735–39; Vaïsse, *La grandeur*, 184–88; Soutou, *L'alliance incertaine*, 198–200.

85. Seydoux (Bonn) to MAE, 13 March 1962, Europe (1961–65): Généralités 1959.

86. Stelandre, "La Belgique et le Plan Fouchet"; Bowman, "'Longing for London,'" in Deighton, *Rebuilding Postwar Europe*, 141–58; Spaak, *The Continuing Battle*, 436–56.

87. Foreign minister meetings, 20 March 1962 and 17 April 1962, Europe (1961–65): Généralités 1962.

88. Blankenhorn to AA on conversations with Quai d'Orsay officials, 19 April 1962,

NL1351/130a; MAE note, undated [July 1962], Europe (1961–65): Généralités 1958; Couve de Murville, *Le monde en face*, 156–60.

89. AA note, 26 January 1961, Referat 200-IA1/371; von Brentano letter to Adenauer, 15 May 1961, Referat 200-IA2/502.

90. Mayer, *Adenauer and Kennedy*, 65–74.

91. Soutou, *L'alliance incertaine*, 177; Lee, *An Uneasy Partnership*, 253–55.

92. AA notes, 16 and 19 June and 7 November 1961, Referat 201-IA1/373; Schwarz, *Adenauer*, 736.

93. AA note, 7 March 1961, B2/79; AA note, 15 August 1961, Referat 201-IA1/372.

94. AA to stations, 19 July 1961, NL1351/116.

95. Blankenhorn note, 17 January 1962, NL1351/126a.

96. Carstens note for Schroeder, 1 February 1962, Referat 201-IA1/374; von Brentano letter to Adenauer, 20 March 1962, NL1239/159.

97. Blankenhorn note on conversation with Adenauer, 12 February 1962, NL1351/128b; de Gaulle–Adenauer meeting, 15 February 1962, 5AG1/161; Seydoux (Bonn) to MAE on conversations with German officials, 20 and 23 January 1962, Europe (1961–65): Allemagne Z174; Kusterer, *Der Kanzler und der General*, 206–9; Osterheld, "*Ich gehe nicht leichten Herzens*," 97–99.

98. Schwarz, *Adenauer*, 736–37.

99. Adenauer letter to von Brentano, 28 March 1962, NL1239/159.

100. Blankenhorn note, 18 April 1962, NL1351/130a.

101. AA note, 14 March 1962, Referat 201-IA1/374; Blankenhorn to AA, 19 April 1962, B2/75.

102. AA note, 3 January 1961, Referat 200-IA2/486; Carstens note, 28 March 1961, B2/77; AA note, 6 October 1961, Referat 200-IA2/526; AA note, 19 September 1962, B2/128 Schwarz, *Adenauer*, 737.

103. Steel to FO, 20 January 1961, FO371/158170; Macmillan–de Gaulle conversations, 28–29 January 1961, Macmillan letter to de Gaulle, 7 February 1961, FO371/158171. FO371/158170 also contains reports from the Paris and Bonn embassies on the political activities of the Six.

104. FO Steering Brief for the Common Market negotiations, 22 August 1961, FO371/158285.

105. Background notes prepared by the FO for Heath's conversations with Italian officials in November 1962, undated, FO371/164807; FO to Stations, 7 September 1961, FO371/158289.

106. FO371/161244; Ludlow, "Le paradoxe Anglais."

107. Macmillan comments to German ambassador von Etzdorf, 21 June 1962, PREM11/3775.

108. Macmillan–de Gaulle conversations, 15–16 December 1962, PREM11/4230.

109. Heath–Hans van Houten (Luns's immediate subordinate in the Dutch foreign ministry) conversation, 12 November 1961, FO371/158303; FO Steering Brief for Macmillan's meeting with de Gaulle, undated [November 1961] FO371/161246.

110. See accounts of Heath's speech in the 11 April 1962 editions of the *Guardian* and the *Times*.

111. Heath comments to Dutch ambassador, 3 May 1962, FO371/164783.

112. Heath conversation with an Italian foreign ministry official, 26 April 1962, FO371/164782; cabinet meetings, 13 April and 2 May 1962, CAB128/36; Macmillan–de Gaulle conversation, 2 June 1962, PREM11/3775.

113. The Hague to State Dept. on embassy conversation with Luns, 14 February 1961, State Dept. paper on Luns's views, 7 April 1961, NSF, box 143.

114. State Dept. to Stations, 24 March 1961, *FRUS* (1961–63), 13:2–4; State Dept. position paper for April 1961 Luns visit to Washington, undated, Lot File 65 D 265, box 4; State Dept. note on the U.S. position on the Bonn Declaration and subsequent developments, undated [November 1961], Lot File 65 D 265, box 4; Ball, *The Past Has Another Pattern*, 259–60.

115. Briefing paper for 28 March 1961 conversations with Dutch leaders, undated, briefing paper for 12–13 April Adenauer visit to Washington, 6 April 1961, Lot File 66 D 54, box 2.

116. Draft of State Dept. circular telegram, undated [November 1961], Lot File 65 D 265, box 4.

117. State Dept. to Stations, 3 November 1961, *FRUS* (1961–63), 13:48–49; Gavin (Paris) to State Dept., 6 November 1961, NSF, box 70.

118. Gavin (Paris) telegrams to State Dept. on conversations with de Gaulle and Quai d'Orsay officials, 14, 18, and 21 February 1962, NSF, box 71.

119. State Dept. paper on European policy, 26 March 1962, Lot File 65 D 265, box 4.

120. State Dept. to Brussels on Ball-Spaak conversations, 23 February 1962, *FRUS* (1961–63), 13:65–67.

121. Gavin (Paris) to State Dept. on conversations with Quai d'Orsay officials, 19 April 1962, NSF, box 71; Rome to State Dept. on embassy conversations with Italian officials, 3 May 1962, NSF, box 120.

122. Rusk to Stations, 27 April 1962, *FRUS* (1961–63), 13:82–84.

123. Rusk (from Athens) to State Dept., 4 May 1962, *FRUS* (1961–63), 13:690–91. See chap. 4 for more detail on the shift in high-level U.S. thinking on de Gaulle in 1962.

124. De Gaulle note to Couve de Murville and Maillard, 20 April 1962, *LNC*, 9:233; Bozo, *Deux stratégies*, 88–98; Peyrefitte, *C'était de Gaulle*, 1:104–11. The text of the 15 May 1962 press conference is in Cabinet du Ministre—Couve de Murville 147.

125. De Gaulle–Dixon conversation, 23 May 1962, DE-CE (1961–65) 516; de Gaulle letter to Spaak, 30 July 1962, CM7; MAE note, 1 September 1962, DE-CE (1961–65) 516; Vaïsse, *La grandeur*, 188–89, and "De Gaulle, l'Italie et le projet d'union politique européenne."

126. De Gaulle–Adenauer conversations, 5 July 1962, 5AG1/161; Maillard, *De Gaulle et l'Allemagne*, 302–4, and *De Gaulle et l'Europe*, 207–8.

127. Couve de Murville–Fanfani conversation, 12 October 1962, Secrétariat Général 17.

128. Couve de Murville–Pompidou–Fanfani conversation, 15 September 1962, Secrétariat Général 17; de Gaulle conversations with German leaders in September 1962, 5AG1/161; de Gaulle–Macmillan conversations, 15–16 December 1962, 5AG1/170.

129. De Margerie (Bonn) to MAE, 16 November 1963, MAE notes, 15 November and 12 December 1963, Europe (1961–65): Généralités 1956.

130. AA note, 27 April 1962, B136/6407; chancellor's office note on Adenauer's views, 27 April 1962, NL1239/185; Schwarz, *Adenauer*, 740.

131. Referat 201-IA1/375; Blankenhorn note, 13 June 1962, NL1351/134b; von Brentano letter to Adenauer, 22 June 1962, NL1239/159; AA note, 25 July 1962, B24/355; Blankenhorn note, 31 July 1962, NL1351/138; Blankenhorn, *Verständnis*, 427–30; Osterheld, "*Ich gehe nicht leichten Herzens*," 127–30, 138; Kusterer *Der Kanzler und der General*, 211–13.

132. De Gaulle–Adenauer conversations, 5 July 1962, 5AG1/161 and NL1351/138; Osterheld, "*Ich gehe nicht leichten Herzens*," 120; Kusterer, *Der Kanzler und der General*, 218–49.

133. AA note, 17 May 1962, B24/339; AA note, 14 June 1962, Referat 201-IA1/374; Schroeder–Couve de Murville conversation, 3 July 1962, Europe (1961–65): Généralités 1958; Carstens (in Geneva) to AA on the Schroeder–Couve de Murville conversation, 22 July 1962, NL1351/138.

134. AA note, 18 January 1963, B102/179470.

135. Adenauer–de Gaulle conversations, 4 July 1963, *Akten*, 2:689–702; AA note, 28 September 1963, Referat IA1/517.

136. AA notes, 18 December 1963 and 28 September 1963, Referat IA1/517; AA note for Erhard, 8 November 1963, Referat IA1/530; Paris to AA, 21 November 1963, B136/2059; AA note, 29 October 1963, B2/131; Schroeder comments to German delegates to the European Parliament, 3 December 1963, Schroeder conversation with new British foreign secretary R. A. Butler, 10 December 1963, *Akten*, 3:1538–40, 1594–1606; AA to stations, 18 December 1963, Referat IA1/517; AA plan for future European developments, undated [January 1964], B2/127.

137. Rusk to Stations, 21 June 1962, *FRUS* (1961–63), 13:725–27; State Dept. note on French plans, late December 1962, Lot File 65 D 265, box 5.

138. State Dept. memo, 9 April 1963, Lot File 65 D 265, box 5; Bohlen (Paris) to State Dept., 28 May 1963, NSF, box 72.

139. Ball–Couve de Murville conversation, 25 May 1963, NSF, box 72; Rusk to Stations, 14 June 1963, *FRUS* (1961–63), 13:202–4.

140. Ball-Erhard conversation, 26 November 1963, Rusk-Luns conversation, 14 December 1963, *FRUS* (1961–63), 13:233–41.

141. FO note, 22 August 1962, FO371/164799; Heath conversations with Benelux foreign ministers, 19–22 September 1962, FO371/164798.

142. Macmillan–de Gaulle conversations, 2–3 June 1962, PREM11/3775; Macmillan–de Gaulle conversations, 15–16 December 1962, PREM11/4230; Macmillan, *At the End of the Day*, 121, 349–55. The French versions of these conversations are in 5AG1/170.

143. Steel (Bonn) to FO, 16 May 1962, FO371/163538; FO371/163543.

144. Dixon (Paris) to FO and FO comments on his telegram, 18 February 1963, FO371/171449.

145. Dixon (Paris) to FO, 23 January 1963, Home minute to Heath on cabinet views, undated, FO371/173340; Ludlow, "Le paradoxe Anglais."

146. Dixon to FO, 31 January 1963, FO371/173340.

147. FO paper, 11 January 1963, FO371/173302. The Foreign Office actually sketched out this policy before de Gaulle's veto, since the failure of the talks one way or another was already on the horizon.

148. FO note, 18 February 1963, FO371/173302.

149. FO note, 17 December 1963, FO371/172071.

150. FO note, 13 November 1963, Bonn to FO on conversations with AA officials, 26 November 1963, FO371/173346.

Chapter Six

1. On the end of the negotiations in January 1963, see Bange, *The EEC Crisis of 1963*. On the technical negotiations, see Ludlow, *Dealing with Britain*.

2. On the political and diplomatic issues, see Greenwood, *Britain and European Cooperation*; Denman, *Missed Chances*; Kaiser, *Using Europe*; Steininger, "Great Britain's First EEC Failure"; Deighton, "La Grande Bretagne et la Communauté économique européenne"; Ludlow and Deighton, "'A Conditional Application': British Management of the First Attempt to Seek Membership of the EEC," in Deighton, *Building Postwar Europe*, 107–26; Sabine Lee, "Staying in the Game? Coming into the Game? Macmillan and European Integration," in Aldous and Lee, *Harold Macmillan and Britain's World Role*, 123–47; Lundestad, "*Empire" by Integration*; Winand, *United States of Europe*; Conze, "Hegemonie durch Integration"; Vaïsse, *La grandeur*; Françoise de la Serre, "De Gaulle et la candidature britannique à la communauté européenne," in *DGESS*, 5:192–202; Christopher Johnson, "De Gaulle face aux demandes d'adhésion de la Grande Bretagne à la CEE," in *DGESS*, 5:202–18; Hölscher, "Krisenmanagement im Sachen EWG"; Toschi, "Washington-London-Paris." A number of recent conference volumes contain contributions dealing with both the technical and political aspects: Wilkes, *Britain's Failure to Enter the European Community*; Griffiths and Ward, *Courting the Common Market*; Deighton and Milward, *Acceleration, Deepening and Enlarging*. The classic work on the British Common Market application is Camps, *Britain and the European Community*.

3. Cabinet meeting, 21 July 1960, CAB128/34; Ludlow, *Dealing with Britain*, 30–33.

4. FO note on the report, 22 June 1960, FO371/150362.

5. Ibid.; cover note for the interministerial report, undated [July 1960], FO371/150362; text of the interministerial report for the cabinet, 6 July 1960, CAB129/102.

6. FO note for Macmillan, undated [June 1960], FO371/150361; Paris to FO, 29 July and 20 September 1960, FO371/154496.

7. Cabinet meeting, 13 July 1960, CAB128/34.

8. FO note, 18 October 1960, FO371/150366.

9. FO talking points for Macmillan conversation with Adenauer, undated [August 1960], FO371/150364; Macmillan-Adenauer conversations, 10–11 August 1960, PREM11/2993.

10. FO note, 18 October 1960, FO371/150366; Heath note, 30 November 1960, FO371/150369; Steel (Bonn) to FO, 8 December 1960, FO371/150369; Macmillan, *Pointing the Way*, 321.

11. Text of the Grand Design, December 1960–January 1961, PREM11/3325.

12. Macmillan–de Gaulle conversations, 28–29 January 1961, PREM11/3322 and FO371/158171, and 5AG1/170; Macmillan talking points for the meetings, undated, FO371/158171; Ludlow, *Dealing with Britain*, 34–36.

13. Macmillan-Adenauer conversations, 22 February 1961, PREM11/3345.

14. Macmillan-Kennedy conversations, 5–8 April 1961, CAB129/105; Rusk to Paris, 8 April 1961, Rusk to Stations, 12 April 1961, *FRUS* (1961–63), 13:4–6, 1035–39.

15. Dixon (Paris) to FO, 12 May 1961, Heath-Chauvel conversation, 21 April 1961, FO371/158176; Dixon (Paris) to FO, 3 February 1961, FO371/158171; FO to Stations, 28 February 1961, FO371/158172; Dixon (Paris) to FO, 28 April 1961, FO371/158174; FO to Geneva,

4 May 1961, Heath memo for the cabinet, 9 May 1961, FO371/158175; Paris to FO, 23 June 1961, FO371/158178.

16. Macmillan conversation with Tory MPs, 9 May 1961, FO371/158269; FO note, 2 March 1961, FO371/158172; Paris to FO, 8 March 1961, FO371/158173; Heath-Chauvel conversation, 21 April 1961, FO371/158176; cabinet meeting, 26 April 1961, CAB128/35; Heath memo for the cabinet, 9 May 1961, FO371/158175; Heath (from The Hague) to FO, 16 June 1961, FO371/158271; Steel (Bonn) to FO, 19 July 1961, FO371/158276.

17. Dixon (Paris) to FO, 12 May 1961, Steel (Bonn) to FO on Adenauer conversation, 31 May 1961, FO371/158176; FO note, 7 June 1961, FO371/158178; Dixon (Paris) to FO, 13 July 1961, FO371/158179.

18. FO note, 8 May 1961, FO371/158270.

19. Prime minister's office note on Macmillan's plans, 15 June 1961, FO371/158273.

20. FO note, 18 July 1961, FO371/158277; Dixon (Paris) to FO, 12 May 1961, FO371/158176; Paris to FO on conversations with French officials, 27 July 1961, FO371/158179.

21. Macmillan minute to Heath, 29 July 1961, FO371/158281; Macmillan memo for the cabinet, 21 June 1961, CAB129/105; cabinet meeting, 21 July 1961, CAB128/35; Macmillan, *At the End of the Day*, 1–32; Lee, "Staying in the Game?," in Aldous and Lee, *Harold Macmillan and Britain's World Role*, 123–47; Kaiser, *Using Europe*, 108–73; Richard Aldous, "'A Family Affair': Macmillan and the Art of Personal Diplomacy," in Aldous and Lee, *Harold Macmillan and Britain's World Role*, 9–35.

22. MAE note on Britain and Europe, 10 March 1961, Europe (1961–65): Généralités 1958; Couve de Murville comments to Austrian foreign minister Kreisky on Britain, 30 June–1 July 1961, Secrétariat Général 14.

23. Seydoux (Bonn) to MAE, 28 August 1960, *DDF*, 19:245–47; MAE note, 18 May 1961, DE-CE (1961–66) 510.

24. MAE note on Britain and Europe, 9 June 1961, Europe (1961–65): Grande Bretagne 1738.

25. MAE brief for de Gaulle–Macmillan meeting, 12 January 1961, Cabinet du Ministre—Couve de Murville 13; MAE note, 10 March 1961, Europe (1961–65): Généralités 1958; Chauvel (London) to MAE, 22 April 1961, Europe (1961–65): Grande Bretagne 1740; Chauvel (London) to MAE, 28 April and 10 May 1961, Europe (1961–65): Généralités 1975. The French accounts of the Franco-British technical meetings are in *DDF*, 19:259–62, 570–73, 934–35.

26. De Gaulle letter to Adenauer, 9 March 1961, 5AG/165; de Gaulle–Adenauer conversations, 20 May 1961, *DDF*, 19:612–24.

27. Chauvel (London) to MAE, 26 April 1961, Europe (1961–65): Généralités 1975; de Gaulle–Kennedy meeting, 2 June 1961, *DDF*, 19:707–10, and POF, box 116a.

28. Chauvel (London) to MAE, 6 July 1961, Europe (1961–65): Grande Bretagne 1738.

29. Seydoux (Bonn) to MAE on Adenauer conversation, 21 April 1961, Europe (1961–65): Allemagne Z220; Seydoux (Bonn) to MAE, 26 April 1961, Europe (1961–65): Généralités 1975; MAE note, 9 June 1961, Europe (1961–65): Grande Bretagne 1738.

30. Osterheld, "*Ich gehe nicht leichten Herzens*," 23–24.

31. Noelle and Neumann, *The Germans*, 266, 271, 281, 509–11, 534, 537–38; Feld *West Germany and the European Community*, 48–49; Schwarz, *Adenauer*, 720–22. See also the letters addressed to the chancellor by German industrial leaders in B136/2553.

32. AA note, 23 May 1960, MB50; Carstens to Stations, 15 June 1960, MB50; Herwarth (London) to AA, 6 August 1960, Referat 304-IA5/182; AA note on British-German relations, undated [November 1960], Referat 304-IA5/181; AA note for Hallstein, 27 December 1960, NL1266/1886; AA note, 26 January 1961, Referat 201-IA1/371.

33. BMWi note, 21 October 1961, B102/65039; Carstens to London, 7 November 1960, Herwarth (London) to AA, 10 November 1960, B2/77; AA notes, 27 December 1960 and 6 June 1961, NL1266/1886; AA note, 16 May 1961, Referat 200-IA2/486; von Brentano letter to Adenauer, 23 May 1961, NL1239/158.

34. Erhard letter to von Brentano, 11 March 1961, MB67; BMWi note, 28 March 1961, B102/65039; BMWi note on conversations with Wormser, 16 May 1961, B136/2553; Steel (Bonn) to FO on conversation with Erhard, 26 January 1961, FO371/158170.

35. AA notes, 24 and 26 January 1961, Referat 200-IA2/486; Carstens, *Erinnerungen*, 247, 277.

36. Chancellor's office notes, 16 and 17 May 1961, B136/2560; de Gaulle–Adenauer conversations, 20 May 1961, *DDF*, 19:612–24; Osterheld, "*Ich gehe nicht leichten Herzens,*" 138–39; Schwarz, *Adenauer*, 729–33.

37. Rusk draft memo for Kennedy on European policy, 12 June 1961, State Dept. paper on the Six-Seven split, undated [April–May 1961], Ball memo to Kennedy, 1 April 1961, Ball memo to British leaders, 2 May 1961, and State Dept. note for Rusk, 11 July 1961, NAUK, box 1; State Dept. brief for U.S.-U.K. conversations, 7 February 1961, State Dept. brief for Adenauer visit to Washington, 6 April 1961, Lot File 65 D 265, box 2; Ball, *The Past Has Another Pattern*, 209–17.

38. State Dept. briefing paper for Macmillan visit, 21 March 1961, *FRUS* (1961–63), 13:1031–35; Winand, *United States of Europe*, 265–71; Lundestad, "*Empire" by Integration*, 65–66.

39. State Dept. to Stations on Kennedy-Macmillan conversations, 12 April 1961, Kennedy-Adenauer conversation, 13 April 1961, Ball-Caccia conversation, 2 May 1961, and Ball (from Geneva) to State Dept. on Adenauer conversation, 24 May 1961, *FRUS* (1961–63), 13:4–12, 21–23; Ball memo to Kennedy, 11 May 1961, NAUK, box 5; de Gaulle–Kennedy conversation, 2 June 1961, *DDF*, 19:707–10 and *FRUS* (1961–63), 13:23–25; State Dept. note for Rusk, 11 July 1961, NAUK, box 1.

40. Kennedy letter to Macmillan, 22 May 1961, NSF, box 171; Kennedy policy directive on the Acheson report, 20 April 1961, NSF, box 220; Rusk draft memo for Kennedy, 12 June 1961, NAUK, box 1; Ball note to Bundy and Kennedy, 7 August 1961, NSF, box 170.

41. State Dept. memo, 25 April 1961, State Dept. European Section note for Ball, 28 April 1961, Ball memo for U.K. leaders, 2 May 1961, NAUK, box 1.

42. In accordance with the requirements of the Six, the British also applied to join the ECSC and Euratom and negotiations on British admission to these two groups took place alongside the negotiations on U.K. entry into the Common Market. However, it was the Common Market application that was the heart of the British effort to join Europe and the other two sets of negotiations were clearly subsidiary. Similarly, even though Ireland and Denmark applied for Common Market membership alongside the United Kingdom and began negotiations with the Six, it was the British application that was the key to everything.

43. Text of Macmillan's speech, in Salmon and Nicoll, *Building European Union*, 69–73;

cabinet meeting, 21 July 1961, CAB128/35; Macmillan minute to Heath, 29 July 1961, FO371/158281; FO to Stations, 10 August 1961, FO371/158282; FO to Stations, 22 August 1961, FO371/158285; FO Steering Brief, 28 August 1961, FO371/158287; Macmillan, *At the End of the Day*, 65; Ludlow, *Dealing with Britain*, 43–73.

44. Heath letter to Spaak, 30 July 1961, FO371/158279; prime minister's office briefing note for Macmillan, 19 December 1961, PREM11/3782; Macmillan-Kennedy conversations, 22 December 1961, FO371/166967.

45. FO note, 15 September 1961, FO371/158290.

46. FO note on Heath's views, 31 October 1961, FO371/158302.

47. Brussels to FO, 22 September 1961, FO371/158292.

48. Heath note for Dixon (Paris), 27 November 1961, FO371/158305.

49. For British long-range planning, see FO371/166972 and FO371/166973.

50. Text of Heath's opening speech, 10 October 1961, FO371/158294; Dixon (Paris) to FO, 9 September 1961, FO371/158181; cabinet meeting, 5 October 1961, CAB128/35; Heath comments at Brussels ministerial meeting, 8–9 November 1961, DE-CE (1961–66) 512; Ludlow, *Dealing with Britain*, 74–77.

51. Macmillan letter to Kennedy, 5 October 1962, FO371/166970; Heath note, 4 February 1962, FO371/164777.

52. MAE note, 24 November 1961, Wormser note, 31 July 1961, Wormser Papers, 47; WEU ministerial meeting, 1 August 1961, MAE note, 9 August 1961, DE-CE (1961–66) 510; Chauvel (London) to MAE, 25 August 1961, DE-CE (1961–66) 509; de Gaulle–Hallstein conversation, 16 December 1961, Secrétariat Général 15.

53. Briefing note for de Gaulle's meeting with Macmillan in June, 22 May 1962, 5AG1/170.

54. MAE note, 26 August 1961, Europe (1961–65): Grande Bretagne 1739; MAE note, 16 November 1961, Europe (1961–65): Généralités 1955.

55. Couve de Murville–Schroeder conversation, 21 July 1962, Europe (1961–65): Généralités 1958; Ludlow, *Dealing with Britain*, and "British Agriculture and the Brussels negotiations: a problem of trust," in Wilkes, *Britain's Failure to Enter the European Community*, 108–19.

56. Debré paper and de Gaulle comments on it, 27 February 1961, CM7; Debré conversation with U.S. ambassador Gavin, 4 September 1961, Secrétariat Général 15; Debré, *Gouverner*, 408–9, 427–28; Vaïsse, *La grandeur*, 208.

57. Wormser to Brussels, 14 October 1961, Couve de Murville–Heath conversation, 12 September 1961, DE-CE (1961–66) 510.

58. De Gaulle–Adenauer conversation, 9 December 1961, Cabinet du Ministre—Couve de Murville 147; French draft response to Heath's opening speech, 6 November 1961, DE-CE (1961–66) 512; de Gaulle letter to Macmillan, 12 December 1961, *LNC*, 9:172–73.

59. MAE note, 4 October 1961, Europe (1961–65): Généralités 1962; Brussels ministerial session, 10–11 December 1962, DE-CE (1961–66) 513.

60. Pompidou–Couve de Murville conversation with Fanfani, 15 September 1962, Secrétariat Général 17.

61. Chancellor's office note, 14 September 1961, B136/2560; AA note, 13 October 1961, Referat 200-IA2/526; German draft response to Heath opening speech, 6 November 1961, DE-CE (1961–66) 512.

62. London to AA, 8 March 1962, Referat 304-IA5/232; interministerial meeting on the British application, 19 February 1962, AA note, 1 March 1962, and interministerial note, 20 September 1962, Referat 304-IA5/234; Erhard note on the British application and undated chancellor's office comments on it, 14 August 1961, B136/2560; London to AA, 8 March 1962, Referat 304-IA5/232; chancellor's office note on AA views, 14 September 1962, B136/2560.

63. AA note, 19 September 1962, B2/128.

64. Cabinet meeting, 8 August 1962, B136/2561.

65. AA note, 2 December 1961, Referat 304-IA5/214; AA note, 19 June 1962, B136/2560; interministerial report, 20 September 1962, Referat 304-IA5/234; AA note for Schroeder, 5 January 1963, Referat 304-IA5/251.

66. BMWi notes, 17 August and 21 October 1961, B102/65039; comments of BMWi representatives at an interministerial meeting, 19 February 1962, Referat 304-IA5/234; Heath note on 25 January 1962 conversation with Erhard, 4 February 1962, FO371/164777.

67. Erhard note to Adenauer, 14 August 1961, B136/2560.

68. Erhard and Schroeder conversation with Heath, 25 September 1962, Referat 304-IA5/234; Heath-Erhard conversation, 9 October 1961, FO371/158296.

69. NSAM 70: Kennedy to Ball, 20 August 1961, NSF, box 331.

70. Ball memo to Kennedy, 23 August 1961, *FRUS* (1961–63), 13:32–38; Ball, *The Past Has Another Pattern*, 215–18; Winand, *United States of Europe*, 291–94.

71. Conversation of State Dept. and Belgian officials, 18 September 1961, Decimal File 840.00/1–460 (1960–63).

72. Ball to Bundy and Kennedy, 7 August 1961, NSF, box 170; Rusk to Stations, 5 September 1961, *FRUS* (1961–63), 13:38–39.

73. Rostow (State Dept.) to Rusk, 24 March 1962, Lot File 69 D 121, box 221.

74. De Gaulle press conference, 5 September 1961, *D&M*, 3:333–49.

75. De Gaulle letter to Macmillan, 12 December 1961, Secrétariat Général 15.

76. De Gaulle–Hallstein conversation, 16 December 1961, Secrétariat Général 15; de Gaulle–Adenauer conversation, 15 February 1962, 5AG1/161; MAE note for de Gaulle meeting with Macmillan, 1 June 1962, DE-CE (1961–66) 516.

77. Heath note on conversation with Chauvel, 12 February 1962, FO371/163499.

78. Dixon (Paris) to FO on de Gaulle conversation, 18 October 1961, FO371/158182; Dixon (Paris) to FO, 27 November 1961, FO371/158306; Macmillan, *At the End of the Day*, 69, 111–13, 118, 337–38.

79. Dixon (Paris) to FO, 16 November 1961, Heath-Chauvel conversation, 21 November 1961, FO371/158183.

80. FO note, 12 December 1961, FO371/164832.

81. MAE briefing paper for de Gaulle, 20 November 1961, de Gaulle–Macmillan conversations, 24–25 November 1961, 5AG1/170; Macmillan, *At the End of the Day*, 32. British documents on the meetings are in PREM11/3338.

82. Paris to FO, 28 November 1961, FO371/158184; Macmillan letter to Commonwealth leaders on the meeting, 2 December 1961, PREM11/3338.

83. Heath conversation with Dutch leaders, 3 May 1962, FO371/164783.

84. FO notes, 24 April and 23 May 1962, FO371/164834; Paris to FO, 16 May 1962, FO371/164835.

85. Paris embassy papers on de Gaulle's foreign policy and Macmillan comments, 9 January and 23 August 1962, FO371/163494.

86. FO notes, 20 and 30 August 1962, FO371/164838; FO371/164797.

87. Macmillan minute on an 8 December 1962 Dixon telegram from Paris, undated, FO371/164841.

88. Dixon (Paris) to FO on Couve de Murville conversation, 1 December 1962, FO371/164840; Dixon (Paris) to FO on conversation with Quai d'Orsay officials, 13 December 1962, FO371/164841.

89. Heath conversation with Italian leaders, 17 September 1962, FO371/164798.

90. Dixon (Paris) to FO on de Gaulle, 10 February 1962, FO371/164832; FO371/163544.

91. Schwarz, *Adenauer*, 721–22.

92. Adenauer dictation on the minutes of 8 August 1962 cabinet meeting, 13 August 1962, B12, STBKAH; Steel (Bonn) to FO on Adenauer comments on British entry, 22 August 1962, FO371/164794; Paris to AA on the French reaction to Adenauer's position, 31 August 1962, NL1351/142; Osterheld, "*Ich gehe nicht leichten Herzens*," 126–27, 138–39, 175–76; Schwarz, *Adenauer*, 722.

93. Cabinet meeting, 8 August 1962, B136/2561; Kai-Uwe von Hassel (minister president of Schleswig-Holstein) letter to Adenauer, 21 August 1962, MB208; Carstens note on conversation with BDI officials, 15 June 1962, AA note, 6 September 1962, and interministerial report, 20 September 1962, Referat 304-IA5/234; Kusterer, *Der Kanzler und der General*, 225, 259–61, 293; Schwarz, *Adenauer*, 760–70.

94. FO to Bonn (account of 1 October Heath-Adenauer conversation), 4 October 1962, FO371/164800; Paris to AA on conversations with Quai d'Orsay officials, 31 August 1962, NL1351/142; Blankenhorn note, 5 October 1962, NL1351/144b; Heath letter to Adenauer, 5 November 1962, AA note, 13 November 1962, MB218; FO to Bonn, 13 November 1962, FO371/164803; Karl Newman, "Legal problems for British accession," in Wilkes, *Britain's Failure to Enter the European Community*, 120–32; Kusterer, *Der Kanzler und der General*, 291–93; Osterheld, "*Ich gehe nicht leichten Herzens*," 146–48.

95. Adenauer letter to the president of the Hamburg senate, 11 September 1962, MB208.

96. Schroeder note to the chancellor's office for Adenauer, 26 September 1962, MB262.

97. Blankenhorn note, 5 October 1962, NL1351/144b; AA note, 20 November 1962, Referat 304-IA5/234.

98. Steel (Bonn) to FO, 21 March 1962, FO371/164784; FO note, 5 March 1962, FO371/164781; FO to Bonn, 10 May 1962, Steel (Bonn) to FO, 11 May 1962, FO371/164783.

99. Bonn to FO, 9 November 1961, FO371/158302; Steel (Bonn) to FO and FO comments on the telegram, 16 August 1962, FO371/164795; FO note, 6 December 1962, Steel (Bonn) to FO, 10 December 1962, FO371/164810.

100. Macmillan letter to Adenauer, 25 July 1962, FO371/164791.

101. Steel (Bonn) to FO, 11 May 1962, FO371/164783; Steel (Bonn) to FO, 16 May 1962, FO371/164784; Steel (Bonn) to FO, 22 June 1962, FO371/164788; Heath conversation with Erich Mende (leader of the FDP), 19 July 1962, FO371/164791; FO note on Heath-Erhard conversation, 26 September 1962, FO to Bonn on 1 October 1962 Heath-Adenauer conversations, 4 October 1962, FO371/164800.

102. Notes on British contacts with Erhard in September 1962, FO371/164800; FO to Stations, 26 November 1962, Steel (Bonn) to FO, 4 December 1962, FO371/164809; Steel

(Bonn) to FO and attached note on embassy conversations with FDP leaders, 12 December 1962, FO371/164811.

103. FO note, 28 August 1961, FO371/158287.

104. Prime minister's office note for Macmillan, 19 December 1961, PREM11/3782; Macmillan-Kennedy conversations, 22 December 1961, FO371/166967; cabinet meeting, 3 May 1962, CAB128/36; Macmillan, *At the End of the Day*, 111.

105. Ball to Paris, 25 July 1962, NSF, box 170; Bohlen (Paris) to State Dept. on Pompidou conversation, 5 November 1962, NSF, box 71a.

106. Ball to Stations on conversations with Heath, 27 January 1962, NSF, box 170; Ball memo for Kennedy, 25 April 1962, NSF, box 175.

107. Ball to Kennedy, 11 May 1961, NAUK, box 5.

108. Paris to State Dept., 20 July 1962, NSF, box 170.

109. Ball-Heath conversation, 6 January 1962, Ball-Heath conversation, 4 April 1962, NSF, box 170; Ball note for Kennedy, 9 August 1962, NAUK, box 4; Ball note for Kennedy, 15 November 1962, *FRUS* (1961–63), 13:123–24.

110. Rusk to State Dept. on conversations in France, 21 June 1962, Gavin (Paris) comments on Rusk telegram, 6 July 1962, *FRUS* (1961–63), 13:725–30.

111. Gavin (Paris) to State Dept., 14 June 1962, NSF, box 71.

112. Ball–Couve de Murville conversation, 21 May 1962, Kennedy conversation with French minister of culture, André Malraux, 11 May 1962, NSF, box 71; Rusk–de Gaulle conversation, 19 June 1962, 5AG1/201; Rusk to State Dept. on conversation with de Gaulle on 19 June, 20 June 1962, *FRUS* (1961–63), 13:718–24; Winand, *United States of Europe*, 304–10.

113. Ball to Bruce (London), 16 February 1962, NSF, box 170; State Dept. note for U.S. conversations with British leaders, 20 April 1962, *FRUS* (1961–63), 13:1064–68.

114. Rusk to Bonn on positions to take with Adenauer, 12 May 1962, *FRUS* (1961–63), 14:142–45; briefing note for Kennedy, 11 January 1963, NSF, box 122.

115. Bundy letter to Jean Monnet on Adenauer conversation, 6 October 1962, NSF, box 71a; Rusk to State Dept. on Adenauer conversations, 23 June 1962, POF, box 88.

116. State Dept. note, 3 May 1962, Lot File 65 D 265, box 4; Gavin (Paris) to State Dept., 6 June 1962, *FRUS* (1961–63), 13:727–30; State Dept. (PPS) note, 9 August 1962, Lot File 69 D 121, box 216.

117. Heath comments at a Brussels ministerial session, 22 March 1962, DE-CE (1961–66) 512; FO brief for Macmillan meeting with Kennedy, undated [April 1962], FO371/166968; cabinet meeting, 4 May 1962, CAB128/36.

118. Cabinet meeting, 4 May 1962, CAB128/36.

119. Heath conversations with Benelux leaders, 19–22 September 1962, FO371/164798.

120. Paris to FO, 13 September 1962, FO371/164838; Heath-Schroeder conversation, 25 September 1962, FO371/164799; FO to Stations, 26 November 1962, FO371/164809.

121. Heath note to Macmillan, 7 February 1962, FO371/164777; cabinet meeting, 13 March 1962, CAB128/36; Labour party position paper, September 1962, Salmon and Nicoll, *Building European Union*, 74–76.

122. Stuart Ward, "Anglo-Commonwealth Relations and EEC Membership: The Problem of the Old Dominions," in Wilkes, *Britain's Failure to Enter the European Community*, 93–107; Macmillan, *At the End of the Day*, 132–40; Ludlow, *Dealing with Britain*, 195–96;

Horne, *Harold Macmillan*, 2:352–59; Vaïsse, *La grandeur*, 202–4; Gallup, *Great Britain*; Moon, *European Integration in British Politics*, 162–212. On the various British domestic interest groups, see the articles in Baker and Seawright, *Britain for and against Europe*.

123. London to MAE, 12 February 1962, DE-CE (1961–66) 524; de Gaulle–Adenauer conversations, 15 February 1962, 5AG1/161; Courcel (London) to MAE, 3 May 1962, Amérique (1952–63): Etats-Unis 376; de Gaulle conversation with an Italian foreign ministry official, 30 May 1962, 5AG1/178; Alphand (Washington) to MAE on Rusk conversation, 6 June 1962, Amérique (1952–63): Etats-Unis 338.

124. De Gaulle comments to German president Heinrich Lübke, 4 September 1962, de Gaulle–Adenauer conversations, 5 September 1962, 5AG1/161.

125. De Gaulle–Adenauer conversations, 15 February, 5 July, and 5–6 September 1962, 5AG1/161.

126. De Gaulle–Lübke conversations, 4 September 1962, de Gaulle–Adenauer conversations, 5 September 1962, 5AG1/161.

127. Prime minister's office note, 28 August 1962, DE-CE (1961–66) 525.

128. French high level meeting on relations with Germany, 31 August 1962, 5AG1/161.

129. MAE brief for de Gaulle's meeting with Macmillan, 1 June 1962, DE-CE (1961–66) 516.

130. MAE note, 8 May 1962, MAE note on de Gaulle–Dixon conversation, 23 May 1962, DE-CE (1961–66) 516.

131. FO brief for Macmillan, 11 May 1962, FO371/166976; FO briefing packet for Macmillan's meeting with de Gaulle in June 1962, undated, FO371/166977.

132. De Gaulle–Macmillan conversations, 2–3 June 1962, 5AG1/170 and PREM11/3775; MAE brief for de Gaulle, 1 June 1962, DE-CE (1961–66) 516; Macmillan, *At the End of the Day*, 119–21; Horne, *Harold Macmillan*, 2:326–30; Ludlow, *Dealing with Britain*, 117–22; Maillard, *De Gaulle et l'Europe*, 183–84.

133. FO note, 4 June 1962, FO371/166977; FO notes, 5 and 15 June 1962, FO371/166978; Dixon (Paris) to FO, 5 and 15 June 1962, FO371/164836; Paris to FO, 31 July 1962, Home to Dixon (Paris), 10 August 1962, FO371/164837.

134. DE-CE note, 2 October 1962, DE-CE (1961–66) 525; MAE note, 24 February 1962, DE-CE (1961–66) 516.

135. Record of 31 July 1962 French planning session, 1 August 1962, DE-CE (1961–66) 516; Couve de Murville comments at meeting of the foreign ministers of the Six, 23 October 1962, Europe (1961–65): Généralités 1962.

136. De Gaulle conversation with Italian foreign minister Piccioni, 17 December 1962, 5AG1/178.

137. Courcel (London) to MAE, 28 September 1962, DE-CE (1961–66) 525; DE-CE note, 2 October 1962, DE-CE (1961–66) 516; Courcel (London) to MAE, 12 October 1962, Europe (1961–65): Grande Bretagne 1739.

138. Dixon (Paris) to FO, 28 November 1962, FO371/166979; Wormser briefing paper for de Gaulle, 12 December 1962, 5AG1/170.

139. FO to Paris, 14 December 1962, FO brief for Rambouillet, undated, and several Dixon (Paris) telegrams containing advice for Macmillan, FO371/164841; prime minister's office note to FO and attached talking points for Macmillan, 6 December 1962, FO371/166979.

140. De Gaulle–Macmillan conversations, 15–16 December 1962, 5AG1/170, and

PREM11/4230; Macmillan, *At the End of the Day*, 340–55; Horne, *Harold Macmillan*, 2:429–32; Ludlow, *Dealing with Britain*, 197–99; Vaïsse, *La grandeur*, 205.

141. FO371/171443; FO371/164784.

142. Nassau meetings, 19–21 December 1962, PREM11/4229.

143. FO paper, 11 January 1963, FO371/173302; FO371/164733.

144. AA note, 15 June 1962, B136/2560; cabinet meeting, 8 August 1962, B136/2561; Adenauer comments to chancellor's office officials, 13 November 1962, cited in a 6 December 1962 chancellor's office note to the BMWi, B102/65051; Adenauer note to Schroeder, 31 December 1962, C42, STBKAH.

145. Ball-Erhard conversation, 14 September 1962, Orville Freeman (secretary of agriculture) note to Kennedy on his European trip, 26 November 1962, *FRUS* (1961–63), 13:116–21, 128–34.

146. State Dept. to Stations, 21 September 1962, Decimal File 651.62a/1–1162 (1960–63); State Dept. talking points for U.S. conversations with Schroeder, undated [late 1962], Lot File 65 D 265, box 5; Ball to Kennedy on the upcoming Nassau meeting, 10 December 1962, Tuthill (U.S. representative to the European communities) to Rusk and Ball, 16 December 1962, U.S. high level planning session on Nassau, 16 December 1962, Kennedy-Macmillan meetings at Nassau, 19–20 December 1962, *FRUS* (1961–63), 13:138–41, 1088–1112; Ball, *The Past Has Another Pattern*, 263–68; Winand, *United States of Europe*, 315–20; Osterheld, "*Ich gehe nicht leichten Herzens*," 162.

147. Ball note to Kennedy, 15 November 1962, Kennedy-Adenauer conversation, 15 November 1962, *FRUS* (1961–63), 13:123–28.

148. State Dept. notes on contingency planning, 11 and 17 January 1963, Lot File 65 D 265, box 11.

149. De Gaulle–Dixon conversation, 2 January 1963, 5AG1/170; Brussels to MAE, 11 January 1963, DE-CE (1961–66) 516; de Gaulle–Luns conversation, 16 March 1963, 5AG1/181.

150. Vaïsse, "De Gaulle and the British 'Application' to Join the Common Market," in Wilkes, *Britain's Failure to Enter the European Community*, 51–69; Greenwood, *Britain and European Cooperation*, 85–93; Urwin, *The Community of Europe*, 123–26; de Gaulle, *Memoirs of Hope*, 171–72, 178, 181, 187–89, 216, 219–20; Peyrefitte, *C'était de Gaulle*, 1:344–55, and 2:16, 225–30; Ludlow, *Dealing with Britain*, 206–12; Kusterer, *Der Kanzler und der General*, 301–6.

151. Text of de Gaulle's press conference, 14 January 1963, *D&M*, 4:61–79.

152. Wormser to Bonn, 11 February 1963, Wormser Papers, 2. The whole "association" idea was intentionally vague and merely served to blunt attacks on France in the period immediately after the press conference.

153. Notes of the Brussels delegation, 17–18 January 1963, DE-CE (1961–66) 526.

154. FO account of 11 January 1963 Heath–Couve de Murville conversation, 16 January 1963, FO371/171445; FO brief for Heath for his meeting with Couve de Murville, 9 January 1963, FO371/175446.

155. FO paper on de Gaulle's motives, undated [February 1963], FO371/169122; Macmillan, *At the End of the Day*, 365–69; Steininger, "Great Britain's First EEC Failure."

156. Dixon (Paris) to FO, 18 January 1963, FO371/169114; Dixon (Paris) to FO on Couve de Murville conversation, 19 January 1963, FO371/169122.

157. Dixon (Paris) to FO, 19 January 1963, FO371/169122.

158. Macmillan to Home, 15 January 1963, Heath to FO from Brussels, 17 January 1963, FO371/171444; FO note, 16 January 1963, FO371/171446.

159. Macmillan letters to Kennedy, 15 and 19 January 1963, PREM11/4593; Dixon (Paris) to FO, 19 January 1963, FO371/169122; Steel (Bonn) to FO, 21 January 1963, FO371/171445.

160. FO to Stations, 20 January 1963, FO371/171445.

161. Charlot, *Les Français et de Gaulle*, 81–85, 277, 280; Vaïsse, *La grandeur*, 221.

162. BMWi response to de Gaulle press conference, 15 January 1963, B102/179470; AA note, 19 January 1963, *Akten*, 1:105–8.

163. Notes of the French delegation in Brussels, 17–18 January 1963, DE-CE (1961–66) 526.

164. De Margerie (Bonn) to MAE, 17 January 1963, Europe (1961–65): Allemagne Z221; Osterheld, "*Ich gehe nicht leichten Herzens,*" 182–88; Blankenhorn, *Verständnis*, 437–38; Hölscher, "Krisenmanagement im Sachen EWG."

165. Franco-German summit, 21–22 January 1963, 5AG1/161, and *Akten*, 1:111–23, 124–30, 137–51; Kusterer, *Der Kanzler und der General*, 319–21.

166. Bonn to MAE, 25 January 1963, DE-CE (1961–66) 526.

167. Blankenhorn note, 28 January 1963, NL1351/152; AA note for chancellor's office, 18 January 1963, B136/2561; chancellor's office note, 18 January 1963, AA note, 19 January 1963, *Akten*, 1:97–102, 105–8; AA note, 22 January 1963, B102/65053; Schroeder letter to Heath, 31 January 1963, MB218; Schroeder to Vienna, 5 February 1963, MB263; AA note, 14 February 1963, Carstens note on de Gaulle, undated [February 1963], MB215, AA; Osterheld, "*Ich gehe nicht leichten Herzens,*" 183.

168. Blankenhorn note on conversation with Pierre Maillard, a foreign policy adviser of de Gaulle, 1 February 1963, NL1351/153b; AA to Washington, 4 February 1963, *Akten*, 1:251–53; Blankenhorn paper, 15 February 1963, NL1351/153a; Schwarz, *Adenauer*, 826; Osterheld, "*Ich gehe nicht leichten Herzens,*" 195.

169. Final Brussels ministerial sessions, 28–29 January 1963, *Akten*, 1:203–15.

170. Ball to Bundy, 23 January 1963, Decimal File 751.11/10–162 (1960–63); Bohlen (Paris) to State Dept., 25 February 1963, NSF, box 72; Bohlen (Paris) letter to Bundy, 2 March 1963, *FRUS* (1961–63), 13:760–61.

171. Meetings of Kennedy and his top advisers (the Excomm), January–March 1963, NSF, box 316. The quotation is from the 31 January meeting. See also Rusk letter to Schroeder, 28 January 1963, B102/65053.

172. Rusk draft letter to Kennedy, 15 January 1963, Lot File 65 D 265, box 11; Brussels to State Dept., 16 January 1963, NSF, box 73; State Dept. paper, 21 January 1963, Lot File 65 D 265, box 11.

173. Tuthill to State Dept., 2 February 1963, *FRUS* (1961–63), 13:167–70; State Dept. note, 1 March 1963, Lot File 65 D 265, box 11; Winand, *United States of Europe*, 331–50.

174. Ball comments at NSC meeting, 2 April 1963, NSF, box 314; State Dept. to Bonn, 24 January 1963, Rusk to Tuthill, 28 January 1963, Bruce (London) to State Dept., 31 January 1963, Tuthill to State Dept., 2 February 1963, and Bruce (London) to Kennedy, 9 February 1963, *FRUS* (1961–63), 13:151–54, 167–70, 188, 1128–30; NSC draft paper on U.S. European policy, 9 February 1963, NSF, box 314.

175. De Margerie (Bonn) to MAE, 30 May 1963, Europe (1961–65): Allemagne Z189; AA note, 14 February 1963, MB215.

176. Schroeder letter to Heath, 31 January 1963, MB218; AA note, 4 February 1963, B2/128; Osterheld, "*Ich gehe nicht leichten Herzens,*" 197.

177. Carstens note, 30 January 1963, NL1337/650; AA/BMWi joint paper on future European policy, 14 March 1963, AA note, 10 April 1963, B102/64781.

178. AA note, 4 February 1963, *Akten,* 1:253–57; AA note, undated [February 1963], Referat 304-IA5/250.

179. AA draft paper, 18 January 1963, B102/179470; AA notes, 4 February and 9 March 1963, *Akten,* 1:253–57, 371–75; AA note, 4 February 1963, Referat IA1/517; Carstens paper on the options facing Germany, undated [February 1963], MB218, AA; Brussels to AA, 4 June 1963, B102/64783.

180. Erhard letter to Adenauer, 27 February 1963, MB208; AA/BMWi joint paper on European policy, 14 March 1963, B102/64781; AA note on interministerial meeting on European policy, 14 May 1963, MB208; Roberts (Bonn) to FO on Erhard conversation, 1 March 1963, FO371/171464.

181. Von Hassel letter to Adenauer, 2 January 1962, MB208; von Hassel letter to Hallstein, 30 July 1962, NL1266/1883; Bonn to FO on conversation of British embassy officials with von Hassel in Kiel, 21 August 1962, FO371/164795; von Hassel letter to Adenauer, 11 February 1963, MB208.

182. The Hague to MAE, 30 January and 7 February 1963, Europe (1961–65): Pays-Bas 1807; The Hague to MAE, 21 and 24 January 1963, Europe (1961–65): Pays-Bas 1808; MAE note, 13 February 1963, 5AG1/178; The Hague to MAE, 11 March 1963, de Gaulle–Luns conversation, 16 March 1963, 5AG1/181.

183. MAE note on Italy, 9 February 1963, Europe (1961–65): Italie 1776.

184. Bonn to MAE, 2 February 1963, DE-CE (1961–66) 401; de Margerie (Bonn) to MAE, 30 May 1963, Europe (1961–65): Allemagne Z189.

185. Courcel (London) to MAE, 22 May 1963, DE-CE (1961–66) 524.

186. FO note, 3 May 1963, FO371/169124; Dixon (Paris) to FO and Macmillan and FO views on Dixon ideas, 11 July 1963, FO371/169116; steering committee paper on future British policy, 20 August 1963, FO371/173303; FO notes on Dixon's views, October 1963, Home to Dixon (Paris), 14 October 1963, FO371/172070; Macmillan, *At the End of the Day,* 374–76.

187. Steel (Bonn) to FO, 28 January 1963, FO371/171301.

188. Home-Bruce conversation, 31 January 1963, FO to Ormsby-Gore (Washington), 1 February 1963, FO371/168421; Heath-Bruce conversation, 31 January 1963, Ormsby-Gore (Washington) to FO on Rusk conversation, 13 February 1963, FO371/171302; Dixon (Paris) to FO, 9 February 1963, FO371/173342.

189. Dixon (Paris) to FO on Couve de Murville conversation, 19 January 1963, FO371/169122; Home to Heath, 7 February 1963, Dixon (Paris) to FO, 12 February 1963, and Heath to Paris, 13 February 1963, FO371/171461; Heath briefing paper for conversations with Benelux leaders, 22 February 1963, FO to Brussels on cabinet views, 28 February 1963, FO371/171463.

190. Dixon (Paris) to FO, 31 May 1963, FO371/169109; Dixon (Paris) to FO and FO comments, 11 July 1963, FO371/169116.

191. De Gaulle–Luns conversation, 16 March 1963, 5AG1/181; Courcel (London) to

MAE on conversation with FO officials, 27 March 1963, Europe (1961–65): Généralités 1531; Courcel (London) to MAE, 10 April 1963, Wormser to Brussels, 10 April 1963, and MAE note, 10 May 1963, DE-CE (1961–66) 526; de Gaulle–Erhard conversation, 4 July 1963, 5AG1/161; Peyrefitte, *C'était de Gaulle*, 2:229.

192. MAE note, 13 June 1963, DE-CE (1961–66) 526.

193. DE-CE note, 19 April 1963, MAE note for Couve de Murville, 1 July 1963, DE-CE (1961–66) 526; conversation of MAE officials with Blankenhorn, 13 February 1963, 5AG1/161; MAE note, 27 June 1963, Wormser Papers, 50.

194. Brussels to MAE on Couve de Murville–Erhard conversation, 1 June 1963, DE-CE (1961–66) 526; MAE note, 27 June 1963, Wormser Papers, 50.

195. AA briefing note for the July 1963 Franco-German summit, undated, Referat IA1/530; Franco-German meetings, 4–5 July 1963, 5AG1/161, and *Akten*, 2:689–728; Schroeder to London, 17 July 1963, MB263; AA note, undated [July 1963], MB209, AA; AA note, undated [September 1963], Referat IA1/517.

196. AA note, 30 September 1963, Referat IA1/518.

197. Roberts (Bonn) to FO on de Margerie conversation, 12 March 1963, FO371/173343; FO to Stations, 29 April 1963, FO371/171428; FO paper, 25 June 1963, FO371/171303.

198. Home to Stations, 15 March 1963, FO371/173343.

199. Macmillan minute to Home and FO comments, 10 March 1963, FO371/169123; FO notes on Macmillan's and Home's views and official British policy, 3 and 6 May 1963, FO371/169124; Macmillan minute, 28 June 1963, cited in a 17 July 1963 FO note, FO371/169116.

200. Draft memo for Kennedy, 30 January 1963, POF, box 116a; Rusk memo to Kennedy, 25 February 1963, POF, box 117; Tuthill to Ball, 25 February 1963, Lot File 65 D 265, box 11.

201. Rostow-Caccia conversation, 18 January 1963, NSF, box 171; Macmillan-Bruce conversation, 4 March 1963, Macmillan letter to Kennedy, 8 March 1963, PREM11/4581; FO to Stations, 28 February 1963, FO371/173302.

202. Courcel (London) to Couve de Murville, 26 September 1963, CM8; Peyrefitte, *C'était de Gaulle*, 2:308.

203. Courcel (London) note on 18 July 1963 Messmer-Thorneycroft (the French and British defense ministers) meeting, 25 July 1963, Couve de Murville–Kennedy conversation, 7 October 1963, Secrétariat Général 19.

204. Wormser note, 13 November 1963, Wormser Papers, 2; Courcel (London) to MAE, 12 December 1963, Europe (1961–65): Grande Bretagne 1739; Wormser note, 18 December 1963, Wormser Papers, 50.

205. Dixon (Paris) to FO and FO comments, 18 February 1963, FO371/171449.

206. R. A. Butler (the new foreign secretary) minute to Home (now prime minister) on contingency planning and Home response, 18 December 1963, FO371/171393; Dixon (Paris) to FO, 6 November 1963, FO371/172075; FO note, 22 November 1963, Dixon (Paris) to FO, 12 December 1963, Brussels to FO, 13 December 1963, and The Hague to FO, 14 December 1963, FO371/171451.

Chapter Seven

1. De Gaulle–Adenauer conversations, 9 February 1961, 5AG1/160; de Gaulle–Macmillan conversations, 24 November 1961, 5AG1/170; de Gaulle–Macmillan conversations, 15–16 December 1962, 5AG1/170.

2. MAE note, 19 May 1961, *DDF*, 19:611–12.

3. Lee, *An Uneasy Partnership*, 278–88; Kusterer, *Der Kanzler und der General*, 319–21.

4. Schwarz, *Adenauer*, 728–29; Schlesinger, *A Thousand Days*, 403–4; Mayer, *Adenauer and Kennedy*, 1–10; Soutou, *L'alliance incertaine*, 211–12, 221; Conze, *Die gaullistische Herausforderung*, 224–26; Vaïsse, *La grandeur*, 249.

5. De Gaulle–Adenauer conversations, 15 February 1962, 5AG1/161; Carstens, *Erinnerungen*, 277.

6. AA study on de Gaulle's political union proposals, 29 August 1960, Referat IA1/517; AA to Stations, 21 February 1961, Referat 201-IA1/372; Blankenhorn, *Verständnis*, 406–7.

7. AA note, 4 April 1961, B32/132; AA note on Franco-German relations, 2 June 1961, B24/359; Bariéty, "Les entretiens de Gaulle–Adenauer"; Schwarz, "Präsident de Gaulle, Bundeskanzler Adenauer und die Entstehung des Elysée Vertrags," in Loth and Picht, *De Gaulle, Deutschland und Europa*, 169–79; Kusterer, *Der Kanzler und der General*, 166–73.

8. Briefing papers for Kennedy's meeting with de Gaulle, 19 and 27 May 1961, POF, box 116a; Gustav Schmidt, "'Master-minding' a New Western Europe: The Key Actors at Brussels in the Superpower Conflict," in Wilkes, *Britain's Failure to Enter the European Community*, 70–90.

9. Rusk draft memo to Kennedy, 12 June 1961, NAUK, box 1.

10. Dowling (Bonn) to State Dept., 11 January 1962, NSF, box 71; Dowling (Bonn) to State Dept., 15 February 1962, Decimal File 651.62a/1–1162 (1960–63); Kennedy-Grewe conversation, 9 February 1962, POF, box 116a; Conze, *Die gaullistische Herausforderung*, 238–50.

11. Steel (Bonn) to FO, 27 July 1960, FO371/154038; Macmillan note to Home, 2 August 1960, PREM11/3003; Macmillan, *Pointing the Way*, 318–20.

12. Paris to FO, 30 September 1960, FO371/154040; Steel (Bonn) to FO, 9 January 1961, FO371/161121; Home-Herwarth conversation, 20 February 1961, FO371/161127; Paris embassy note on de Gaulle, 9 January 1962, FO371/163494; Macmillan, *Pointing the Way*, 320.

13. Soutou, *L'alliance incertaine*, 203–59; Vaïsse, *La grandeur*, 225–62.

14. MAE note, undated [Summer 1962], MAE note on Adenauer's position in Germany, 30 June 1962, Europe (1961–65): Généralités 1958.

15. De Gaulle letter to Adenauer, 26 April 1962, *LNC*, 9:234–35; Blankenhorn (Paris) to AA on conversation with Couve de Murville, 19 April 1962, B136/2056; Bonn to MAE, 27 August 1962, DE-CE (1961–66) 516.

16. Von Brentano letter to Adenauer, 22 June 1962, NL1239/159.

17. Blankenhorn note, 18 April 1962, NL1351/130a; Blankenhorn notes, 23 and 29 May 1962, NL1351/132a; Blankenhorn note, 13 June 1962, NL1351/134b.

18. Chancellor's office note on Adenauer's views, 27 April 1962, NL1239/185; Schwarz, *Adenauer*, 721–22, 728–29, 745–46, 751, 755–56; Osterheld, "*Ich gehe nicht leichten Herzens*," 120–27; Kusterer, *Der Kanzler und der General*, 211–13.

19. De Gaulle–Adenauer conversations and Franco-German plenary sessions, 5 July

1962, 5AG1/161; Peyrefitte, *C'était de Gaulle*, 1:150–56; Blankenhorn, *Verständnis*, 427–28; Osterheld, "*Ich gehe nicht leichten Herzens*," 130–35; Schwarz, *Adenauer*, 757–63; Burin des Roziers, *Retour aux sources*, 138–40; Vaïsse, *La grandeur*, 249–52; Maillard, *De Gaulle et l'Europe*, 175–76; Kusterer, *Der Kanzler und der General*, 216–50.

20. Adenauer letter to Rusk, 10 July 1962, B2/79.

21. AA note on de Gaulle press conference, 17 May 1962, B24/339; AA note on Franco-German relations, 1 July 1962, B24/354.

22. MAE note, 30 June 1962, Europe (1961–65): Généralités 1958.

23. De Gaulle letter to Adenauer, 15 July 1962, 5AG1/165. These were, of course, the same four areas that had been the heart of the Fouchet negotiations.

24. French planning session for de Gaulle's trip to Germany, 31 August 1962, 5AG1/161; MAE memo on Franco-German cooperation, 6 September 1962, Europe (1961–65): Généralités 1958.

25. AA protocol section note, 9 July 1962, MB196.

26. AA to Stations, 8 September 1962, B24/360; AA note on conversation between German and Italian officials, 18 October 1962, Referat 201-IA1/375.

27. Cabinet meeting, 8 August 1962, B136/2561.

28. De Gaulle–Gavin conversation, 19 September 1962, 5AG1/201; de Gaulle–Lübke conversations, 4 September 1962, de Gaulle–Adenauer conversations, 5 September 1962, 5AG1/161; Pompidou–Couve de Murville conversation with Fanfani, 15 September 1962, Secrétariat Général 17; Vaïsse, *La grandeur*, 250–52; Maillard, *De Gaulle et l'Europe*, 208–12, and *De Gaulle et l'Allemagne*, 176–80; Peyrefitte, *C'était de Gaulle*, 1:157–63; Blankenhorn, *Verständnis*, 428–30; Burin des Roziers, *Retour aux sources*, 140–42; Schwarz, *Adenauer*, 765–69; Osterheld, "*Ich gehe nicht leichten Herzens*," 139–44; Kusterer, *Der Kanzler und der General*, 250–90; Gerhard Kiersch, "De Gaulle et l'identité allemande," in *DGESS*, 5:304–12.

29. Pompidou–Couve de Murville–Fanfani conversation, 15 September 1962, Secrétariat Général 17.

30. French draft memo, 6 September 1962, Secrétariat Général 17; Text of the French memo sent to the Germans, 19 September 1962, 5AG1/165; Maillard, *De Gaulle et l'Europe*, 216–17.

31. De Margerie (Bonn) to MAE, 15 October 1962, Europe (1961–65): Allemagne Z220.

32. De Gaulle letter to Adenauer, 26 October 1962, Secrétariat Général 17.

33. Blankenhorn note, 22 November 1962, NL1351/146.

34. Blankenhorn notes, 1 and 10 September 1962, NL1351/148; AA note on conversation with McGeorge Bundy, 25 September 1962, B2/79; Blankenhorn note on the French memo, 5 October 1962, NL1351/144b; Carstens note, 5 November 1962, Carstens–von Brentano conversation, 7 November 1962, and AA conversation with Italian officials, 19 November 1962, B2/75.

35. Text of the German reply, 8 November 1962, Cabinet du Ministre—Couve de Murville 68; French translation, 5AG1/165.

36. De Margerie (Bonn) to Couve de Murville on conversation with an AA official, 5 November 1962, Cabinet du Ministre—Couve de Murville 68; Couve de Murville–Schroeder conversations, 16–17 December 1962, 5AG1/161; AA note, 7 January 1963, Carstens note, 10 January 1963, and AA note, 12 January 1963, *Akten*, 1:19–29, 42–45,

56–60; German cabinet session, 16 January 1963, cited in a 21 February 1963 chancellor's office note, B136/3954; Final treaty text, Soutou, *L'alliance incertaine*, 445–49; Vaïsse, *La grandeur*, 253–54; Carstens, *Erinnerungen*, 251; Mayer, *Adenauer and Kennedy*, 75–94.

37. DE-CE note on the German response, 26 November 1962, Wormser Papers, 1.

38. Note of the AA legal section, 14 January 1963, *Akten*, 1:73–74.

39. Bonn to MAE, 18 January 1963, Europe (1961–65): Allemagne Z228; Osterheld, "*Ich gehe nicht leichten Herzens*," 174; Schwarz, *Adenauer*, 817–25, and "Präsident de Gaulle, Bundeskanzler Adenauer und die Entstehung des Elysée Vertrags," in Loth and Picht, *De Gaulle, Deutschland und Europa*, 169–79.

40. AA note, 20 January 1963, *Akten*, 1:108–9; AA note on de Gaulle's press conference, 16 January 1963, B24/470; AA note for meeting with Bundestag foreign affairs committee, 16 January 1963, B24/470; von Brentano letter to Adenauer on the expectations of the Bundestag, 21 January 1963, NL1239/159; Blankenhorn, *Verständnis*, 437–39.

41. De Margerie (Bonn) to MAE, 17 January 1963, Europe (1961–65): Allemagne Z221.

42. Alphand (Washington) to MAE, 22 January 1963, Europe (1961–65): Allemagne Z230.

43. Pompidou–Adlai Stevenson conversation, 27 March 1963, 5AG1/201; Couve de Murville–Kennedy conversation, 7 October 1963, Secrétariat Général 19.

44. Carstens note on conversation with Dowling, 24 January 1963, NL1337/650; Vaïsse, *La grandeur*, 255–62; Soutou, "Les problèmes de sécurité."

45. Franco-German summit, 21–23 January 1963, 5AG1/161, and *Akten*, 1:111–30, 137–51.

46. State Dept. (PPS) paper, 6 February 1962, Lot File 69 D 121, box 215; Tuthill (Paris) to Ball on Blankenhorn conversation, 28 May 1962, Lot File 65 D 265, box 4.

47. State Dept. (INR) paper on Germany, "West Germany: Political and Economic Prospects," 3 August 1962, NSF, box 75; Gavin (Paris) to State Dept., 7 July 1962, NSF, box 71.

48. Brussels to State Dept. on Spaak's views, 7 and 13 September 1962, NSF, box 79; State Dept. to Stations, 21 September 1962, Decimal File 651.62a/1–1162 (1960–63); Rusk letter to Kennedy, 8 October 1962, NSF, box 71a; Conze, *Die gaullistische Herausforderung*, 241–50.

49. Adenauer letter to Kennedy, 23 August 1962, POF, box 116a.

50. Dowling (Bonn) to State Dept., 13 September 1962, Decimal File 751.11/5–362 (1960–63); Rusk-Alphand conversation, 7 September 1962, *FRUS* (1961–63), 15:311–13; Ball-Erhard conversation, 14 September 1962, *FRUS* (1961–63), 13:116–21.

51. Paris to State Dept., 11 September 1962, Decimal File 751.11/5–362 (1960–63).

52. Bonn to State Dept., 5 October 1962, Decimal File 651.62a/10–162 (1960–63); Rusk letter to Kennedy, 8 October 1962, NSF, box 71a.

53. Ball-Schroeder conversation, 14 November 1962, Decimal File 651.62a/10–162 (1960–63); State Dept. study of Franco-German relations, 22 November 1962, Lot File 65 D 265, box 4.

54. Paris to FO, 9 January 1962, Paris to FO, 23 August 1962, FO371/163494.

55. Macmillan comments on 23 August 1962 Paris embassy memo, undated, FO371/163494.

56. Dixon (Paris) to FO, 5 July 1962, FO371/163543; Paris to FO on embassy conversations with French officials, 10 August 1962, FO371/164838; Steel (Bonn) to FO, 15 August 1962, FO371/164794.

57. FO note for Heath on Herwarth-Carstens-Steel conversation, 11 July 1962, FO371/164789; Steel (Bonn) to FO, 30 July 1962, FO371/164791.

58. Macmillan letter to Adenauer, 25 July 1962, FO371/164791.

59. FO briefing paper for Heath, undated [August 1962], Dixon (Paris) to FO and attached memo, 13 September 1962, FO371/164838; Bonn to FO, 7 September 1962, PREM11/4129; Home to Stations, 14 September 1962, Bonn to FO, 15 September 1962, FO371/163544.

60. FO note, 23 October 1962, FO371/163544.

61. Steel (Bonn) to FO on Herwarth conversation, 15 October 1962, FO371/163544; Dixon (Paris) to FO on conversation with de Gaulle on 29 September 1962, 1 October 1962, FO371/164839; Dixon (Paris) to FO, 2 October 1962, Bonn to FO, 8 October 1962, FO371/163544; Heath-Schroeder conversation, 7 January 1963, FO371/173340.

62. Dixon (Paris) to FO, 19 November 1962, FO371/163544; Dixon (Paris) to FO, 21 and 22 December 1962, FO371/171443.

63. FO371/171443; FO371/171301.

64. Maillard, *De Gaulle et l'Allemagne*, 203–20, and *De Gaulle et l'Europe*, 222–25; Kosthorst, "Die Unerwünschte Liaison."

65. The treaty text can be found in Soutou, *L'alliance incertaine*, 445–49.

66. State Dept. memo on de Gaulle's foreign policy, 23 January 1963, Lot File 65 D 265, box 5; Unsigned draft comments on the treaty, 23 January 1963, POF, box 117; Rusk briefing paper for Kennedy, 23 February 1963, POF, box 117; Ball paper for Kennedy, 1 March 1963, NSF, box 9; Winand, *United States of Europe*, 334–36; Mayer, *Adenauer and Kennedy*, 89–94; Ball, *The Past Has Another Pattern*, 271–73; Conze, *Die gaullistische Herausforderung*, 257–75.

67. Kennedy note to Bundy, 1 February 1963, POF, box 62a.

68. Dowling (Bonn) to State Dept., 24 January 1963, State Dept. note on conversation with German embassy officials, 31 January 1963, Decimal File 651.62a/10–162 (1960–63).

69. Dowling (Bonn) to State Dept. on Carstens conversation, 24 January 1963, Decimal File 651.62a/10–162 (1960–63).

70. Rusk briefing paper for Kennedy, 23 February 1963, POF, box 117.

71. Karl Knappstein (the new German ambassador in Washington) to Bonn on conversations with Clay and Acheson, 28 and 30 January 1963, and Adenauer letter to McCloy, 28 January 1963, *Akten*, 1:200–2, 228–29; John J. McCloy letter to Adenauer, 4 February 1963, POF, box 31.

72. Adenauer letter to Kennedy, 22 January 1963, *Akten*, 1:153–55.

73. Adenauer-Dowling conversation, 24 January 1963, Adenauer-Gilpatric conversation, 13 February 1963, *Akten*, 1:162–65, 302–12.

74. Carstens note on his trip, 9 February 1963; Carstens conversation with State Dept. officials, 5 February 1963, Carstens to Schroeder on Kennedy conversation, 6 February 1963, *Akten*, 1:269–76, 289–94; Ball, *The Past Has Another Pattern*, 272–73; Winand, *United States of Europe*, 334–35.

75. 28 January 1963 Adenauer letter to John J. McCloy, *Akten*, 1:201–2.

76. Carstens–de Margerie conversation, 7 February 1963, B2/131.

77. Erhard letter to Adenauer, 4 February 1963, B136/3952; Hallstein-Erhard meeting, 18 February 1963, *Akten*, 1:332–34.

78. Osterheld (chancellor's office) note on the views of the various parties and cabinet ministers, 21 February 1963, B136/3954; Bulmer and Paterson, *The Federal Republic of Germany and the European Community*, 135–36. The SPD and FDP initially favored al-

tering the treaty itself rather than simply passing a resolution along with it or attaching a preamble.

79. Noelle and Neumann, *The Germans*, 271–74, 534–37; Noack, "Er kam und ging als Fremder," in Loth and Picht, *De Gaulle, Deutschland und Europa*, 83–94.

80. AA note on the Franco-German treaty, 29 March 1963, *Akten*, 1:443–46; Carstens, *Erinnerungen*, 253; Bulmer and Paterson, *The Federal Republic of Germany and the European Community*, 127–30; Mayer, *Adenauer and Kennedy*, 90; Hildebrand, "'Atlantiker' versus 'Gaullisten.'"

81. Golo Mann, *Die Zeit*, 14 February 1969, cited in Osterheld, "*Ich gehe nicht leichten Herzens*," 237; German text of the preamble and treaty, in Möller and Hildebrand, *Die Bundesrepublik Deutschland und Frankreich*, 3:793–95; Osterheld, "*Ich gehe nicht leichten Herzens*," 170, 222; Schwarz, *Adenauer*, 825–26, 834. With the preamble attached, all the German parties voted overwhelmingly for ratification.

82. Bonn to MAE, 18 January 1963, Europe (1961–65): Allemagne Z228.

83. De Margerie (Bonn) to MAE, 10 February 1963, Europe (1961–65): Allemagne Z221.

84. De Margerie (Bonn) to MAE, 31 January, 23 March, and 22 April 1963, Europe (1961–65): Allemagne Z221.

85. Alphand (Washington) to MAE, 22 March 1963, Europe (1961–65): Allemagne Z182; Osterheld, "*Ich gehe nicht leichten Herzens*," 196–97.

86. De Margerie (Bonn) to Couve de Murville on Adenauer conversation, 4 February 1963, CM8.

87. Schroeder letter to Couve de Murville, 1 February 1963, *Akten*, 1:238; de Margerie (Bonn) to MAE, 1 February 1963, DE-CE (1961–66) 526; Wormser to Bonn, 1 February 1963, Wormser Papers, 2.

88. Wormser note on de Gaulle's views, 6 July 1963, DE-CE (1961–66) 526; Peyrefitte, *C'était de Gaulle*, 2:219–30.

89. Pompidou-Brandt conversation, 26 April 1963, 5AG1/161; Soutou, *L'alliance incertaine*, 255.

90. De Margerie (Bonn) to MAE, 8 February, 26 March and 29 March 1963, Europe (1961–65): Allemagne Z221; de Margerie (Bonn) to MAE, 3 April 1963, Europe (1961–65): Allemagne Z182; Burin des Roziers, *Retour aux sources*, 145; Vaïsse, *La grandeur*, 261–62.

91. De Margerie (Bonn) to MAE, 22 April 1963, Europe (1961–65): Allemagne Z221.

92. Adenauer conversation with Alain Peyrefitte (de Gaulle's minister of information), 12 May 1963, 5AG1/161; de Margerie (Bonn) to MAE, 17 May 1963, Europe (1961–65): Allemagne Z229; MAE note on the treaty, 31 May 1963, Europe (1961–65): Allemagne Z222; de Gaulle press conference, 29 July 1963, *D&M*, 4:112–30.

93. Blankenhorn paper, 15 February 1963, *Akten*, 1:315–23; Blankenhorn notes, 28 January and 12 February 1963, NL1351/152; Blankenhorn note, 14 August 1963, NL1351/160.

94. AA note, 9 April 1963, B2/127.

95. Erhard letter to von Brentano, 1 March 1963, NL1239/170; BMWi notes, 15 January, 5 February, 13 February, 14 February, and 19 February 1963, B102/179470.

96. MAE note, 23 April 1963, Europe (1961–65): Allemagne Z221; Kusterer, *Der Kanzler und der General*, 314.

97. MAE note, 6 May 1963, Cabinet du Ministre—Couve de Murville 70.

98. Text of the government's declaration on the treaty, Cabinet du Ministre—Couve

de Murville 70; MAE note, 31 May 1963, Europe (1961–65): Allemagne Z222. The French ratification vote was less uniform than that of the Bundestag, with the communists and many socialists voting against it and the Radical party abstaining.

99. Quai d'Orsay–AA conversations on application of the treaty, 9–10 May 1963, B24/473; AA note, 12 June 1963, Referat IA1/517.

100. De Margerie (Bonn) note on Kennedy's actions in Germany, 26 June 1963, Europe (1961–65): Allemagne Z230; Couve de Murville, *Une politique étrangère*, 235–84.

101. Ibid.; de Margerie (Bonn) to MAE, 27 June 1963, Amérique (1952–63): Etats-Unis 382; Peyrefitte, *C'était de Gaulle*, 2:26–28.

102. De Gaulle–Adenauer conversations, 4 July 1963, 5AG1/161, and *Akten*, 2:689–702.

103. De Gaulle conversations with Erhard, Schroeder, Lübke (as well as Adenauer in some sessions), 4–5 July 1963, 5AG 1/161, and *Akten*, 2:702–28.

104. Carstens notes, 15 and 22 June 1963, *Akten*, 2:631–32, 654–56; Blankenhorn note, 27 June 1963, NL1351/158a; Osterheld, "*Ich gehe nicht leichten Herzens*," 233–34.

105. Blankenhorn note, 28 June 1963, NL1351/158a; Blankenhorn letter to Schroeder, 10 July 1963, NL1351/159b.

106. Text of the press conference, 29 July 1963, *D&M*, 4:112–30; MAE to Stations, 6 July 1963, Secrétariat Général 18.

107. Schroeder to Paris, 6 August 1963, Blankenhorn (Paris) to AA, 8 August 1963, *Akten*, 2:939–40; Peyrefitte, *C'était de Gaulle*, 2:231; Kusterer, *Der Kanzler und der General*, 430–44.

108. AA note, 19 September 1963, B24/475.

109. Adenauer letter to de Gaulle, 14 August 1963, de Gaulle letter to Adenauer, 23 August 1963, 5AG1/165; Europe (1961–65): Allemagne Z182; Peyrefitte, *C'était de Gaulle*, 2:30–31; Conze, *Die gaullistische Herausforderung*, 288–89; Osterheld, "*Ich gehe nicht leichten Herzens*," 240–53.

110. De Gaulle notes to Couve de Murville, 11 and 23 September 1963, CM8; Soutou, *L'alliance incertaine*, 265; Peyrefitte, *C'était de Gaulle*, 2:33–35.

111. Couve de Murville–Schroeder conversations, 17 September 1963, 5AG1/161, and *Akten*, 2:1139–43.

112. Couve de Murville conversations with Rusk, Kennedy, and Ball, 7–9 October 1963, Secrétariat Général 19, and NSF, box 73.

113. Wormser note, 16 November 1963, Wormser Papers, 2; Wormser note, 18 December 1963, Wormser Papers, 50.

114. De Gaulle–Adenauer conversations, 21–22 September 1963, 5AG1/161, and *Akten*, 2:1185–87, 1192–1210; Schwarz, *Adenauer*, 857–58; Peyrefitte, *C'était de Gaulle*, 2:235–37.

115. Alphand (Washington) to MAE, 14 October 1963, Europe (1961–65): Allemagne Z182; de Margerie (Bonn) to MAE, 11 November 1963, DE-CE (1961–66) 401; MAE note on the Erhard government, 15 November 1963, Wormser Papers, 2; Washington to MAE on Erhard-Johnson meetings, 30 December 1963, Europe (1961–65): Généralités 1956.

116. Erhard–de Gaulle meetings, 21–22 November 1963, 5AG1/161, and *Akten*, 3:1455–86.

117. Bonn to MAE, 24 November 1963, Europe (1961–65): Allemagne Z182; de Margerie (Bonn) to MAE, 29 November 1963, and MAE note on Erhard-Johnson meetings, 2 January 1964, Europe (1961–65): Allemagne Z186; MAE note on Erhard-Johnson meetings,

30 December 1963, de Margerie (Bonn) to MAE, 4 January 1964, Europe (1961–65): Généralités 1956; Vaïsse, *La grandeur*, 549–51; Peyrefitte, *C'était de Gaulle*, 2:250–51.

118. AA note, 19 September 1963, B24/475; AA note, 15 November 1963, B24/479.

119. MAE notes, 10 and 26 June 1963, Europe (1961–65): Allemagne Z230.

120. MAE note, 17 September 1963, Europe (1961–65): Allemagne Z230.

121. MAE note, 6 February 1964, Europe (1961–65): Allemagne Z230.

122. State Dept. briefing paper for Kennedy's European trip, 16 June 1963, Lot File 65 D 265, box 1; Bruce (London) note for Kennedy, 9 February 1963, *FRUS* (1961–63), 13:188; State Dept. paper on Germany, 9 February 1963, NSF, box 316; Discussions of Kennedy and his top advisers (the "Excomm") on European policy, January–February 1963, NSF, box 316.

123. Bohlen (Paris) to State Dept. on conversation with Couve de Murville, 1 October 1963, NSF, box 73; Schlesinger, *A Thousand Days*, 882–84, 887–88; Winand, *United States of Europe*, 335–36; Conze, *Die gaullistische Herausforderung*, 276–94; Osterheld, "*Ich gehe nicht leichten Herzens*," 231; Kusterer, *Der Kanzler und der General*, 336–40; Ball, *The Past Has Another Pattern*, 272–73.

124. Paris to State Dept., 21 August 1963, NSF, box 72; Bohlen (Paris) to State Dept., 20 November 1963, NSF, box 73.

125. Tuthill (Paris) letter to Ball on conversation with Erhard in Bonn, 31 October 1963, Lot File 65 D 265, box 5.

126. State Dept. note, 24 October 1963, Lot File 65 D 265, box 5.

127. FO to Steel (Bonn), 17 January 1963, FO371/171443; Dixon (Paris) to FO, 19 January 1963, FO371/169122.

128. FO note on the treaty, 13 February 1963, FO371/169176; Dixon (Paris) to FO on Blankenhorn conversation, 20 January 1963, FO371/169175; Home comments to Bruce on British conversations with German leaders, 31 January 1963, FO371/168421; Horne, *Harold Macmillan*, 2:447.

129. Dixon (Paris) to FO, 22 January 1963, FO371/169175; Steel (Bonn) to FO, 21 January 1963, FO371/171445; FO to Stations, 13 February 1963, FO371/169176; Frank Roberts (the new British ambassador in Bonn) to FO, 17 July 1963, FO371/169179.

130. Dixon (Paris) to FO, 7 October 1963, FO371/172070; Dixon (Paris) to FO, 30 October 1963, FO371/172071.

131. Roberts (Bonn) to FO, 17 July 1963, Paris to FO, 13 August 1963, FO371/169179.

132. MAE note, 31 May 1963, Europe (1961–65): Allemagne Z222; de Gaulle–Adenauer conversations, 21–22 September 1963, 5AG1/161, and *Akten*, 2:1185–87, 1192–1210.

133. Gerbet, "Le rôle du couple France-Allemagne dans la création et développement des Communautés Européennes," in Picht and Wessels, *Motor Für Europa*, 69–119; Peyrefitte, *C'était de Gaulle*, 2:257–87, 305; Soutou, *L'alliance incertaine*, 261–309; Vaïsse, *La grandeur*, 563–92; Couve de Murville, *Le monde en face*, 76–86, and *Une politique étrangère*, 235–84; Simonian, *The Privileged Partnership*.

Conclusion

1. This pattern is detailed well in the concluding chapter of Kaiser, *Using Europe*.
2. This is the thesis of Garton Ash, *In Europe's Name*.

BIBLIOGRAPHY

Archives

FRANCE

Archives des Services du Premier Ministre, Fontainebleau
  Debré Cabinet Papers
Archives Nationales, Paris
  Papers of the Presidents of the 4th Republic (4AG)
  Papers of the Presidents of the 5th Republic (5AG1)
Fondation Nationale des Sciences Politiques, Paris
  Maurice Couve de Murville Papers (CM 1–10)
Ministère des Affaires Étrangères, Paris
  Amérique
  Cabinet du Ministre
  Coopération Économique (DE-CE)
  Europe
  Secrétariat Général
  Olivier Wormser Papers
Office Universitaire de Recherche Socialiste, Paris
  Archives Guy Mollet (AGM)

GERMANY

Archiv der Sozialen Demokratie, Bonn
  Willy Brandt Archive Papers
Bundesarchiv Koblenz, Koblenz
  Herbert Blankenhorn Papers (NL1351)
  Heinrich von Brentano Papers (NL1239)
  Karl Carstens Papers (NL1337)
  Chancellor's Office Papers (B136)
  Franz Etzel Papers (NL1254)
  Walter Hallstein Papers (NL1266)
  Ministry of Economics Papers (B102)
Politisches Archiv des Auswärtigen Amtes, Bonn
  Büro Staatssekretär (BSTS/B2)
  European Economic Integration (Referat 200-IA2)
  European Political Integration (Referat 201-IA1 and Referat IA1)
  France (B24)
  Great Britain (Referat 304-IA5)
  Ministerbüro (MB)
  United States (B32)

Stiftung Bundeskanzler Adenauer Haus, Bonn
  Konrad Adenauer Papers

UNITED KINGDOM
Public Record Office, London
  Cabinet Papers (CAB128–129)
  Foreign Office Papers (FO371)
  Prime Minister's Office Papers (PREM11)

UNITED STATES
Dwight D. Eisenhower Library, Abilene, Kansas
  Council on Foreign Economic Policy Chair Records
  Council on Foreign Economic Policy Records
  John Foster Dulles Papers
  Christian A. Herter Papers
  National Security Council Special Assistant Papers
  National Security Council Staff Papers
  White House Central Files
  White House Office—Office of the Special Assistant for National Security
    Affairs Records
  White House Office—Office of the Staff Secretary Records
  Ann Whitman File
John F. Kennedy Library, Boston, Massachusetts
  National Security Files
  President's Office Files
  White House Central Files
National Archives, College Park, Maryland
  State Department Diplomatic Branch Papers (Record Group 59)

Published Documents

Akten zur Auswärtigen Politik der Bundesrepublik Deutschland 1963. Bonn: Politisches
  Archiv des Auswärtigen Amtes, 1994.
Aussenpolitik der Bundesrepublik Deutschland: Dokumente von 1949 bis 1994. Köln: Ver-
  lag Wissenschaft und Politik, 1995.
Commission de Publication des Documents Diplomatiques Français. *Documents
  Diplomatiques Français.* Paris: Imprimerie Nationale, 1987–.
Foreign Relations of the United States. Washington: United States Government Printing
  Office, 1861–.
Möller, Horst, and Klaus Hildebrand, eds. *Die Bundesrepublik Deutschland und
  Frankreich: Dokumente 1949–1963.* Munich: K. G. Saar, 1997.
U.S. Department of State Historical Office. *Documents on Germany, 1944–1961.* Wash-
  ington: U.S. Government Printing Office, 1961.
———. *Documents on Germany, 1944–1985.* Washington: U.S. Government Printing
  Office, 1985.
U.S. Government Printing Office. *Public Papers of the Presidents of the United States:
  John F. Kennedy, 1962.* Washington, 1963.

Memoirs

Adenauer, Konrad. *Briefe.* Edited by Hans Peter Mensing. Vols. 11 (1953–55) and 12 (1955–57). Berlin: Siedler, 1983–.

———. *Erinnerungen.* 4 vols. Stuttgart: Deutsche Verlags-Anstalt, 1965–68.

———. *Teegespräche.* Edited by Hanns Jürgen Küsters and Hans Peter Mensing. Vols. 5 (1955–58), 7 (1959–61), and 10 (1961–63). Berlin: Siedler, 1986–92.

Alphand, Hervé. *L'Étonnement d'être: Journal 1939–1973.* Paris: Fayard, 1977.

Ball, George. *Diplomacy for a Crowded World: An American Foreign Policy.* Boston: Little, Brown, 1976.

———. *The Past Has Another Pattern: Memoirs.* New York: W. W. Norton, 1982.

Blankenhorn, Herbert. *Verständnis und Verständigung: Blätter eines politischen Tagebuchs 1949 bis 1979.* Frankfurt am Main: Propyläen, 1980.

Bohlen, Charles. *Witness to History, 1929–1969.* New York: W. W. Norton, 1973.

Brentano, Heinrich von. *Sehr verehrter Herr Bundeskanzler!: Heinrich von Brentano im Briefwechsel mit Konrad Adenauer, 1949–1964.* Edited by Arnulf Baring, Klaus Mayer, and Bolko von Oetinger. Hamburg: Hoffmann und Campe, 1974.

Bundy, McGeorge. *Danger and Survival: Choices about the Bomb in the First Fifty Years.* New York: Random House, 1988.

Burin des Roziers, Etienne. *Retour aux sources: 1962, l'année décisive.* Paris: Plon, 1986.

Carstens, Karl. *Erinnerungen und Erfahrungen.* Boppard am Rhein: Harald Boldt Verlag, 1993.

Couve de Murville, Maurice. *Le monde en face: Entretiens.* Paris: Plon, 1989.

———. *Une politique étrangère 1958–1969.* Paris: Plon, 1971.

Debré, Michel. *Entretiens avec le Général de Gaulle.* Paris: Albin Michel, 1993.

———. *Gouverner: Mémoires 1958–1962.* Paris: Albin Michel, 1988.

Dixon, Piers. *Double Diploma: The Life of Sir Pierson Dixon, Don and Diplomat.* London: Hutchinson, 1968.

Eisenhower, Dwight D. *Mandate for Change, 1953–1956.* Garden City, N.Y.: Doubleday, 1963.

———. *Waging Peace, 1956–1961.* Garden City, N.Y.: Doubleday, 1965.

Fouchet, Christian. *Mémoires d'hier et de demain: Au service du Général de Gaulle.* Paris: Plon, 1971.

Gaulle, Charles de. *La discorde chez l'enemmi.* Paris: Plon, 1972.

———. *Discours et messages.* 5 vols. Paris: Plon, 1970–71.

———. *Le fil de l'épée.* Paris: Éditions Berger-Levrault, 1944.

———. *Lettres, notes et carnets.* 13 vols. Paris: Plon, 1980–97.

———. *Mémoires de guerre.* 3 vols. Paris: Plon, 1954–59.

———. *Memoirs of Hope: Renewal and Endeavour.* Translated by Terence Kilmartin. New York: Simon & Schuster, 1971.

———. *Vers l'armée de métier.* Paris: Berger-Levrault, 1944.

Grewe, Wilhelm G. *Rückblenden 1976–1951.* Frankfurt am Main: Verlag Ullstein, 1979.

Heath, Edward. *The Course of My Life: My Autobiography.* London: Hodder & Stoughton, 1998.

Kiesinger, Kurt. *Stationen 1949–1969.* Tübingen: Rainer Wunderlich Verlag Hermann Leins, 1969.

Kusterer, Hermann. *Der Kanzler und der General.* Stuttgart: Neske, 1995.

McGhee, George. *At the Creation of a New Germany: From Adenauer to Brandt: An Ambassador's Account.* New Haven: Yale University Press, 1989.

Macmillan, Harold. *At the End of the Day, 1961–1963.* New York: Harper & Row, 1973.

———. *Pointing the Way, 1959–1961.* London: Macmillan, 1972.

———. *Riding the Storm, 1956–1959.* New York: Harper & Row, 1971.

———. *Tides of Fortune, 1945–1955.* New York: Harper & Row, 1969.

Maillard, Pierre. *De Gaulle et l'Allemagne: Le rêve inachevé.* Paris: Plon, 1990.

———. *De Gaulle et l'Europe: Entre la nation et Maastricht.* Paris: Éditions Tallandier, 1995.

Malraux, André. *Les chênes qu'on abat.* Paris: Gallimard, 1971.

Osterheld, Horst. *"Ich gehe nicht leichten Herzens": Adenauers letzte Kanzlerjahre-ein dokumentarischer Bericht.* Mainz: Matthias-Gruenewald Verlag, 1986.

———. *Konrad Adenauer: Ein Charakterbild.* Bonn: Verlag Bonn Aktuell, 1995.

Peyrefitte, Alain. *C'était de Gaulle.* 3 vols. Paris: Fayard, 1994–2000.

Pineau, Christian. *1956/Suez.* Paris: Éditions Robert Laffont, 1976.

Rusk, Dean. *As I Saw It.* As told to Richard Rusk and edited by Daniel S. Papp. New York: W. W. Norton, 1990.

Schaetzel, J. Robert. *The Unhinged Alliance: America and the European Community.* New York: Harper & Row, 1975.

Schlesinger, Arthur M. *A Thousand Days: John F. Kennedy in the White House.* Boston: Houghton Mifflin, 1965.

Schroeder, Gerhard, Alfred Müller-Armack, Karl Hohmann, Johannes Gross, and Rüdiger Altmann, eds. *Ludwig Erhard: Beiträge zu seiner politischen Biographie: Festschrift zum fünfundsiebzigsten Geburtstag.* Frankfurt: Propyläen, 1972.

Seydoux, François. *Dans l'intimité Franco-Allemande: Une mission diplomatique.* Paris: Éditions Albatros, 1977.

———. *Mémoires d'Outre-Rhin.* Paris: Bernard Grasset, 1975.

Sorensen, Theodore C. *Kennedy.* New York: Harper & Row, 1965.

Spaak, Paul-Henri. *The Continuing Battle: Memoirs of a European, 1936–1966.* Translated by Henry Fox. Boston: Little, Brown, 1971.

Strauss, Franz Josef. *Die Erinnerungen.* Berlin: Siedler, 1989.

Secondary Works

Adamthwaite, Anthony. "Marianne et John Bull: la mésentente cordiale 1945–1957." *Matériaux pour l'histoire de notre temps* 18 (1990): 38–43.

Aldous, Richard, and Sabine Lee, eds. *Harold Macmillan and Britain's World Role.* New York: St. Martin's Press, 1996.

Allin, Dana H. *Cold War Illusions: America, Europe and Soviet Power, 1969–1989.* New York: St. Martin's Press, 1995.

Ambrose, Stephen E. *Eisenhower.* Vol. 2, *The President.* New York: Simon & Schuster, 1984.

Artaud, Denise. "Le grand dessein de J. F. Kennedy: Proposition mythique ou occasion manquée." *Revue d'histoire moderne et contemporaine* 29 (1982): 235–66.

Association Georges Pompidou. *Georges Pompidou et l'Europe*. Brussels: Éditions Complexe, 1995.

Baker, David, and David Seawright, eds. *Britain for and against Europe: British Politics and the Question of European Integration*. Oxford: Clarendon Press, 1998.

Bange, Oliver. *The EEC Crisis of 1963: Kennedy, Macmillan, de Gaulle and Adenauer in Conflict*. New York: St. Martin's Press, 2000.

Bariéty, Jacques. "Les entretiens de Gaulle–Adenauer de Juillet 1960 à Rambouillet: Prélude au Plan Fouchet et au Traité de l'Élysée." *Revue d'Allemagne* 29 (1997): 167–76.

Bell, Philip. "Les attitudes de la Grande Bretagne envers l'Europe et l'intégration européenne, 1940–1957." *Revue d'histoire diplomatique* 108 (1994): 113–27.

Bernstein, Serge. *The Republic of de Gaulle, 1958–1969*. Translated by Peter Morris. Cambridge: Cambridge University Press, 1993.

Bernstein, Serge, Jean-Marie Mayeur, and Pierre Milza, eds. *Le MRP et la construction européenne*. Brussels: Éditions Complexe, 1993.

Binoche, Jacques. *De Gaulle et les Allemands*. Brussels: Éditions Complexe, 1990.

Bitsch, Marie-Thérèse. *Histoire de la construction européenne de 1945 à nos jours*. Brussels: Éditions Complexe, 1996.

Bled, Jean-Paul. "Les conceptions européennes du Général de Gaulle à la veille de son retour au pouvoir." *Revue d'Allemagne* 29 (1997): 159–66.

Bloch, Charles. "De Gaulle et l'Allemagne." In *La Politique étrangère du Général de Gaulle*, edited by Élie Barnavi and Saul Friedländer, 112–36. Paris: Presses Universitaires de France, 1985.

Bluth, Christoph. *Britain, Germany, and Western Nuclear Strategy*. Oxford: Oxford University Press, 1995.

Bossuat, Gérard. "Le choix de la petite Europe par la France (1957–63): Une ambition pour la France et pour l'Europe." *Relations internationales* 82 (Summer 1995): 213–35.

———. *L'Europe des Français: La IVe République aux sources de l'Europe communautaire*. Paris: Publications de la Sorbonne, 1996.

———. "Guy Mollet: La puissance française autrement." *Relations internationales* 57 (1989): 25–48.

———. "Le rêve français d'une Europe franco-britannique." *Matériaux pour l'histoire de notre temps* 18 (1990): 3–11.

Bozo, Frédéric. *Deux stratégies pour l'Europe: De Gaulle, les Etats-Unis et l'Alliance atlantique*. Paris: Plon, 1996.

Bozo, Frédéric, and Pierre Mélandri. "La France devant l'opinion américaine: Le retour de de Gaulle (début 1958–printemps 1959)." *Relations internationales* 58 (1989): 195–215.

Brusse, Wendy Asbeek. *Tariffs, Trade and European Integration, 1947–1957: From Study Group to Common Market*. New York: St. Martin's Press, 1997.

Buffet, Cyril. "The Berlin Crises, France, and the Atlantic Alliance, 1947–62: From Integration to Disintegration." In *Securing Peace in Europe, 1945–1962: Thoughts for the Post–Cold War Era*, edited by Beatrice Heuser and Robert O'Neill, 84–104. New York: St. Martin's Press, 1992.

———. "De Gaulle et Berlin: Une certaine idée d'Allemagne." *Revue d'Allemagne* 22 (1990): 525–38.

————. "La politique nucléaire de la France et la seconde crise de Berlin, 1958–1962." *Relations internationales* 59 (1989): 347–58.

Bulmer, Simon, and William Patterson. *The Federal Republic of Germany and the European Community*. London: Allen & Unwin, 1987.

Burgess, Simon, and Geoffrey Edwards. "The Six plus One: British Policy-making and the Question of European Economic Integration, 1955." *International Affairs* 64 (Summer 1988): 393–413.

Burr, William. "Avoiding the Slippery Slope: The Eisenhower Administration and the Berlin Crisis, November 1958–January 1959." *Diplomatic History* 18 (Spring 1994): 177–205.

Camps, Miriam. *Britain and the European Community*. Princeton: Princeton University Press, 1964.

Cerny, Philip. *The Politics of Grandeur: Ideological Aspects of de Gaulle's Foreign Policy*. Cambridge: Cambridge University Press, 1980.

Charlot, Jean. *Les Français et de Gaulle*. Paris: Plon, 1971.

Clark, Ian. *Nuclear Diplomacy and the Special Relationship: Britain's Detterent and America, 1957–1962*. Oxford: Clarendon Press, 1994.

Cogan, Charles C. *Charles de Gaulle: A Brief Biography with Documents*. Boston: St. Martin's Press, 1996.

Cohen, Samy. *La monarchie nucléaire: Les coulisses de la politique étrangère sous la Ve république*. Paris: Hachette, 1986.

Conze, Eckart. *Die gaullistische Herausforderung: Die deutsch-französischen Beziehungen in der amerikanischen Europapolitik, 1958–1963*. Munich: R. Oldenbourg, 1995.

————. "Hegemonie durch Integration?: Die amerikanische Europapolitik und ihre Herausforderung durch de Gaulle." *Vierteljahrshefte für Zeitgeschichte* 43 (April 1995): 297–340.

Costigliola, Frank. "The Failed Design: Kennedy, de Gaulle, and the Struggle for Europe." *Diplomatic History* 8 (Summer 1984): 227–51.

————. "The Pursuit of Atlantic Community: Nuclear Arms, Dollars, and Berlin." In *Kennedy's Quest for Victory: American Foreign Policy, 1961–1963*, edited by Thomas G. Paterson, 24–56. New York: Oxford University Press, 1989.

Defrance, Corine. "La culture dans les projets d'union politique de l'Europe (1961–1962)." *Revue d'Allemagne* 29 (1997): 289–302.

Deighton, Anne. "La Grande Bretagne et la Communauté économique européenne (1958–1963)." *Histoire, économie et société* 13 (1994): 113–30.

————, ed. *Building Postwar Europe: National Decision Makers and European Institutions, 1948–1963*. New York: St. Martin's Press, 1995.

Deighton, Anne, and Alan Milward, eds. *Acceleration, Deepening and Enlarging: The European Economic Community, 1957–1963*. Brussels: Nomos/Giuffrè/LGDJ/Bruylant, 1997.

Denman, Roy. *Missed Chances: Britain and Europe in the Twentieth Century*. London: Cassell, 1996.

Deutsch, Karl W., Lewis J. Edinger, Roy C. Macridis, and Richard L. Merritt. *France, Germany and the Western Alliance: A Study of Elite Attitudes on European Integration and World Politics*. New York: Charles Scribner's Sons, 1967.

Dimbleby, David, and David Reynolds. *An Ocean Apart: The Relationship between Britain and America in the Twentieth Century.* New York: Random House, 1988.

Doerr, Juergen C. *The Big Powers and the German Question, 1941–1990: A Selected Bibliographic Guide.* New York: Garland, 1992.

Dreyfus, François-Georges. "L'opinion française et le Traité de l'Élysée." *Revue d'Allemagne* 29 (1997): 201–9.

Duchêne, François. *Jean Monnet: The First Statesman of Interdependence.* New York: W. W. Norton, 1994.

Ellison, James R. V. "Perfidious Albion?: Britain, Plan G and European Integration, 1955–1956." *Contemporary British History* 10 (Winter 1996): 1–34.

Ellwood, David W. *Rebuilding Europe: Western Europe, America, and Postwar Reconstruction.* New York: Longman, 1992.

Feld, Werner J. *West Germany and the European Community: Changing Interests and Competing Policy Objectives.* New York: Praeger, 1981.

Frank, Robert. "France–Grande Bretagne: La mésentente commerciale (1945–1958)." *Relations internationales* 55 (1988): 323–39.

Friend, Julius W. *The Linchpin: French-German Relations, 1950–1990.* New York: Praeger, 1991.

Gallup, George H., ed. *The Gallup International Public Opinion Polls: Great Britain, 1937–1975.* Vol. 1, 1937–64. New York: Random House, 1976.

———. *The Gallup Poll: Public Opinion, 1935–1971.* 3 vols. New York: Random House, 1972.

Garton Ash, Timothy. *In Europe's Name: Germany and the Divided Continent.* New York: Random House, 1993.

George, Stephen. *Politics and Policy in the European Community.* 2nd ed. New York: Oxford University Press, 1991.

Gerbet, Pierre. *La construction de l'Europe.* Paris: Imprimerie nationale, 1994.

———. *La France et l'intégration européenne: Essai d'historiographie.* Berne and New York: P. Lang, 1995.

Giauque, Jeffrey G. "Offers of Partnership or Bids for Hegemony?: The Atlantic Community, 1961–1963." *International History Review* 22 (2000): 86–111.

———. "The United States and the Political Union of Western Europe, 1958–1963." *Contemporary European History* 9 (2000): 93–110.

Gillingham, John. *Coal, Steel, and the Rebirth of Europe, 1945–1955: The Germans and French from Ruhr Conflict to Economic Community.* New York: Cambridge University Press, 1991.

Girault, René, and Gérard Bossuat, eds. *Europe brisée, Europe retrouvée: Nouvelles réflexions sur l'unité européenne au XXe siècle.* Paris: Publications de la Sorbonne, 1994.

Gordon, Colin. *The Atlantic Alliance: A Bibliography.* London: Nichols, 1978.

Gordon, Philip H. *A Certain Idea of France: French Security Policy and the Gaullist Legacy.* Princeton: Princeton University Press, 1993.

Greenwood, Sean. *Britain and European Cooperation since 1945.* Oxford: Blackwell, 1992.

Griffiths, Richard, ed. *Socialist Parties and the Question of Europe in the 1950s.* Leiden: E. J. Brill, 1993.

Griffiths, Richard, and Stuart Ward, eds. *Courting the Common Market: The First Attempt to Enlarge the European Community, 1961–1963*. London: Lothian Foundation Press, 1996.

Grosser, Alfred. *Affaires extérieures: La politique de la France 1944–1984*. France: Flammarion, 1984.

———. *La politique extérieure de la Ve république*. Paris: Éditions du Seuil, 1965.

Guillen, Pierre. "L'Europe remède à l'impuissance française?: Le gouvernement Guy Mollet et la négociation des traités de Rome (1955–1957)." *Revue d'histoire diplomatique* 102 (1988): 319–35.

———. *La question allemande 1945 à nos jours*. Paris: Imprimerie nationale, 1996.

Hanrieder, Wolfram. *Deutschland, Europa, Amerika: Die Aussenpolitik der Bundesrepublik Deutschland 1949–1994*. 2nd ed. Paderborn: Schöningh, 1995.

Hanrieder, Wolfram, and Graeme P. Auton. *The Foreign Policies of West Germany, France, and Britain*. Englewood Cliffs, N.J.: Prentice-Hall, 1980.

Hayward, Jack, ed. *De Gaulle to Mitterand: Presidential Power in France*. New York: New York University Press, 1993.

Heller, Francis H., and John R. Gillingham. *The United States and the Integration of Europe: Legacies of the Postwar Era*. New York: St. Martin's Press, 1996.

Heuser, Beatrice. *NATO, Britain, France and the FRG: Nuclear Strategies and Forces for Europe, 1949–2000*. New York: St. Martin's Press, 1997.

Hildebrand, Klaus. "'Atlantiker' versus 'Gaullisten' zur Aussenpolitik der Bundesrepublik Deutschland während der sechziger Jahre." *Revue d'Allemagne* 22 (1990): 583–92.

———. *Integration und Souveränität. Die Aussenpolitik der Bundesrepublik Deutschland 1949–1982/Intégration et souveraineté. La politique étrangère de la République Fédérale d'Allemagne de 1949 à 1982*. Bonn: Bouvier, 1991.

Hoffmann, Stanley. *Decline or Renewal?: France since the 1930s*. New York: Viking Press, 1974.

Hogan, Michael J. *The Marshall Plan: America, Britain, and the Reconstruction of Western Europe, 1947–1952*. Cambridge: Cambridge University Press, 1987.

Hölscher, Wolfgang. "Krisenmanagement in Sachen EWG: Das Scheitern des Beitritts Grossbritanniens und die deutsch-französischen Beziehungen." In *Von Adenauer zu Erhard: Studien zur Auswärtigen Politik der Bundesrepublik Deutschland 1963*, edited by Rainer A. Blasius, 9–44. Munich: R. Oldenbourg, 1994.

Horne, Alistair. *Harold Macmillan*. Vol. 1, London: Macmillan, 1988; vol. 2, New York: Penguin, 1989.

Immerman, Richard H. "Confessions of an Eisenhower Revisionist: An Agonizing Reappraisal." *Diplomatic History* 14 (1990): 319–42.

———, ed. *John Foster Dulles and the Diplomacy of the Cold War*. Princeton: Princeton University Press, 1990.

Institut Charles de Gaulle. *De Gaulle en son siècle*. 6 vols. Paris: Plon, 1991–92.

———. *De Gaulle et ses premiers ministres*. Paris: Plon, 1990.

Institut Français de l'opinion publique. *Sondages: Revue français de l'opinion publique*. Vols. 17–25. Paris: IFOP, 1955–63.

Kaiser, Wolfram. "The Bomb and Europe: Britain, France, and the EEC Entry Negotiations, 1961–1963." *Journal of European Integration History* 1 (1995): 65–85.

———. "To Join or Not to Join: The 'Appeasement' Policy of Britain's First EEC Application." In *From Reconstruction to Integration: Britain and Europe since 1945*, edited by Brian Brivati and Harriet Jones, 144–56. Leicester: Leicester University Press, 1993.

———. *Using Europe, Abusing the Europeans: Britain and European Integration, 1945–63*. New York: St. Martin's Press, 1996.

Kocs, Stephen A. *Autonomy or Power?: The Franco-German Relationship and Europe's Strategic Choices, 1955–1995*. Westport, Conn.: Praeger, 1995.

Kolodziej, Edward A. *French International Policy under de Gaulle and Pompidou*. Ithaca: Cornell University Press, 1974.

Kosthorst, Daniel. "Die 'Unerwünschte Liaison': Thesen zur Vorgeschichte des deutsch-französischen Vertrages vom 22. Januar 1963." *Revue d'Allemagne* 29 (1997): 177–94.

Kuper, Ernst. *Frieden durch Konfrontation und Kooperation: Die Einstellung von Gerhard Schroeder und Willi Brandt zur Entspannungspolitik*. Stuttgart: Gustav Fischer, 1974.

Kusterer, Hermann. "Intention und Wirklichkeit: Von der Konzeption zur Ratifizierung des Deutsch-Französischen Vertrages." *Revue d'Allemagne* 29 (1997): 195–200.

Lacouture, Jean. *De Gaulle*. 3 vols. Paris: Éditions du Seuil, 1984–86.

Lamb, Richard. *The Macmillan Years, 1957–1963: The Emerging Truth*. London: John Murray, 1995.

Ledwidge, Bernard. *De Gaulle et les Américains: Conversations avec Dulles, Eisenhower, Kennedy, Rusk 1958–1964*. Paris: Flammarion, 1984.

Lee, Sabine. *An Uneasy Partnership: British-German Relations between 1955 and 1961*. Bochum: Brockmeyer, 1996.

Lefebvre, Denis. *Guy Mollet: Le mal aimé*. Paris: Plon, 1992.

Loth, Wilfried. "De Gaulle et la construction européenne: La révision d'un mythe." *Francia* 20 (1993): 61–72.

———. "De Gaulle und Europa: Eine Revision." *Historische Zeitschrift* 253 (1991): 629–60.

Loth, Wilfried, and Robert Picht, eds. *De Gaulle, Deutschland und Europa*. Opladen: Leske & Budrich, 1991.

Ludlow, N. Piers. *Dealing with Britain: The Six and the First U.K. Application to the EEC*. Cambridge: Cambridge University Press, 1997.

———. "Le paradoxe Anglais: Britain and Political Union." *Revue d'Allemagne* 29 (1997): 259–72.

Lundestad, Geir. *"Empire" by Integration: The United States and European Integration, 1945–1997*. New York: Oxford University Press, 1998.

Lynch, Frances M. B. "De Gaulle's First Veto: France, the Rueff Plan and the Free Trade Area." *Contemporary European History* 9 (2000): 111–35.

Mayer, Frank A. *Adenauer and Kennedy: A Study in German-American Relations, 1961–1963*. New York: St. Martin's Press, 1996.

Mayers, David. *George Kennan and the Dilemmas of U.S. Foreign Policy*. New York: Oxford University Press, 1988.

Mélandri, Pierre. "Le Général de Gaulle, la construction européenne et l'Alliance atlantique." In *La Politique étrangère du Général de Gaulle*, edited by Élie Barnavi and Saul Friedländer, 87–111. Paris: Presses Universitaires de France, 1985.

Menudier, Henri. *Le couple franco-allemand en Europe*. Asnières: Publications de l'Institut d'allemand d'Asnières, 1993.

Merkl, Peter H., ed. *The Federal Republic of Germany at Forty.* New York: New York University Press, 1989.

Milward, Alan S. *The European Rescue of the Nation State.* Berkeley: University of California Press, 1992.

Moon, Jeremy. *European Integration in British Politics, 1950–1963: A Study of Issue Change.* Brookfield, Vt.: Gower, 1985.

Ninkovich, Frank. *The Wilsonian Century: U.S. Foreign Policy since 1900.* Chicago: University of Chicago Press, 1999.

Noelle, Elisabeth, and Erich Peter Neumann, eds. *The Germans: Public Opinion Polls, 1947–1966.* Translated by Gerard Finan. Allensbach: Verlag für Demoskopie, 1967.

Northedge, F. S. *Descent from Power: British Foreign Policy, 1945–1973.* London: George Allen & Unwin, 1974.

Nouschi, Marc. *En quête d'Europe: Construction européenne et légitimité nationale.* Paris: Librairie Vuibert, 1994.

Nugent, Neill. *The Government and Politics of the European Union.* 3rd ed. Durham, N.C.: Duke University Press, 1994.

Pagedas, Constantine. *Anglo-American Strategic Relations and the French Problem, 1960–1963: A Troubled Partnership.* London: Frank Cass, 2000.

———. "Harold Macmillan and the 1962 Champs Meeting." *Diplomacy & Statecraft* 9 (March 1988): 224–42.

Park, William. *Defending the West: A History of NATO.* Brighton: Wheatsheaf Books, 1986.

Passeron, André. *De Gaulle parle 1962–1966.* Paris: Fayard, 1966.

Paxton, Robert O., and Nicholas Wahl, eds. *De Gaulle and the United States: A Centennial Reappraisal.* Oxford: Berg, 1994.

Picht, Robert, and Wolfgang Wessels, eds. *Motor für Europa: Deutsch-Französischer Bilateralismus und europäische Integration/Le couple franco-allemand et l'intégration européenne.* Bonn: Europa Union, 1990.

Preussen, Ronald W. *John Foster Dulles: The Road to Power.* New York: Free Press, 1982.

Reynolds, David, ed. *The Origins of the Cold War in Europe: International Perspectives.* New Haven: Yale University Press, 1994.

Rimbaud, Christiane. *Pinay.* Paris: Éditions Perrin, 1990.

Risse-Kappen, Thomas. *Cooperation among Democracies: The European Influence on U.S. Foreign Policy.* Princeton: Princeton University Press, 1995.

Rose, François de. *European Security and France.* Urbana: University of Illinois Press, 1984.

Salmon, Trevor, and William Nicoll. *Building European Union: A Documentary History and Analysis.* Manchester: Manchester University Press, 1997.

Scherz, Adrian W. *Die Deutschlandpolitik Kennedys und Johnsons: Unterschiedliche Ansätze innerhalb der amerikanischen Regierung.* Cologne: Böhlau, 1992.

Schröder, Hans Jürgen. "Chancellor of the Allies?: The Significance of the United States in Adenauer's Foreign Policy." In *Transatlantic Images and Perceptions: Germany and America since 1776,* edited by David E. Barclay and Elisabeth Glaser-Schmidt, 309–31. Cambridge: Cambridge University Press, 1997.

———. "Deutsche Aussenpolitik 1963/64: Die 'Akten zur Auswärtigen Politik der Bundesrepublik Deutschland.'" *Vierteljahrshefte für Zeitgeschichte* 43 (July 1995): 521–37.

Schwabe, Klaus, ed. *Adenauer und die USA*. Bonn: Bouvier, 1994.

Schwartz, David. *NATO's Nuclear Dilemmas*. Washington, D.C.: Brookings Institution, 1983.

Schwartz, Thomas Alan. *America's Germany: John J. McCloy and the Federal Republic of Germany*. Cambridge: Harvard University Press, 1991.

Schwarz, Hans-Peter. *Adenauer: Der Staatsmann: 1952–1967*. Stuttgart: Deutsche Verlags-Anstalt, 1991.

———, ed. *Adenauer und Frankreich: Die deutsch-französischen Beziehungen 1958 bis 1969*. Bonn: Bouvier, 1985.

———. *Berlinkrise und Mauerbau*. Bonn: Bouvier, 1985.

Schweizer, Cyril. "Le gouvernement italien et le projet d'union politique de l'Europe, 1961–1962." *Revue d'Allemagne* 29 (1997): 231–42.

Serfaty, Simon. *France, de Gaulle, and Europe: The Policy of the Fourth and Fifth Republics toward the Continent*. Baltimore: Johns Hopkins University Press, 1968.

Shennan, Andrew. *De Gaulle*. London: Longman, 1993.

———. *Rethinking France: Plans for Renewal, 1940–1946*. Oxford: Clarendon Press, 1989.

Sherwood, Elizabeth D. *Allies in Crisis: Meeting Global Challenges to Western Security*. New Haven: Yale University Press, 1990.

Simonian, Haig. *The Privileged Partnership: Franco-German Relations in the European Community, 1969–1984*. Oxford: Clarendon Press, 1985.

Soutou, Georges-Henri. *L'alliance incertaine: Les rapports politico-stratégiques franco-allemands, 1954–1996*. Paris: Fayard, 1996.

———. "Le Général de Gaulle, le Plan Fouchet et l'Europe." *Commentaire* 13 (1990–91): 757–66.

———. "Le Général de Gaulle et le Plan Fouchet d'union politique européenne: Un projet stratégique." *Revue d'Allemagne* 29 (1997): 211–20.

———. "Les problèmes de sécurité dans les rapports franco-allemands de 1956 à 1963." *Relations internationales* 58 (1989): 227–51.

Steinbruner, John D. *The Cybernetic Theory of Decision: New Dimensions of Political Analysis*. Princeton: Princeton University Press, 1974.

Steininger, Rolf. "Great Britain's First EEC Failure in January 1963." *Diplomacy & Statecraft* 7 (1996): 404–35.

Stelandre, Yves. "La Belgique et le Plan Fouchet." *Revue d'Allemagne* 29 (1997): 221–30.

Stuart, Douglas, and William Tow. *The Limits of Alliance: NATO Out-of-Area Problems since 1949*. Baltimore: Johns Hopkins University Press, 1990.

Toschi, Simona. "Washington-London-Paris: An Untenable Triangle (1960–1963)." *Journal of European Integration History* 1 (1995): 81–109.

Trachtenberg, Marc. *A Constructed Peace: The Making of the European Settlement, 1945–1963*. Princeton: Princeton University Press, 1999.

———. *History and Strategy*. Princeton: Princeton University Press, 1991.

Turner, John. *Macmillan*. London: Longman, 1994.

Urwin, Derek. *The Community of Europe: A History of European Integration since 1945*. 2nd ed. London: Longman, 1995.

Vaïsse, Maurice. "Aux origines du mémorandum de septembre 1958." *Relations internationales* 58 (1989): 253–68.

————. "De Gaulle, l'Italie et le projet d'union politique européenne, 1958–1963: Chronique d'un échec annoncé." *Revue d'histoire moderne et contemporaine* 42 (1995): 658–69.

————. "De Gaulle et la premiere 'candidature' britannique au Marché Commun." *Revue d'histoire diplomatique* 108 (1994): 129–50.

————. "Le Général de Gaulle et la défense de l'Europe, 1947–1958." *Matériaux* 29 (1992): 5–8.

————. *La grandeur: Politique étrangère du Général de Gaulle.* Paris: Fayard, 1998.

Vaïsse, Maurice, Pierre Mélandri, and Frédéric Bozo, eds. *La France et l'OTAN 1949–1996.* Brussels: Éditions Complexe, 1996.

Varsori, Antonio. "La classe politique italienne et le couple franco-allemand." *Revue d'Allemagne* 29 (1997): 243–57.

Wilkes, George, ed. *Britain's Failure to Enter the European Community, 1961–63: The Enlargement Negotiations and Crises in European, Atlantic and Commonwealth Relations.* London: Frank Cass, 1997.

Williams, Charles. *The Last Great Frenchman: A Life of General de Gaulle.* New York: John Wiley & Sons, 1993.

Willis, F. Roy, ed. *France, Germany and the New Europe.* London: Oxford University Press, 1968.

Winand, Pascaline. *Eisenhower, Kennedy, and the United States of Europe.* New York: St. Martin's Press, 1993.

Wurm, Clemens, ed. *Western Europe and Germany: The Beginnings of European Integration, 1945–1960.* Oxford: Berg, 1995.

Young, John W. *Britain and European Unity, 1945–1992.* New York: St. Martin's Press, 1993.

————. "'The Parting of the Ways'?: Britain, the Messina Conference and the Spaak Committee, June–December 1955." In *British Foreign Policy, 1945–56*, edited by Michael Dockrill and John W. Young, 197–224. New York: St. Martin's Press, 1989.

Zubok, Vladislav, and Constantine Pleshakov. *Inside the Kremlin's Cold War: From Stalin to Khrushchev.* Cambridge: Harvard University Press, 1996.

INDEX

Acheson, Dean, 210

Acheson Report, 108

Action Committee for the United States of Europe, 167

Adenauer, Konrad: and European integration, 5–6, 12–13, 19, 30, 43, 166; on World Wars I and II, 12; and Common Market, 12, 23–27, 41, 42, 52, 56, 64, 75, 81, 194, 230, 250 (n. 74); and France, 13, 20, 37, 38, 44, 57, 77, 78, 80–97, 111, 119, 129, 131–35, 142, 144, 148, 155, 160, 164, 165, 176, 186, 189, 194, 196–223, 228, 235, 275 (n. 28); retirement of, 13, 125, 150, 216, 222, 231; and failure of EDC, 19; and Messina conference (1955), 22; and Brussels negotiations and Treaty of Rome, 23–27; and Britain, 37, 38, 43, 52, 65, 81, 95, 165, 175–77, 179, 180–81, 184, 186, 194, 197–200, 205, 208, 220, 235; and de Gaulle, 37, 44, 77, 78, 80–81, 84–86, 88–89, 92–97, 111, 119, 129, 131–34, 142, 144, 148, 155, 160, 164, 165, 176, 186, 189, 196–217, 221–23, 231, 275 (n. 28); and Soviet Union, 38, 81–82, 95–96, 220–21; and Macmillan, 38, 177, 208, 230–31; and FTA, 49, 52, 57, 58, 59, 63, 67, 70, 81, 176; and EFTA, 71; and United States, 81, 93, 111, 136–38, 144, 197–98, 205, 207, 209–10, 215, 222; and Eisenhower, 81, 93, 136–37, 144; and Bad Kreuznach meeting (1958), 85, 86–87; and Colombey-les-Deux-Eglises meeting (1958), 85–86; in Paris meetings in 1959–60, 88, 90–91, 96–97; resignation considered by, 89; and West German territorial losses from World War II, 89; successors for, 89, 92; and Paris East-West summit (1960), 91–93; and Atlantic Community, 102,
111, 118, 217; and OECD, 106; and Kennedy, 111, 138, 144, 205; and Nassau accord, 119; and Fouchet plan, 133–36, 138, 139, 143, 144, 149, 150, 197, 200, 277 (n. 63); and British membership in Common Market, 158, 165, 175–77, 179, 180–81, 184, 186, 190, 194, 204, 208, 210; and Franco-German relationship between July 1960 and April 1962, 196–99; and Franco-German treaty (1963), 199–215, 221–22, 231; state visit to France by, 200–201, 206; and Franco-German relations in 1963, 209–20; and French veto of British membership in Common Market, 212; and East Germany, 220–21; personal diplomacy of, 230. See also West Germany

Agriculture: and France, 26, 189, 190, 192, 195, 215–19; and Britain, 48, 159, 160, 162, 163, 167, 169, 175, 179, 182, 184, 185; and Brussels negotiations (1956–57), 50; and FTA, 54, 58, 59; and EFTA, 68, 70; and CAP, 142, 145, 149, 151, 167, 169, 170, 172, 189–92, 195, 215–19, 228

Algeria, 17, 24, 58, 61, 83, 85, 113, 142

Atlantic Community: origins of, in Eisenhower administration, 44, 74, 98, 99–100, 106; and Kennedy, 44, 74, 98, 100, 103, 106–17, 124, 225; purposes of, 98–100, 225, 237; U.S. role in, 98–101, 124, 193; historiography on, 99; and Britain, 99, 101–2, 111–12, 120–23, 125, 165; and West Germany, 99, 102, 110–11, 112, 118–20, 123, 124–25, 217; and France, 99, 102–3, 108–10, 112–24, 143, 147; goals and components of, 100–101, 107, 113–14, 124; and nuclear weapons, 101, 107–9, 111–24; and NATO, 101, 120; and de Gaulle, 103, 112–23, 147; forma-

149, 195, 200; and NATO, 65, 87, 105, 109, 125, 131, 134, 135, 147, 205, 218; Himmler's message to, 77–78; and Soviet Union, 78, 82, 84, 86, 91, 95–96, 125, 221; Third Force goals of, 78, 94, 109, 113, 124, 128, 129, 140, 155, 160, 168, 184, 198, 211, 213, 222; on France as global power, 79, 84–85; and Erhard, 83, 84, 90, 189, 191, 214–18, 222; and Bad Kreuznach meeting (1958), 85, 86–87; and Colombey-les-Deux-Eglises meeting (1958), 85–86; and Berlin crisis (1958), 87–88, 89, 96; Paris meetings in 1959–60 between Adenauer and, 88, 90–91, 96–97; and Khrushchev, 91; and Paris East-West summit (1960), 91–93, 131–32; and East Germany, 96; and Kennedy, 103, 108–9, 129, 148, 151, 155, 164, 228; and Atlantic Community, 103, 112–24, 147; and OECD, 104–5; and nuclear weapons, 109, 112, 114, 115, 117–18, 175, 205–6, 215; and monetary system, 125; on politics, 126; and Fouchet plan, 126–57, 179, 196–97, 199, 226, 229, 277–78 (n. 76); and Franco-German treaty (1963), 149, 181, 185, 189, 199–215; and British Common Market membership, 163–64, 167, 172, 173–75, 180–83, 185–88; and veto of British membership in Common Market, 178, 180–95, 197, 204, 209, 212, 222, 223, 225; presidential powers of, 183; parliamentary victory of, in November 1962, 183, 203, 204; and direct election of president, 183, 204; and "empty chair" episode (1965), 194–95, 229; resignation of, 195, 221; and Franco-German relationship between July 1960 and April 1962, 196–99; state visit to West Germany by, 201–2, 206; and Franco-German relations in 1963, 209–20; and Bundestag resolution with Franco-German treaty (1963), 212–13, 231; personal diplomacy of, 230; and Treaties of Rome, 259 (n. 78). *See also* France

De Margerie, Roland, 212, 213
Denmark, 68, 70–72, 284 (n. 42).
  See also Seven
Disarmament, 27
Dixon, Sir Pierson, 152, 167, 181, 183, 186, 208, 220
Dulles, John Foster: and European integration generally, 5, 13, 14–15, 22; and Messina conference (1955), 22; on France, 32; and Common Market, 55; and Euratom, 55; and FTA, 55–56, 67; and Franco-German relations, 93, 94; and Adenauer, 144

Eastern Europe, 1, 60, 76, 86, 227, 236, 246 (n. 1)
East Germany: and Common Market, 24; and France, 96, 267 (n. 102); recognition of, 144, 219; and Test Ban Treaty, 219; and Adenauer, 220–21
ECSC. *See* European Coal and Steel Community
EDC. *See* European Defense Community
Eden, Anthony: and European integration generally, 6; and Common Market, 16; and France viewed as rival of Britain, 16; and Germany as tool of France, 16; and Messina conference (1955), 23; and Suez crisis (1956), 25; and Franco-British union proposal (1956), 29; and atomic community, 30; and FTA, 51–52
EFTA. *See* European Free Trade Association
Egypt, 6, 17
Eisenhower, Dwight D.: and European integration generally, 5, 11, 13–14, 18, 100, 136, 237; and EDC, 5, 15; and NATO, 5, 87, 114, 129, 137; on "Third Force," 14, 15, 107; and Messina conference (1955), 22; on France, 32, 39, 92–94, 109, 129, 155; and de Gaulle, 39, 92–94, 109, 129, 155; and Common Market, 41, 43–44, 56, 70; and Atlantic Community's origins, 44, 74, 98, 99–100, 106; and FTA, 49,

143–45, 149, 155, 196–97, 199; and beginning of political cooperation from 1958–60, 130–38; and NATO, 131, 134, 136, 141, 146; and Common Market, 132, 134, 135, 138, 140, 141, 143, 145, 278 (n. 76); Rambouillet meeting (1960) on, 132, 134–35, 160, 196, 199; Paris summit (1961) on, 138–39, 277 (n. 63); study commission on, 139, 140; Bonn summit on, 139–40, 144; draft treaties on, 141–48; failure of, 148–51, 156, 157, 199, 200, 226, 229

France: and Franco-German treaty (1963), 1, 102, 119, 149, 150, 181, 185, 187, 188, 189, 199–215, 220–23, 227, 231, 299 (n. 98); and EDC, 4, 11, 17, 19–20, 23, 24, 28, 31, 61, 251 (n. 109); and Suez crisis (1956), 6, 17, 25–26, 29, 30, 37, 130; Fourth Republic in, 6, 17, 33, 34, 37–38, 50, 60, 61, 74–75, 77, 83–84, 128, 133, 232, 233, 235; Fifth Republic in, 6, 17, 62, 75, 79; and NATO, 6, 37, 65, 78, 84, 87, 89–91, 93, 94, 96, 105, 109, 125, 131, 134, 135, 137, 147, 153, 197, 205, 207, 208, 212, 213, 215–16, 225, 229, 232; and European integration generally, 6–7, 16–19, 27–28, 43, 225–26, 232–33; and West Germany, 13, 20, 44, 57, 80–82, 133–35, 194, 196–223, 227, 233, 235–36; and Adenauer, 13, 20, 44, 57, 80–82, 133–35, 194, 196–223, 235; distrust between West Germany and, 13, 21–22, 24, 36–37, 44, 88–91, 96, 254 (n. 162); and Erhard, 13, 58–59, 83, 84, 90, 92, 189, 191, 194, 214, 217–20; and Britain, 16–17, 29, 31, 34–35, 37–38, 45, 47, 79, 94–95, 96, 109, 120, 125, 127–28, 137–38, 146, 151–57, 161, 163–64, 168–70, 173–75, 180–95, 197–98, 202, 208–9, 222–23, 225–26, 228, 233; and Indochina, 17; and Algeria, 17, 24, 58, 61, 83, 85, 113, 142; colonialism of, 17, 26, 28, 32, 36, 171, 190; and supranationalism, 17, 37, 63, 85, 95, 127, 149, 195, 200; and Common Market, 17–18, 21,

22, 25–31, 33–46, 53, 56–62, 67, 75, 79, 94, 96, 149, 154, 186, 190, 202, 217, 218, 228–29; public opinion in, 18–19, 186, 200; and WEU, 20, 28, 191; and Messina conference (1955), 21–22; and atomic community, 25, 26, 27; and agricultural policy, 26, 189, 190, 192, 195, 215–19; and Brussels negotiations and Treaty of Rome, 27–30, 86, 136, 189; in World War II, 29; and Franco-British union proposal (1956), 29, 31; and Paris as capital of Europe, 29, 35, 131, 135; and United States, 32, 39, 44–45, 65, 90, 92–94, 108–10, 112–23, 125, 128–30, 142, 149, 151, 153–57, 175, 187–88, 194, 197–99, 206–7, 209–11, 218–20, 225–26, 228, 233, 266 (n. 87); and de Gaulle's foreign policy, 34–35, 78–80, 84–85, 89–90, 92, 94, 95, 102–3, 108–9, 126–30, 153–54, 157, 163–64, 167, 178–79, 190–91, 196–98, 222–23, 225–26, 231–32; currency and finances of, 40; external tariffs of, 40, 86; and FTA, 49–50, 52–54, 56–68, 73–76, 86, 96, 194, 222, 255 (n. 22), 258 (n. 67); and Euratom, 53; economy of, 53–54; and European Economic Cooperation Union, 60–61; and Seven, 68–69; and EFTA, 72–73; personalities and parameters of Franco-German relationship, 77–83; detente between West Germany and, from 1958–60, 77–97; and Third Force goals of de Gaulle, 78, 94, 109, 113, 124, 128, 129, 140, 155, 160, 168, 184, 198, 211, 213, 222; as UN security council member, 79; and nuclear weapons, 79, 108, 109, 112, 114, 115, 117–19, 122, 152, 175, 192, 205–6, 213–16; and United Nations, 79, 153; and East Germany, 96, 267 (n. 102); and Atlantic Community, 99, 102–3, 108–10, 112–24, 143, 147; and OECD, 104–5; veto by, of British Common Market membership, 116, 117, 120, 122, 149–52, 177, 178, 180–95, 197, 204, 209, 212, 222, 223, 225, 231,

Napoleon, 40

Nassau accord, 115–19, 121–22, 185, 186, 206, 231

National Security Council (NSC), 32, 94, 114

NATO: creation of, 1, 2; American dominance of, 2; and Soviet military threat, 3, 129; and Eisenhower, 5, 87, 114, 137, 155; and West Germany, 5, 90, 110, 134, 144, 206, 207, 208, 210, 211, 215–16, 219; and France, 6, 37, 65, 78, 84, 87, 89, 90, 91, 93, 94, 96, 105, 109, 125, 131, 134, 135, 137, 147, 153, 197, 205, 207, 208, 212, 213, 215–16, 225, 229, 232; and Britain, 51, 70, 87, 111, 138, 146, 152, 167, 185, 190; and de Gaulle, 65, 87, 105, 109, 125, 131, 134, 135, 147, 205; and FTA, 66, 76; reform of, 87, 132; and Atlantic Community, 101, 120, 124; and Bowie Report, 107; and Kennedy, 107, 110, 114, 129, 155; and Acheson Report, 108; and nuclear weapons, 108, 111, 112, 114–16, 122, 123; Soviet fears of, 127; fears about future of, 131; and Fouchet plan, 131, 134, 136, 141, 146; and Franco-German treaty (1963), 210

Nazi Germany. *See* Germany: Nazi

Netherlands: opposition to Fouchet plan by, 112, 128, 136, 137, 139, 143–51, 153, 156, 200; and Britain, 140, 189, 190; and French veto of British membership in Common Market, 189

Norway, 68. *See also* Seven

NSC. *See* National Security Council

Nuclear weapons, 79, 86, 101, 107–9, 111–24, 152, 161, 183–84, 192, 205–6, 213–16. *See also* Atomic community; Euratom

OECD. *See* Organization for Economic Cooperation and Development

OEEC. *See* Organization for European Economic Cooperation

Organization for Economic Cooperation and Development (OECD): creation of, 1, 103–4; membership of, 103, 104;

and France, 104–5; and Britain, 105, 167, 184; and West Germany, 105–6; signing of convention for, 106; limited role of, 106, 227; and Bowie Report, 107; Ball's concerns about, 107–8; and Kennedy, 110; and United States, 110, 172; and EFTA neutrals, 171

Organization for European Economic Cooperation (OEEC): creation and purpose of, 2, 11; and Britain, 23, 28, 31, 51; and Erhard, 25; and FTA, 48, 51, 55–59, 66, 67; and European Economic Cooperation Union, 60–61; and Common Market, 63–64; and Atlantic Community, 101; transformation of, into OECD, 103, 227

Ostpolitik, 233, 235

Paris East-West summit (1960), 91–93, 131, 254 (n. 161)

Paris peace conference (1919), 15

Pétain, Marshal, 77

Pinay, Antoine, 19–22, 27

Pineau, Christian, 27–29, 33, 53

Pompidou, Georges, 128, 169, 182, 233

Portugal. *See* Seven

Quai d'Orsay. *See* France

Rambouillet meeting (1960), 132, 134–35, 160, 196, 199

Rhineland, 84

Rome Treaties (1957). *See* Common Market; Treaties of Rome

Rusk, Dean, 100, 148, 151, 165–66, 178, 179, 188, 207

Saar, 84

Schroeder, Gerhard: as West German foreign minister, 118–19, 133, 231, 235; and Fouchet Plan, 119, 133, 134, 144, 150, 151, 155; and Franco-German treaty (1963), 119, 187, 189, 200, 203, 205, 210, 211, 213, 215, 221, 222; and Atlantic Community, 120; and British membership in Com-

(n. 26). *See also* Atlantic Community; Eisenhower, Dwight D.; Kennedy, John F.; State Department, U.S.; *names of other government officials*

Uruguay Round of GATT, 252 (n. 115)

USSR. *See* Soviet Union

U-2 incident, 92

Vaïsse, Maurice, 99

Versailles Treaty, 15

Vietnam, 231

Von Brentano, Heinrich, 13, 30, 38, 42, 82, 133, 200, 222

Von Hassel, Kai-Uwe, 189, 215

Warsaw Pact, 1

Weimar Republic, 84

Western Europe. *See entries beginning with Europe*

Western European Union (WEU), 11, 19–20, 23, 24, 28, 31, 51, 133, 137, 138, 145, 146, 152, 191, 192

West Germany: rearming of, 1; and Franco-German treaty (1963), 1, 102, 119, 149, 150, 181, 185, 187, 188, 189, 199–215, 220–23, 227, 231, 297–98 (n. 78); economic recovery of, 2; and NATO, 5, 90, 110, 134, 144, 206, 207, 208, 210, 211, 215–16, 219; and European integration generally, 5–6, 12–13, 18–19, 154–55, 225, 227, 229, 235–36; and reunification of Germany, 6, 86, 87, 198, 235; and Common Market, 12, 17, 20–27, 35–37, 40–46, 52, 56, 57–58, 64, 67–68, 75, 81, 91, 105–6, 120, 133, 202, 218; distrust between France and, 13, 21–22, 24, 36–37, 44, 88–91, 96, 254 (n. 162); and Britain, 16–17, 36, 52, 94–95, 96, 119, 144, 164–65, 170–72, 175–77, 179, 180–81, 184, 189, 190, 194, 197–200, 208–9, 220, 222–23, 236; Social Democratic party (SPD) in, 18, 42, 83, 88–90, 199, 211, 212, 221, 222, 235; Christian Democratic/Christian Socialist parties (CDU/CSU) in,

18, 49, 89, 200, 211; public opinion in, 18–19, 49, 134, 165, 211–12, 235; and supranationalism, 20–21, 85, 95, 235–36; and Messina conference (1955), 20–22, 37; and Brussels negotiations and Treaty of Rome, 23–27, 210; and atomic community, 25, 26; and de Gaulle, 35–37, 44, 77–80, 83–97, 124, 126, 153, 196–223; and Berlin crisis (1958), 37, 38, 64, 87–88, 89, 96; external tariffs of, 40; FTA, 49, 52, 56, 57–59, 63–67, 74–75, 81, 86, 94, 96, 176; FDP in, 49, 211; and trade with Seven, 69; and EFTA, 70, 71–72; and GATT, 72, 119, 120, 125, 151, 218; personalities and parameters of Franco-German relationship, 77–83; Franco-German detente, from 1958–60, 77–97; and Soviet Union, 81–82, 91–92, 170–71, 198, 210, 220–21; and nuclear weapons, 86, 115, 118–20, 205–6, 215, 216; territorial losses of, from World War II, 89; and United States, 93–94, 110–11, 134, 155, 197–99, 203, 206–7, 209–11, 215–20, 222, 227, 236; and Atlantic Community, 99, 102, 110–11, 112, 118–20, 123, 124–25, 217; and OECD, 105–6; Kennedy's trip to, 116–17, 124, 214–15, 216, 219; and Kennedy Round of GATT, 119, 120, 125, 151; and Fouchet plan, 128–29, 132, 133–35, 138–39, 143, 144–45, 149, 155, 196–97, 199, 200; and WEU, 133, 191; and British membership in Common Market, 164–65, 170–72, 175–77, 179, 180–81, 184, 186–90, 194; and Brussels negotiations on British entry in Common Market, 170–72, 175–77, 180–81, 184, 186–87, 212; Franco-German relationship between July 1960 and April 1962, 196–99; de Gaulle's state visit to, 201–2, 206; Franco-German relations in 1963, 209–20; and Bundestag resolution with Franco-German treaty (1963), 210, 211–14, 219, 220, 222; and Test Ban

Treaty, 216; arms agreements with U.S., 216, 219; and *Ostpolitik*, 233, 235; and France since 1960s, 233, 235–36; foreign policy of, since 1960s, 235–36. *See also* Adenauer, Konrad; East Germany; Five; Six; *names of other government officials*

WEU. *See* Western European Union

Winand, Pascaline, 99

World Trade Organization (WTO), 252 (n. 115)

WTO. *See* World Trade Organization

Yugoslavia, 60

Zollverein ("Tariff Union"), 12

Jeffrey Glen Giauque, *Grand Designs and Visions of Unity: The Atlantic Powers and the Reorganization of Western Europe, 1955–1963* (2002).

Chen Jian, *Mao's China and the Cold War* (2001).

M. E. Sarotte, *Dealing with the Devil: East Germany, Détente, and Ostpolitik, 1969–1973* (2001).

Mark Philip Bradley, *Imagining Vietnam and America: The Making of Postcolonial Vietnam, 1919–1950* (2000).

Michael E. Latham, *Modernization as Ideology: American Social Science and "Nation Building" in the Kennedy Era* (2000).

Qiang Zhai, *China and the Vietnam Wars, 1950–1975* (2000).

William I. Hitchcock, *France Restored: Cold War Diplomacy and the Quest for Leadership in Europe, 1944–1954* (1998).